# *Untitled*

## AND OTHER RADIO DRAMAS

*Also by Norman Corwin*

THIRTEEN BY CORWIN
MORE BY CORWIN

# *Untitled*

## AND OTHER RADIO DRAMAS

BY NORMAN CORWIN

NEW YORK: HENRY HOLT AND COMPANY

PRINTED IN THE UNITED STATES OF AMERICA

*To my sister Beulah*

# CONTENTS

# FOREWORD

I HAVE no apology to make for the affirmative tone of these scripts. I am convinced that ultimately we will get where we want to go. It will be grim 'en route, but I think there is nothing to be said for cynicism and despair, and everything to be said for getting out and working toward a better world.

The pieces in this book were written for radio during a war that we like to think ended on 14 August, 1945. But the phase of the war with which most of them are concerned—the moral war—is still going on.

Since completing the notes to these plays, I have traveled around the world on a project which brought me in contact with leaders of state as well as with common people. As a result of the experience, I find myself revaluating only a few of the opinions stated, and confirming most.

I thank Lou Ashworth, Hugh Garvey, Robert Heller, Charles Lewin, William H. Fineshriber, Jr., Edward R. Murrow, and Davidson Taylor for counsel and services bearing on the contents of this book.

N. C.

*New York City*

*Untitled*

AND OTHER RADIO DRAMAS

# THE UNDECIDED MOLECULE

First produced in Hollywood on July 17, 1945, under the direction of the author. Groucho Marx played the Judge, Robert Benchley was the Interpreter, Vincent Price was the Prosecutor, Norman Lloyd the Clerk, and Sylvia Sidney appeared as Miss Anima. Keenan Wynn performed no less than four roles, quadrupling as Defense Counsel, Spokesman for both the vegetable and mineral kingdoms, and the Conductor. Elliott Lewis was the Vice-president in Charge of Physiochemistry. The musical score was by Carmen Dragon and was conducted by Lud Gluskin.

# THE UNDECIDED MOLECULE

*Music: Opening.*

ANNOUNCER. Lucky you! You have happened to dial
This program in time to attend a trial
Stranger than any since we first learned the
knack
Of breathing—and that was a long time back.
The poor folks listening to other stations
Will lose all this. But congratulations
To *you* for being no such fool
As to miss *The Undecided Molecule!*

*Music: An upsurge, and down behind:*

ANNOUNCER. (*Opening announcement, credits, etc.*)

*Music: Opening up and out.*

*A heavy, raucous alarm bell drills the air. When it stops:*

VICE-PRESIDENT IN CHARGE OF PHYSIOCHEMISTRY.
Oh, dear! Oh, dear!
The cosmic alarm!
Which means, I fear,
Some woeful harm
Is afoot or awing
In the universe.
Some deplorable thing,
Some active curse
Like a falling sky
Or a new star-cluster,

Been banged up by
A cluster-buster.

*The alarm sounds again.*

VICE-PRESIDENT.    Sounds to me like a dried-up sea
Or another Ice Age for a spell,
Or maybe it's only a freezing hell.
On the other hand it might possibly be
That Hitler is alive and well.
But after all, there is no point guessing.
If it rings again in a manner pressing
I'll answer the interstellaraphone.
I wish they'd leave a feller alone.
Why, only last eon, the—

*The alarm again, even more insistently. Receiver off hook.*

VICE-PRESIDENT.    Hello? Hello? . . . Yes, this is he.
What? Who? What's that? Say that
again? . . .
But where? But how? But why? But
when?
Individually and solely?
Now wait a minute—take it slowly!
It *did?* Oh, no! Oh, no, not *that!*
Holy jumping Jehoshaphat! . . .
I'll call a session right away.
You bet. Uhuh. Mm-hm. Okay.

*Receiver down.*

VICE-PRESIDENT (*to himself*).
O grunt! O moan! O dammit, we
Are faced with a calamity!

I must be cool as liquid air.
Hold on! Who's that? Who's pulling
    my hair?
Why, it is *I!* What am I scary at?
Nonsense! I'll phone the secretariat.
Oh, dear, I *am* in such a tizzy!

*He dials three numbers and gets a busy signal.*

VICE-PRESIDENT.    The obvious rhyme: the line is busy.

*Receiver up.*

VICE-PRESIDENT.    I'll try again. There's no harm trying.

*Again he dials three numbers.*

VICE-PRESIDENT    (*to self*). Oh, I am dying, Egypt,
    dying.
(*Into phone.*) Hello? Say, this is the
    Fifth V.P.
In charge of physiochemistry.
Now listen here: an especially perk-
y molecule has gone berserk!
It has refused to be confined,
Incorporated, or assigned
To *anything.* It simply sits
With a calm expression, and it knits.
Now by all means we must prevent
Such an utterly dangerous precedent.
One holdout molecule, unpent,
Can cause the cosmos great ferment!
We must arraign this beast and try it!
The charge? Inciting particles to riot!
Okay! Arrange—I mean arraign.
I mean all three—I mean the twain.

Oh, never mind! Just get it booked,
Or else the universe is cooked!
Oh, me, oh, my!
G'by. G'by!

*Hangs up.*

*Music: An important fanfare, on long, thin horns, announcing an event of importance to the inner cosmos.*

CLERK.            Hear ye, hear ye!
The Court of Arbitrations and Adjudications of Physiochemical Relations, Department of the Interior of the Atom, Criminal Sitting, Division of Investigation, Charge, Countercharge, Accusation, and Confession,
Is now in session.

*Music: Another fanfare.*

CLERK.            The court will rise and face
The justice who will adjust this case.
See that your concentration centers
On His Honor the Justice just as he enters—
Which he is doing even now.
Everybody bow. Everybody bow.

JUDGE (*coming on*).
Arrumph . . . garrump . . . ahem
. . . to wit . . .
Contrary notwithstanding . . . you may sit.

*Sound of a court sitting.*

JUDGE.      Clerk, read the charge.

CLERK.      May it please the court, et al., to wit—

JUDGE.      It pleases the court. Get on with it.
Who's versus whom?

CLERK.      The Cosmos and all the spheres, systems, clusters, galaxies, orbits,
planets, satellites, together with
all species of animals, vegetables,
and minerals appertaining thereto,
of all conditions of age, social
standing, and sex
Versus
The anonymous molecule hereinafter
referred to as X.

JUDGE.      Mm. What's the charge against said
molecule?

CLERK.      Unwilling to be named.
Rebelling when defined.
Declining to be blamed,
Objecting when assigned,
Protesting when selected,
Resisting an attack,
Refusing to be directed,
And talking back.

JUDGE.      Most serious. Most dangerous.
So strange it's almost strangerous.
Insidious. Precarious.
A shade below nefarious.
The possibilities in sight
Are frightful (meaning full of fright)

And rueful (meaning full of rue)
And gruesome (meaning rather grue)—

CLERK.    Providing, your Honor, the charges are true.

JUDGE.    Why, yes, they must be proven true.

CLERK.    Which is something we have yet to do.

JUDGE.    Quite right, but who was asking you? Now—is the prosecutor here?

PROSECUTOR.    Present.

JUDGE.    Well, then, appear, appear. The trial's on. Try not to miss it. Step up and state your case, and be explicit.

PROSECUTOR.    May it please the court, this case involves a very small matter. By this I don't mean mere trivia or idle chatter, But a particle of matter best described as little.

JUDGE.    Smaller than a jot?

PROSECUTOR.    Even smaller than a tittle.

JUDGE.    Are you referring to Molecule X?

PROSECUTOR.    Yex.

JUDGE.    Then why don't you say so?

PROSECUTOR.    I will, if I may so.

The point, your Honor, is that should
    X be acquitted here,
Catastrophe will follow, since it must
    then be admitted here
That all control of elements has given
    way to anarchy,
And every substance will perforce be
    jittery and panicky.
Thus when we wish a molecule to join
    up with some others
To make a cop or lemon drop or the
    Karamazov brothers,
To be a fog or a catalogue or a lawn
    to be idyllic on,
A beagle or a bagel or a mountain
    made of silicon,
They may refrain, they may desist—
    and if enough of them should
    do so
There'll never be another tenor singer
    like Caruso;
No dog to bark, no lark to hark, no
    grand old man like Talleyrand;
No bee will be, you'll see no sea, no
    ostrich fan for Sally Rand!

JUDGE.

It's staggering! It's awesome!
The damage X could wreak
By simply playing possum!
It makes me rather weak!
Clerk, order me a pony—uh—
Of spirits of ammonia.

PROSECUTOR.    Now there you are! If X's rebellion is indulged,
I think it only safe to say (and fair to be divulged):
There'll never be another atom of the element ammonium.
So take *that* home and play it on Your Honor's own euphonium!

JUDGE.    Young man, I blast at you a disapproving snort
And warn you: one more phrase like that—garrumph—contempt of court! . . .
Now who is here for the defense?

DEFENSE COUNSEL.    I am, your Honor.

JUDGE.                            Well, commence!

DEFENSE COUNSEL.    I will. I do so. Now you see, sir—

JUDGE.    I see nothing of the sort. Who's paying you your fee, sir?

DEFENSE COUNSEL.    No one at all. The way it is with me, sir,
I'm acting out of interest in civil libertee, sir.

JUDGE.    What's liberty to do with it, if you will be so kind?

DEFENSE COUNSEL.    Just this: Where in the universal law books can you find
It's criminal for anything to be of open mind?

PROSECUTOR.         The precedent is ample.

DEFENSE COUNSEL.    It is? Let's have a sample.

PROSECUTOR.         Blackstone on the Elements. Case of
                    Bismuth versus Mo*lyb*denum.

DEFENSE COUNSEL.    Oh, drat the books. Our legal fore-
                    bears doubtlessly all fibbed in 'em.

JUDGE.              Hold on there, you! Why, you up-
                    start!
                    Is not the horse before the cart?
                    Where would we be without tradition?

DEFENSE COUNSEL.    In some advanced, improved position.

JUDGE.              What, what? Young man, are you a
                    red?
                    Have you been to the crimson bred?

DEFENSE COUNSEL.    Neither to crimson nor to purple.

JUDGE.              Well, no whippersnapping twerp'll
                    Challenge me. What do you take me
                    for?

DEFENSE COUNSEL.    A most distinguished expert on the law.

JUDGE.              First sensible thing you've said today.
                    Where were we in this trial, by the
                    way?

DEFENSE COUNSEL.    On the right of X to have an open
                    mind.
                    Now surely Justice is not yet so blind
                    As to be unfavorably disposed—

JUDGE.              Toward openness of mind my mind is
                    closed!

DEFENSE COUNSEL. Your Honor, this is scandal! This—

JUDGE. Now see here: I can handle this.
Let's have no more of your bold to-do.
*A molecule must do what it is TOLD to do!*
Now that's decided, suppose we break for lunch.
I'm famished. Been a tiring day. I sure would like to crunch
A nice fresh salad bowl of crispy, tangy hasheesh!

DEFENSE COUNSEL. Your Honor, I cannot refrain from calling you a Fasceesh!

JUDGE. Contempt of court! Clerk, fine the counsel for defendant, please.
He has the brass to charge the bench with having Fascist tendencies.
Ridiculous and ludicrous! Make it a heavy fine!
How could I be a Fascist? Why, I am so benign
I hardly ever beat my wife; my children bow before me.
I'm much admired by rattlesnakes, and birds of prey adore me.
I'm tender and I'm sensitive and anti-insurrectionist;
I wouldn't hurt a cobra, and I'm anti-vivisectionist.

DEFENSE COUNSEL. I'm sure that's absolutely true and that you're not the sort

Who would deny a prisoner his right
    to speak in court.
Your might is mixed with mercy, and
    wisdom's interfused;
So how about a word or two from X,
    who is accused?

JUDGE.    Oh, very well, since your appeal is to
    the better side of me,
Let no one say my conduct here is prej-
    udiced or snide of me.
We'll hear from X, but make it short.
    Where is the little dope?

DEFENSE COUNSEL.  Right here beneath the new 'lectronic
    supermicroscope.

JUDGE.    Swear him in.

CLERK.    Put your right hand on the atomic
    table
And say as loud as you are able:
"I do solemnly swear to tell the truth,
    the whole truth, and buzz-fuzz
    the muzzawalla buzzawalla hut-
    sut floogle-bugle putt-putt scuttle-
    butt and nothing but the truth.
So help me I."
Now testify.

*An oscillator peeps in a fluttery and poignant fashion,
but with perfect syntax and grammar.*

JUDGE.    What's that squeaking?

DEFENSE COUNSEL.  My client speaking.

JUDGE.                    Well, how do you expect me to under-
                          stand?

DEFENSE COUNSEL.    There's an interpreter at hand.

JUDGE.                    Where? I don't see any.

DEFENSE COUNSEL.                  Right at your elbow.

JUDGE.                    Oh, yes. How de do.

INTERPRETER.                          I'm very well, bo.

JUDGE.                    *Bo?* . . . Aren't you getting a bit
                          famil?

INTERPRETER.         I spoze I am, but please think nil
                     Of it.

JUDGE.                    Can you understand what the molecule
                          says?

INTERPRETER.         Yez.
                     That's my biznit, iznit?

JUDGE.                    A fey character.

INTERPRETER.                       Like in a film by Disney.

JUDGE.                    Disney's not involved in this.

INTERPRETER.                              Why isney?

JUDGE.                    I don't know. Where does all this
                          lead?

INTERPRETER.         Nowhere.

JUDGE.                              Then please proceed
                     To interpret X for the court of Lex.
                     (Lex is Latin for Law, I guess—
                     Which shows I *too* enjoy access

To more than one tongue. I'm a giant
Intellect.) Now let's hear your client.

DEFENSE COUNSEL. Proceed if you will, Mr. Molecule. Let
your story fairly leap from you.
Come on, come on, we're waiting now.
The court wants to hear a peep
from you.

MOLECULE. (*Peeps forlornly. At length:*)

INTERPRETER.    X says as follows:

I cannot bring
Myself to be
Just anything
That's asked of me.

I cannot chide
My inner soul:
I must confide
I've set a goal.

I've thought it through
And cannot bear
To be shampoo
For oily hair.

My spirit sings,
My fiber spiels
Of nobler things
And high ideals.

I'll fairly bust
My heart within
If I am just
An onion skin.

I worry some:
What's drearier
Than to become
Bacteria?

And when I tried
Hard to obey,
My conscience cried:
"But hold! But stay!"

A worm for bait?
I have my pride!
I vacillate.
I can't decide.

Though Hamlet had
A hard time, why,
He wasn't so sad
As little I.

You see my lot?
It's not, for me,
To *be* or not,
But *what* to be?

My plight inside
Is bona fide.
I can't decide,
I can't decide.

JUDGE. I've never been so touched or moved.
  I sniffle and I blubber.
I thought my heart was made of steel,
  but it is made of rubber.
Poor little thing! Tormented so by
  dreams of the eugenic—

PROSECUTOR.

O fiddlesticks! This molecule is but a
    schizophrenic!
How is it that in all the time since
    matter first appeared
Each separate iota has loyally adhered
To universal law, without a solitary
    beef
Until this pipsqueak came along? Now
    suddenly there's grief:
The heavens shake and earthquakes
    quake and oceans heave and
    slither,
And dogs and cats and acrobats are in
    a frightful dither—
A timid snip has lost its grip and
    whines of its neurosis.
If you condone this freak you'll reek
    of moral halitosis.
I strongly urge Your Honor purge X
    to its smallest decimal,
Or else the infinite will bow before the
    infinitesimal!

JUDGE.

You're right! What was I thinking of
    to pity yon schlemiel?
I thought my heart was fairly soft, but
    it is made of steel!
I shall not spoil this molecule by spar-
    ing it the rod,
And so I sentence it to die before a
    firing squad!
Perhaps a little torture first, like singe-
    ing at the stake

And drops of water on the head; and
    for variety's sake
A little twist of the garrote, a slice of
    guillotine—
And X shall mark the spot where X
    was boiled in vaseline!

DEFENSE COUNSEL. I ask this sentence be appealed!

JUDGE. Impossible. Your client's fate is sealed.

DEFENSE COUNSEL. Ah, no! The court's decision is far
    from ineluctable.
I must remind you, my good sir, that
    *matter's indestructible!*

JUDGE. Gadzooks, it *is!* I had forgot. We can't
    destroy a particle!
It seems we're in the power of this
    clever young upstarticle!

PROSECUTOR. The case is lost! I must withdraw. If
    punishment's not capital
And X cannot be executed, I don't give
    a rap at all!
We can't imprison it, for we'd be in a
    most infernal stew,
With cosmic checks and balances eter-
    nally askew.

JUDGE. Oh, dear, oh, dear, vay's mir, vay's
    mir, what will become of all of
    us?
This little jerk and his strange quirk
    will surely be the fall of us!

DEFENSE COUNSEL. May I suggest a means by which disaster be evaded?

My client is no pighead and may likely be persuaded

To join some element or other. X is not a softy.

It merely wishes to belong to something fairly lofty.

Its point of view is forward, its attitude is global,

Its heart is set on being part of something good and noble.

So I suggest you demonstrate—and this will never hurt you—

That being this or that or t'other has a point of virtue.

JUDGE. Well, how do you propose we do it?

DEFENSE COUNSEL. I have a plan, and I was coming to it.

Invite a representative of each important kingdom—

JUDGE. You mean like Dempsey for the ring or Artie Shaw for swingdom?

DEFENSE COUNSEL. No, but you're warm.

JUDGE. A lion for the jungle or an eagle for all wingdom?

DEFENSE COUNSEL. Keep on—remember: three of them, and one for every kingdom.

JUDGE. Oh, I know—animal and mineral (*pause*)—and I forget the third—

DEFENSE COUNSEL. The *vegetable* kingdom!

JUDGE.                    Why, yes, of course! Absurd!
                  That's splendid! We could get them
                      here and each could make a pitch,
                  And X could then make up its mind to
                      which it wished to hitch.
                  I'll call a recess in this trial while we
                      round up a trio.
                  Meanwhile, some music! Clerk!

CLERK.            Yes, sir?

JUDGE.                    Can you sing "Sole Mio"?

CLERK.            No, but the court musicians would be
                      very glad to play for you.

JUDGE.            Where's the conductor?

CONDUCTOR.                        Here.

JUDGE.                    Is everything okay for you?

CONDUCTOR.       You bet. Shall I begin, Your Honor,
                      with a prelude by Stravinsky
                  Or toccata for the G string by the
                      famous Brothers Minsky? [1]

JUDGE.            Have you anything around that Dmitri
                      Shostakovitch wrote?

CONDUCTOR.       Oh, yes. A passacaglia, and I'm sure
                      that you will love itch note.

JUDGE.            I've changed my mind. I'll have a slug
                      of music by Lyn Murray—

---

[1] The numbered notes will be found on page 43.

> The one he calls "Verklärte Nacht von
>> Chicken mitten Curry."
> Is that title correct?

CONDUCTOR.                    I fear it is.

JUDGE.        Okay, then. Play it.

CONDUCTOR.                    Here it is!

*Music: "Verklärte Nacht," but plenty verklärte. It resolves in the fanfare motif on the thin horns, as before.*

*The recess is over, and we are about to resume the proceedings.*

CLERK.        Hear ye, hear ye!
> The spokesman for the vegetable kingdom will rise and address the court concerning the advantages to Molecule X of joining this classification, with handy allusions to paleontology, plant psychology, stems and flowers, roots and fruits, and outstanding examples of horticulture and botany—
> If he's got any.

VEGETABLE SPOKESMAN.
> I doubt that X will ever see
> An atom lovely as a tree.
> Why, nothing has got quite the charm
> Of the most ordinary palm.
> We've coffee beans and turpentine
> And grapes that make imported wine,
> And as for molds and types of fungus,
> We have some noted ones among us

(Penicillin is a spore
Noble beyond metaphor).
Life is earnest, life is sweet
For the common sugar beet.
Cotton, spinach, hemp, and hop—
One could really never stop
Singing vegetary praise
For years and months and weeks and
            days—

MOLECULE. (*Interrupts with an observation which our
            Interpreter presently translates.*)

INTERPRETER.    X says that trees
Are chopped for wood,
And that he sees
No special good
In being a beet,
Which people eat.

X says a palm,
Though fine in main,
Can come to harm
In a hurricane.

The grape's a curse
(Since drink is evil),
And cotton is worse
For the boll weevil.

X does not wish
To look for trouble.
It's not his dish,
The vegetable.

JUDGE.    For a molecule that's supposed to be
            meek,

The choosy Mr. X has a lot of cheek!
Step down, Vegetable; let Mineral
    speak.

CLERK.

The spokesman for the mineral kingdom will address the court concerning the advantages to Molecule X of joining this classifica-
tion, with allusions to metallurgy,
gypsum, filiform silver, motor-
cars, nickel bars, pickle jars, and
manganese.
Please.

MINERAL SPOKESMAN.

Now the way that X can best insure
His choice of substance will endure
Is to stop his flopping about and settle
Down to being a respectable metal.
O fiddle-dee-dee and fiddle-dee-dum,
Yum yum, O boy, aluminum!
If he likes the work of Byron, he
Can be the iron in irony.

JUDGE.

That sounds to me like pure
Unalloyed non sequitur.

MINERAL SPOKESMAN.

If he wishes to be a worker, he
Can serve in a column of mercury.
If he'd rather be gay and giddysome,
There's radium, uranium, iridium.
O tantalum, tungsten, talcum, tin,
Ipsy, pipsy, bitters and gin,
Alto sax and carpet tacks,
Rackety rax borax borax—

Merrily, beryly, chalybite, chin,
Tripolite, zinc, and kaolin . . .

JUDGE.    Are these football yells necessary?[2]

MINERAL SPOKESMAN.
Yes, sir—very.

JUDGE.    What do they mean?

MINERAL SPOKESMAN.
Well, amphibole, sphene and pyroxene,
Being amygdaloidally idiochromatic,
May create a stalactitic static
Affecting the scalenohedral speed.

JUDGE.    That clears it up very well indeed.
Proceed.

MINERAL SPOKESMAN.
If X wants glamour, need he be told
Of silver, platinum, and gold?
And the safest job on any planet
Is to be a nice strong rock of granite.
If he likes good cooking, a dinner'll
boil
Very nicely over mineral oil.
Does he cry to be a wagon hitched to a
star?
Then apply to be a Hollywood motor-
car.
Oh, I could pour mineral lore before
you
Forever and a day, if it wouldn't bore
you.

MOLECULE. (*States his position with reference to the fore-*

*going, uttering many persuasive and incisive peeps and
squeaks.*)

INTERPRETER.  X says, says he,
That any jury'll
Find mercury
Somewhat mercurial.

Iron gets rusty;
Bare rock's too nude.
Talc is too dusty;
Oil is crude.

The automobile
Is not his bent;
One elliptical wheel
Means an accident.

Gold you can keep.
He simply balks
At lying deep
Beneath Fort Knox.

JUDGE.  I've never heard such utterly rash
Hypercritical balderdash!
If I weren't so stately and dignified
I'd take that molecule outside
And bop him right on his little beezer.
Who does he think he is—Little
    Caesar?
Growl. Let the animal kingdom present
*Its* spokesman. Come on, where *is* the
    gent?

CLERK.  Right here. But, Your Honor—

JUDGE.                    All right, begin.

CLERK.   It's a *her*.

JUDGE.   Never mind. Swear him in, swear him in.

CLERK.   The spokesman for the animal king-dom, et cetera, species of bird, bee, dog, flea, hen, men—does solemnly swear, et cetera, in the name of llama, gnu, auk, yak, kangaroo, Slippery Dan, Charlie Chan, the Common Man, and so forth—
That he (or she) will please go forth
And testify to the legal corps.

ANIMA.   Thank you. I gladly take the floor.

JUDGE.   Mm. Rather pretty. *Eh bien. Alors.*

ANIMA.   I could fascinate X with the mystery
Of our considerable natural history,
    And tell him the fame
    Of each colorful name—

JUDGE.   Go on. I'm goose-pimply and blistery.

ANIMA.   I could tell of a bird named the smew
And another yclept urubu—
    Of the dziggetai, dzo,
    And of zingel roe—

JUDGE.   And a fish that is called inconnu.

ANIMA.   Quite true.

JUDGE.   And a monkey that's called wanderoo.

ANIMA.   Quite true.

JUDGE.      Oh, I just love to listen to you.

ANIMA.      I could tell of the vinegaroon,
The squacco, the gweduc, baboon,
     The antelope bongo,
     The crow known as drongo—

JUDGE.      Will you join me for lunch one day
     soon?

CLERK.      For the record, may I ask whether
     these names are real or fictionary?

JUDGE.      Don't interrupt. They're all in your
     dictionary.[3]

ANIMA.      Now the capercaillie has a whistle
Distinct from the ling and dickcissel,
     The zebu and zivet
     And terek of Tibet—

JUDGE.      I cling to your words like a thistle.

ANIMA.      I urge X to join the toucan
Or some other nice animal clan
     Like the beautiful cootie
     Or charming agouti—

JUDGE.      But what of the species of man?

ANIMA.      Oh, that's another subject entirely. I
     do *not* recommend that X get in-
     volved in the affairs of mankind.

JUDGE.      Mmm. Is that because you believe in
     the principle of matter over man's
     mind?

ANIMA. No. But being human would surely hex
A sensitive molecule like X.

JUDGE. Just how do you mean, queen?

ANIMA. Well, it's not so easy to be a common
man.
No matter how much you work and
plan,
It's still a neat trick to live the span
Commonly allotted to the common
man.

A wandering breeze'll
Affect your pump—
If not a measle,
Then a mump.

You can pull a tendon,
Get roundly hissed,
Or have to depend on
An analyst.

You can get ptomaine
Or be undersold.
Then there's Franco Spain
And the common cold.

A review can stink.
You can miss a guess
Or be told how to think
By the yellow press.

JUDGE. Did I tell you I greatly admire your
dress?

ANIMA.

There's water on the knee
And athlete's toes,
The doctor's fee
And the running nose—

Aching bursitises,
Rashes and rickets,
Colitis and *worse* itises,
And parking tickets.

You can get diabetes
Or caught in the rain,
You can run out of Wheaties
Or into a train.

You can get neuras*the*nia;
A blizzard can chill you;
Your wife can be meannya;
A dentist drill you.

A plaintiff can sue you,
A bite give malaria.
If no lover woo you,
Alas, misereria!

JUDGE.

Re legal embroilments just let *me* take
care o' ya.

ANIMA.

A Fascist will fight you,
And then there is asthma.
Vampires can bite you,
And wine on your plasma.

You can be badly reared
And flunk out in Latin
Or tangle your beard
In spaghetti au gratin.

> You can get a flat tire,
> Drop teeth in the drain,
> Or suffer a dire
> Escutcheon stain.
>
> You can drown in the Dnieper
> Or suffer the bends;
> You can wind up a leper
> And lose all your friends.
>
> You can settle in Philly
> Or step in a pail,
> Or feel willy-nilly
> And cease to inhale.

JUDGE. How morbid! Depressing—in fact, suicidal! . . .

By the way—have you ever an hour that's idle?

DEFENSE COUNSEL. Your Honor, my client has something to say!

JUDGE (*to Anima*). I could meet you— (*Slow take.*) What's that about X again? Eh?

DEFENSE COUNSEL. He's ready, I said.

JUDGE. Well, let him go ahead.

MOLECULE. (*Takes the stand.*)

INTERPRETER. X says as follows:

> I'm glad to know
> The awful truth:

Man has such woe,
Forsooth! Forsooth!

Yet what he's done
Proud hands can clap:
He's beaten the Hun
And will the Jap.

He flies the air
Just like a smew
And swims for fair
Like the inconnu.

He has a soul,
He reads Descartes;
Like me, his goal
Is a thing apart.

He's learned to kill
The harmful bug
By serum, pill,
And sulfa drug.

He beats the band
And goes to school
To understand
The molecule.

In face of odds
He makes his way:
Gives birth to quads,
Builds TVA;
Displays his charms,
Plays blindfold chess,
Listens to Brahms
And CBS.

The common guy
Both thinks and feels.
Nothing's too high
For his ideals.

Though it cost him sadly
To put down jerks,
He's not done badly—
Look at his works!
For all his pains
We owe him thanks.
And I do gladly
Join his ranks.

The human flock
Has golden fleece
Grace to its stock
And lasting peace!

JUDGE.            O splendid! What a moving speech!
                 I had thought X a worm, a leech,
                 But now I see he's a regular fellow.
                 He's twanged me so, I quiver like jello.
                 O joy! O rapture! Fields of clover!

CLERK.           Looks to me like the trial is over.

JUDGE.           Quite so. My dear X, forgive the di-
                     gression,
                 But I'm sure you'll be happy in your
                     chosen profession.
                 As for you, Miss Anima, you were
                     great.
                 It's slightly extralegal—but have you a
                     date

For later in the evening? Do you like
   to dance?
Have you any marked tendency toward
   romance?

ANIMA.
I have; but what about the *wife* you
   seldom beat
And the children you have mentioned
   who grovel at your feet?

JUDGE.
Ho, ho, mere rhetoric and figmentary
   frippery!
The legal mind behaves this way—it's
   very smooth and slippery
When arguing. I have no wife or any
   such a fixture.

ANIMA.
In that case I will marry you, as in a
   Class B picture.
We'll create a happy ending, plus two
   children of each sex.

JUDGE.
To be a part of one of them, shall we
   invite friend X?

ANIMA.
Magnificent idea, that. Is our future
   child agreed?

MOLECULE. (*A brief statement of acceptance, translating
   as follows:*)

INTERPRETER.
X says indeed
And asks you speed
Your visit to the Reverend
So he can have a life to lead
And bring this to a clever end.

CLERK.    Hooray! I thought you'd never end.
Will the court musicians kindly ad-
vance
To the mike and play a wedding dance;
And then, after that, please segue and
sally
Into a sort of a kind of finale?

*Music: A sort of a kind of finale.*

# THE UNDECIDED MOLECULE

The atomic bomb was several weeks east of Hiroshima when this was first broadcast; so it wasn't *that* which got me writing about Mr. X. Fact is, I'd had doubts about the stability of matter ever since I almost blew up a house at 36 Perkins Street, Winthrop, Massachusetts, when I was a high-school student. I was in love with a chemistry course at the time and built myself a laboratory in the cellar. It was for sheer exhibitionism, and not, I am sorry to say, for quiet research. Far from working on the isolation of positrons, I was happy to dissolve gold leaf in fluoric acid while the younger kids of the neighborhood watched in awe. I was also a specialist in noxious odors, and my mother often had to speak to me sharply about distillates of hydrogen sulphide. But the experiment that finally ended in my father's seizure of the laboratory was the cooking of nitro-glycerine in a double boiler.

The trial of X was something I had been wanting to write for years, simply because that kind of rhyme is such fun to do. Not since "The Plot to Overthrow Christmas" in 1938 had I made a pass at a fantasy in verse, for I felt there were more urgent and serious things to be said during a war. But with victory in Europe, and the personal catharsis of producing a V-E show, I finally relaxed my strictures against even *thinking* of jingles and took up the case of the undecided molecule.

Certainly the stand taken by X, if permitted to spread, would have touched off dangerous developments among the elements. You have only to grasp the outlines of the quantum theory to sense how vast a transfigmentation of the amordify would be involved. Indeed, as one character hints, there would be the risk of creating a stalactitic static. What the character does not get around to saying is that this disturbance might very well generate such friction against negatrons of nitrogen and oxygen that the whole atmosphere of the earth might burst into flame and consume itself —leaving, when the smoke lifted, an Oboleresque planet, cratered, shriveled, lifeless.

The Prosecutor, you must admit, has a case. X is antisocial, antiuniversal. It is bad enough that man, the end product of certain molecular combinations, should be more or less neurotic. But if his raw material—the dust from which he cometh and to which he returneth—if that, too, goes off into a psychic sulk, then woe to everybody and everything.

Justice and law, both of the highest type, are on the side of the cosmic government that brings action against X. That the judge is an unprincipled bully and quasi-Fascist does not alter the fact that the good of the whole has been gravely jeopardized by the fractiousness of a part—and a very small part at that. However plaintive our hero may be (and I am most sympathetic about his vacillation, because I'm that way myself), there is no denying he stands to cause the cosmos great ferment.

It is worthy of note that the happy ending is arrived at not by due process of law. No legal triumph is scored by either side. When finally the action is defeated, it is only because the defense has pointed out the impossibility of sentencing X to death. A keener prosecution would have challenged as obsolete the theory of indestructibility, and the Judge, if he were as quick on the trigger as on the libido, would have remanded X to a cyclotron, to be split asunder.

As for the airy assumption that a molecule could possibly be undecided, the court overlooked an important fact: the molecule is not the ultimate particle of matter. By the time atoms team up to form a molecule, the combination is already *something*—like borscht, say; or a false tooth. The molecule is a big boy among corpuscles. My spies tell me there are certain molecules big enough to be seen under a microscope. Yet as I take pains publicly to discredit the scientific platform of the case against X, I wot of the Heisenberg principle of indeterminacy. Maybe, after all, X need not have been so predetermined as you think, professor; nor these apologies so elaborate.

*Acting.* The Vice-President in charge of Physiochemistry has plenty to worry about, especially now that atomic energy is on the open market. At any moment some high-school boy in a cellar in Weehawken, experimenting with matter in a double boiler, may succeed in splitting the hydrogen atom, and the planet will explode into a star. Such an incident would automatically ring an alarm bell in the office of the V.P.; and he would have to go to work. He doesn't like to work. He doesn't like the responsibility. It is his job to keep a rough kind of balance in the universe, and if a continent should sink too deep, or a nova get too hot, or a glacier drift down over lush tobacco country, he is likely to catch hell from a higher-up in heaven. It is this reluctance to apply himself, to put down his copy of *Thirteen by Corwin* * and attend to work, which accounts for the fact that the alarm clangs twice before he decides that if it sounds *again,* he'll answer the interstellaraphone. Once aroused, he is in a dither; he springs, as the saying goes, into action. He is essentially the rattled, fussy type—

* Henry Holt and Company, $3.00.

ideally, Edward Everett Horton or Franklin Pangborn. At the time of the original production both these actors were away from Hollywood; so I cast the ever-reliable Elliott Lewis in the role. Lewis played it as well as anybody could, but his voice is on the heavy side and carried too much authority. A light, nervous quality is what is needed.

The clerk is any and every clerk of court—perfunctory, dry, legal, with now and then a wry observation beyond the call of duty. Norman Lloyd, then playing in the Actors' Laboratory production of *Volpone,* was the perfect model.

I don't know of an actor in the world who could preside over so eccentric a court as efficiently as Groucho Marx. Our Justice is a blue-plate special of temperaments—easily angered, mollified, and moved; suspicious, gullible, peremptory, sadistic, vain, lecherous. The original broadcast had the benefit of Groucho's irrepressible ad-libbing, and some of his improvisations during rehearsal were used in the air show. When the Mineral Spokesman gyrated into a sales talk resembling a college yell, Groucho cried, "Team, team, team!" as though he had been carried away; then, recovering from his reflex, he sternly asked, "Are these football yells necessary?" When Miss Anima, cataloguing the woes of mankind, mentioned Franco Spain, Groucho spat, "Pfui!" When she listed parking tickets, he interposed, "Not in this court!" And a moment later, at the reference to Wheaties, he repeated, commandingly, "Not in this court!"

Perhaps the most sensible way of conveying what the role of the Judge requires is to recommend that you see Groucho in any of his movies. I am hipped on the subject of Groucho Marx; so don't expect a level judgment. I think he is a supreme artist. It is one of the gross and morbid signs of our degenerating humor that Chaplin, the Marx

Brothers, W. C. Fields, Buster Keaton, Harold Lloyd, Raymond Griffith, Chester Conklin, Harold Langdon, Laurel, Hardy, all the other great film comics of yore, have been succeeded by comics of not even faintly comparable stature. Instead, we have Abbott and Costello, Red Skelton, and the unbelievably bad films of two great radio comics, Jack Benny and Fred Allen. Of them all, past and present, Groucho is for me the funniest to watch, even funnier in action than Chaplin. Of course, the two do not share the same broad talents—Chaplin's gift of situation, for example. But Groucho—

We were discussing the casting of "The Undecided Molecule." The Prosecutor is properly indignant about X's defection, and his tones are the most ringing of anybody's, with the possible exception of the clerk's. Vincent Price gave our attorney a learned and cultured quality—he was a cross between the influences of Pomona and Oxford. Naturally the State would not trust its case to a mere shyster from Harvard Law. Mr. Price was forceful and eloquent, his only fall from grace being something that happened in rehearsal, not on the air. It seems Mr. Price said *"bah-gel"* when he meant bagel. Stunned, the rest of the cast asked him if he knew what he had done—mispronounced one of the great pastries of the world. Price confessed he had never met the word before: worse, had never eaten a bagel. Mrs. William Ashworth, then vice-president in charge of bagels for the Columbia Broadcasting System, quickly got him a specimen of the famous glazed doughnut. He had no trouble with the word after that.

The defense counsel is a clever Joe and knows how to handle a Judge like Groucho. He challenges, discredits, defies, then suddenly flatters; charges the bench with scandalous behavior, calls the Judge a Fascist, then in the next

breath wins a point by praising him. After rescuing X from
sentence of death, he rescues the court from embarrassment
by proposing a way out of the dilemma. At this moment
in the original production, I directed Keenan Wynn, who
played Counsel for the Defense, to request a conference at
the bench. The Judge readily agreed, and the passage beginning, "May I suggest a means by which disaster be
evaded," down through Groucho's demand for music in the
court, was played in the low, half-whispered key of all such
conferences between bench and counsel.

Mr. Wynn, whose mugs and drunkards on the screen are
among the immortal character bits of all time, was found
everywhere one turned. He was not only Defense Counsel,
but Spokesman for the Vegetable and Mineral Kingdoms
and Conductor of the Court Musicians. Wynn's Counsel
had a nasal, wheedling tone; as Spokesman for high vegetable circles he was suave, like a lobbyist for a California
farmers' association. His orchestra conductor was from
Galicia, and very short in this country. For the Mineral
Spokesman, Keenan invented a New Yorkese compounded
of the worst speech characteristics of all five boroughs, including:

> If he wishes to be a woiker, he
> Can soive in a column of moicury. . . .

> If he likes good cookin', a dinner'll berl
> Very nicely over mineral erl.

In the production, X himself had no voice, save that of
the oscillator which is described below under "Sound." I do
not believe in animals or inanimate objects speaking on the
radio. In a talking cartoon, that is another matter—the
eye accepts the image, and the ear tags along. But when the
spectator is blind, as in radio, there is no image to bridge

the gap between the dimensions of real people (in this case the Judge, counsels, clerk, et cetera) and the image of a caterpillar, or of a talking locomotive, or an argumentative fish. The inconceivably small image of a molecule could not have been compressed into anything resembling a realistic voice. Therefore I used an interpreter, and he was in the image of Robert Benchley. This was four months before Benchley's untimely death—a loss mourned by thousands of his fans, including myself.

That part of Benchley's versatile style which bore most directly on the role of the Interpreter was his half-fey, amiable, slightly hesitant, suppressed-chuckle quality. He kept a kind of blithe neutrality about him, never permitting the content of X's testimony to color his reading.

Miss Anima is a sultry number, who understands a thing or two about human and molecular nature. She has the Judge in the palm of her hand (or the calf of her leg) the minute she begins to speak; she wastes little time trying to impress anybody but X with the force of her argument. Simply by using reverse English and basic feminine psychology, she interests the undecided molecule in the condition of being a man.

The limerick section, beginning with

> I could fascinate X with the mystery
> Of our considerable natural history,

should be played at strict tempo, with the Judge's interpolations coming right on the proper musical beat.

Sylvia Sydney made Miss Anima sexy, yet dignified and aloof; desirable to the wolfish chief justice, yet punctilious as Portia. And by the way, make sure that her name is pronounced clearly by hizzoner; that it is in no way confused with a medical term of similar sound.

*Sound.* The old handyman of sound effects is the oscillator. It is an electrical device that looks like a small receiving set, and it produces a squeal not unlike that which arose from an early radio when closely approached. The musical instrument called the theremin (after its inventor, Alexander Theremin—and what has happened to both?) was based on the principle of the oscillator. No more versatile piece of baggage exists in the sound department. Its tone can be held steady or interrupted, as in code; its pitch can be varied; it can be made to flutter, whine, or imitate the inflections of speech. The last of these talents is the one I selected to serve as the voice of X. I myself (every director is a ham at heart and wants to perform in some way or other) operated the spark key and tuning dial that gave expression to the molecule's inner struggle. I found it was best to use the effect sparingly, else it became monotonous. And the inflection should parallel that of a child's sing-song recital of a poem.

The alarm bell should be of the heavy type used in fire stations and should awaken the dead from the local cemetery. As for the court's sitting ("Contrary notwithstanding . . . you may sit"), the best way to get this is to ask the members of the orchestra please to rise and sit on cue from the control room. If you use recorded music in your production, you will have to think of something else.

*Music.* Carmen Dragon wrote exactly the right score for the original production, and the way to insure results if you are using a live orchestra is to get in touch with Dragon through the office of Lud Gluskin at Columbia's Station KNX in Hollywood. The job was no pushover for a composer, since I had stipulated that the music be not whimsy-whamsy and that it contain the same element of tongue-in-cheek as the script. None of the passages should be *backed* by music. This ain't the Lux Radio Theater; and the only thing resembling a love scene is the dialogue between the Judge and Miss Anima. I have known directors who would back even such converse with mellow 'cellos. They should be hanged on the highest hill.

*Additional Notes.* 1. The upcoming generation, inheriting a peaceful, clean, burlesqueless world, may not understand the allusion. The G string, in strip-tease parlance, was a small triangular vestment doing the work of a fig leaf. The Minsky Brothers were famous entrepreneurs of burleycue, circa 1920-40.

2. Please, you shouldn't pronounce this "ness'ry." It is meant to rhyme three ways with "Yes, sir—very."

3. The Judge is right: they *are* all in your dictionary. I had enormous fun weeding strange animal names out of an unabridged Webster. It would take days to track down all the odd names, but if you select only those that are illustrated, you will come up with an astonishing catalogue. I was most happy with the dziggetai-dzo-zingel combination, especially since the latter's "z" is pronounced "ts," so that it quite alliterates with the others.

# UNTITLED

Produced first for radio on April 18, 1944, as the seventh of the "Columbia Presents Corwin" series. It was repeated by popular request five weeks later, on the eve of Memorial Day. On both occasions Fredric March appeared as Hank Peters, the Voice throughout, and the author directed. The script has since been performed widely by Stage for Action and by the personnel of hundreds of United States Army camps, centers, hospitals, and overseas units.

The most notable of its foreign productions up to the end of 1944 was that done by the Australian Broadcasting Commission on November 19, 1944. John Stacy appeared as Hank Peters, and John Cairns directed.

# UNTITLED

*Music: Introduction.*

VOICE. With reference to Hank Peters—he is dead.
That much is certain.
The fact of his death is common knowledge to himself and to the files of the War Department
in Washington, D. C.,
And has been duly reported in his home-town newspaper,
And has been taken into consideration by his relatives and friends.

Perhaps you knew Hank Peters.
Perhaps if you didn't know him you saw him somewhere and didn't know it was he. Quite possible—
Because at one time or other he rode on the coaches
of the Santa Fe, the Union Pacific, the New
York Central, and the Nickel Plate;
He mingled with crowds in depots across the land,
and at various times was among the audiences
at widespread Orpheum and Loew theaters;
He strolled, on leave, down Broadway, Wilshire
Boulevard, Wabash Avenue, and the main
streets of Killeen, Texas; Gulfport, Mississippi; and Des Moines, Iowa.
He frequently ate blueplates at scattered Childs
restaurants; was known to have purchased

> sodas, razor blades, and magazines at Liggett
> Drug Stores;
> And before he was apprenticed to the war, he drove
> many a mile over many a state highway, also
> over secondary and dirt roads not represented
> on the Socony maps.
> So it is quite possible that at some time or other
> you may have passed him, seen him, talked to
> him.
> Well, anyway, he's dead now.
>
> A couple of the boys sorted out his belongings and
> put them in a canvas bag and sent them home.
> There wasn't much to send.

SERGEANT. Wrist watch.

CORPORAL. Check.

SERGEANT. Shaving kit.

CORPORAL. Check.

SERGEANT. Wallet.

CORPORAL. Check.

SERGEANT. Fourteen American dollars.

CORPORAL. Fourteen bucks.

SERGEANT. Sixty-two lire.

CORPORAL. What'll his family do with lire?

SERGEANT. Never mind. Put it down there. (*Pause.*)
Portable radio.

CORPORAL. Check.

SERGEANT. Deck of cards.

CORPORAL. Check.

SERGEANT. Pack of letters.

CORPORAL. Check.

SERGEANT. Four snapshots.

CORPORAL. Lemme see.

SERGEANT. Come on, come on. (*Pause.*) Marksman's
medal.

CORPORAL. Right.

SERGEANT. That's all.

CORPORAL. Next. . . .

VOICE. These things were sent home in a neat package.

But what could not be sent home were items un-
assorted and unrelated that died within his
head when he was hit:

Telephone numbers;

The taste of good hot grub on a cold, rainy day;

The image of the evening plane caught in a skein
of searchlights over the town, pulling the
whole web with it across the sky;

The paralyzed newsboy on Maple and Elm who
could barely hold coins in his hand while he
counted change;

The shimmer and float of summer, and the bright
bare legs of a woman;

The posture of his dog, faking exhaustion, lying
with his head down on the floor, but watching
his every move—

Oh, a great many corny things and a few others,
including the antique smell of books in the
public library;

The pinch of his favorite pipe after two hours of
smoking;

And the moon going down over the shoulder of his
girl Marian as they sat on the porch into the
hours of the forming of dew.

These items of course cannot be reconstructed as he
felt them, and neither can Hank Peters be re-

constructed, at least in the form by which you may possibly have known him.

As for his life, there is no straightforward account available, but there are several people who could piece it together, although they cannot always be relied on to give you a true interpretation of the facts.

Let us start, then, with two men who saw him last and first—neither friends nor relatives, but professional men, and thus unprejudiced this way or that.

*Music: Transition and preparation, coming out before:*

MEDICAL OFFICER. I am a medical officer attached to the Sixth Company, Twenty-second Regiment, Tenth Division. In this coffin, we have reason to believe, is the body of Hank Peters, Private First Class. I shall read you the contents of his death certificate: "Henry Charles Peters, twenty-six, Identification Number 8406912, killed in action of the following injuries: Abdominal lacerations, lower left quadrant; fracture of the sternum; ruptured spleen; internal hemorrhages; severed right arm." That is all.

*Music: Punctuates sharply, fading down behind:*

VOICE. Ah, but you have left out the important things:
He died also of a broken Jew [1]
And multiple abrasions of the skin of a Chinese.
And where in the report have you mentioned what happened in a little Spanish town in 1938?

[1] The numbered notes will be found on pages 73-76.

*Music: An angry upsurge, which subsides quickly as the next man speaks.*

OBSTETRICIAN (*quietly*). I am the doctor who twenty-six years ago delivered Henry Charles Peters. My file says: "Primipara; normal labor, of about six hours, no complications; anesthesia, ether; weight, six pounds, four ounces." It was a simple birth.

*Music: A quiet, almost rustic theme in the strings. It fades slowly under:*

VOICE. Ah, but it was not a simple birth,
> His mother's womb having inward connections with Scandinavia and the springs and winters of that region,
> The seed of his father being out of the cross-fertilizations of restless migratory peoples, and the silt and backwash of a thousand continental waters;
> And at his birth his pulse was one hundred thirty and his States were forty-eight,
> His respiration normal and his rights equal,
> And there were fifty-one teeth implicit in his gums [2]
> And twenty-one amendments in his Constitution.
> And although he was blind at birth, and without a mind of his own,
> He was nevertheless automatically a citizen of his country,
> Certain privileges having been obtained in his name and underwritten by many men,
> Among them some too famous to be mentioned,
> And others less famous who died in battles too familiar to be here recounted.

Do you call that a simple birth?

*Music: A brief, untroubled passage of an American patriotic flavor, but not too obvious. It fades before:*

MOTHER. I am his mother. His hair was light when he was born, but it turned dark later. He was a bottle baby after three weeks.

When he was still in knee pants he got into a fight with some other boys at the corner of our street and got cut with a piece of metal. That's how he got the scar on his chin.

He was a dreamer, Henry was, with all kinds of ideas. It seems like he was never one for the girls, hardly, until he met Marian, whom he got engaged to the day he got the good job at McAndrew's Department Store.

I remember how I was hoping he wouldn't be drafted, but he went and enlisted. And when he went away to the war he said he knew exactly why he was going and said he'd be back when the war was over and not to worry. But I worried.

Why did he have to get killed? Why did it have to happen to my boy?

He kissed me good-by on a Thursday morning—it was August twentieth, 1942—he had to get up very early that morning—and I cried, and the last I saw of him was when he went out of the front door, and I hurried into the front room and watched him through the front window, going down the street.

*Music: A dark passage; quiet; poignant. It backs all of the following:*

VOICE. Down the street a piece there was fighting, Mother,
And your boy got hit with a piece of metal.

Who will come to the door and tell her why?

It was a long street he started down, Mother,
All the way on Maple and continuing on Piccadilly
and the Nevsky Prospekt,
Winding down around the main drag of Canberra
And connecting with footpaths in the Solomons.

Many mothers and many windows on that street,
Mother,
And many a turning and a sudden intersection.

Where it leads to is, of course, the question of our
time.

*Music: Continues alone for a moment.*

TEACHER. I was his teacher.

*Music: Out.*

TEACHER. He was a fair student. Nothing out of the ordinary. His average grade was B minus, overall, rating
a C in English, A in history, D in geography, and B
in chemistry. Best mark was in history. He was in the
lower third of his graduating class. That is all we
have in the record.

*Music: A statement very close to a fanfare. It de-
velops and sustains under:*

VOICE. There is more to the record.

Sir, he went beyond you in geography, learning that
an ocean is a strait, a continent an isthmus:

Learning that the sky is the limit of the letting of
blood;
Learning the lie of the darkest land.

Sir, he has been graduated with honors,
And he shall have a good mark in history forever.

*Music: The spirit of the music that preceded the
Teacher, but segueing now to a homely folk quality,
which fades under:*

MUSIC TEACHER. It was I who gave him music lessons. He
started with the violin at the age of twelve and went
as far as the third position. I'm sorry to say he wasn't
a very good pupil. I understand his mother had a hard
time making him practice. When he was about fifteen
he got a sudden passion to be a drummer, and so he
gave up the violin. I advised against his doing it, but
he was all caught up with traps and snares and para-
phernalia, and I suppose he had to have his fling.
There's no accounting for the tastes of adolescents.

When he was nineteen or so, he got to appreciate
good music, and in fact the last time I talked with him
was at a concert at the Memorial Building in town.
He was there with his girl, and we met at intermission
and made a date to meet afterward, and Mr. Draper
and I and Henry and Marian went to an ice-cream
parlor, and we had a fine time talking about things in
general, and I got to like him very much. I saw him a
couple of times after that, at the movies, but I never
again got to speak to him. I was really sorry to hear
about him. I mean about what happened to him.

*Music: A poignant and adolescent passage, solo violin
against somber woodwinds. It is punctuated by sym-*

*bolic tympani and drums as the following speech indi-
cates:*

VOICE. Who was it fiddled while Rome was burning the
native huts of Abyssinia?

Very respectable gentlemen indeed, including old
King Carol and his fiddlers three—

Paganini Baldwin, Joachim Blum, Sir Johnny One-
Note,[3]

And choirs of fiddlers, whole companies of fiddlers,
nations of fiddlers, senatorial and parliamentarian [4]—

All of whom may now sound A's for a dead soldier
And then go into a pavanne.

Call it "None but the Purple Heart."

Private First Class Peters was a good-enough music
pupil soon to see relationships between the concert repertoire at home

And how the boys were doing on the beachhead,

And good enough to recognize that whereas four-
forty would buy two good seats to the municipal auditorium to hear the symphony,

It was a hot and smoking seventy-five did the arguing for Mendelssohn and Gershwin and the
deeply non-Aryan St. Louis Blues.

Among the heavy drums he sat and played the
bazooka, played the sweet bazooka, played it
sweet and low and ducked his head from time
to time as chords crashed all about him;

And when the raid was over he would rise and pick
his pack up and go on against the kettledrums,

against the snares and booby traps and para-
phernalia of the well-rigged enemy.

And by such tactics, he and others of his band storming the Appian hill up as far as the third position,

The comfort of a box seat at the Met was being
made secure,

And the undivided concentration of the music-lover
in his home was being convoyed safely through
the program on the radio.

*Music: The spirit of the passage that preceded the
Teacher, but it segues now to a tender mood and holds
briefly under:*

GIRL. We'd been keeping company for three years before
the war broke out, and I wanted to get married right
after Pearl Harbor, but he enlisted immediately and
said he'd rather wait until after the war, because he
didn't want me tied down to him in case he might
get crippled or blinded or something and be a burden
to me.

We used to go to the movies once a week, depending
on who was playing, or to a concert, and occasionally
we went dancing at the Palladium on a Saturday night.
We were both crazy about photography, and used to
keep a picture album together, in which we pasted pictures of all the places we had been, and all the people
who were important to us, like our families and the
boy who first introduced us at a party. Hank became
very serious toward the end, though, and he used to
talk a great deal about the world and its problems.

When Hank went away, I felt sure he'd come back,
and I still can't get used to the idea that he won't.

*Music: Development of the theme that introduced the Girl, but it erases quickly under:*

VOICE. While you were going to the movies once a week,
The Weimar Republic failed you.
While you were fumbling on a sofa,
A paperhanger laid waste your plans.

In your picture album
Have you not left out the gallery of senators who
      voted down the League of Nations?
And a group shot of the Chinese of Mukden—dead
      since 1931?
And a close-up of the greaseproud face of Franco? ⁵
These people were important to you also.

Tonight your arms lie empty of your lover
Because it was assumed in local legislative circles,
      after one such war as this,
The world was none of our concern.

The empty pillow beside your own
Is stained with oil we sold the enemy.
Our foreign policy was set against the occasional
      Saturday night at the Palladium,
Or so it turned out when the scrap reserve got high
      enough in Yokohama.

*Music: A commentary.*

EDITOR. I got a letter from him once, practically telling me
how to run my newspaper. He demanded to know why
we took the stand we did, in our editorials, about certain fundamental and constitutional things. He accused
us of being anti-war and against the United Nations
simply because we hammered away at bureaucracy in

Washington and kept pointing out the dangers of trusting our Allies too far. He indulged in the fruitless and misguided pastime of calling names and took occasion, in his letter, to label us Fascists simply because we took a strong position against the excesses of labor and warned the public not to encourage racial equality among population groups for whom equal rights would obviously create problems that would upset the entire social structure.[6] It was typical of letters we received from numerous victims of propaganda, and so, naturally, we did not print it.

VOICE. Yes, he was the type to trust an ally in all seasons
of travail.
For in the summer of the year,
When the star close by us shone upon the midlands
And the grasses grew exuberantly on the moors,
The varicolored currents sparkling and curling in
the channel,[7]
He trusted the young men of an ally up as far as
thirty thousand feet against the finest squadrons of the obviously unvanquishable Luftwaffe;
And in the spring of yet another year,
When the dandelions in cool disdain of the communiqués appeared among the corpses,
And spice-carrying breezes from neutral orchards
to the south blew softly over the ammunition
dumps, he trusted the young men of another
ally as far as the border of Rumania and still
farther.

He was also the type to enjoy the excesses of labor
As they appeared in the shape of the gun in his
hands,

As they flew by the hundreds over his head,
And as they rolled on tracks and treads down the
paths of most resistance.

He was the type who insisted upon the open candors
of labeling,
His nose contending Fascists by any other name
smell just as bad.
He was an easy victim to the propaganda that all
men were equally created,
This being not especially a doctrine short-waved
from abroad, but rather early American.
On the day he died, reconnaissance had told them
that the foe lay straight ahead, but Pete knew
very well some of the enemy was back at
home—
Publishing daily and Sunday.

*Music: A stern comment, brazen and harsh. The music
cuts off for:*

NAZI SOLDIER. I killed him. It was early in the morning
when we shelled the road. I did not see him, of course,
because I was miles away. I merely pulled the draw-
string that fired the eighty-eight-millimeter shell.

As far as I am concerned, it was merely a puff of
smoke on the side of a hill.

I had nothing against this man personally. I was
merely doing my duty for the Führer and the Father-
land in the struggle to save the world from the Bolshevik democrats.

It was entirely an impersonal matter.

Heil Hitler!

*Music: A pompous and Wagnerian strain, going out
quickly under:*

VOICE. When the last bomb has crumped
And the tank is garaged
And the cruiser wheels about and makes for port,
When the tape is scraped off the windows in London
And the delicatessens of Copenhagen once again
break out in green neon,
When the wives and children go down to the station
in Council Bluffs,
Knowing that victory comes in on the 5:45,
Mrs. Peters will be sitting alone at the front-room
window listening to the bells and the whistles.

What will *you* be doing then, blitz boy?
Where will you be going then, warmaker extraordinary?
What impersonal matter will absorb you on that
day, master of Europe?

The mother of the smoke puff on the hillside
Will finger a worn gold star,
Remembering the son you killed merely in the name
of the mystic of Munich.

*Music: A variation on the previous cue. It fades
under:*

FERRITER. I'm Charlie Ferriter. Me and Hank was crawling on our bellies up a slope one morning, and there was a stinking big red flash;[8] and when I looked around again, Hank was just a mess of rags and a couple of bones stickin' through.

Me and Hank used to get into arguments about the war. He used to talk about freedom, and he said that's what we were fighting for.

Well, for Christ's sake,[9] I knew that—he didn't have to tell me that; anybody except a Fascist louse [10] would agree it's the best thing in the world you could fight for. But what I'd like to know is, why do you have to fight for it every twenty-five years? Can't somebody figure a way around that?

What bothers me is whether I'm being a sucker. Because if this war don't add up to something big— bigger than ever came out of any other war—then I don't know what I'm doing in this outfit.

I used to say to Hank, if the people who are still alive when this one's over—if those people don't do something sensible about it, then what the hell is the use? What's the good of guys like Hank Peters getting knocked off if nobody knows what to do over their dead bodies?

(*Angrily.*) What are *you* going to do about it?

*Music: A very angry passage, cutting out suddenly and sharply for:*

VOICE (*the same as we have been hearing after each speech*).

I was Hank Peters.

I assure you I hated to go; it is not easy to leave a woman crying at a train gate; it is not easy to leave a mother standing at a window—to walk away and not look back.

You can get lonesome, no matter what, when you are far from home, especially if you don't know when, if ever, you are coming back.

I am dead of the mistakes of old men,[11]
And I lie fermenting in the wisdom of the earth.

I am very dead, but no deader than the British who
    struck at Alamein, the Reds who crossed the
    Dnieper going west.

I am silenced, but no more silent than the partisans
    of Yugoslavia who fought tanks with their
    bare hands and a bottle of benzine.[12]

I am missing, but not farther than a famined Greek.

I am buried, but no deeper than the children of
    Chungking.

I know, I know,
How there will be the jubilation at the end,
And how the proclamations will be sent out on the
    waiting air.
They will gather in committee,
Pose for pictures,
Sign the papers.
Territories will be wrangled, and big punishments
    performed.
It will be seen to that the ruins are most carefully
    policed.

(Will someone give my best to Marian the day that
    Palestine is taken up?) [13]

Ah, there will be a stirring and a busyness about
    the capitals,
And Charlie Ferriter will wonder if perhaps he's
    being answered.
The charters will be sealed in wax above the bodies
    of the dead,
And all the words will make a noise of truth and
    sensibility.

But let me tell you—

From my acre of now undisputed ground I will be
    listening:

I will be tuned to clauses in the contract where the
    word Democracy appears

And how the freedoms are inflected to a Negro's
    ear.

I shall listen for a phrase obliging little peoples of
    the earth:

For Partisans and Jews and Puerto Ricans,

Chinese farmers, miners of tin ore beneath Bolivia;

I shall listen how the words go easy into Russian

And the idiom's translated to the tongue of Spain.

I shall wait and I shall wait in a long and long sus-
    pense

For the password that the Peace is setting solidly.

On that day, please to let my mother know

Why it had to happen to her boy.[14]

*Music: Conclusion.*

# UNTITLED

*This free man is a rare bird and when you meet him take a good
look at him and try to figure him out because
Some day when the United States of the Earth gets going and runs
smooth and pretty there will be more of him than we have now.*
                                                    —CARL SANDBURG

When I wrote "Untitled," I half feared Hank Peters
was too rare a bird to be more than a symbol, a vision, a
figment of literary wish-fulfillment. I was corrected in this
by a number of his comrades-in-arms who happened to hear
playbacks of the broadcast or who read the script in magazines that found their way overseas. Soldiers wrote me from
France and New Guinea and Germany, from hospitals in
Holland and California, confirming the life and death of
Peters. The letters came in not by thousands—I wasn't selling soap or giving away cigarettes—they came in slowly,
over a long period of time; there were not more than three
hundred and fifty altogether. I was moved and pleased by
their corroboration, because it meant that the men best
qualified to judge—G.I.s wearing combat stars—found, in
my attempt at a portrait, a reasonable likeness of a man
they knew and loved.

To me the citizen who hated Fascism before it was fashionable to do so, was and is the first patriot of our time. It
is to his everlasting glory in the eyes of mankind, that
Mukden and Madrid were to him as Pearl Harbor; that
the murder of Matteotti and the sellout at Munich were
moral Dunkirks.

Such men organized the Flying Tigers and flew against the Japs well before 7 December, 1941. Such a man was Robert Montgomery, who drove an ambulance in France before it was a popular hazard for Americans. Such a man was Herman Bottcher, who fought Fascism all the way from Jarama to Leyte, where he died wearing a U.S. Distinguished Service Cross. Such a man also was Hank Peters, though less conspicuous, and not the kind to be decorated.

For a long while it was apparently the policy of government investigators to stigmatize men of this sort for having too early understood the nature of the enemy. It was one of the more classic bonehead attitudes in that shameful period of our history when we were literally racing legislation through Congress in order to stop a poor straggling ship named the *Mar Cantabrico* from delivering supplies to the Loyalists (meanwhile we were stepping up shipments of scrap and oil to Japan); when a man could not contribute a dime to the medical relief of Spanish republicans, or make a speech in their behalf, without being denounced by professional patriots and headline-muggers.

Once when I was a reporter in my native Massachusetts, an organization of dubious lineage and connections which called itself "Italian Red Cross," wanted to hire Springfield's big municipal auditorium for a "benefit." The proceeds were to alleviate the suffering of Italian soldiers then slaughtering Ethiopians for Mussolini and the King. The application for permission so to use civic property was contested by a Negro pastor and four anti-Fascists who had been reading the papers and drawing their own conclusions. A hearing was held at which spokesmen for the American Red Cross showed up to support the Italians; and after much debate permission was granted to go ahead with this humanitarian enterprise. I attended, to cover the story for my newspaper. I saw the Fascist salute freely given, and I watched old women and young mothers drop gold wedding rings into a kitty. Meanwhile the local anti-Fascists were denounced in the usual quarters as Communists. It was all part of the great tableau of the times. Multiply the incident by thousands, and you have a picture of the political immaturity of the United States of 1935.

Hank Peters grew into manhood during the long spiral downward into war. He was intelligent enough to wonder about the respect shown in high places of state for bums like Musso and Ciano. The fact that a thug was the head of a nation did not, in Hank's view, make him any less a thug. Hank was naïve that way. He thought Hitler an evil and dangerous man from the start, and held those who did business with him to be accessory before the fact.

Being prematurely against Mrs. Lindbergh's *Wave of the Future*, Hank was uneasy among several societies: his highest contempt was for appeasers, noninterventionists, and isolationists; he hated the Washington-New York-Chicago newspaper axis and their hirelings no less than he hated Goebbels; he was vexed by the sophistries of the whole wing of American radicals, including Communists, who begrudged aid to an embattled Britain; he was bitter against liberals who flopped about like seals on perilous issues; he cursed the professional Russia-baiters for playing into the hands of the Axis anti-Comintern racket. By the tendencies of his world he was much disturbed, as all free men had a right to be. He knew that his life and the life of his whole generation was involved and committed, and that disaster and death were in the cards.

Hank was no genius, no seer, no prophet. He wrote no columns, radiated no opinions on the air. He merely used his head. One needs no special dispensation from God or

Yale to be able to smell a stink in Denmark. Hank was by no means unique—he was typical and ordinary among people who were ahead of their time. And there were enough of them to fill Madison Square Garden several times over.

The reaction to this broadcast from civilians was warm and widespread, but I had never expected the response I was to get from G.I.s. I should have known better. Many a soldier, during the dark days, needed assurance that the people back home weren't *all* basking in the sun and going to the races and eating filet mignon and supporting the reactionary press. If he *was* going to die, he wanted it to be for a purpose—and the higher the purpose, the better. The war never became "less ideological" to him, as it did to Winston Churchill on the occasion of the mid-war speech in which he announced he had "kind words" to say for Franco Spain.

A pilot named Lt. Robert E. McCumber wrote me from France during the Ardennes counteroffensive: "Your Hank Peters still lives. I know, because my Hank Peters by another name, a copilot, still lives, although we saw him crash on enemy territory last spring. He lives within us; and will, unless we quit. In 'Untitled' you have told much that I think my friend would like people to know, if he could tell them now. . . . Why write this to you? Because I hope writers can do it again, time after time, until the unenlightened and unappreciative surviving beings finally realize what it is that makes life so precious. And until, having learned this, they learn also to work hard and long to find a means to guard this treasured way of life—to guard it well enough to prevent having to ransom it again with the blood of good men. But is there any hope, really? . . . What of the survivors this time, can more be hoped from *them?* I think so and apparently you do. But only if they are well taught."

Also from France, the same questioning from Private Jack Rudin: "Hank Peters was my brother. I mourn his death as a brother. . . . He was more than a puff of smoke on a hillside; he was everyone fighting oppression, intolerance, and bigotry. He was right about the enemy at home, the one with the largest daily circulation in the world. I have seen the once-proud Nazi frightened and humbled, but the sleek, smug enemy at home remains as firmly entrenched as ever. What can we do to ferret him out? The struggle is for you . . . [who] have the ammunition to fight him—truth. If I'm lucky enough to settle down after the war, I'll think of Hank whenever I feel that I'm smug and safe in my world. To forget Hank in the gay years of peaceful relief to come would be an admission to our children that we have failed them."

Such letters made me realize that a good many of our fighting men were carrying with them not only guns and K rations, but doubts and misgivings; that they were hungering for the simple reassurance that somebody *cared*, in a political way, back home.

One of the large majority of those back home who did indeed care a good deal was the man who appeared as Hank in the first two productions of the script—Fredric March. March had not long before returned from a tour of the European theater, where he had been enormously popular among the troops. He had performed in his camp appearances neither comic routines nor vignettes by Noel Coward, but had gone to early American sources. He read from Thomas Paine, and the boys took to it hungrily. Again, the great need was reassurance. Even reassurances one hundred and sixty-five years old. Tom Paine had cared.

It was a matter of record that this country was worth the trouble in 1776, but some of the boys needed to know whether the same held true for 1944. They needed to know, because according to some advertisers, it was the old corner drugstore and not a new, united world that our boys were fighting for—an America blissfully unchanged, and no hare-brained social reforms behind their backs, either. A rugged manufacturer, unworried about his own power and milk supplies, snorted about TVA's on the Danube and milk for Hottentots, as though such tokens of victory, such practical manifestations of recovery from chaos, were too utterly ridiculous. One of our representatives coined "globaloney" as the war cry that would frighten visionaries like Mr. Roosevelt. Naturally some of our boys wanted to know whether this person represented the whole nation or was merely an isolated globilliterate.

The McCumber-type soldier was not much reassured by the Bilbo-type statesman, and the Colonel Blimps of the home press. He preferred Paine and Lincoln and F.D.R., and war aims that he could sink his teeth and heart into. Hence his approval of Hank's disclosure at the end, a speech that certainly did not burst upon the world as something new. The war aims of Hank Peters are, roughly, the war aims of any man who cares about the how, what, and why of freedom. They paraphrase the platforms of a dozen statesmen and a hundred million people, and are as ordinary as hope itself.

As to the business of producing this script: This is Hank's piece. He is the Narrator, and without a good Hank you have no show. Though his age is indicated to be twenty-six, he can be older. Certainly he should not be much younger, because the attitude of his thinking is not that of a stripling. Mr. March was closer to his forties than his twenties; yet he was completely acceptable, agewise, as young Peters. Sense-wise, he was just about perfect. He modulated beautifully from the matter-of-factness of the introductory passages to the faintly chiding accent of his reply to the medical officer; there was a glow of quiet patriotic pride in the commentary on the obstetrician's report; a sadness without bitterness after the mother's speech; an open sardonic contempt to-ward the editor.

There are several occasions when Hank fringes on anger, but never does he contain it less than in his apostrophe to the Nazi soldier. By the time Ferriter has finished, Hank is on his way back to his grave, and there is about him the resignation of a man who knows he cannot rest until he gets word that the coming peace is on the up-and-up.

It is important that the characters who people this script be carefully chosen and painstakingly directed. Once, when Stage for Action first presented a stage adaptation of "Un-titled," the medical officer was so grief-stricken over Hank's death that one expected him to break down and cry. No, that's not the way. Hank is one of thousands of dead sol-diers within the experience of this officer, and the recital of the file on Peters is routine business. The same goes for the obstetrician.

The mother should be a reasonable facsimile of Charmé Allen, the Mrs. Peters of the original production, and one of radio's few genuine mother types. The role must be rinsed clean of soap, for if there is the slightest resemblance between this woman and the kindly old bores of the morn-ing serials, the Archangel Raphael will answer with plagues and migraine headaches.

The music teacher should be the most relaxed of all. Those who heard the first CBS production may recall the brilliance of Hester Sondergaard in this role. To sound calm, ordinary, and mike-free on the air is one of the most difficult things you can ask an actor to do, and in the case of the music teacher that is precisely what is called for. Unlike others in the script who are formal or else emotionally involved, the music teacher is in a halfway position: she knew Hank, but not well. He wasn't a bright pupil, so they were never closely bound by common interest. She was on the periphery of his life, a zone that included accidental meetings in ice cream parlors. Mrs. Draper is honestly sorry about Hank's end, but no more than you are about the death of the boy who ran one of the elevators in your building three years ago.

The girl Marian is a delicate problem in casting, for she should sound neither too mature and knowing nor too girlish. Hank would not have been interested in a giggler or a debutante; yet it is clear from Marian's speech that he was considerably ahead of her in an understanding of the world's ways. She was no doubt a childhood sweetheart; they grew up together. Had Hank lived, she would have learned enough from him to become an ardent citizen, a Sandburgian rare bird, on her own. As things stood, she was a good, substantial, attractive girl and would have made Hank a fine wife.

The editor is a jerk, of whom we have many distinguished prototypes in this country. Kermit Murdock made a composite portrait of them in as keen a characterization as the script enjoyed. Assured, stuffy, yet not overbearing; genteel; a scoundrel who has convinced himself of his integrity on all issues, concerning the truth of which his office boy knows better.

The Nazi is a party product, the kind who bears himself proudly in prison camp, and sasses his captors about articles of the Geneva Convention as though his stripe ever had any use for them. The speech is spoken coldly, without boasting of any kind, but you gather nevertheless that you would like to punch his nose. The "Heil Hitler" should be snapped with the fanatical fervor of the well-inculcated *Jugend*. In the original broadcast, Michael Ingram as the Nazi was perfectly Nuremberg.

Charlie Ferriter is a solid hombre. He is McCumber and Rudin, but roughhewn. He speaks his mind more simply and bluntly than anybody else in the play. There is no room for nuance in his interpretation of things. Even more than Hank, Ferriter flings the challenge direct. His tagline— "What are *you* going to do about it?"—points a demanding finger at the listener.

*Music.* Bernard Herrmann's score was austere over most of its pages, but its moments of relief (as in a pastoral strain behind Hank's speech on the birthright of an American and in a tender violin solo preceding the entrance of the music teacher) were lyrical and deeply felt. The music managed somehow to superimpose reflections of its own upon what was being said, and did not simply nod and bow before and after every speech. I don't mean that the score ever went in a direction opposite to the script, but the music was always in there pitching instead of sitting on the bench.

*Sound.* None is required, and no production should improvise where possibilities for sound may be felt to exist. I refrained from indicating an explosion to punctuate Ferriter's description of the "stinking big red flash" because of its obviousness. Every now and then amateurs who undertake to produce my plays also undertake to rewrite them without authorization or consultation. It is nice of them to take the trouble, and if they succeeded in improving the plays, I should be grateful forever, but in the meantime it would perhaps save a lot of time, trouble, and threatening noises from the constabulary if the plays were left roughly as they are. An old idiosyncrasy.

*Additional Notes.* 1. During rehearsals of the first broadcast, some of the cast thought I had intended "broken Jew" as a pun on "broken jaw," and I was so horrified at the thought that I changed the phrase to "broken Hebrew." It appeared this way in some of the early printed versions, notably in *PM* and *Coronet,* but I later restored the original word because "Hebrew" seemed to me, on reflection, to be not what Hank would say.

2. There was some confusion about the number of teeth implicit in the human mouth. One dentist told me forty-eight, and I broadcast this bit of misinformation to the world. Dentists in my audience soon set me straight. Twenty baby teeth, they advised me, and thirty-two "second" teeth.

3. Sir Johnny is an allusion to Sir John Simon, in the cabinet of Stanley Baldwin. Sir John was one of the Whitehall clique who felt Franco was a decent type and took a dim view of intervention. All of which was of aid and comfort to the rebels.

4. This line originally bore the additional phrase, "senatorial and parliamentarian," but Columbia's photoelectric ear, William Fineshriber, pointed out that some listeners might get the impression I was slurring the Democratic Process. I huffed and puffed and took the phrase out. It is perfectly true, of course, that guilt does rest heavy on the between-wars national assemblies of Britain, France, and the United States, but I did not want to risk any misconstruction on the point.

5. Eight years since the fall of Madrid, and still we do business with Franco. Eight years of mounting evidence of Falange terror, photographic documentation by the *March of Time,* even repudiation by Sir Samuel Hoare, an early

apologist and Franco-lover, yet *still* we recognize this openly Fascist government. It will be hard to explain to the class of 1985.

6. Out of considerations of political policy, a few among the scores of Army orientation groups that produced "Untitled" deleted this sentence, and some others eliminated entirely the editor's speech and Hank's rejoinder. I would never have condoned such deletions had I known of them in advance, because I consider this exchange of speeches, and most especially the reference to equal rights, as hewing very close to the core of the script.

7. This line is literary rather than functional, and twice I have cut it from broadcasts; but I have been prevailed upon to leave it to the option of the reader-director. If you feel certain your listener will know you are speaking of the English Channel, include it. But to *say* English Channel obviously wouldn't do.

8. Herrmann composed a series of ominous ground-swelling crescendi for the transitional passage going into Ferriter's speech. They were spaced to fill natural pauses in Charlie's speech, and the biggest and last surge came right after the words "big red flash." It was much better than a literal explosion.

9. Changed to "criney's sake" for the American air. The British Broadcasting Corporation permits a man to swear, and such words as "damn," "hell," "devil," and "bastard" flash uncensored to the far ends of His Majesty's Empire. But we are pure, we are, so you must unman Ferriter and make him say "criney."

10. "Louse" is a euphemism for the original term. Most stage versions prefer "bastard."

11. How the sins of the fathers *are* visited upon the heads of the children! The young man of this war, as of

others, paid for the indifference of a generation of seniors. The eighteen-year-old conscript of 1945 was a kid of nine when Hitler marched into the Rhineland. He was only four when the German people gave Hitler enough votes to make trouble in the grand manner.

I had an uncomfortable moment when, during the 1944 election campaign, the script was performed at Carnegie Hall to climax a rally attended by Mrs. Franklin D. Roosevelt. The phrase "old man" was being used cynically by Republicans against the president; and as I happened to be involved in the campaign to re-elect him, I winced when Paul Mann, playing Hank Peters, came to this line. Nobody connected with the production had thought of it in advance, and the implication almost knocked me out of my seat. However, it was apparently accepted in its proper context by most of the audience, including Mrs. Roosevelt, who made a complimentary reference to the production in her speech later in the evening.

12. Why do most narrators want to pronounce this "benzedrine"? It is a fine drug and all that, but even its manufacturers don't claim that it could stop a tank.

13. Palestine is one of those subjects that His Majesty's government would rather you didn't bring up. My fondness for the British people is, I think, expressed somewhat in the pages of "An American in England," but I have never been an admirer of the way British diplomacy has fumbled, ducked, and double-talked its way around the problems of Palestine and India. Hank, no respecter of the Baldwin-Simon-Halifax-Chamberlain-Churchill-Bevin colonial policy, had a right to be especially pointed on this question.

14. An earlier version of this play, distributed for morale and orientation purposes at the request of numerous army, school, and amateur groups, went four lines beyond this end-

ing. The appendage, though innocuous, was an inadvertence of printing, and was never used in the broadcast or in major stage productions. Should the earlier script fall into your hands, and should you be of a mind to make comparisons, pay no attention to the discrepancy.

# EL CAPITAN AND THE CORPORAL

Produced on July 25, 1944, as the nineteenth of the "Columbia Presents Corwin" series, under the direction of the author. Katherine Locke and Joseph Julian were co-starred as Betty and the Corporal, with Kermit Murdock as the Fat Man. Burl Ives was the traveling minnesinger. The score was composed and conducted by Alexander Semmler.

# EL CAPITAN AND THE CORPORAL

**P.A. AMPLIFIER** (*being the one in Union Station, Los Angeles*). Attention. Santa Fe Train Number 22, the El Capitan, for Albuquerque, Dodge City, Kansas City, and Chicago, now loading at Track 5 for departure at 11:30.

*Music: A bustling introduction, dropping behind:*

**CAL.** Well, I had seat No. 18 on this train, the El Capitan, and the way I figured, it wasn't quite right for two people to have the same seat on the same train; so I said to the man who was sitting in it when I got there: "You sure you got the right seat, sir?" and he looked kind of startled and said:

**MAN.** Why, yes. My ticket here says seat 18, and this is 18.

**CAL.** Well, so does mine say 18.

**MAN.** Guess the thing to do is to take it up with the conductor. . . .

**CAL.** So we took it up with the conductor and got it straightened out. Seems he had seat No. 18 in the *next* car. I got settled in my seat, and there was a little time before the train started, and I was wondering who was going to sit next to me. You see, in all the times I'd been riding on trains I never had a pretty girl sit next to me, and this time was no exception, because a guy came along who must have weighed three hundred pounds, and he plunked down beside

79

me. The poor fellow was puffing and panting, because he'd thought he was going to miss the train. . . .

FAT MAN. Phewy! I'm winded. I'm not built for this kind of thing, as you can see.

CAL. What'd you do? Run up the ramp?

FAT MAN (*puffing*). All the way from the street. Guess I couldn't have been looking where I was going. I went up the wrong track and found myself on a train for *San Diego!* Isn't that a silly thing to do?

CAL. Well, I don't know. It's easy to make a mistake.

FAT MAN. That ever happen to you?

CAL. No, can't say it has.

FAT MAN. Look at this handkerchief—wringing wet. Boy, I won't catch my breath till I get to Santa Barbara.

CAL. Santa Barbara? This train doesn't go to Santa Barbara.

FAT MAN. You mean—you mean this isn't the Beaver for San Francisco?

CAL. Heck, no. This is the El Capitan going to Chicago.

FAT MAN (*in a panic*). Oh, dear! Oh, my Lord! Will you help me down with that bag?

CAL. Sure thing.

*There is a bustle of baggage and general retreat, under which effect Cal explains:*

CAL. I went to help the poor guy off the train, and I started down the aisle, sort of running interference for him, but before I went five steps, I bumped smack into a girl.

*An oomph, and a suitcase on the floor.*

CAL. We collided so hard she dropped her suitcase and almost fell over it. . . .

GIRL (*in an injured tone, sharply*). Will you *please* watch where you're *going!*

CAL. I beg your pardon. (*Down.*) She gave me a look that would wither your left arm, and I said to her: "I'm just trying to help a man catch a train," but she didn't answer and went by with her nose in the air, and I felt like saying to her: "Don't you know there's a war on?" But what's the use of arguing with a dame in a situation like that? So I tumbled off the train with the guy's suitcase and helped him on his way. Well, I got back on the car, and who was sitting in *my* seat by the window but this same girl? She looked at me as though I had just slugged her grandmother, and I gave the courtesy right back to her.

(*Up; icily.*) I'm very sorry, miss, but you're sitting in my seat.

GIRL. You must be mistaken. This ticket says seat 18.

CAL. But mine is 18 *window.* Yours is 18 *aisle.*

GIRL (*zero degrees centigrade*). In that case I'll move.

CAL. If you don't mind. I'd just like to sit in my own seat, that's all.

GIRL. Very well, excuse it. . . .

CAL. I moved in and sat next to the window, and the train started.

*Train starting, under:*

CAL. She picked up a magazine and thumbed through it, and now and then looked up out of the window as we mooched along toward Pasadena, but her glance was strictly the impersonal type, and it went right past me with no local stops. After a while I must have got interested in the pictures in her magazine and started looking at them over her shoulder, because suddenly it struck me that this girl had a very interesting profile, to say the least. I was in the middle of admiring it when . . .

GIRL. *Well?*

CAL. Well what?

GIRL. What are you looking at?

CAL. Your nose.

GIRL. Oh. Does it meet with your approval?

CAL. Sure does.

GIRL. I'm so relieved. . . .

CAL. After that I kept pretty much to myself until we'd left San Berdoo[1] and had started to climb through Cajon Pass. Then I volunteered to point out some of the features of interest. I didn't know too much about the country, but I made off like I was an authority and named a couple of mountain peaks that have been anonymous since the Mojave Indians were running the place.

She paid no attention to me at all until I said to her: (*Up.*) That one there is called Mount Glickstein.

GIRL. Now, look—who do you think you're annoying? That happens to be Mount Baldy.

CAL. It is? Well, maybe you're right. It *does* seem unlikely they'd be naming a mountain after my commanding officer.

GIRL. You know, you're the least smart aleck I've ever had the—

CAL. The name is Cal, not Aleck.

GIRL. Short for callow, I presume.

CAL. Short for what?

[1] The numbered notes will be found on pages 107-108.

GIRL. Let it go. . . .

CAL. I tried not to let it go, but she buried herself in a book, and we were past Victorville before I spoke to her again. I finally said: (*Up.*) Look—I'm sorry if I was rude. After all, I didn't *intend* to bump into you in the aisle. I was helping that fat man off the train. Poor fellow, you know what happened to him? First he got on a train headed for—

GIRL. I'm not interested.

CAL (*deflated*). Well—all right. If you don't want to accept an apology, why, then—after all, if we're going to be sitting next to each other for a couple of days, I— (*Pause.*)

(*Down.*) She simply stared at her book and ignored me, and I shut up, feeling pretty foolish for wasting my time on a cold potato just because she happened to have a cute profile.

She probably would never have spoken to me of her own accord if it hadn't been for a little accident just before we got to Barstow. Seems she wanted something in her suitcase; so she got up and reached for it in the rack. . . .

GIRL. Excuse me.

CAL. Can I help you there?

GIRL (*reaching*). No, thank you. I can manage. . . .

CAL. Well, she didn't manage so good, because the train gave a little lurch, and down went the bag on my noggin. . . .

CAL AND GIRL. (*Ad libs of action wherein the girl loses her grip on the bag and it comes down heavily on the head of our hero.*)

GIRL. Oh, I'm sorry! I'm terribly sorry. Are you hurt?

CAL (*down*). Actually the bump didn't hurt much at all,

because the grip wasn't heavy; yet it made such a loud noise when it dropped on my head that she must have thought I was killed. I played it for sympathy, naturally. . . .

GIRL. Are you all right? Here, let me—

CAL (*without conviction; faintly*). I—I'm okay—I'm all right.

GIRL. I'm *so* sorry, really I am. What's the matter, is it bleeding?

CAL. No. The only thing I'm worried about is an old skull fracture I got six years ago.

GIRL (*scared now*). Why—do you think you've—does it feel—can I *do* anything for you?

CAL (*again without conviction*). No, no, I'm all right. (*Down.*) Well, she was so scared about the idea of having refractured my skull—which had never been fractured in the first place—and so regretful about the way she'd treated me, that she just took right over, and the first thing I knew she was massaging my scalp.

GIRL. Does that feel better now?

CAL. Much better. You have the healing touch.

GIRL. I'm sorry if I seemed mean—but you must admit you were pretty fresh.

CAL. But I apologized, didn't I?

GIRL. Yes, and I should have accepted your apology. That wasn't very nice of me.

CAL. Okay, then—are we friends?

GIRL (*chuckling*). Yes—we're friends. . . .

CAL. The train stopped for a few minutes at Barstow, and we got off and walked around in the hot desert sun.

*Background sound of normal train traffic at a typical railroad division point.*

CAL. It didn't take us long to get acquainted as to who we were and what we were doing. I found her name was Betty Frisby, that she worked on jigs in an aircraft factory in California, and that she was going to . . .

BETTY. . . . Chicago, to bring my brother back from the marine hospital in Markleton, Pennsylvania.

CAL. What's he doing there?

BETTY. He was badly wounded in the merchant marine. He got torpedoed twice, and the second time he lost an arm and his spine was broken.

CAL. Gee, that's tough. I'm sorry to hear it.

BETTY. He may never be able to walk again.

CAL. Terrible.

BETTY. He's done a lot of fighting for a boy his age. Before he was in the merchant marine, he fought in Spain.

CAL. He did?

BETTY. He was with the American volunteers.

CAL. So this is really his second war, eh?

BETTY. No, it's all one war, wouldn't you say?

CAL. Well—this one really began in 1939, and the other—

BETTY. Surely by now you know better than that.

CAL. Well, I didn't follow that Spanish war very much.

BETTY. Well, I did—not only because Sandy was in it up to his neck, but I guess because my own heart was in it, too.

PORTER (*far off*). Board! All aboard!

CAL. That's us.

BETTY. Yes—let's get aboard.

CAL. This way, Betty.

BETTY. No, that's not our train. That's a Union Pacific train.

CAL (*laughing*). If I don't watch out, I'll be doing just

what that fat man did. Don't know what's come over me. I'm not usually absent-minded.

BETTY (*genially*). Maybe it was the blow on your head. . . .

CAL. We returned to the train and continued our talk, and Betty asked a lot of questions about me. . . .

BETTY. Are you on a furlough?

CAL. No, I'm just returning from one.

BETTY. What happens when you get to New York?

CAL. Well, then I go to a port of embarkation.

BETTY. Oh. (*Pause.*) Are you married?

CAL. No.

BETTY. Got a girl?

CAL. Well, nobody I'm really in love with. How about you?

BETTY. Oh, just about the same as you, I suppose.

CAL. Yeah?

BETTY. There's a boy at home who wants me to marry him, but I'm afraid we'd never get along.

CAL. Why?

BETTY. Well, we don't agree much about the world.

CAL. About the *world?*

BETTY. Yes. You see, to my way of thinking—

*A fellow passenger who has come up the aisle interrupts.*

SALESMAN. Pardon me, folks, would you like to get in on a little game of pinochle?

BETTY AND CAL. (*Decline with thanks.*)

*The passenger moves off, and Cal resumes.*

CAL. What did you mean, you and your friend didn't agree about the world?

BETTY. Well, the way I see it, there are two main—uh—let's say *points of view* about being alive on this earth. Now you're either an active human being with all that implies, or else—

CAL. Wait a minute. What *does* that imply?

BETTY. Well, it implies a certain amount of responsibility—it implies the idea of giving to as well as receiving from your country—

TOT (*who has come wandering up the aisle*). Hello.

BETTY. Well, hello.

TOT. What's your name?

CAL. Oscar Fiddlefuddle. What's yours?

TOT. Marylou Slezak.

CAL. Well, hello, Marylou. How are you?

TOT. I'm fine, thank you. How are you?

CAL. Splendid.

TOT. What's your name?

CAL. That's where we came in. Where's your mother, Marylou? Where do you live?

TOT (*by rote*). Two hundred sixteen Walnut Street, Ventura, California.

CAL. You better go to your mother now, or you'll get lost. Good-by, Marylou.

TOT. By-by. . . .

CAL. You were saying there are two kinds of people—active human beings, and what's the other kind?

BETTY. Well, for want of a better word I'd say vegetables.

CAL. Vegetables? (*Laughs.*) How do you mean?

BETTY. I mean just people who vegetate. They're planted and they grow, and you know just what to expect from them; and if their father was a head of lettuce, that's good enough for them; so *they're* a head of lettuce.

CAL. Well, now, what kind of person exactly do you mean?

BETTY. Well, look, I'll give you an example. Let's take the first privilege of citizenship in a democracy.

CAL. Yes?

BETTY. What is it, do you know?

CAL (*caught unprepared*). Uh—well, uh—I suppose it's a free press, and freedom of religion, and the other— No, that's not what I mean. Well, what is it?

BETTY. The first privilege of a citizen in a country like ours is the right to *vote*.[2]

CAL. Oh, well, of course.

BETTY. Well, I call a voter who doesn't vote—as far as I'm concerned, he qualifies as a vegetable.

CAL. A vegetable.

BETTY. Yes. He's vegetating. Voting is the *least* thing you could expect him to do. I mean, the least he could do is take a slight interest in his country. Why, when you consider how many men have *died* just for the simple right to *vote*—which we take so much for granted— when you consider how *little* trouble it is to go to the polls, then you look around at the person who stays at home on election day, and you say: There goes a cabbage. Because after all—the— (*Stops short, diverted by what is happening at the far end of the car.*)

PARTY. (*An uproar of laughter and ad libs, advancing.*)

BETTY. What's all the jollity about?

CAL. Looks to me like a wandering minstrel show. Just some soldiers and sailors on the way to the smoker, I guess.

SAILOR (*the first distinguishable voice in the hubbub*). Wait a minute, wait a minute—listen to this one. Listen! This guy says to another guy: "Did you ever have an accident?" So the other guy says: "No, but a dog bit me once." And the first guy says: "Well, wasn't that an accident?" So the second guy says: "Heck, no, he did it on *purpose!*" [3]

PARTY. (*Great laughter.*)

*They pass through the vestibule door. It closes after them, and the group is lost to us.*

CAL. Well, where were we?

BETTY. I was talking about voting. You see, to me that's only *one* way of expressing what I call a basic interest in being alive. You can be *interested* or *disinterested* in the kind of education your children are going to get—or in the wages you'll be making after the war— or in the kind of highway the town is going to build— or in a struggle for democracy, whether it's in Spain or in your own back yard.[4] Now the trouble with— (*She stops short.*) What are you looking at?

CAL. Your eyes. You have very beautiful eyes.

BETTY. And you haven't been listening to what I've been saying?

CAL. Yes, sure. But nothing you have said so far alters the fact that you have very beautiful eyes.

BETTY (*injured*). Excuse me.

CAL. Betty—where are you going? Betty! (*Raising his voice.*) Betty!

(*Down.*) People turned around and looked at me, and I felt sort of foolish; so I stayed in my seat for a while, pretending to read, and then after a few minutes I got up to look for Betty in the club car. She wasn't there, and I went through the train twice looking for her and couldn't find her; so I guessed she must have gone in the ladies' lounge. We got to Needles and still no Betty; so when the train stopped I got out, hoping to find her on the platform, and sure enough, there she was at a newsstand, buying a paper.

(*Up.*) Betty! Listen, I've been looking all over for you.

BETTY. Well, here I am. I'm the girl with the beautiful eyes.

CAL. Aw, cut it out, will ya? You want a paper?

BETTY. I have one, thank you. I don't suppose you ever read such things.

CAL. No, never.

BETTY. Afraid you might find out what's going on in the world?

CAL (*pleasantly; not miffed*). Listen, Betty—other people can read the news, but guys like your brother and I, we're the ones who have to go out and make it. Look, I'm not a vegetable, Betty, honest I'm not—and don't get mad at me. Here I am on my way to a POE,[5] and you're going back to California with your brother, and don't you think you're being just a little—

BETTY (*smiling*). All right, Cal. . . .

CAL. That's all she said. She said: "All right, Cal," and she smiled and took my arm, and we went back on the train. We got hungry around Kingman, Arizona, and went in the diner and had the ninety-cent meal, which she insisted should be Dutch, and then we returned to our car. As we opened the door off the vestibule . . .

SINGER. (*A folk tune to the accompaniment of a guitar, under Cal's speech. It is a slow, sweet ballad.*)

CAL. . . . we found there was a sort of concert going on. One of the passengers had unmasked a guitar, and there was a whole cluster of people around him listening in silence as the El Capitan streaked along in the night.

SINGER. (*The song ends.*)

PASSENGERS AND SINGER. (*The group around the singer urges him ad lib to go on. They offer suggestions, but he's particular about what he sings, and finally he selects one of his own favorites, announcing it as he strikes the first chord. It is "Black Is the Color of My True Love's Hair." At length:*)

CAL (*over singing*). After a while we returned to our seats and listened from there.

SINGER. (*The song stands out clear again for a few moments, but at a reduced perspective. It continues under:*)

CAL. Most of the lights in the car were low now, and Betty's eyes had a dark glow that made them seem more beautiful than ever. . . .

BETTY (*low*). What are you thinking?

CAL. Hm? Oh—I was just thinking there's a place in the world for this, too.

BETTY. What do you mean? For what too?

CAL. For love, and songs about love, and for singing.

BETTY. I'd hate to think what the world would be without it.

CAL. Well, that's not so hard to imagine.

BETTY. Hm? What do you mean?

CAL. Just look how it is in Germany. Why, love in Germany is under the control of the Nazi Party, and they tell people who shall breed and who'll be sterile. I don't think it's hardly possible for a Fascist to be really in love, do you know that? I mean, not if he's been brought up to believe a woman belongs only in the kitchen and the nursery. Isn't that what the Japs and Nazis think?

BETTY. Yes, it is.

CAL (*down*). Betty put her head on my shoulder, and after a while she went to sleep. I took one of her hands in mine, and I guess that was all right with her, because when I moved her hand she opened one eye sleepily, and a corner of her lip smiled at me, and she went back to sleep.

After a while I dozed off myself, with the guitar and the wheels still singing in my ears.

SINGER. (*The song continuing, over:*)

*Train wheels.*

*Music: The orchestra takes over the melody of the song; it carries the guitar along with it. The music is sleepy and sweet, but soon it freshens into a lively passage, which serves both to convey movement and to bridge the night. It goes out quickly under:*

CAL. When I woke up the train was going through Wagon Mound, New Mexico, and Betty had already eaten breakfast and was in her chair reading *Strange Fruit.* . . .

BETTY. Oh, are you awake?

CAL (*sleepily*). Yeah. Good morning.

BETTY. Good morning.

CAL. What time is it?

BETTY. Time for you to be up and about. I've already had my breakfast.

CAL. What a woman! Do you always get up so early and look so pretty in the morning?

BETTY. Daily except Sunday.

CAL. You're wonderful. Excuse me while I scrape my beard off.

BETTY. You're excused.

CAL (*again narrating*). For a day that started off so good, I suffered a great many annoyances. In the first place, the car we were in got so chummy that everybody was practically sitting in our laps, including young Miss Slezak of Walnut Street, Ventura. . . .

TOT. What's your name?

CAL. I told you yesterday. Fiddlefuddle.

TOT. Why? . . .

CAL. And then a girl going through to the diner spotted Betty, and it had to turn out they were classmates in college. . . .

BETTY. Miriam, I'd like you to meet Corporal Hollister— Miriam Maizlish.

CAL. How do you do, Miss Maizlish.

MAIZLISH. How do you do.

CAL (*down*). And they sat and gabbed for hours about their old schooldays, and believe me, there's nothing more boring than for a neutral party to hear about Bud Phillips, who's in the South Pacific, and Bob Lee, who's just written a book on television, and Gazella Cronkite, who married a furniture salesman from Far Rockaway. . . .

MAIZLISH. Yes, and I hear she's expecting. . . .

CAL. And Miss Maizlish of course came along to lunch, and when the train stopped at La Junta and we got out to stretch our legs, she tagged along with us. So that I never really got any time alone with Betty all day. Worse than that, a fellow right in back of my chair, a music-lover who should have been born a canary, started whistling and kept it up until it got on my nerves.

WHISTLER. (*He has been faded in behind the end of Cal's speech. He whistles "As Time Goes By" in an arrangement for two front teeth. We should sympathize with Cal.*)

CAL. I went into the club car to get away from him, and everybody had all the regular magazines already; so I read the *Railroad Age* and the Standard Book of Timetables. Dinner was even worse. Maizlish was along—and not only that, but two good-looking Marines went on the make for Betty, and I had all I could do to keep from taking a hand in the situation. But I curbed myself, figuring what right would I have to interfere—she's not my girl, after all; I'd just met her yesterday—so I took the whole thing philosophically. . . .

BETTY. What's the matter, Cal?

CAL. Oh, nothing.

BETTY. You seem so glum all of a sudden.

CAL. No, nothing, really.

BETTY. You sure? . . .

CAL. I said I was sure, just to end that line of inquiry. But it wasn't until the latter part of the evening that I really had her to myself, and that was only because everybody began to get so fagged that they couldn't keep their eyes open. We sat back in our seats and talked in a very low voice. . . .

BETTY. You tired?

CAL. A little.

BETTY. So am I.

CAL. You know what?

BETTY. What?

CAL. I missed you all day.

BETTY. *Missed* me?

CAL. Yeah. Between Maizlish and the Marines, I hardly got to talk to you.

BETTY. Why, Cal—you sound as though that were important to you.

CAL. Well, it is.

BETTY. But we only met yesterday.

CAL. I know, I know—we're not exactly engaged to each other or anything, are we?

BETTY. That's right.

CAL. But would that be so bad?

BETTY. Would what be so bad?

CAL. Being engaged?

BETTY. What a silly question!

CAL. Well, I know *I'd* like it.

BETTY. You're silly.

CAL. Am I? (*For a moment neither speaks.*) I'm sorry if I've made a fool of myself again.

BETTY. You haven't made a fool of yourself. What time is it?

CAL. Eleven. Why?

BETTY. We get to Kansas City in fifteen minutes, and I want to get out there.

CAL. Yes? What for?

BETTY. Well, Sandy wrote me he wanted me to bring him a book, and I didn't have time to get it at home, and it'll be so early when we get to Chicago that I won't have time to get it before catching my connecting train; so—

CAL. What's the book he wants?

BETTY. *The People, Yes,* by Carl Sandburg.

CAL. Oh, yes. He's the one wrote that poem about the fog with the little cat's feet or something—didn't he?

BETTY. Yes. Have you seen that new biography of Tom Paine?

CAL. No, but I heard of it. He was quite a guy, Tom Paine, according to what Major Glickstein says. I like Glickstein, although he's a tough disciplinarian.

BETTY. You ought to read Paine some time.

CAL. Jefferson—that's *my* boy.

(*Down.*) We got to Kansas City and went up the stairs to the station, and Betty bought her book. Then we walked around outside the station to get a breath of fresh air, and we stood there looking at the lights. Betty put her arm in mine, and it felt to me as though it belonged there, and I couldn't help thinking to myself how nice it would be if we were married and this was our honeymoon.

BETTY. Cal—how long does the train stop here?

CAL. Huh? Oh—uh—seven minutes. It leaves at 11:22.

BETTY. Well, what time is it now?

CAL (*galvanized*). Holy smokes! 11:21! We've only got one minute.

BETTY (*beginning to run*). We'd better run for it! What track is it on?

CAL. I think it's Track 4.

BETTY. Well, don't you *know?*

CAL. I'm pretty sure it's four.

BETTY. Well, here's the staircase down for Track 4. I hope you're right.

*They scramble down a flight of stairs. The dialogue takes place mostly in full flight. They reach the bottom.*

CAL. Porter, is that the El Capitan?

PORTER. No, suh, this here's a westboun' train.

CAL. Well, what track is the El Capitan on?

PORTER. Ah doan know.

CAL. Come on, let's get back upstairs.

*They tear upstairs, and as they're running:*

BETTY. And all my stuff is on the train!

CAL. Mine too. And I've got to report on time! Come on, hurry, Betty.

*They reach the top, breathless and worried.*

CAL (*frantically*). Mister—which is the stairway for the El Capitan? [6]

MISTER. Sorry, I don't know. Ask the conductor at the train gate.

CAL. What train gate?

MISTER. Right there.

CAL. You wait here, honey. I'll ask the conductor.

*We hear Cal hotfooting it down a corridor. His footsteps stop after a moment, and we hear him, about twenty feet away, addressing a couple of conductors:*

CAL. Say—what track's the Capitan on?

CONDUCTOR. On six, I believe.

SECOND CONDUCTOR. No, I think it's on seven tonight.

CONDUCTOR. Well, I believe you've missed it anyway. It's 11:25.

CAL. Oh, great!

SECOND CONDUCTOR. Try seven, soldier.

CAL. Okay—

*Cal hurries back, getting short of wind.*

BETTY (*off*). Did you find out?

CAL. Seven . . . try seven.

BETTY. Oh, Cal!

*Both scramble down the stairs. At the bottom:*

CAL. Porter! What train is this?

PORTER. El Capitan eastbound.

CAL AND BETTY. (*Ad libs of relief.*)

CAL (*narrating*). We staggered on our car, winded and disheveled, and thanked our stars the train hadn't pulled out on time. But to top it all, that train just stood there another twenty minutes. So we'd given ourselves a scare and a workout for nothing.

It was about midnight when the train got under way . . .

*Wheels starting.*

CAL. . . . and we were pretty tired, and Betty slumped down and put her head on my shoulder and went off to sleep. She looked so pretty with her head on my shoulder, and her hair smelled kind of nice, you know, and I guess I felt pretty sentimental toward her, although it was true that we had only met yesterday.

I stayed awake quite a while, but then I must have dozed off, because the next thing I knew, I was suddenly aware that light was just beginning to come up in the east. The train was slowing down to go through Streator, Illinois, and the car was quiet. I looked at Betty to see how she was doing, and to my surprise I found she was wide awake. She was looking at me out of those big eyes. . . .

BETTY (*low*). Good morning, Corporal.

CAL. Morning, Betty. Can't you sleep?

BETTY. I slept some. I've been thinking a lot.

CAL. So have I.

BETTY. About what?

CAL. About you.

BETTY. What about me?

CAL. I'm sorry we're not going on together after Chicago.

BETTY. Want to know something?

CAL. What?

BETTY. So am I.

CAL (*pleased and touched*). *Are* you, Betty?

BETTY. Yes. (*Pause.*) I like you. . . .

CAL. I squeezed her hand a little, and we sat there for a while without saying anything, just watching the sky go from purple to pink. Finally I said to her: (*Up.*) Betty—

BETTY. What?

CAL. I'd like to ask just one thing before we get to Chicago, because I know you'll have to rush to make your connection.

BETTY. What is it, Cal?

CAL. Can I kiss you just once?

(*Down.*) She looked at me for a moment without saying anything. Then she put her hand under my chin and drew me toward her, and—and she kissed me. I don't know how to describe it exactly, but all kinds of things suddenly began singing in my head—lines of poems that I learned in school and thought I'd forgotten, and there was a kind of music, too, and all the time the dawn was coming up in the east, and there was a glow outside that seemed to go along with the glow inside *me*.

I couldn't really trust my Adam's apple for a while, so I didn't say anything. . . .

BETTY. Do you think you'll remember me after today?

CAL. Well, I don't know about after the war, but that kiss will carry me through the duration.

BETTY. You're a sweet boy, Cal. I suppose it's silly, in war, to say "Take care of yourself" to a soldier. But—I guess it's more or less in the hands of God, isn't it?

CAL. God and Major Glickstein.

BETTY. Nevertheless, *you* be careful.

CAL. I'm coming back, Betty. And you know who I'd like to see first right I step off that boat? You.

BETTY. I—I'm glad you feel that way. I really am.

CAL. Just you don't go getting hitched to some vegetable before you've given *me* a chance, now, will you?

BETTY (*smiling*). Don't worry.

CAL. Betty, if I write you, will you answer me?

BETTY. Of course I'd answer you.

CAL. But you haven't told me your—

MAIZLISH (*advancing; bright and cheery*). Hi! Good morning, folks. Greetin's and salutations!

BETTY. Good morning, Miriam.

CAL (*none too cordially*). Good morning.

MAIZLISH. Well, we get in in ten minutes. Have you got all your stuff together?

CAL. Yep.

MAIZLISH. How much time've you got to get over to the other station, Betty?

BETTY. Half hour.

MAIZLISH. None too much.

BETTY. No.

*Young Miss Slezak has pattered down the aisle in the direction of our people.*

MAIZLISH (*spotting her*). Look, isn't this a cute kid? (*Up.*)

Good morning, young lady. (*To Betty and Cal.*) Isn't she cute?

TOT. Hello.

CAL. My name is Fiddlefuddle. Good-by.

TOT. Good-by.

CONDUCTOR (*from off*). Chicago! Chicago! Please make sure that you've left nothing behind. . . .

CAL. We got off the train, and I helped Betty with her bags, and on the sidewalk there in front of the Dearborn Station I said good-by to her. . . .

BETTY (*hurriedly*). Good-by, Cal. Good luck. Come back.

CAL (*talking fast to get it all in*). Good-by, Betty. Tell your brother Sandy that I'm going over there and avenge that lost arm. Tell him I'm going to help finish the job he started in Spain. And also tell him I love his sister.

BETTY. I'll tell him. I'll tell him all that. Good-by, dear. . . .

CAL. She smacked me right on the lips and turned and ran and got into a taxi and disappeared inside. I stood there rooted to the intersection of Polk and Dearborn Streets, looking after her. And it must have been all of five minutes later, with me in a perfect daze all this time, that I realized with a sinking feeling that I hadn't given her my address, and I didn't have hers, either.

I started to run automatically in the direction the taxi had gone, but I stopped after a few steps, because I knew that was silly. And then, while I was still wondering what to do, I looked down in my hand, and there was a piece of paper—a plain white piece of paper with some writing on it. So help me, I don't remember how it got there, but she must have put it in my hand when she kissed me good-by, and I was too dumbstruck to notice it. It said:

*Music: Betty's theme, behind:*

BETTY. Betty Frisby. 7692 North Elmwood Drive, Long Beach, California. At home after the armistice.

*Music: Dips down for:*

CAL. I put it in my breast pocket and started for the train that would take me to Long Beach—via Germany.

*Music: And the curtain falls.*

# EL CAPITAN AND THE CORPORAL

I have long wanted to write a rhapsody on a timetable, in which the romance of time, space, and bus connections could be interwoven with incidental information on dogs, cats, corpses,φ and drinking cups. The typographical excitement and congestion of a transcontinental timetable could, it seems to me, be translated excitingly into radio or concert performance—or for that matter, into film or ballet.

The ambition to write such a piece hits me every time I cross the country, and it was especially troublesome one day in July 1944, when I got on the eastbound Chief at Los Angeles without a word written for a program due six days later ⌒ from New York. The idea of a rhapsody, however, was dismissed immediately because there would not have been time for a composer to score the work. But the impulse died hard, and I settled for an itinerant love story based on a routine sailing✗ of Train No. 22.△

The conditions under which I wrote "El Capitan" may be of clinical interest to writers like myself who have had to turn out copy in barber chairs, subways, and delicatessens. I had just recovered from a flu that left me with a bleeding nose. Ordinarily I compose on a typewriter or in longhand, but this time I dictated. The effect was weirdly nasal,

φ Baggage car space not available for handling corpses on El Capitan.

⌒ Most of my programs in an extended series are written from week to week—a shame on radio's and my own methods.

✗ It seems to me odd and wonderful that railroads speak of train departures as "sailings."

△ Stops to discharge from La Junta and beyond or receive for Kansas City and beyond.

since one of my nostrils was plugged with cotton; but, for all that, I found the system quite helpful in leavening dialogue. Syntax usually takes a beating in ordinary conversation, and one of the best ways to produce ungrammatical language is to write it out loud. Such a line as "You know who I'd like to see first right after I step off that boat?" comes straight from the oral approach.

Radiomen often ask me how long it took to write a particular script. This one took from Pasadena to Pittsburgh, as the Chief and the General ‡ sail. Roughly, three days. I would rather have taken three months, and I'm not especially lazy. There is no excuse for the way American radio burns up program material. The BBC rightly considers our pace uncivilized. Good radio drama should be repeated without apology, and as often as a good symphony. Every time I write a play in less than a week, I want to cleanse myself in a Ganges. The chance to revise is denied most radio writers, and as a lot we look with envy on screen writers. They sometimes seem to us gypsies without a care in the world, although of course we know better. They have many burdens, including producers and stars.

But to get back to El Capitan, the story of Cal and Betty was written hurriedly, and it plays in a hurry. Its pace, if you crowd it into twenty-nine minutes and thirty seconds, is brisk, and the almost constant movement in underlying sound should help to balance the occasional andante of the Corporal's narration.

The dope regarding stops, train equipment, ◈ and the kind of company you have on El Capitan is fairly straight. The scene involving the multiple stairways in the Kansas City station was inspired by an incident that shortened the

‡ Train No. 48 on the Pennsylvania R.R.
◈ As of the A.T. & S.F. timetable of August 5, 1945.

lives of Bernard Herrmann and me. Once, when we were on our way to Hollywood to do a broadcast, we got off the train at K.C. and went upstairs to browse in the excellent bookstore of that depot. There we fell into a literary-type argument,@ and we were furiously scoring points when I noticed that our train was scheduled to have left (along with our baggage and Pullman space) fully a minute before. We ran up and down more flights of stairs (and faster) than Cal and Betty and at last found the train still taking on mail. I didn't catch my breath until Trinidad. ◊

Betty has absorbed some political knowledge from her brother who fought in Spain, some from reading, most from the events of her lifetime. Cal's instincts are every bit as good as Betty's, but he has been less exposed to discussion and argument. He has learned little from the average Hearst-fed G.I. around him and has been fighting his war day to day. Maybe at his camp the commanding officer didn't think orientation important. That happened all too often in the Army. Even in high places (as at the top of the Armed Forces Radio Service) there were colonels who censored friendly words about Britain and Russia and rejected out-and-out anti-Fascist material. They placed heavy stress on the "entertainment" value of radio programs exported to soldiers overseas and kept many of the best war documentaries from being circulated. This policy was also prominent in the Radio division of the Office of War Information, especially during the first years of the war. So commercial-minded were its officials that the OWI's war came to be known as "the war that refreshes—in six delicious flavors."

@ Herrmann thinks Hardy is God.
◆ Colorado.

*Acting.* Katherine Locke, who up to this writing had done far too little radio for an actress of her superlative talents, performed the role of Betty and made her keen, yet warm; discerning and restrained, yet nicely sentimental. Joseph Julian, as Cal, had the same direct and simple quality of his narration in the "American in England" series. Obviously, the role does not want an actor who sounds like a speaker of poesy on a sponsored mortuary program. Cal should be as American as corn flakes.

The fat man, the casual passengers, Miriam Maizlish (played by Minerva Pious in the original production) should be relaxed and natural, with never a suggestion of caricature.

*Sound.* This is a busy half-hour for the sound crew. A series of subdued and varied recordings of interior coach effects is vital to the atmosphere of the piece. Special care must be taken to avoid monotony in the tempo and timbre of the clicking wheels. Actually, sound inside a train varies according to the roadbed, rate of speed, topography of embankment, and the nature of objects passed. I took pains to keep this pattern realistic, even in small details. When El Capitan was climbing Cajon Pass, the tempo was slow. On the level plateau "past Victorville," the wheels rolled merrily. On the down-sloping home stretch toward Chicago, the train breezed along at about 70 m.p.h. At all times the idea is to keep your sound low and unobtrusive. It is background, not foreground. The starting of the train, the stopping, the passage from standing to full flight, must be sneaked. If the listener becomes aware of mechanics, he will lose interest in what is being said.

The stairway business will be most difficult even under the best conditions, and you had better give up all ideas of doing it with standard studio equipment. The converted soapboxes that pass for stairs in the average studio should be taken outside and burned in an alley back of the sound department. To get a believable effect, I had to extend mike cables to the nearest actual stairwell and make Cal and Betty do their own running up and down. Cal moved from a standing microphone in the studio to a portable mike that was handed to him (without a break in his narration), and he walked out, speaking all the way, through an open door to the stairwell. There he was relieved of the portable mike and picked up freshly on microphones placed strategically at the bottom of the stairs. This enabled him to make his own footsteps, and the effect sounded far more natural than if he had been stationary while a soundman covered the course. All the exercise, moreover, left Cal convincingly out of breath by the time he found his train.

*Music.* No particular problems. You will be lucky if you can get a Semmler or Burl Ives for any production you may contemplate, £ but we can't all strike oil, can we? What you need in the way of a score is warm, ingratiating stuff, with bright movement that now and then takes note of the special poignance of wartime romance.

*Additional Notes.* 1. Native for San Bernadino.

2. The 1944 political campaign was shaping up at the time this was written, and emphasis was being placed by both major parties on the importance of registering and voting. The discussion had topical intention, but the gist of it naturally applies to all election years and elections.

3. This item came out of a monstrous publication called *Soldier Jokes,* sold at newsstands along the Santa Fe. I studied an issue hoping to find a typical G.I. joke, and the best of the lot was the dog gag, which gives you an idea

£ After due negotiation with Henry Holt and Company, a most pleasant group of people.

of the general level. Most of the jokes must have been handed down from Egyptian vaudeville.

4. Including Jersey City.

5. Port of embarkation.

6. *"The* El Capitan," as Cal says here, is, literally, "The *the* Captain." But that is how it is commonly used, and Cal never studied Spanish.

# SAVAGE ENCOUNTER

Produced for the first time on March 28, 1944, as the fourth of "Columbia Presents Corwin." Carl Frank performed the role of the Pilot, Joan Alexander played Ara, Arnold Moss was the Native, and the author appeared as the Prosecutor. Bernard Herrmann composed and conducted an original score. The author directed.

# SAVAGE ENCOUNTER

*Music: Introduction.*

PILOT. My name is unimportant, and you will understand soon enough why I must omit certain details from the telling of this story.

I was flying a seaplane in an area of the South Pacific, en route to my base, when I ran into a heavy electric storm.

*Plane sounds in and continue under:*

PILOT. It seemed to me the ship must have been struck by lightning several times, because although no apparent damage was done to the body of the plane, I noticed that both compasses, the radio, and half my instruments had stopped working.

For upward of three hours I flew blind, not knowing where I was, and unable to see what lay below me. It was getting dark, and I had about twenty minutes of fuel left, when suddenly an upcurrent caught the plane and lifted it with cyclonic force six or seven thousand feet in a few seconds.

And then, as though I were coming out of a dream only to enter another, I was above the storm, and I saw rising before me . . .

*Music: Suggests his sensation.*

PILOT. . . . a mountain peak, silhouetted against the pearly wash of a clearing sky lit by the full moon.

I knew I must be over a land mass not immediately

111

recognizable on my map. There was nothing to do now but fly with the wind, negotiate the extremely narrow pass, and bail out on the other side.

But once through the pass, I was dismayed to see dense forests on the other side. I jumped—having no other choice; and the wind was so strong it carried my descent for miles. I finally hit the treetops with such force that I must have been knocked out, because the next thing I knew I was lying on the ground in pitch darkness, bruised and aching.

When I awoke it was day. I was in a forest of vine-covered trees that rose straight for a hundred feet, interlocking at their tops to form a ceiling of leaves. There was a green glow all about; occasionally a shaft of sunlight slanted through when a tree swayed in the wind. Gradually I felt an instinctive alarm, and for good reason: there was something behind me. Something had been in the brush watching me for I know not how long.

I got to my feet, but whatever it was that was standing in the gloom didn't move. I took a step toward it. Only then did it stir. With a quick movement the branches between us parted and there came forward a native. He was about seven feet tall, justly proportioned, his skin a coppery bronze in the shadows. I addressed him.

(*Up.*) Speakee English?

He looked at me with fixed expression. I tried again.

(*Up.*) You know how speakee? You friend white fella?

He came closer, studied the wounds on my face for a moment, and then did an astonishing thing. He touched my brow where it had been bleeding and said:

NATIVE. What dialect of a decent tongue are you mouthing?

PILOT (*surprised and relieved and happy*). You speak
*English!* That's wonderful! I was afraid I might've
come down in enemy territory. What island is this,
anyway? Where's the base around here?

NATIVE. Base? Enemy territory?

PILOT. Yeah.

NATIVE. What does that mean?

PILOT. Why—don't you know——the enem— (*Pause.*)
Japs. You mean you—you don't—?

NATIVE. Has your wound diswitted you?

PILOT. Diswhat?

NATIVE. Mm. Whatever this cumbrance round your feet,
cast it off and come with me.

PILOT. This is a parachute. I bailed out in it last night.
Saved my life.

NATIVE (*gravely*). An extern kindly and familiar, yet a
tongue wilder than the chatter of a tree-chirro leap-
ing the vines.

PILOT. Uh—what did you say the name of this island was?

NATIVE (*after a pause; tolerantly, almost with amusement*). Come with me. Come. Follow me. . . .

PILOT. He led me down to a stream, along which we
traveled for some time. During this he said very little.
Most of the way he preceded me on the narrow trail
and so couldn't speak conveniently. But at one point
he stopped and turned to me with a wide grin. . . .

NATIVE. Yes, we speakee English. (*Laughs.*) . . .

PILOT. Where on earth, and on what, had I stumbled? Was
I in a delirium? How else to explain the language of
this native? His speech was certainly English, but it

was a kind *I'd* never heard before—antique, archaic, stilted, strangely formed.

We arrived at length at a place which, by my own promise, and by all I hold sacred, I cannot describe to you. It was a fair place—a beautiful place; that's almost the only way I can describe it. It was modest and livable. Above all, there was a dignity of life in that place I had never seen before.

My rescuer and guide took me through curious and animated crowds to a place of assembly where a council was in session. They rose at my entrance, greeted me with silent nods, and listened to my friend's report. He delivered it with high humor, telling how while hunting he had looked up and seen an odd object descending in the sky. . . .

NATIVE. . . . and I thought: What? A riggish pollen coming on the wind to breed with trees and make new combines of flora? For we see so much of jesting nature here—fish flippant to the fin tip and birds jocose from sunrim to nightpeep—I was prepared for some outcountry creature conceived upon a mountain riverbed by low-lying vapors.

COUNCIL. (*Laughter.*)

NATIVE. And as he had not been discharged by any cloud that I could see above me, I discounted him a dewdrop.

COUNCIL. (*Laughter.*)

PILOT. I saw the laughter was not at my expense, for they seemed kindly disposed; and when my discoverer had finished, the leader of the council came over to where I was standing and took my hand. . . .

TARAM. We welcome you to these woods, to the fruit of our gardens and the produce of our hands. We invite

you to take of us and be of us, to convive haply, both
in our own name and in the name of Thomas, your
brother, whose memory is quick and ageless in our
nation. . . .

PILOT. I was too dazed at the moment to make any special
note of his reference to "Thomas," for immediately
the others of the council approached and took my
hand, and each greeted me with sentiments similar to
those of their leader. Something was said about my
needing rest, and I was taken to a cottage overlooking
the gardens of the—. But I must be careful not to describe too much of this place—again, for reasons you
shall see.

I was numb from my head wound and intoxicated
by the brilliance of my surroundings, but once I had
eaten, I yielded to fatigue and fell into a deep sleep.
And as though every level of my consciousness had
been affected by this experience, even my dreams, unlike the nightmares of the previous night, were pleasant and full of exotic music.

*Music: A nocturne expressing the South Sea island you
remember from your fondest imaginings. Healthy lusts
and red flowers and blue sky and bare breasts are all
mixed up in it.*

PILOT. Whether out of my own resilience or something
tonic in the atmosphere, I awoke fresh and clear-
headed, my injury well on its way to healing and my
spirits unaccountably light. The war, of which so lately
I had been a part, seemed remote and unreal. And the
events of that day served only to heighten this feeling.

To begin with, I was regarded by all with the sort
of open affection I'd always thought the possession

only of lifelong friends. Children flocked around me when I went about in the streets as though I were a favorite uncle. There was no superstition or mystic awe mixed up in it—the people of this place simply were happy to see me and did not hesitate to show it.

On the fifth evening there was an occasion in my honor: music and dancing and the speaking of poetry.

*Music: Begins far off, under last sentence, along with:*

*Sounds of festivity. We are fading in on a Polynesian ballet, which grows closer.*

PILOT. The poetry seemed to me Shakespearean—I almost thought I recognized certain passages, though my acquaintance with Shakespeare is small. The dancing and the music were obliquely sensuous, yet at times solemn and restrained.

Altogether there were many startling and happy devices for the eye and ear, and I was aware that some of the natives kept watching me, probably to savor my enjoyment. But even if that night had not been otherwise charged with sensation, I should remember it all my life for one thing. It was then and there that I met Ara, daughter of the leader of the council—Ara of the blue-black hair and eyes that outshone the proudest constellation in the heavens. Ara—O blessed name!

*Music: Up from the background comes love music.[1] It holds long enough to color the scene, then dips down behind:*

PILOT. It was Ara who told me about Thomas as we walked by the lake shore afterward, hands clasped—

[1] The numbered notes will be found on pages 135-136.

how a man was cast up on the far shores of their
island three centuries ago, the only survivor of a ship-
wreck . . .

ARA. . . . tall as we; your color; white-haired. A legend
writ of him in after years swore that a cloud sate on
his brow, a very cumulus of considerations. . . .

PILOT. How he had been a profound and good and forceful
man, and a student of the great poets of his time . . .

ARA. Shakespeare and Marlowe and Webster—he bore
their sea-soaked pages as a libbard [2] carries her young,
purposefully, tenderly, yet with a haughty and a pride-
ful eye. . . .

PILOT. How he had found her people—in the words of his
own journal, which I later was to read—so gifted of
intellect, so benignly civil, so acquisitive of knowledge,
that he gave up all thought of returning to his own
country. He lived among them, telling them little of
the temporal matters of his own world, but teaching
them all the best of its poetry. And so great was the
native genius for the spoken word, so complete their
fascination in it, that soon English came to be their
second tongue. . . .

ARA. And growing supple with usage, became at last our
elected speech, for we pitched upon it. . . .

PILOT. This, then, explained the peculiar idiom spoken
here.

ARA. Yes. Quite as you say . . . a transplanted language,
flourishing like some wind-blown and accidental seed
dropped in rich foreign soil. . . .

PILOT. It was obvious that since they'd had no example of
vulgar English speech,[3] they emulated only the kind
Thomas allowed them to know, for Thomas was
hitherto the only white man they had ever seen, and I

was, in effect, the first bulletin from the outside world in more than three hundred years. Thus I suppose it was natural they should think me of the same stripe as the sainted Thomas, especially since at my best I am not exactly unpresentable. For my part, I fully reciprocated the kind attitudes they displayed toward me.

And as for my feelings for Ara—

*Music: The love theme rises to say for him what he has to tell.*

PILOT. It started the night I dined, or convived, as they put it, at the place of Taram, Ara's father.

CAST. (*Background of laughter, talk, etc., under:*)

PILOT. We were discussing the great festivity of the planting, soon to draw together the people from the far-lying provinces, the hill people, the lake people, for the great celebration of the year. I was talking with an elder named Chargo when, in the course of conversation, I began to expand on the subject of my adventures in the war. Quickly the room fell silent. (*Which it does.*)

I attributed this to the interest they took in my story, and with growing eloquence—I admit I was somewhat animated by drink, and perhaps more loquacious than usual—I recounted briefly the history of the outer world since the time of Thomas—its wars, its industrialization, its panics, its depressions. I told them about the wonders of radio and the airplane, as well as the various uses to which they had been put. They listened without a word, at times looking at each other quizzically, but never interrupting. I told them of the first World War and of the intervening years—of the

origins and career of World War II. At length Taram
made a little gesture as if to speak. I stopped. . . .

TARAM. You tell us, then, that thirty years agone your
peoples slaughtered twenty millions of each other with
cruel murdering-pieces?

PILOT. Yes, 1914 to 1918. About twenty million were
killed.

TARAM. And now, today, simult with our sitting here, your
nations are at killing once again?

PILOT. Yes. Already about twenty million killed in this one
so far, and it's not over yet by any means.

TARAM. And nothing learnt between? Nothing extraught
from the many wars and bloody garboils? [4]

PILOT (*lightly*). Oh, sure, in a way. We've learned how to
kill more efficiently. War's a full-blown science now.

TARAM. Tell us more. . . .

PILOT. I went on, encouraged by the amazement and aston-
ishment on the faces of my hosts. And when I had
finished I sat back, pleased with my account. For a
moment nobody spoke. Then Taram rose. . . .

TARAM. The night is old, and the moon is set. We must
part now. Our fellowly guest shall be escorted home,
but I would have the council remain. . . .

PILOT. I thought it peculiar that the party, which began
so informally, should end in this manner and that I
should be assigned an escort, when up to now it had
been considered quite all right for me to go about
alone. And I was still more puzzled when, as I was
leaving and started to cross the room to say good
night to Ara, I was intercepted by Chargo, ostensibly
for the purpose of asking me a question. It was a small,
pointless question and, I'm sure, merely a ruse to de-

lay me. For upon disengaging myself from Chargo I noticed Ara was no longer in the room.

*Music: Tension cue, not so much of danger as of puzzlement.*

PILOT. The attitude of my hosts seemed to have changed. They were still courteous and kind, but I found that fewer people spoke to me, and these less freely than before. I was detained close by my cottage on this excuse and that, and when finally I strolled down to the central area of the place, no children were about. What concerned me even more was the fact that though I had been seeing Ara daily since we met, she was now mysteriously absent from her father's house. I made inquiries for her, and Taram explained. . . .

TARAM. Ara has gone to the lakes on errand.

PILOT. When will she be back?

TARAM. I cannot say. . . .

PILOT. I returned, sullen, to my cottage and was shocked to find that on the pretext of needed repairs to its roof, I was being moved up into what they called the high holt—a wooded section some distance from the gardens. The new place was even larger and more luxurious than the old, and I was given plentiful services. But I was aware that the warm and open hospitality of the country had deteriorated to a sort of protective custody. And as this process continued I became uneasy and wretched—the more so for want of news of Ara.

Then late one sleepless night—a night when all the wild beauty of the land lay tranquil under a southern moon—I started up from my brooding at an unaccustomed noise. There was someone at the window. With an eye half open I feigned sleep, but at the same time, with a stealthy movement of my hand under my blanket, I grasped the knife I had been keeping under my pillow ever since being removed to the holt. I waited. For minutes nothing stirred. Then something happened that made my blood freeze.

For no sooner had a cloud drifted across the moon and darkened the woods than a figure slipped swiftly through the curtain of the window, noiseless as a shadow, and was standing in the room above me. I rose to my elbow, my fingers tight around my knife. (*Pause. Then up, but in a low, tense voice.*) Who is it? Who is there?

ARA. It is I, Ara.

PILOT. Ara—my love. Ara, Ara, I'm so glad— (*Down.*) I leaped from bed and seized her in my arms.

ARA. O my alderliefest![5] I am forbod to see you, but I have stolen the way here to tell you of the danger.

PILOT. What danger?

ARA. They have markt you out a savage.

PILOT. I a savage?

ARA. Yes. They say you come of ugsome people and societies forewasted by greed and savage instincts.

PILOT. But, Ara, how can they—

ARA. I must go quickly, else I am found out. O my lief, my soote,[6] my love, be you of caution for your life.

PILOT. But why? What have I done?

ARA. They dread you will subvert our youth by story and example. And we are people of such—

PILOT. What do they intend to do with me?

ARA. I fear they will kill you on an unsuspecting moment.

PILOT. But I thought they liked me.

ARA. They look on you fondly, but they're fearful lest, all

innocent, you plant the cancer of your dispiteous world
among us.

PILOT. But I—I couldn't—I *wouldn't* do that.

ARA. I must go, beloved, or they discover me.

PILOT. But, Ara—you're not safe. Why did you come?

ARA. Because I love you and I am forlore—

PILOT. Ara, my—

ARA. I am spiritless and all amort without you; I— (*She
stops, arrested by what she sees.*)

PILOT. There, standing in the doorway, were two native
guards. Silently they came to Ara. One gently took her
arm, and she went out between them, speaking not a
word. They said nothing to me, beyond apologizing
for the disturbance. . . .

FIRST GUARD. We regret to have intruded on your privacy.
Good night, sir, and deep sleep to you.

*Music: An upsurge into an unhappy variation of the
love theme.*

PILOT (*down*). I expected my food to be poisoned, and so
I ate little. I expected to be killed in my sleep, and
so I slept not at all. . . .

GUARD. Shall the bed be readied?

PILOT. No, I am not tired.

GUARD. You have not rested since noonstead two days.

PILOT. I tell you I'm not tired. I'll let you know when I am.

GUARD. We await your pleasure. . . .

PILOT. I expected them to pounce on me when I walked
about in the holt, but nobody came near. After a while,
unable to stay awake longer, I fell asleep in a chair—
and awoke many hours later in a bed to which I had
apparently been carried like a child. Then, uncomfort-
ably hungry, I ate the food set out on my table. It

was not poisoned. But Ara had risked her life to warn me, and I knew that at any moment of the night or day a sentence of death might be carried out upon me. Finally I could stand it no longer. (*Up.*) Guard!

GUARD. You called, sir?

PILOT. See here, I've had enough of this. I demand to see Taram immediately, do you understand?

GUARD. He shall be told. . . .

PILOT. I was sure this would do me no good, but to my great surprise, later that day Taram arrived at the holt. He was downcast and seemed much older than when I saw him last, as though he had been through a terrible ordeal. He bore bad news. Ara was being held for treason, and the council had decided I must die. I asked him what they would do to Ara. . . .

TARAM. She too is under sentence.

PILOT (*after a pause to think it over*). You have made up your minds?

TARAM. All but to hear you.

PILOT. Hear me?

TARAM. Our code is to inform the accused one of our charges, then to hear him out.

PILOT. What good will that do?

TARAM. Little—less than little; nought unless you are persuasive against the damning testaments of your own lips. But there will be to hear you a deputation of our people. A council of judgment will give tendance to the last of what you have to say.

PILOT. You're putting me on trial, is that it?

TARAM. Yes. We are putting you on trial.

*Music: Preparation for the trial. The passage fades down under the first three lines of the Prosecutor's speech that follows.*

*We are in a large council room, and there is a slight echo under:*

PROSECUTOR (*fading on*). . . . and however painful to our ancient hospitalities, do it we must, for then and only then, good judges, can we be proof against unimaginable woes.

The war, by his report, engluts all of the oceans of the world, save for this haply mirage-hidden island. How long, if he escape and does rejoin his barbaric company, should we stay unconsidered in their strategies?

PILOT (*off*). But you have my *word* I'd tell them nothing about you.

PROSECUTOR. His *word!* Respected judges, he himself has told us of the history of treaties in his forlorn society.

PILOT. You're deliberately misinterpreting what I said the other night!

PROSECUTOR. This prosecution is small pleasure to us all. Consider him: in face, resembling Thomas; in language, uncouth but understandable; a brave and hardy fellow; outwardly, a worthy and a gracious man. Yet inward, what decay sits still and waits? How else than by a vile inheritance of blood could lusts and fratricidal passions so control the children of the fighters of the wars that they persist in making up and fighting *new* wars of their own? Is there no love among their schemes?

Good judges, these are the risks of an acquittal: First, that he escape. Next, that staying in our midst alive, he, by ingratiation and insisture, by devices uncanny such as that which he calls radio, by the same perversions of wit and skill that have rendered this race of savages sovereign over the bird, will subtly and wickedly corrupt our people. Already he but touches a maiden, the noble daughter of our noblest leader, and she so deep contracts the special sickness of this savage that she hurries through the night to betray her people by forewarning him.

We all agree and are together saddened that this very personable and, by certain lights, this innocent young man should, for the sake of the tranquillity and peace of generations yet unnumbered on this island, be forfeit of his years and die under the sentence of this council. Yet these are good causes that I account here—these are the highest of all; and he, alas for him, is overmatched by them.

For in his world, by all that he has freely told the many of us here, there is such bale, such epidemic misery, hunger amid great riches, and the lessons of catastrophe continuing unlearned, we cannot but assume some awful growth is rampant in their blood, breeding in cycles, and affecting finally the very seat of reason. Our guest—so logic and quiescent now, like Thomas of that old and better world—may be the carrier of a black and mortal plague striking the inner organs of the soul.

We cannot risk this prospect in our nation. I call upon you to pronounce the edict of his execution, in the name of the various peoples by whom you have been here deputed.

JUDGE. These are the weights against you. We shall listen if you wish to speak.

PILOT (*his perspective advancing*). I certainly do wish to speak. First of all, get rid of any idea that I'd willingly stay here if you were to reprieve me on condition I don't try to escape. Because I *would* try.

COUNCIL. (*Reaction.*)

PROSECUTOR. He pleads the case against himself better than we.

PILOT. I would try to escape to the very war that you've condemned and by whose conduct you consider me a savage.

PROSECUTOR. Why?

PILOT. Because I have a share of fighting yet to do in that war, and not even for this sublime island and the dignity and sweetness of your life here would I remain while other men are dying for a cause that I consider just as sacred as you do your own.

Listen. Any fool could understand your caution to keep the thing you have. But let me ask you something. Was it always this way here? Did you come out of the earth complete with laws and culture? Were your landscapes already gardened when you took this place away from the animals? It doesn't matter whether you came up from the tadpole or the ape . . . somewhere along the line you had to fight; you had to conquer beasts or else be conquered.

Well, that's the way it is with us today. *We're* fighting beasts—animals far wilder than anything you've ever had to face. We fight the *makers of wars,* and that's not easy for people who, like you, are brought up to prefer peace.

If you kill me, then there is one man less against the beast. And if *he* wins, don't be so sure he won't eventually find you, for all the freakish storm fronts protecting you. *I* found you, didn't I?

You make the mistake of lumping together as savages the makers of war and the breakers of war. There's a difference between the two, and men are willing to die for that difference. We call them men of good will, and there are millions of them, fighting in places that are as terrible as this place is beautiful, fighting for some semblance of the kind of life that you've got here.

Do you mean to say you would deny to others the blessings you have found? Can you mean that you're willing to take, but not give?

You took what Thomas had to offer, and you found it good enough to make a saint of him. Well, I can tell you there are many other Thomases, present and future, who can bring you countless good and wonderful things—and will, after we've finished with the Fascists.[7]

Before this war all of our countries were islands like yourself, each one of us cut off in spirit from the rest of the world as you are cut off in fact. But now we're together, and the leaders are meeting, and one nation gives to the other commonly what it needs, as you people do here among yourselves.

Well, that's where *we* stand. As for you—you can sit alone, if you choose, and hoard your riches like a miser counting gold; or else you can help those who are poor in wisdom to reach what seems to you so obvious and easy, simply because you reached it so long ago. In a very small way you can start helping by letting me return to the fight. But whatever you decide to do to *me*, what about Ara? She's accused of treason. Why? Because she ran through the woods to warn the man she loves? That's not treason. Treason is deliberate and studied, not a girl's panic for the safety of her lover in the night. Is there no love among *your* schemes?

I say to you, release us. Let her go. Let me go. I will make a vow to tell nobody where to look for you—at least not until our civilization is worthy of your acquaintance.

That's all I have to say.

*Music: The scene is bitten off. There is nothing to convey the decision of the court—only the passion of the pilot's plea and his love for Ara. It sinks behind:*

ARA. Good-by, my alderliefest. Go safely, and my love be constant with you.

PILOT. Good-by, beloved, beloved Ara.

ARA. May you find the way to your people, and may your people find their way to peace.

PILOT. I will try to come back, Ara; and if I can't, my world will come to you—and it will be a part of me, as I am a part of it.

ARA. I shall dream forever of the all of you.

PILOT. Once more I fill my eyes with your face, and then I go. (*A long pause.*) All right, friend, the blindfold.

NATIVE. Here. Does it bind you too close?

PILOT. No, that's comfortable.

NATIVE. So, take my hand.

PILOT (*down; narrating*). And thus, blindfolded, I was led up the slopes and through the pass. It was an extra precaution on the part of my hosts, but quite unnecessary. (*He pauses, takes a long breath.*)

(*Quietly.*) One day, when all the savagery of inhumanity to man is rooted out, when all the many inequalities are evened up over the whole of our known world—when we have *won* [8]—I shall borrow a plane. I shall head for a certain quadrant of a certain ocean. And then I shall look for a storm to get lost in.

*Music: Conclusion.*

# SAVAGE ENCOUNTER

I wrote this piece as an exercise, just as, I suppose, painters try out new forms and color combinations and composers fool around with harmonic intervals. I was experimenting not with style or structure, but with a psychological concept: terror, set deep in an atmosphere of kindness and gentleness.

The terrors of war are wholesale and palpable. One expects the enemy to kill and destroy, and it is the simplest thing in the world to hate him. Such terrors as attach to warfare, gross and appalling as they are, have the grimly redeeming virtue of being shared. But the terror of the individual, alone against society, against nature, against perhaps a malignance in his own body or mind—that is something else again.

"Out of peace and great contentment," wrote Heywood Broun, "fantasies of utter desolation may arise." He was speaking of the introverted mind, which psychoanalysis has latterly come to understand and relieve. But I was interested in an experiment involving no such inward problem: I wanted to keep my terror-out-of-kindness above ground, completely extrovertive and "normal."

I wanted to see what would happen if I took a superior young man, decent, healthy, articulate, aware, and put him among kind people, also superior, in a benign land. To this test tube of happy ingredients I wanted then to add a situation that would curdle the whole brew. I wished my opposing elements to respect and even love each other on the plane of the individual, but to lock in conflict as symbols of forces greater than themselves. And I wanted to resolve my problem rationally, by argument and not by tricks. This was a rash order, and whether or not I succeeded must be left entirely to the verdict of listener and reader.

I am aware, as I write this, that my "experimental exercise" may have been done already in twenty forms and thirty languages. If so, I did not then, and do not now, know of any. And even if I did, I am sure I would have proceeded exactly as you have seen. There is nothing wrong with a variation on a theme, providing the theme is worth while to begin with and the variation interesting.

The business of selecting locale and the language of the natives turned out to be fun. One of the most rewarding assignments for a muser type is to conjure up all the nice places he has ever been in. A physician once told me that the best way to overcome insomnia is to relax by thinking of restful places you have seen or visited—to wander among thought associations of quiet, sunny afternoons in the country, of indolent moments becalmed in a sailboat. I went over all the pleasant vistas in my limited log (just for warmup purposes—I could not select a *known* country) and then turned to the exotic places of our earliest imaginings. I wound up where you yourself would probably wind up—in a far Pacific isle. Surely the reportage of this war should have disabused us of the idea that South Sea isles are idyllic. They are like hell. They are stinking, humid, full of malarial mosquitoes, chiggers, snakes, elephantiasis, filariasis, dengue fever, and now and then a leper or two. But romance will persist, and not even the solemn word and the morbid evidence of our terrible campaigns in that part of the world will quite rid us of the conviction that the islands are a division of paradise.

To a dream-bound isle in the Pacific, then, our Pilot was

to go. The notion that he could actually fall into an un-
charted area turned out to be not so wild when, late in the
war, an American transport plane crashed in an area of
New Guinea that had never been visited by white men.
There are at this late date vast tracts of Brazil, Borneo,
and other leafy territories so little known that they appear
blank on the best maps.

When it came to the language of the natives, I determined to detour as widely as possible to avoid the Bwana-
Massa-Him-See-Plenty-Big-Bird-Drop-Egg-Go-Boom variety of Polynesian. It seemed to me that just about the
furthest from such language would be the archaic tongue
of early England. I wist well of an early fascination with
Chaucer and the poets who pined away in fourteenth-cen-
tury love-longings:

> Ich libbe in love-longinge
> For semlokest of all thynge,
> He may blisse bringe,
> Icham in hire bandoun.

I didn't want quyte that mutche of berdis on the bewis in
the olde manere, because that might make a bestly impression on listeners in Akron and Chicopee, but I figured
a small sprinkling of archaisms and a general antique tone
would give me a strong and credible effect and at the same
time permit Ara and Taram to be understood here and
there around the network.

Our Pilot is distinctly not a dese-and-dem guy. I deliberately raised his narrative style several pegs above ordinary
conversational story-telling, in order to imply an effect upon
his speech of life among the unnamed people on the island.
He never adopts their idiom, but certainly his lingo is better than it was when he enlisted in the Navy. Few pilots I

have met would say, "Whether out of my own resilience or something tonic in the atmosphere," but our boy, after some months among Ara's tribe, would have acquired respect for such kind of talk.

Some correspondents accused me of having been influenced by *Lost Horizon,* wherein a pilot discharges a plane load of characters in Shangri-La, a superior land where no one ever dies. Or hardly ever. That is like charging any new tragic love story with having been influenced by *Romeo and Juliet,* or a current tale of Arctic adventure with having borrowed from Freuchen. I don't recall that James Hilton ever claimed *all* unexplored territories and advanced civilizations for the British crown.

*Acting.* This piece was a casting headache of the migraine order. The distance between ordinary narration and the speech of the Pilot, to say nothing of the language of the natives, was apparently too great for even some of radio's ablest and most versatile actors. I usually cast new roles from memory or from a list of actors whose qualities and performances I know at first hand, but for "Savage Encounter" I had to spend hours auditioning. And, to my pleasant surprise, it was an actor whose identification with soap operas had led me to believe he was limited to this sort of work who gave by far the most understanding and sensitive reading. Carl Frank made the Pilot at all times believable and switched from direct narration to participation with the ease of an automatic relay. The objectivity with which he began his tale gradually merged, as the play progressed, into a complete identification with events, mood, and atmosphere. One of the best pieces of acting I have ever heard on a monitor was Frank's speech to the court. He did not fall into the mistake (made by so many actors in circumstances of this sort) of treating a courtroom argu-

ment as a *speech*. It came out of him with the urgency of
*necessity:* he was fighting for his life, and these were the
best weapons he knew.

The role of Ara was another tough one—in some ways
tougher than that of the Pilot. She had, first of all, to
sound like a native girl, not a debutante at the Stork Club.
She had to transmit a warm and compelling quality that
would justify the Pilot's fascination by her: she had also
to carry the play's tensest scene on the back of some of its
most formal language. After much auditioning I cast Joan
Alexander in the part. Miss Alexander is a jill of all roles
and one of the busiest actresses in the industry. But it took
all of her prowess and experience to make Ara the kind of
girl our flier (and your writer) would have you believe she
was.

The natives speak with quiet dignity, especially the good-
humored fellow (played by Arnold Moss, the Prospero of
Margaret Webster's *Tempest*) who discovers the "outcountry creature" lying tangled in his parachute among the trees
of the forest. The Prosecutor is the only island character
who speaks with more than conversational force, and even
then he is not at all a conventional state's attorney. True,
he gets a little irritated at moments. When he is nettled by
the Pilot's charge of willful misinterpretation, he retorts,
"This prosecution is small pleasure to us all," and that is as
close as any of the islanders get to snapping at their "fellowly guest." Taram is a nice old bird, as he would have to
be to win the honor of heading the supreme council of so
talented a people.

*Sound*. No problems.

*Music*. Herrmann was faintly bored by this story and did
not extend himself to his full length in the score. He
warmed over a few previously used cues, which, being good

Herrmann to begin with, made good listening. But the broadcast did not enjoy the finished carpentry usually evident in Herrmann's work.

*Additional Notes.* 1. The idea and plot of "Savage Encounter," unlike those of most plays I have written for radio, seemed to me too hefty to be contained in twenty-nine minutes of playing time, and I felt from the beginning that it might make a better stage play or movie than radio show. In order to pack essentials into an arbitrary time limit, I capsuled the romance between the Pilot and Ara and called upon music to help out. The love theme at this point is no mere punctuation: it is intended actually to take over the narration. Just as it does a few moments later when the Pilot says, "As for my feelings for Ara—"

2. Leopard.

3. From a strictly philological point of view, the preservation for three centuries of an almost pure Elizabethan idiom without considerable development, coinage, and corruption would be either totally impossible or, at best, unlikely. I was aware of this at the time of writing, but one can't afford to worry about such technicalities when developing a fantasy. It belongs in the record, however, that no philologist arose, after either network production of this play, to take issue with me on this score.

4. Uproar, commotion.

5. Means "most loved of all." "Lief" by itself means a dear one, a sweetheart.

6. Sweet. Sometimes spelled suete.

> Lo, how finely the Graces can it foote
> To the Instrument:
> They dauncen deffly, and singen soote. . . .
>
> —SPENSER

7. One of the most enthusiastic responses to this broadcast came from a man who telephoned from Washington to say he thought it was the greatest show he ever heard, et cetera. But he had an objection. "Why did you use the word Fascist?" he wanted to know. "It was the only false note in the play."

"What's false about using the word Fascist?" I asked.

"Well, everybody these days is calling everybody else a Fascist or a Communist," he said.

I explained that even if this were the case, there *were* such things as Fascists, and we were fighting them, and it would be well if we called them what they were. He agreed, with reservations.

8. This should be read to convey the *larger* victory—the ultimate and millennial triumph of good over evil.

# LONDON BY CLIPPER

Produced in London under the direction of the author on July 27, 1942, and short-waved to the United States for simultaneous transmission by CBS. The first of the "American in England" series, it was based on the author's eastward crossing a month earlier. The broadcast of July 27 was lost to atmospheric disturbances over the Atlantic; so the program had to be repeated the following week.

The score was composed by Benjamin Britten and performed by the symphony orchestra of the Royal Air Force under Wing Commander R. P. O'Donnel. The author imported Joseph Julian to perform the title role. Members of the BBC repertory company appeared in most of the supplementary roles. Edward R. Murrow, CBS European chief, was associate producer.

The entire series was later produced in Australia under the direction of Lawrence H. Cecil, with Hal Thompson, American-born actor, in the role of Joe. Individual programs from the series were also produced over the Canadian network, and by U. S. Army radio units in Egypt.

# LONDON BY CLIPPER

JOE (*annoyed*). Hello! . . . hello! . . . What's the matter with this line?

*Jiggling hook.*

JOE. Hello, reservations? I guess we were cut off. I was asking how much baggage I can take on the Clipper tomorrow . . . yes, to England. Huh? (*Incredulous.*) *Forty-four pounds!*[1] Is that all? (*Protesting.*) Why, my suitcase and a couple of neckties weigh forty-four pounds! . . . Well, can't I take more if I *pay?* . . . (*Amazed.*) You mean to say I'd have to get an order from the War Department if I want to carry more baggage? . . . Well, no, not in that case. . . . No. Take too much time. . . . All right. . . . When do I show at the airport? . . . Four in the *morning?* And you leave at six. . . . Okay. Thank you. . . . G'by.

*Receiver up.*

*Music: Passage conveying the excitement of anticipation. Suddenly it segues, retarding, into good-natured morning music. Over the concluding phrases:*

JOE. I took exactly forty-four pounds of luggage with me, and I said good-by to my folks and my girl and my friends, and at 6:30 in the morning I walked down a ramp to board a Clipper bound for England. . . .

OFFICER. Good morning, sir.

---

[1] The numbered notes will be found on pages 169-171.

JOE. Good morning.

OFFICER. I'm afraid we're a little late getting started, but we're going to fly direct. We ought to be there in good time.

JOE. That's fine. Thank you.

OFFICER. Yes, sir.

JOE (*to audience*). That was an officer of the crew. Did you hear what he said? *Direct!* Atlantic *non-stop!* . . .

OFFICER. All passengers aboard, please. . . .

JOE. You get on board and take an assigned seat. You look around at your fellow passengers. Nothing odd about them. Pretty much like the average pay load on the eight o'clock plane to Washington. . . .

BISHOP.[2] Do you mind if I put my bag on your seat for a moment?

JOE. Go right ahead. Perfectly all right. (*To audience.*) That was a bishop. You had an idea only generals and diplomats and business executives went on these flights. . . .

GIRL (*fifteen years old*). Pardon me, how soon do we take off?

JOE (*startled*). What?

GIRL. How soon do we take off?

JOE. Why, any minute now, I should think.

GIRL. Thank you.

JOE (*to audience*). Where did she come from? A *kid!* Can't be more than fifteen years old, if she's that. What kind of war is this, anyway? Kids flying the oceans nonstop in a Clipper! Trouble with that kind of thing, it puts you in your place. Up to then you were feeling important. (*Low; apprehensively.*) Oh-oh . . . looks like we won't get to see the take-off! . . .

STEWARDESS. I'm sorry, but curtains must be pulled down over the windows until we're twenty minutes out. War regulations. . . .

JOE. Stewardess. For a while you thought she might be English, but you find out later she comes from New Jersey. Life can be just a series of disillusionments sometimes. Jersey takes care of the curtains; then she goes down the passageway to shut the door of the ship.

*Door slams.*

JOE. That, you say to yourself, is no ordinary door. That door won't be opened again until you've crossed an ocean. . . .

OFFICER. Tell the captain we're all set back here, Miss Malone.

STEWARDESS. Yes, sir. . . .

JOE. Well, so we're all set. And with our nose pointed in the general direction of war, we take off.

*Music: A brief passage symbolic of take-off. It cross-fades to:*

*Effect of engines in full flight, as heard from inside the cabin. This sustains behind all but the indicated musical interpolations in the following:*

JOE. Twenty minutes out, and the curtains go up. You look below and see your country gliding westward; you see the farms and woods and towns of two of the forty-eight States, and the blue Atlantic. It's a calm day— a fine North American summer morning, just a little mist—

PASSENGER. I say, aren't those some warships down there?

JOE. Where? (*Patronizingly; to audience.*) Obviously this passenger hasn't traveled much by air. Can't gauge altitudes. (*To passenger.*) No, those aren't warships. Just a couple of fishing boats.

PASSENGER. But they're bigger than fishing boats. We're up pretty high. They must be destroyers.

JOE. No, we're only up a couple of thousand feet.

PASSENGER. All the same they're good-sized ships.

JOE (*genially*). Okay. (*Pause.*) The last of the land is slipping away now. Only islands ahead. The ship flies steady. The air is smooth; cabin's settled down now. Everything's quiet. . . .

PASSENGER. Hey, what's that stuff on the water there?

JOE. What stuff? (*Pause; to audience.*) You look out of the window and see something that hits you like a sledgehammer.

*Music: A sudden and dark presence, forte. It sustains, somberly and sinuously, under the following:*

JOE. Oil. Thick oil. Far as the eye can see. Great patches of oil, spread out over mile after square mile of water, covering the ocean with a gray-green scum. That's war, drifting inshore with the tide. These patches are all that's left of American and Allied ships torpedoed recently along the coast.[3] You wonder how many good men lie in those waters—how many thousands of tons of munitions and food for England and Russia are rotting beneath the surface of this oil. Gives you a new slant, looking down on this tremendous oil slick, about people who act careless with the dim-out, as though it were a kind of nuisance, a kind of make-believe.[4] Well, it's not. That oil down there ain't kidding.

*Music: Crosses with sound.*

*Motors again.*

JOE. You find yourself thinking about the boys who sail those ships. You wonder whether you would have the guts to sign on to the crew of a tanker. . . .

PASSENGER. Will you have a cigarette?

JOE (*coming out of it*). Oh—yes, thanks.

PASSENGER (*qualifying his offer*). It's English—

JOE. That's okay. I like English cigarettes.

PASSENGER. Then that's *one* problem you won't have to face in England.

JOE. Yeah. (*Chuckles; to himself.*) Say, that's right. You *are* going to *England,* aren't you? Almost forgot that in the last-minute rush. You pinch yourself and wake up to the fact that you're very much on your way—that you're actually flying the Atlantic nonstop. Been out of sight of land for some time now.

Sure enough, going to England. You wonder whether you will like the people as much as you like their cigarettes. Are the people a mild, mixed blend, like their tobacco? Nonirritating? It occurs to you that we Americans as a whole know very little about Britishers, although we've been speaking their language all our lives, and half our cities are named after theirs. We know more about English dogs and muffins and tweeds than about English people. According to what we've always imagined, England is made up of three or four distinct types. There's the upper-class old-school-tie Lord Smudgepot type, who's filed away in your mind as a stuffed shirt, and who talks like this:

*Motors out.*

SMUDGEPOT. Absolutely ripping, old fruit. I remember at Ascot one year early in June. It was really remarkable.

Believe it or not, the jolly old horse actually stopped running.

*Motors in.*

JOE. That's the fellow you blame for the loss of Singapore. And then there's another type you're sure represents most of Great Britain—the cockney. You gather from the movies that all cockneys are natural-born comedians who break into song at the slightest opportunity, like this:

*Motors out.*

COCKNEY.[5] Talk about a toff—blimey, you ought to see him sitting around Covent Garden in a—

*Music: Tremendous exaggerated opening to song, which then reduces rapidly to a mere patter of accompaniment. The whole effect fades under:*

*Motors in.*

JOE. And then there's the high-spirited type who founded the Empire and has been losing it, cheerfully, ever since. . . .

*Motors out.*

CHEERFUL. Chin up, cheerio, carry on, old chap—bear up, righto, wot? . . .

*Motors in.*

JOE. So altogether, when you try to picture the average Englishman, he seems to you mainly one of two things: a cold, calm, aloof highbrow, or a funny little guy who sings.

Oh, well . . . you look out of the window at a sky

full of broken clouds and wonder where you got some
of those ideas. Maybe from the movies, or the novels,
or the short-wave radio. BBC news broadcasts, perhaps—very calm, very cultured they are about the
news. They don't go in for the shouting and wheezing
and high-pressure opinionizing that we do at home. No
question about it—they're a cool bunch. Why, if the
world were to come to an end at three tomorrow afternoon, they'd wait until the regular six o'clock broadcast and go on as usual. . . .

*Motors out.*

NEWS. This is London calling. Here is the news, and this
is John Snagge reading it. The world came to an end
at two minutes after three this afternoon, during a
debate in the House of Commons. A summary of the
debate will be given at the end of this bulletin. Due
to the unusual nature of the event and also to the fact
that he was away at the time, Mr. Churchill could not
be reached immediately to comment on the policy that
His Majesty's Government intends to pursue regarding the situation. . . .

*Motors in.*

JOE. Yes, that's about how it would be. (*Chuckles; then
sobers suddenly.*) Hey, look—there's a convoy directly
beneath you. Ten freighters. Headed the same way
you are. Wonder if there were more than ten when
they started out? Your friend in the seat opposite also
sights the ships. . . .

PASSENGER. Say, isn't that a convoy down there?

JOE. Either that or a reasonable facsimile.

PASSENGER. They seem to be pitching, don't they? Must

be a heavy sea. Certainly looks like a millpond from up here.

JOE. Certainly does. (*After pause; to audience.*) We're leaving them behind pretty fast now. So long, convoy. You take the low road and we take the high road, and we'll get to London before you. (*Abstractedly humming "Loch Lomond."*) Getting a little stuffy in the cabin now. Let's see, you were figuring how much you know about the British. Hmmmm. (*New thought.*) What's the lowdown about them as *fighters?* That's the important thing right now, isn't it? Not how they talk and broadcast news. You wonder how much one can believe of what one hears. Are they really starving, for example? Eating horsemeat and seaweed? Have they lost confidence in themselves after the shellackings they took? Maybe they're just sitting back waiting for America and Russia to win the war for them.

Someone said the island was chock-full of well-trained, fully-equipped troops hanging around doing nothing because they lack the courage and the audacity to attack. Were they really hard and tough during the bombings, or was that just propaganda? Well—all these things are what you're going over to find out about. Have to check into those stories about their sympathy for Russia and the rubbing out of old class distinctions. Yes, you'll see—you'll give a good look around when you get there. Oh, dear—yawn coming on. (*Yawns.*) Pretty tired now. No sleep for the past two nights.

You yawn two or three more times, and then you decide that war or no war, you're going to leave the Clipper to its crew and the Atlantic to its weather and England to tomorrow—and get some sleep. You crawl into your berth and do acrobatics to undress, and then you lie in a sort of stupor, drugged by the noise of the motors.

*Motors behind this.*

JOE. After a while you become conscious of a sound from the bridge—radio code. . . .

*Slow code. A fat spark—dot-dot-dot-dash.*

JOE. Isn't that the V symbol? V for victory? What's it doing on that receiver? You're too tired to wonder. . . . And then, for no good reason, you begin to think of *music.* Maybe because of the rhythms set up by the vibration. You try to recall what little English music you've heard, and it isn't at all hard to remember. It very obligingly runs through your head.

*Music: A mnemonic melange, sneaking in as:*

*Motors fade slightly. The effect goes on under:*

JOE. And somehow or other, as you drop away into a spongy sleep, it all gets mixed up like a radioman's nightmare—code, and motors, and Gilbert and Sullivan, and static, and "Pomp and Circumstance" and V for victory—and the night. . . .

*Music: A disturbed montage as described, with sounds of motors and code interspersed ad libitum. At length a sustained quiet passage suggestive of sleep. Then suddenly a flourish of awakening.*

STEWARDESS (*announcing*). An hour and ten minutes to your destination! One hour and ten minutes to your destination! . . .

JOE. That's how the passengers are awakened. By Miss

Malone of New Jersey, the self-winding cuckoo clock with the English accent. Of course she doesn't say "Your destination"—she names the place. Naturally we can't do the same on the air for obvious reasons— censorship. . . .

STEWARDESS. Good morning.

JOE. Good morning, Miss Malone. (*To audience.*) War-time censorship isn't a gag—it's a protection. (*Yawning.*) Heeaaww. That wasn't much sleep. Flying east as fast as we've flown, the night gets folded up like an accordion. (*Returning to the thought.*) Why is it nobody loves a censor? He's like a baseball umpire— everybody wants to kill the bum. Yet he does an important job—a vital job, in fact. Any man who keeps information away from the swine is a friend of mine. Well, so the Clipper (which you feel you've been on all your life by now) makes a beautiful landing at a place called—

CENSOR. Censored.

JOE. And she tears around in the water like a speed boat for a while, and then finally she moors; and you disembark; and you go through the customs in a building overlooking the beautiful—

CENSOR. Censored.

JOE. Then you have breakfast, and you all pile into a—

CENSOR. Censored.

JOE. And you travel for a censored number of miles to a censored place, where you are met by a censored type of camouflaged airship whose windows are censored by white paint. It's a white-out—allows light to come through, but keeps you from seeing anything. And you get into that plane and fly for a censored number of hours, and then—well, then you're *there!*

*Music: Landing; arrival; a stern passage with suggestion of excitement and premonition of grimness. It sustains for some time under:*

JOE. You are on the soil of England. You're on the island that fought the Nazis alone for a year. You look around. . . .

OFFICER. This way, please. . . .

JOE. And on your way to the customs and censorship you catch a glimpse of the airfield on which your plane landed. It's heavily guarded, heavily camouflaged— warplanes perched here and there—you walk right under the nose of a big Lancaster bomber, and it lifts your heart to see it. It's a strange sensation. You've seen brand-new Flying Fortresses fresh off an American assembly line, and that was a pleasant enough sight—but that was nothing compared to seeing this grizzly old battle-worn giant with bullet holes in his fuselage and one of his wings slightly ruffled. This fellow, you can wager, was over Germany last night. This baby has been carrying the war to where it belongs—right on the front doorstep of the Fascists. . . .

CUSTOMS. Passport, please? . . .

JOE. You're asked some questions by customs officials. . . .

CUSTOMS. Have you credentials? . . .

JOE. You have, and you show them. . . .

CUSTOMS. How long do you plan to stay, please? . . .

JOE. You tell him. . . .

CUSTOMS. Where will you be living in England? . . .

JOE. You tell him. . . .

CUSTOMS. What is the purpose of your visit? Have you documents in your possession? What are your references in England and the United States? . . .

JOE. It's all cordial and routine, and then you move along to the censor. He inspects the contents of your brief case. . . .

CENSOR. Any letters or articles?

JOE. Yes. These. (*Pause.*) He reads them. One is a clipping from the New York *Times*—an article damning the British for the loss of Tobruk.[6] Another is a carbon of a letter you wrote to a friend, in which, among other things, you criticize certain British government policies.[7] . . .

CENSOR. Interesting letter, this.

JOE. Thank you.

CENSOR. And this clipping is from the New York *Times?*

JOE. Yes.

CENSOR. These are quite all right. You may go through, sir. I hope I haven't delayed you from catching the special train to London.

JOE. Oh, that's quite all right. (*To audience.*) It develops that you *have* lost the train, but in doing so you've gained the comforting knowledge that here, in this small detail, is one of the thousand yardsticks by which one can measure the issues in this war. If anybody in Germany were foolish enough to be found carrying literature critical of the government, he'd either be shot or slapped into a concentration camp.

*An auto horn blows, about fifty yards away.*

JOE. That's the coach that takes you to the London train. It's going to be a long ride to the city, and you're hungry enough to eat a horse. Are horses rationed, by the way? (*To driver.*) Driver, I take it there's a dining car on the train to London?

DRIVER. Oh, no, sir. No dining cars on any of the trains. Haven't had them for some time now.

JOE (*dryly*). I see. (*To audience.*) When you reach the station, you have four minutes in which to get something to eat. You rush into a place marked "Refreshments" and dash up to the counter. . . .

WAITRESS. Yes, sir. What will you have?

JOE. A sandwich, please.

WAITRESS. We have meat pastes, that's all.

JOE. Any milk?

WAITRESS (*scandalized*). *Milk?* Of *course* no milk. Coffee!

JOE. All right. Coffee. (*Down.*) The train saves you from having to drink the coffee. You feel such coffee is a blow to the Allied cause. And with your forty-four pounds of luggage you board your first English train.

*Starter's whistle. Then train effect, starting up. It continues in the background all the way under:*

JOE. The train is crowded. It's a warm Sunday, and people are apparently returning to London from outings in the country. Everybody in the compartment looks tired, but none can be as tired as you.

You look at their faces. Good, average, unspectacular, kindly people. No signs of malnutrition in this batch.[8] A little shabby, perhaps—not a new hat or suit or dress in the lot. For a long while you ride in silence. Then you look up, look casually out of the window; and there—right in front of your eyes . . .

*Music: Shock. It tapers off under:*

JOE. . . . are the first bomb ruins you have ever seen. It's an ordinary suburban house such as you'd find in Chevy Chase, Oak Park, Glendale—any of ten thousand towns in the States. But the roof of this one is burnt away and the insides blasted out . . . and now you're passing a church, a little church like the one in Winthrop, Massachusetts, or Kent, Ohio, or Pleasantville, Mississippi. Only this one is just four hollow walls.

It's different from the pictures in the roto, somehow; different from the newsreels—it's the difference between seeing an actress on the screen and seeing her in person. *This* is the brick and mortar—this is the flesh and blood. It makes you mad—mad enough to forget your fatigue. You catch the eye of the man sitting opposite. (*To the man.*) When did they have a crack at this place?

MAN. Fairly recently. About three weeks ago.

JOE. That's the first I've seen.

MAN. Oh. Just come over?

JOE. Well, uh, yes. I'm an American.

MAN. I'm afraid you'll see a good deal more.

JOE. Might be a good idea to ship one of these ruins intact to America and set it up stone by stone in Times Square, so we could see what a bombed house really looks like.

MAN (*good-naturedly*). Why do that?

JOE. Because I'm afraid it's hard for some of us to visualize these things at such a distance. To a lot of us the war exists mainly in the newspapers. Here it's blown up your houses and killed your neighbors.

MAN. Yes, I see what you mean.

JOE (*after a pause*). You have a long conversation with this fellow. He speaks seriously of the war, its aims, the peace after victory. . . .

MAN. You see, I really believe this war is part and parcel

of a great revolution which began long before Munich.
It's bigger than just a world *war*.

JOE. In what way do you mean?

MAN. Well—things are never going to be the same as they
were. That's all done with. The people who are fighting this one and paying for it and suffering its agonies
are simply not going to let the old systems take up
where they left off.

JOE. Are you talking about all people, or the people of
England?

MAN. All people, I *hope*—the English certainly. We've discovered that the idea of every-man-for-himself, that
the old class distinctions have outlived their useful-
ness—if they ever *were* useful. We've found out that
when people allow incompetents and blunderers to
manage their affairs, they run up a big bill in blood
and grief and money.

JOE. But how are you going to do anything about it?

MAN. Well, by insisting on a new life—by demanding that
the same tremendous sacrifice and energy, the same resources of men and material that are put into a successful war be put into a successful peace. (*Pause.*)
It staggers the mind to think of what could be done
in the way of housing and health and education for the
cost of what it takes to run a week of this war. The
idea is first to win the war—and then to see that what
*can* be done after this war *will* be done. (*Pause.*)
That's what we're fighting for. Not the old stuff.

JOE (*after a pause*). A silence falls between you; for a
while you think over what he's said. Then fatigue sets
in again, and you stop thinking and just sit.

The train hurries on. You must be approaching
London, because the barrage balloons are getting

thicker. Look like stubby fish, all swimming the same way—into the wind. The train's slowing down now, and you make ready to get off. As you collect your forty-four pounds of luggage, your friend comes over and takes you aside. . . .

MAN. One thing I wish you'd keep in mind when you're looking about the country. Don't judge us by the occasional bounder you may come across . . . there's that kind in every country. And don't judge us by the lobbies of a few hotels in London. See us as we are— see us in the towns and villages and on the streets and in the factories and pubs and army camps and aerodromes and schools. I think you'll like us. . . .

JOE. By this time the train has arrived, and passengers are crowding out. . . .

MAN. It's been terribly good talking to you.

JOE. Thanks. It's been a pleasure for me.

MAN. I'm Flying Officer Hill, Royal Air Force. . . .

JOE. You tell him who you are, and you shake hands. . . .

MAN. Good-by. Good luck.

JOE. Good-by. Good luck, sir. (*Pause.*) And he's lost in the crowd. You get out with your luggage and try to get a taxi. (*Up.*) Taxi! Hey, taxi!—Hey, you, how about it?

TAXI. Finished. Just enough petrol to get home.

JOE. What about you, there? (*Whistles.*) Hey!

SECOND TAXI. Sorry. Through for the day.

JOE. If you think trying to get a taxi at the depot in *Washington* is tough! (*Up.*) Taxi! (*Down.*) You wait an hour, and then finally one comes along that has enough petrol to take you to your hotel. You arrive. You get into your room. The curtains are drawn over all windows. The bathroom window is painted black. You're hungry. You feel you can eat *two* horses by now. You order something to eat. . . .

WAITER. Did you ring, sir?

JOE. Yes. I'm starved. Can you bring me some milk?

WAITER. Oh, no, sir. Too late for that.

JOE. Soup?

WAITER. Sorry, sir. All gone by now.

JOE. What *can* you bring me?

WAITER. Some cold meat?

JOE. Okay. . . . The meal arrives, but when it's set on the table, you can't eat it, because you're even more tired than you are hungry.

It's getting on toward midnight now. You take a warm bath and stagger into a robe. Then you switch off the lights and go over to the window and pull back the curtains.

*Music: London in the gloom of mid-war blackout.*

JOE. London is blacked out. The greatest city in the world lies in a vast hush between battles. You see rooftops faint in the light of the waning moon. And you make out the Thames. You make out the tall silhouette of Big Ben; you're surprised to find it this close. (*Pause.*) And as you stand at the open window, suddenly you hear airplanes overhead. They must be friendly planes, or else you'd hear a siren—or wouldn't you? Is that distant gunfire, or a train crossing a bridge somewhere? Is that a siren, or a bus starting up in low gear?

The planes keep droning above you. They're heading east to the attack. They'll be flying over swastikas twenty minutes from now.

*Big Ben begins to strike, off in Westminster. It is midnight.*

JOE. Ah! Big Ben! Fine, upstanding, outspoken Ben—telling the world midnight has come again to this island in the third year of its siege. You wonder how many midnights more will sound before the siege is turned and *we* do the besieging? How many midnights more before Big Ben is joined by all the bells in England and in the whole wide world, proclaiming victory and peace and the new world of Flying Officer Hill? (*He pauses and reflects.*)

Another plane flies up there somewhere in the black night of England, bent on making that new world.

*The twelfth bell, dissolving into:*

*Music: Conclusion.*

# LONDON BY CLIPPER

A summer storm came down the Potomac on its way to the sea. It was a pelting, sweet-smelling rain, having picked up fine qualities on its way over the Blue Ridge Mountains. I watched the downpour with the kind of acuteness that comes after forty-eight hours without sleep, when the mind goes antic with skittering impressions. Somehow it resembled a movie storm, for the people on the street ran like extras to get out of it, and the Capitol dome loomed like a process-shot through the curtain of rain. It seemed utterly impossible to me, riding in a cab to the State Department, that the space between Pennsylvania Avenue and Charing Cross Road could be compressed into thirty hours.

Only a hick could feel the way I did in anticipation of this flight to Britain. The Atlantic had already been criss-crossed by thousands of pilots and passengers, and the route was known by the comfortable name of shuttle; but it was to be *my* first transoceanic flight, and I had a right to be reasonably steamed up about it. Four months later I was to make a return flight three times longer, and four years later I was to fly around the world, but I had no way of knowing those things then.

"An American in England" was handicapped by lateness in getting under way. The series had an immovable opening date and a limited number of Tuesdays available to it. I had hoped to spend two months observing the people of Britain at war before starting to write the first program, scheduled for July 27. But here it was June 26, and I was still in Washington, winding up business so that I could depart the next morning.

I picked up my passport at the State Department, and then, by one of those little ironies with which life abounds, had to clear my first visa with the embassy of a country which was at that time almost as hostile to Britain as the Axis—Eire. This formality was to permit me passage through Foynes, the Shannon port used as a terminus for North Atlantic clipper flights.

Because of the lateness of the hour and the imminence of sailing, Seumas Noonan, Irish minister, decided to telephone Dublin directly. He placed the call, and after a moment I heard him sputter, "Why in God's name should I have to wait six hours for *London* to clear a call to *Dublin?*" He listened with growing irritation, then hung up the receiver. "They can *have* their telephone circuit," he said. "I'll give you a visa myself and explain it to Dublin afterward."

With the sign of the harp stamped in my passport, I dashed over to the British Embassy. There I was impressed by a girl, a clerk, who took my fee for a visa. She seemed low in spirits, as she had a right to be, what with the current fortunes of war. "We really shouldn't be taking ten dollars from you for a visa when you are going over to help us," she said.

I told her I was going to do nothing more than tell Americans exactly what I saw in England, and if that amounted to help, then I hoped it would be worth that much. She replied wistfully that the essential truth about a people was too seldom known outside their political boundaries, and that whenever this "essence" managed to cross those boundaries and reach another people intact, both benefited from the experience.

Later I had occasion to appreciate how basic to post-war

international relations was this girl's comment. For there are few peoples in the world, who, relieved of pressures, anxieties, or actual dangers, are not kindly, hospitable, decent, democratic. The British, even under the pressure and danger of a powerful enemy as close to them as Yonkers to Staten Island, never for a moment lost a jot of the "essence" for which many an American, including Joe, came to admire them.

However, there is too often a division between a people— as an essence—and the statesmen representing them. Plainly the statesmanship of a country automatically *becomes* that country in the eyes of other nations; so that by the most natural process, John Doe finds himself disliking a people when actually the focus of his dislike is a premier, a cabinet, a cabal.

There were perfectly sensible Americans who had never been able to respect British colonial policy and who were exasperated by British statesmanship up to and including Munich. Later, from the fall of France to Pearl Harbor, Britain was suspected by thousands of additional Americans, especially isolationists and their bedfellows, of doing her best to draw us into her "imperialist" war. But the blunderings of Whitehall, bad as they were, never were permitted by the British people to degenerate to the level of attempting a negotiated peace. Chamberlain was relieved, rather tardily to be sure, but bounced properly. And the heroic stand of the British through the long blitz, when they were being blasted by everything the Nazis had, when their food supplies were so low that every transport sunk in the Atlantic was a blow distinctly felt, had placed the entire free world in their debt.

By the time CBS invited me to produce "An American in

England," the isolationists had been answered at Hawaii, the British had broken the Luftwaffe, and the fear of an immediate invasion of Britain had been relieved. But there was still very little American love being exported with lend-lease, notwithstanding valentines like *Mrs. Miniver* and *The White Cliffs of Dover*. British armies had been swept out of Greece and Crete and for a third time were being driven back in North Africa. Only four days before the girl at the Embassy spoke so philosophically of the essences of people, the British garrison at Tobruk, 25,000 strong, had fallen to Rommel after twenty-four hours of battle. The British were being damned up and down as poor fighters who, beginning with Dunkirk, had done nothing but pull out of foreign countries.

I expected and understood (though I did not condone) a certain measure of American antipathy toward the British. But the scope and the utter senselessness of most anti-British sentiment puzzled me. I wanted to get significant data on the subject before setting out for England and therefore requested from both British and American sources all available intelligence on anti-British attitudes in this country: their extent, how they started, where they flourished, and why. I might as well have asked for an interview with the governor-general of the moon. Nobody knew anything about anything. It developed later that during the war the Federal Bureau of Investigation did a superb job of tracking down actual anti-British activity inspired by Fascist agents, but the information on anti-British attitudes and their expression was apparently unavailable to press and radio at that time.

The absence of help from official quarters warned me against a common sequel to this sort of thing: meddling, once a project is going. There are thousands of people who never have a suggestion to make when work is in progress. But once the hard task of clearing the forest and digging a foundation and building the house is safely out of the way, they are happy to come around and suggest how the job could have been improved. They tell you solemnly that it was a great mistake to clear this particular patch in preference to the one down by the river.

Just before the English trip was proposed, I'd had my fill of protocol during a four-network, quasi-governmental series called "This Is War!" Instructed by this experience, I soon proposed conditions of authority affecting the English junket, and these were accepted. My memorandum on the subject was as blunt as I could make it:

There should be a clear understanding at the outset that once general agreement has been reached on the directives, scope, and form of this series, the author-director and the producer shall not be answerable to American or British governmental or any other agencies on aesthetic or other grounds, beyond the ordinary and reasonable requisites of military necessity and good taste; further, that they will not be responsible to radio agencies other than the CBS; and that while counsel and co-operation from qualified sources will of course be welcome and necessary, no attempt shall be made to influence the writer and producer against their own scruples.

This is stipulated to avoid the confusion and contradiction that would unquestionably result if orders, directives, suggestions, and formal criticisms were to be made by several interested agencies such as the U.S. Embassy, the State Department, the Office of Facts and Figures, the Co-ordinator of Information, the BBC, and departments of the British government. It was the experience of "This Is War!" that multiple points-of-view always canceled out; that, for example, what one half of the OFF liked, the other half didn't; that what a Navy liaison man found objectionable in a production program was the very thing that made the War Production Board very happy to have said on the air.

I accompanied this with a statement of objectives (cf. notes on "Passport for Adams," pp. 367-368), and these were simple enough:

To promote understanding between the peoples of Great Britain and the United States toward the closest collaboration in the prosecution of the war.

To create, through such understanding, a fuller appreciation of the indivisibility of the fight.

To countervail anti-United Nations sentiment and the propaganda of division within the United States.

To establish the character of the British people through the eye and idiom of the inquiring American.

To establish identity of interests between the British people (and, inferentially, among all of our allies) and ourselves; our traditions, language; our stake in the war; common future in a better world.

To allow for realistic consideration of all issues of the war pertinent to the series. There should be a definite squaring-away against anti-British propaganda that has already gained currency in the United States or that may develop out of the fortunes of war in the course of the series. In this respect the program should be dedicated to the principle of wiping old slates clean—of obliterating the regrettable history of appeasement and embracing the new determination of the united peoples to crush forever the forces of aggression.

This much settled, it remained now only to get there, and the American Export Lines took care of that. The flight was exactly as described in the script, save for minor unreported incidents such as the loss of my glasses during the night of strange time and the uprooting of half the ship's upholstery in order to find them.

Though the need for censorship of place names and other details has long since passed, I have printed the script as broadcast, for the purpose of preserving as nearly as possible the atmosphere of the moment. The flight was from the marine basin adjoining LaGuardia airport to the town of Foynes, Limerick County, where the Fergus and the

Shannon meet. From Foynes we traveled by bus through the town of Limerick to an airdrome miles beyond, where a British land plane picked us up. We then flew east over Eire and the Irish Sea, to land in Bristol.

I was the last of fourteen passengers to clear through customs and censorship and the only one to miss the special train that carried clipper customers to London in a nonstop run taking about a third of the time required by other trains. I was miffed at the moment, being tired and hungry, but I soon realized I'd had a lucky break. The special train could not have been nearly as stimulating and colorful as the slow, untidy crawler that stopped every few signal-blocks to let freight trains whistle by. It was this hot, crowded train, with dirty windows, no drinking water, and flushless toilets, that presented me with the ending to my script, and I was grateful. Not so much to the train itself, but to one of the passengers on it. The man's name, incidentally, was not Hill, but Flying Officer *Smith*—only what listener would have believed that? He was a remarkable man, and, like the absent-minded dolt that I am, I neglected to get his first name or address. It would have been good to compare notes with him later, perhaps to see something of the island in his company. Our conversation was substantially as Joe reports it, except that I have not done justice to Hill's articulateness and eloquence.

I checked in at the Savoy, stretched my legs, rang for the waiter, and indulged in cold meat and midnight reverie as related in the script. And in the morning I set about preparing for the series.

First of all I had to look for a studio that would serve my needs, much as a worker migrating to a strange city would first look for lodging. A studio may be beautiful and equipped with the latest technical improvements, but still be no good for one's purposes. It may, for example, be suitable for a concert orchestra, but not for an intimate scene in a drama; it may be right for long-wave transmission, but wrong for short-wave.

Then there was the matter of who would enact my pieces when they were written. To an alien writer-director like myself, with no previous experience in British radio, this was a problem. I auditioned about fifty actors in order to familiarize myself with the color, timbre, and range of their voices, their dialects, their histrionics. Since I was no expert on British speech, I had to acquire at least a superficial familiarity with sectionalisms before pretending to be a judge of them.

If the English part of "An American in England" were to be authentic, it was no less important that the American be so. I had hoped to find an American actor in London, but the eight candidates I auditioned were either hopelessly British or not good narrators. At length I imported Joseph Julian, an underestimated actor who had appeared in a major role for me only once before and who was virtually unknown outside a small circle of radio-wise people in New York. He arrived by bomber less than twenty-four hours before this script was to go on the air, and he had time only for a sleep and a shave before beginning rehearsals.

Casting the series was one thing, getting the right kind of music another. The resources of the BBC were limited, having been drained by heavy drafts of manpower into the armed forces. Moreover, because of enemy action it had long ago been necessary to disperse the facilities and personnel of the corporation. Thus some of the best orchestras were in Bedford, about fifty miles north of London, others in Manchester, considerably farther away. I went with two BBC men to Bedford with the idea of originating my broadcasts from there. But we found the Bedford troupe already laboring under a demanding schedule. For a moment it seemed that I would have to settle for an organ, a balalaika, and a wandering mezzosoprano. Then somebody suggested the orchestra of the Royal Air Force, consisting largely of the peacetime personnel of the London Philharmonic. The suggestion was taken up *con spirito* by the RAF, and lo, I had at my disposal a sixty-two-piece symphony orchestra—reputedly the best in the land.

Then came the hunt for a composer. By a stroke of good luck we were able to engage Benjamin Britten ("Sinfonia da Requiem"), whose name was appropriate for the series and whose music was even more so. But not yet could I turn my attention to writing. There were long preliminary conferences with Britten; with Sergeant John Hollingsworth of the RAF, representing the symphony; with Wing Commander O'Donnel, its conductor; with Murrow; with studio engineers regarding construction of special accoustical facilities; with CBS New York via short-wave telephone.

Once cast and music were straightened out, I went into the business of sound. Certain effects, I realized, would not do for transmission across an ocean. They would get gobbled up by atmospherics on the way over. So I made test records and played them over a telephonic circuit to Davidson Taylor at CBS in New York. He listened to the sound of a door slamming. "No good," he said; "sounds like a bomb going off." The sound of an airplane motor came out the other end as an avalanche of indefinable mush. An auto horn registered perfectly. Interhemispheric telephone tolls being what they are, Taylor's comments were brief. "Good . . . bad . . . impossible . . . fair . . . try a higher frequency . . . no, no better . . . mushy . . . very clear . . . too much echo."

The sound-effects test ruled out at least two-thirds of my intended reportoire of sound, and that was that. Then the work really began. All I had to do now was write the script. It got written somehow and went into rehearsal. A company of more than a hundred musicians, actors, technicians, made its way through the blackout to the barnlike studios at Maida Vale, on the outskirts of the city. The clock went round toward the zero hour of the première.

Then there was an alert. Guns were firing in the city. My CBS and BBC colleagues stood by in case we'd have to take the program to an emergency studio and paraphrase it for two or three voices, sans production and music. But the "All clear" came just before the clock reached 4 A.M.—and we were on the air in New York. It was 10 P.M. there.

Julian and the men of the RAF and the British actors and Engineer Cox and Soundman Smart and Soundgirl Jamblin and Announcer Snagge and Composer Britten and Producer Murrow and Liaison Monroe and Conductor O'Donnel and Timer Hall, all of the crew worked mightily, and there was sweat and thirty minutes of cue-knitting, and ten-second timings called out, and interstudio telephonic messages, and signals, and decisions, and twiddling of dials, and the managing of fades and cross-fades, and all of the hocus-pocus that goes into studio production.

And then it was over, and we sighed a sigh, and there were congratulations, and I thanked everybody, and everybody thought it was just dandy. Which it was, with the exception of only one thing: The program never got through!

I had outsmarted myself. The opening device of Joe's trouble with a telephone connection ("Hello! . . . hello! What's the matter with this line?") I had intended deliberately to attract the ear of the listener. I had merely worked on the principle that nothing will rivet attention to a loudspeaker so much as something going wrong on the studio or transmitting end. We are all by nature eavesdroppers, and it was with this in mind that I set out the way I did. The idea may have been a honey, but by an inadvertence nobody in London had informed master control in New York that I was opening with a *simulated* disconnection. The engineers on the American side, hearing a voice complain about the telephone service in a convincing tone of irritation, assumed that the routing of the circuit had been snafu'd between the studio and the receiving towers, and pulled their plugs. The network control went to a standby dance 'band. Whole minutes later, the engineers, hearing what seemed like a reasonable semblance of a dramatic script on the short-wave monitors, switched back to London, but by this time, atmospheric conditions had so deteriorated that the transmission was impossible anyway. The broadcast was cut off at the New York end before it was ten minutes along. No one knew this in the London studio during the actual broadcast, save Murrow and D. H. Monroe of the BBC. They kept the knowledge to themselves in order not to dismay the company. It was not until the next day that all were told.

We did the program over again the following week.

*Acting.* Perhaps the best way to suggest the requirements for the American is to repeat what I wrote in my production notes to "Cromer," sixth of the series, in a previous collection: "The Joe of your company wants to be the things Joseph Julian was in the original production: young, thoughtful, friendly, impressionable, curious, neither standing in awe of the British nor patronizing them. Mostly he's just looking around and thinking about what he sees. He never forces the narration, never feels obliged to sell the

British to Americans, never consciously 'acts.' This is a report, not a play."

The only other character to worry about is the man (Hill) whom Joe meets on the train. He should be played earnestly and quietly. Actually there were six other people in the compartment with Hill and me, and this factor conditioned his speech. Being solid British types, the others pretended not to hear us, and none at any time broke into our conversation. It is noteworthy that when Hill had something extra-special to say—when he was in effect summing up as we neared London—he took me aside. This he did on the pretext of pointing out Windsor Castle from the south side of the train. But as soon as we were alone he urged me not to judge the British "by the occasional bounder you may come across." It was the sort of thing he could not well have said before his compatriots in the compartment, and his tact was but another fine quality in a man whom I was eager to acclaim as a true representative of the true England.

*Sound.* The four-motors of the NC41882 make a mature and steady drone and are constant behind Joe's narration throughout the flight. The effect never has time to become monotonous, because the narrative is frequently interrupted by passengers making small talk or by the *dramatis personae* of Joe's own thoughts. However, it is important not to treat the "motors in" and "motors out" as though the soundman were going through a revolving door. The engines should be faded rather than cut in and out—not slow, lingering fades, but quick ones, quick as a dissolve in a movie.

The soundman should be inducted into the orchestra for the "disturbed montage" describing Joe's restless sleep. John Smart, one of the BBC's finest sound engineers, mixed a cocktail of motors and code that blended perfectly with Britten's score. It was a moment of wry radiogenic humor.

*Music.* The British have a healthy attitude toward music in radio drama, and this is reflected in their superior scores. When Louis MacNeice in 1942 wrote a ninety-minute program commemorating Columbus Day, none less than William Walton was commissioned to do the score. The American equivalent would be the commissioning of a Barber or a Copland. Britten's music for this series must rank with the best of Herrmann and Murray, at the very top of radio's serious original work. The cues that Britten composed for the takeoff and blackout passages were so powerful and graphic that I urged him to develop what he had written and to make a suite of it. Such music seemed too good to be lost after a single hearing. On the level of the top composers who specialize in films and radio, even bridge and background music is distinguished, and often contains material worth developing into full-grown works. Few such scores have been expanded into suites for concert performance, but these are so successful that they demand more attempts. Among the best are the *Lieutenant Kijé Suite* by Prokofiev; *Welles Raises Kane* by Herrmann; Aaron Copland's *The City;* Lyn Murray's *Cromer Suite;* Deems Taylor's *Job* music; Alexander Semmler's suite from *Between Americans.* Listeners who recall Murray's *Daybreak* and *Esther,* Semmler's rich work in *Psalm for a Dark Year,* and Herrmann's backstopping of *We Hold These Truths* and *Untitled,* will perhaps agree that such scores should be creations by themselves.

*Additional Notes.* 1. This limitation dismayed me as it did Joe, because my lightest suitcase weighed eighteen pounds by itself. I hastily bought two canvas bags weighing only two pounds each. A few months later, the maximum load was raised to fifty-five pounds. Except to Havana, which is still forty-four. (Subject to change without notice, I might add.)

2. I was short of believable American voices; so I put the bee on Charles Collingwood to play the role of the Bishop. I don't usually cast one-line roles with such distinguished figures, but the series, being the first of its kind, was looked upon by CBS London as an expensive and exciting lark, and the whole crew of 49 Hallam Street came down to the studio to watch and, if needed, to help.

3. This was at the height of the submarine war off our Atlantic coast. Only a few days before, a German submarine had sunk the merchant ship *Rio Tercero* 120 miles off New York City, and the patch of oil could have been from that sinking.

4. The night glow of the world's best-lit city was such that it would silhouette ships many miles at sea and thus make them easy prey for enemy submarines. A dim-out was ordered, which meant that the advertising signs could no longer blaze on Broadway and that shops must cut down the candlepower of their window lighting. This was little enough to ask when the lives of sailors and merchantmen were at stake; yet a good many burghers, commentators, and columnists complained. It was this sort of arrogant smugness throughout the war that made me so angry in scripts like "There Will Be Time Later" (page 407).

5. This speech was ad-libbed by Arthur Somers and came so fast that beyond the first few phrases it was incomprehensible. It was an inspired bit of Cockney gibberish—so inspired that neither Somers nor I could quite make out what he had said when we listened to the record. The song itself can be any fast, funny Cockney vaudeville patter. Better if clean, of course.

6. James Aldridge in the New York *Times* of June 24, 1942, dispatched from the Egyptian theater an article sharply criticizing the British command—one of the few articles I encountered during the war in which anti-Fascist orientation of troops was regarded as a military *necessity*. "Death," he said, "is what a soldier expects, but he does not like to die unless you keep telling him sensibly what he is going to die for."

7. The censor found this so interesting he wanted to hold it for study. As the letter contained a good deal of yeasty profanity, I did not want it knocking around England over my signature. It was the time spent arguing him out of holding this letter that made me lose the Clipper train.

8. England's level of nutrition reached an all-time high during the war, in spite of food shortages and severe rationing. The reason was that poor people, under wartime control, were better fed. Unemployment had been absorbed by war industries; wages were high, and so was purchasing power. Canteens were installed at pit-heads of mines where there had been none before, and the so-called British Restaurants, government owned and operated, fed low-income groups economically and well. Also, certain dietary absurdities of normal times, such as the overrefinement of flour, were eliminated; instead of the best part of wheat being fed to animals, it was put into bread—called national bread —85 per cent wheat extraction by law.

9. Actually I was not left to my own resources here. I was met by Robert and Kitty Trout at Paddington, and the three of us went off on separate taxi hunts. We were almost an hour at it, until Bob finally showed up triumphant on the running board of a cab.

# HOME IS WHERE YOU HANG YOUR HELMET

Produced on December 8, 1942, as the seventh in the "American in England" series. Lyn Murray composed and conducted, and the author directed.

# HOME IS WHERE YOU HANG YOUR HELMET

*Music: Introduction, fading under:*

JOE. If you've never met a soldier away from his country, you have no idea how much a man can carry that isn't in a pack. The faces of his people and the taste of home grub and the smell of turf and fallen leaves in football time and the way his dog looks when you holler: "Get down off that sofa!"—all these he carries with him tucked away in the little kit bag behind his forehead. He thinks of the silly porcelain horse on the top shelf of the china closet, and that first dance in June, when he drove her home and they necked briefly on the front porch before her old man came out and said: "What's the idea of keeping my daughter up so late?" These things a soldier keeps filed away under his helmet, and every now and then he takes them out and thinks them over and puts them back.

Yes, every soldier who goes abroad takes his country with him—a thousand square miles of it, and also his favorite home-grown stories and homemade songs. And when he sings, he may not sound like much, but at least he knows what he's singing about.

VOICE. (*Faintly we hear a soldier who knows what he's singing about. It's a Polish folk tune; there's an accordion accompanying him. We advance toward the music.*)

JOE. One night in a village in Surrey I came across two

RAF pilots who were having a fine time singing. I figured they both belonged to a Polish squadron, because they looked, and the song sounded, Polish. I went over . . .

VOICE. (*We are alongside the music now. The song finishes.*)

JOE (*tentatively*). Speak English? (*No answer.*) Parlez-vous français?

BEN (*in perfect English: good-naturedly*). Why, yes, both languages. Especially English, as I'm an Englishman.

JOE (*laughing it off*). Oh. I thought you were Polish. Wasn't that a Polish song you were singing?

BEN. Yes. It's one my friend here taught me. *He's* Polish. . . .

JOE. We introduced ourselves at this point—Ben, the Briton, and Stan, the Pole. Stan explained, mostly in Polish, that except for Ben's slightly Galician accent, he could easily pass for a street singer in Warsaw. . . .

BEN. Yes, the kind they throw shoes at from the windows.

STAN. Ben uczył mnie jak to sing niektóre English and Scotch songs jak "Loch Lomond" and "Londonderry Air." Po wojnie będę uczył tych piosenek moich pupils in Przasnyż, my school.

BEN. I suspect he's saying that he's learned some English songs, and when the war is over he's going to teach them to his pupils in Przasnyż.

JOE. Does he sing any request numbers?

STAN. What does he say?

BEN. He says sing "Loch Lomond."

STAN. "Loch Lomond." Yess. Righto. (*Stan sings "Loch Lomond" in English, but with a deep Polish accent.*

*He is accompanied by an accordion. After a while both voice and accordion dip under to make way for:*)

JOE (*over music*). Comrades in more than one kind of air, these flying men from Oxfordshire and Przasnyż. They liked each other and swapped songs and stories and took turns buying the beers. A good time was being had by both. They knew that tomorrow, just as last night, they would be out hunting the Hun, and maybe they wouldn't get back, and there would be no more "Loch Lomond" and no more polska and no more laughter in the pub by the sign of the Rose and Crown.

The fact of the matter is that within five weeks . . .

*Music: Orchestra sneaks in here to take over "Loch Lomond," as Stan's singing fades out; music sustains through the end of the speech.*

JOE. . . . Stan was killed over Belgium, and Ben didn't get back from escorting some Fortresses into France. Both took the high road; and it's in the records, perfectly plain for anybody to see, that they went out and fought day after day, sincerely, without compromise, without pose or politics, for a world that would be better for themselves and other people in a lot of countries.

Well, if the statesmen of their countries fight as honestly and hard and for the same things as Stan and Ben, there may well be occasion later on for considerable swapping of songs and beers, and maybe at last a good time might be had by *all*—Malaya to Loch Lomond.

*Music: "Loch Lomond" is up and away.*

JOE. Soldiers are wonderful people. At a dock in Liverpool . . .

*In with dock background, light; it sustains intermittently behind the entire scene.*

JOE. . . . I was watching some American army engineers supervise the unloading of a transport. They had the job well under control and were willing to talk as soon as they were satisfied I wasn't a spy. I told them my name, but they insisted on calling me Mac. And they plied me with questions. . . .

PETE. Been here long, Mac?

JACK. What d'ya think of English girls?

PETE. What kind of a town is London?

JACK. Do you know Ed Murrow who's on the radio?

PETE. How'd you come over, by plane? . . .

JOE. One of the boys was from St. Louis, and I asked him if he knew how the world series was coming out (that was the week the series started).[1] His answer shocked me as it would probably shock St. Louis. . . .

PETE. Aah, I don't know and I don't care. How the hell can you get excited about a baseball game when you're getting ready to bust into Europe somewhere with a couple of million tanks and guns! Lookit the stuff coming off this one ship. I don't care if the Cards win, lose, or draw. Besides, my team has always been the Browns, anyway.

JACK (*deprecatingly*). Haw! What an ambition! Rootin' for the Browns!

JOE. What's *your* team, Jack?

JACK. Reds. The Cincinnati Reds. Best team in baseball.

[1] The numbered notes will be found on pages 193-195.

PETE. How about the *Russian* Reds! I bet they're not playing baseball in *Russia* right now.

JACK. I bet they *are*. Maybe not baseball, but soccer or
something.

JOE. I suppose you could say there's a kind of world series
going on there too.

PETE. What an army those Reds got, hey?

JACK. Aw, Russia—if they only had names you could
pronounce. Smallyensk—Bryansk—Minsk—Pinsk—
Starry-eye Russka, Novachord—

PETE (*disgusted*). *Novgorod*, not Novachord!

JOE. It's Star*aya Russa,* isn't it?

JACK. I can't pronounce *any* of them Russian names.

PETE. Christ sakes, you ought to be ashamed to say that,
coming from where you do.

JOE. Why, where does he come from?

PETE. Tell him, tell him where you come from.

JACK (*evasively*). I come from Texas.

PETE. But where in Texas? Tell him the name of the town.

JACK (*somewhat sheepishly*). Odessa.

PETE. (*A broad horselaugh.*)

*Both laughter and dock noises fade quickly under:*

JOE (*after a pause*). More Americans know more about
more English today than ever before in our joint history. And vice versa.

Far as I'm concerned, that's all to the good, because
once you get to know the British *people,* you can't
help liking them. Of course that doesn't necessarily go
for their country or their climate; there's some difference of opinion about that. Sergeant from Pittsburgh,
stationed in a city in the Midlands, said to me:

SERGEANT. What a hole! What a country! Black, dirty,

rainy, smoky! Sometimes I think I'd rather be in Jersey City. . . .

JOE. Whereas a private from Montana,[2] whom I met near Henley-on-Thames, said to me:

PRIVATE. Do I *like* it here? (*Reverently.*) I think this is as close to heaven as a man can get. . . .

JOE. He was drinking ginger beer, which is non-alcoholic; so it couldn't have been that. He meant it. . . .

PRIVATE. Yessir, as close to heaven as you can get.

JOE. Like to stay here after the war?

PRIVATE. I sure would. . . .

JOE. Don't think he was slighting Montana, either. That Thames Valley district has some of the most beautiful country in the world. Soft and green and rolling and happy-looking. Affects you like a poem by Keats or a Morris dance or a young country girl with a bloom on her cheeks and no paint on her lips.

Which reminds me of the Land Army girl (that's a volunteer farm worker) who showed up late on the job at a farm in Kent one morning and apologized to the farmer. . . .

GIRL. I'm sorry to be late, but the Jerries were over last night and dropped a bomb on the house I'm living at, and I'm afraid the rescue squad took a bit long digging me out.

JOE. Now what about that? What about the British and their famous stiff upper lip and their genius for understatement? What about the capacity of the man at home to stand up under punishment? The phrase, "He took it like a soldier," is no idle phrase in Britain, for *all* her people in this war are soldiers. Do you remember those store signs in London during the blitz? . . .

FIRST STORE. Bombed out, flooded out, but not sold out.

SECOND STORE. Buy one of our camp beds and be bombed in comfort. . . .

JOE. Soldier shopkeepers. Kept their helmets on the wall behind the counter. Why, the British are even good soldiers between *stops*. A Chelsea housewife told me the story of how she was riding in a train, and (*overlapping with the woman's speech*) there was only one other passenger—

WOMAN (*simultaneously*). There was only one other passenger in the compartment, a woman, and we were both reading. The train was going at a pretty good speed when a raider spotted us and dropped a bomb. Now when you're riding in a train with the windows closed you don't hear planes and don't get any warning of bombs, because you can't hear them whistle on the way down.

JOE. Lovely.

WOMAN. Well, I happened to glance up, casually, as you do when you're reading, and just as I looked out of the window I saw a bomb land in a culvert at the side of the railway—and there was a big explosion. Well, the train rocked and shook, but it held the tracks and kept right on going. This woman still sitting across from me seemed a little startled, but she returned to her magazine as though nothing had happened, and I returned to my book. About three minutes passed, and she looked up and said very quietly: "I beg your pardon—that *was* a bomb, wasn't it?"

"Yes," I said, "that was a bomb."

She nodded and went back to her reading, and we rode the rest of the way to Cardiff in perfect silence. . . .

JOE. The British are obviously brave and soldierly people. But—unlike the Germans—there's also a little shyness mixed up there somewhere. Fellow who works for the BBC told me:

BBC. We're inclined to be self-conscious, as a people. We get scared the same as anybody else, but we don't show it for fear of making fools of ourselves. If a man were walking down the street and bombs started falling, he probably wouldn't *run* for shelter; he'd keep on walking—if anything, he'd walk a bit slower. If he ran, he'd think he was making a spectacle of himself. . . .

JOE (*after a pause*). I was staying at a farm in Great Dunham in Norfolk one week end, and my host, a farmer in the home guard named Everington, invited me into his office to take a look at his morning mail. He thought it might amaze me, and it did. In one delivery there were *seven* different forms to be filled out. . . .

ONE. Form One: Application for a permit to obtain supplies of sugar for the purpose of feeding a colony of bees.

TWO. Form Two: Form concerning vegetable and glasshouse cropping program, 1943-4. Return must be completed within seven days. Penalties for failure.

THREE. Form Three, Code Number OWL 1136: Application for building license.

JOE (*parenthetically*). Fifty-four separate questions in this one. Question 1a, for example, read:

THREE. State if the work is necessary as a result of enemy action.

FOUR. Form Four: Application for the retention of men born in 1924 from military service under the special scheme for farm workers.

JOE (*again commenting*). Fifty-two questions in this one. The second got right to the point:

FOUR. If any of the work on the farm is prima facie suitable for a woman, give reason why a woman substitute cannot be employed.

FIVE. Form Five: Application for potato subsidy.

SIX. Form Six: Questionnaire from the Grass Dryers Association, Ltd., requesting information of all owners of combine harvesters.

SEVEN. Form Seven: Application to enter stock for marketing. . . .

JOE. The significant part of this form fest, to me, was Everington's attitude. He didn't grouse about red tape, but believed that answering questionnaires was a patriotic service. The way he explained it was simple. . . .

EVERINGTON. It's really very little to ask of a man when you think of the tremendous job being done. Before the war we used to raise only one-third of the country's food requirements. Now we're raising two-thirds.

JOE. Gosh! What that means just in terms of ship tonnage saved must be nobody's business.

EVERINGTON. Ah, but it's *everybody's* business—every last farmer, every last—

JOE. No, you see, I mean, that's an expression—"nobody's business"—it's an American expression.

EVERINGTON. I know it's an expression. It's a British expression too. But it's *still* everybody's business. The amount of corn and sugar beets and potatoes we raise here in England has a great deal to do with the amount of munitions you're able to ship to your men in the Solomons.

Certainly our Ministry has to ask questions. How

else can they know how to plan for the feeding of our civilian population, to say nothing of our own armed forces and the forces of our Allies stationed on our soil? . . .

JOE. I couldn't help thinking of the letter I'd got that week from a friend in the States, complaining bitterly about questionnaires from Washington. According to him, a simple matter like the forms for mileage rationing got into such complications that it practically took an advanced university course to fill one out. I got the impression, from the low, wailing tone of his complaint, that he was being asked by Mr. Ickes:

A. A: If you use your car on week ends, state whether, assuming the initial motion of said car is X and its proportionate velocity is Y, and your wife is in the back seat, the constant of integration of both front tires is greater or lesser than the logarithm of the smiff, which is Z.

B. B: If your driving license has been suspended at any time between 1927 and 1942, do *not* answer the second and third of these questions: (1) Can you whistle with three fingers in your mouth? (2) Have you noticed any undue wear and tear either on your flywheel dowel pin or on the center line of your gudgeon pin? (3) Where are the snows of yesteryear, and do you own chains for both sets of tires? (This question *must* be answered.) . . .

JOE. That, according to my friend's letter, was how the United States was torturing its citizens; but I wasn't for a minute taken in by it. I had very little sympathy for his complaint, to begin with; and Everington's example of good cheer gave me less. Here was a British farmer, already weighed down by taxes, living on rations, liable at any moment to be bombed, working hard on his farm to increase production, doing home-guard duty on Sundays, serving without pay on the District War Agricultural Committee—and inciden-tally bringing up a family to be useful citizens of his country. So when he gets the morning mail and finds seven forms to fill out, what does he do—squawk? No. He supports the Ministry of Agriculture, which sent him those forms, and explains to a visiting Ameri-can why certain questions are necessary and why a government at war must know the answers. . . .

Everington took me for a walk on his farm and showed me, with justifiable pride, his green fields, his orchards, his barns, his animals. He stopped to pick an apple off a tree and said:

EVERINGTON. This orchard I planted for my son's educa-tion. When he's old enough to go to the university these trees will be in their prime, yielding enough to pay for his tuition.[3] . . .

JOE. We walked through fields of barley and beet and grass and potatoes and wheat. The sky was clean and blue after the early rain, and the morning was heavy and still, as though with the peculiar wisdom of autumn, with the quietness of things grown and ready to be reaped. And somehow, in the tranquillity of those Nor-folk acres, the trees thinning, the time being fall, the air being innocent of war as a newborn lamb, I could think of nothing but bombs and food quotas and ques-tionnaires. And it occurred to me that the civilian who objects to answering questions might do well to think of the very simple, uncomplicated forms filled out for soldiers who have given the best they have to give. . . .

FORM (*slowly, quietly*). Name . . . age . . . identity number . . . cause of death . . . next of kin.

JOE. And I wondered about the *ultimate* questionnaire, about the great question to be asked in the final reckoning:

VOICE (*echo*). And what did *you* do for the race of man in the time of the greatest struggle ever on your earth?

*Music: Under the following speech, fade in Mozart Piano Concerto in D, slow movement.*[4]

JOE. At the National Gallery in London one fine day, the RAF symphony orchestra was playing a benefit concert with Myra Hess, the celebrated pianist. Now this orchestra goes around the country playing for workers in factories, for soldiers in the camps, for wounded men in hospitals; and Miss Hess, who before the war gave perhaps a dozen concerts a year, now gives almost that many in a week. She, too, plays in canteens and factories; but this afternoon she was playing before a London audience that included the Queen.

*Music: Up alone for a moment.*

JOE (*over music*). There are very possibly boxes in the National Gallery, including a royal box, but the Queen was not in one. She was sitting in the audience like everybody else.

There was nothing to distinguish the Queen from such commoners as the Waafs in the same row, from the ushers who stood at the back of the hall, from the RAF men who had saved Britain and were listening raptly to the music, or from the German-speaking composer who wrote it.

*Music: Alone again for a stretch.*

JOE. What impressed me as I listened was the democratic attitude of the heads of our Allied nations. The King and Queen of England eating hot dogs at Hyde Park; [5] Mrs. Roosevelt riding in the New York subway; Joe Stalin taking two hours out of a busy war, with the Hun at the gates of Moscow, to talk with the editor of a liberal American newspaper named *PM.* [6]

*Music: Alone.*

JOE. Soldiers? The Duke of Kent was killed on active duty. Stalin's son helped to smash the Germans on the central front. Churchill's daughter is in the ATS [7]; the Roosevelt boys are scattered around the earth. A big war, this one; and whether you hang your hat in the White House, Whitehall, or the Kremlin, it's a *helmet* your hanging.

*Music: Again, the concerto alone for a moment. It fades quickly under:*

JOE. It would take a year of programs to tell you half the curious and amusing and touching little things one meets up with in the course of a few weeks.

For example, I was standing on the banks of the Cam River in Cambridge one day, watching some ducks paddling around. Their coloring seemed to me unusually beautiful, and I said to an instructor of RAF cadets: (*Up.*) Tell me, are these ducks native to this part of the country?

INSTRUCTOR. Oh, no. They're very foreign. You see, they escaped from the Cambridge zoo a few years ago and nobody's had the heart to put them back. [8] . . .

JOE. The British like punning. On the wall of a convoy

conference room in Liverpool there's a large poster showing a Nazi Focke-Wulf 190 being shot down in flames by a British armed trawler. The legend under the poster says:

LEGEND. Who's afraid of the big bad Wulf? [9]

JOE. I was at an RAF Bomber Command station one night when the boys came back from raiding Wilhelms-haven.[10] The bombardier of the first crew to report came into the intelligence room looking very happy over the night's work, and when the flight captain asked him:

CAPTAIN. Well, how did it go? . . .

JOE. He answered:

BOMBARDIER. We hit 'em right in the eye! . . .

JOE. The captain put his hand on the boy's shoulder and said:

CAPTAIN. *Which* eye? . . .

JOE. And then there was the little East End school-kid évacuée at Bill Skipsey's school in Hindhead, Surrey. A teacher asked her what two things in the world she loved best, expecting the kid to say her mother and father. But she answered in dead earnestness:

KID. Fish and chips, and Jesus.

JOE (*after a pause*). The sailor in Liverpool who stopped me to ask the way to St. James's Cathedral, and fell to talking, and gave me a slant I never realized before about fighting at sea . . .

SAILOR (*Lancashire*). If somebody wants to invent a use-ful new weapon, let him find a cure for seasickness. Try aiming a gun at a dive bomber when the ship's rolling over on her side every three seconds and *you're* rolling over on your *inside*. And with a freezing wind blowing and the decks awash, to make it all the nicer.[11] . . .

JOE. Then there was the time I was on a train, and a young Scotch tank driver was telling me [12] how he had lost his mother and father in a bombing raid on the un-military village where he lived—or used to live. . . .

SCOTSMAN. Oh, I'm stoic about it; perfectly stoic, you know. You have to be philosophic about these things. I don't mind it any more. Bothered me at first, I grant you that, but I'm well over it now. I'm well over it. . . .

JOE. We rode along for another twenty minutes, and after a while he took his wallet out of a pocket and said:

SCOTSMAN. Would you . . . would you like to see a picture of my mother and father? . . .

JOE. Soldiers, soldiers, millions of them, hanging their helmets in all kinds of homes except their own, hanging them in camps, hotels, pubs, trains, ships, palaces, pup tents, hospitals, cinemas, dugouts—soldiers of a dozen Allied nations, crowded into these little British Isles, carrying helmets for the express purpose of one day pulling them down over their heads and going out after the Huns wherever they may be.

Two months ago, the soldiers I've told you about were moving here and there over the face of England —they were shooting at targets, unloading transports, drinking beers, watching ducks, ducking bombs, listening to Mozart. But sooner or later, if they're not already doing it, they'll be shooting at Fascists and un-loading block busters and fighting in the night on frozen earth and awakening in the black hours before the dawn for the attack; they'll be flying and slugging and running and crawling and sniping and flanking, and making with the grenade and the bayonet. And one day—may it be a soon day—they'll be hanging their dusty helmets on a peg somewhere in Germany,[13] and the swastikas will come down, and the boys from Pont-à-Mousson and St. Louis and the fjords of Norway and the lochs of Scotland and the mountains of Montana—they'll be there to see the pay-off, the fruit of their labors: Hitler, Hess, and Goering, Goebbels and Laval, Quisling—all the slimy crowd, including opportunist generals and ratting statesmen,[14] will go climbing up the gallows for the last and most popular of their public appearances.

In the meantime England is the temporary home for the Allied avenging armies—the last house on the street, this side of Liberty.

# HOME IS WHERE YOU HANG YOUR HELMET

It seems that short-wave atmospherics between England and our eastern seaboard are not usually at their best between 02:00 and 02:30 Greenwich Mean Time, the half-hour during which "An American in England" was transmitted. Sunspots, auroras, cosmic rays, faulty spark plugs, X-ray machines, vacuum cleaners, and power plants knocked one another down in their hurry to get into the act whenever we went on the air. Out of six tries on consecutive Tuesday nights (U.S. time), our broadcast reached American listeners clearly only twice. Two programs had fair conditions, and the remaining two (the first and last) were magnetic pincushions for every disturbance in the zodiac.

Up to a point it is great fun to contest with the electrical tides of the solar system, just as it is fun to dive into breakers at a beach. But when the storm is overwhelming you might as well go home and read comic strips in a dry corner. After tough luck with my sixth broadcast, I complained about God to Ed Murrow, and we decided the best solution would be to discontinue the short-wave transmissions and prepare the rest of the programs for production in America. To this end I spent the following month gathering notes and data before returning to the States.

It was a bleak month for me. The accumulated fatigues of four years of constant, chain-smoking radio, unbroken by vacations, had begun to tell. At first I thought my new dispiriting weariness was simply more of a well-nurtured hypochondriasis and paid it no more honor than to gripe about it to Joe Julian and my poor secretary. But physical symptoms began to appear, for I was now prey to every passing bug. A bit of food poisoning (probably nothing more than a virulent dose of typhoid) laid me flat and dragged the floor with me, after which I caught a low-grade grippe, which made it small pleasure to sit in cold and draughty rooms. Since life in England is lived entirely in cold and draughty rooms, even in peacetime, I was in a fix. Nevertheless it was better to travel about the country than to sit in London and brood about the war and myself; so I went on junkets to Liverpool, Manchester, Dover, Nettlebed, Hindhead, Cambridge, Norwich, Cromer, Sandringham, King's Lynn. I was looking for broad impressions rather than specific objectives—with the exception, that is, of Cromer, a little shore town that I cased in a couple of days (results on exhibit in *More by Corwin,* Holt, 1944); but the rest of the time I spent wandering fairly aimlessly.

At intervals I returned to London to have hot, unpoisoned dinners at the flat of Robert and Mrs. Westerby in Old Barrack Yard and to listen to the master of the house play the trombone. Westerby worked in the Ministry of Food by day, and by night wrote brilliant short stories and played the trombone very poorly indeed. Dear God, what a fearsome trombone! Bob told me that in the first days of the war, when he and his wife were living in the country, he used his trombone as an auxiliary to the local air-raid warning system, since the siren in the church steeple didn't carry very far. If I seem to attach undue reverence to Westerby's trombone in these notes, it is perhaps because it symbolized to me the wonder that is the English spirit. A second-hand trombone against the Luftwaffe, the minor moo of a patched-up sackbut against the arrogant drone of enemy bombers. Obviously people like that could not possibly lose a war.

"Home Is Where You Hang Your Helmet," like the piece that follows it here, is a collection of notes, strung loosely together like beads on a string. The string in this case happens to be the Fighting Man, a term broad enough to take in women, farmers, shopkeepers, instructors, and the royal family. Some of the material in these two scripts was based on incidents outside my own experience, but they were authentic, and I believe they belong in the report. The story of Stan and Ben was told me by an English newspaper-woman; that of the Scotch tank driver ("Would you like to see a picture of my mother and father?") by an American Red Cross worker stationed in London. I did not myself attend the concert by Myra Hess in the National Gallery, but saw an excellent film of the event, in which the whole setting, and much of the music, was reproduced.

*Additional Notes.* 1. That was the year the Cards beat the Yankees, four games to one.

2. Does rugged and forbidding country produce mild, sweet-tempered people? This soldier came from one of the wildest parts of Montana, yet a gentler-mannered soul I have never met. The only other Montanans I know, all three of them, are likewise soft-spoken and affable. But let's see now—Senator Wheeler comes from Montana, doesn't he?

3. To me this was a touching and beautiful idea. Just imagine being put through Cambridge by thousands of little apples, growing quietly at home.

4. I strongly advocate the use of musical quotation, wherever justified, as material for mood and atmosphere behind narration or dramatic scenes. Not often is the opportunity as good as in this instance, but everyday life affords us considerable music (restaurants, movie houses, radio, etc.), and such music may thus be legitimately put

to work in scripts. In cases where it is behind speech, it is best to employ slow passages, for if figuration is too rapid and bright, it will divert the listener from what you are trying to say.

5. Laurence Gilliam told me that when a recording of this broadcast was played over the BBC, this phrase had to be blacked out. To a Briton, Hyde Park means a park in the heart of London, the park of Rotten Row and the Serpentine. To Americans since 1932 it has meant the estate of the Roosevelts on the east bank of the Hudson, which indeed was where the first families of both the U.S. and U.K. ate hot dogs one summer day. The English listener would have been shocked by the idea of H.M. George VI and Elizabeth picnicking on mustard-covered franks in a park hard by Buckingham Palace. I can understand the BBC's caution.

6. An allusion to the conversations between Josef Stalin and Ralph Ingersoll, then editor of *PM*, in October 1941.

7. Auxiliary Territorial Service—British equivalent to our WAC.

8. The British apparently have great reserves of sentimentality. When this was broadcast, an Englishman living in New York phoned to tell me that the detail of the ducks made him weep; said it inspired in him acute nostalgia.

9. This motto was roundly damned by pilots and bomber crews. At one aerodrome a similar poster was answered by a large sign reading "WE ARE" and signed by the entire complement of the station.

10. William S. Paley and I visited an RAF aerodrome in Cambridgeshire on a night when Stirlings took off to raid Wilhelmshaven. Every plane of the eleven that left the field returned safely; so we were considered lucky fetishes to have around, and wouldn't we please come back soon.

Superstition was at its height in the RAF at this time, for the American air forces were not yet heavily committed, and almost the entire burden of aerial warfare fell on the over-worked and hard-pressed British crews.

11. This sailor, fresh off a destroyer, stopped me to ask the way to the Liverpool Cathedral. He must have mistaken my black Homburg for the mark of an Englishman. We began to chat, and before I could stop him he told me that his ship was part of a force that had just planted a tremen-dous mine field in the North Sea. "Just a minute," I said, "how do you know I'm not a German spy? Isn't that the kind of information you shouldn't be giving out?" He looked at me silently for a moment and then said, "Well, I didn't tell you the *course,* did I?"

12. The "me" in this case was Mary Y. Munford, at-tached to the George Washington Club of the American Red Cross in London.

13. It was to be almost two long years to that day (twenty-one months and three days, to be exact) when the American First Army crossed the German border in the vi-cinity of Aachen.

14. The "opportunist general" was a reference to Ad-miral Darlan, not yet assassinated. Of the "slimy crowd" named in this speech, two (Laval and Quisling) have been executed up to the time of this writing.

# AN ANGLO-AMERICAN ANGLE

Produced in London on September 8, 1942, as the sixth program of the "American in England" series. Joseph Julian narrated, and Betty Hardy appeared as Betty. The score was composed by Benjamin Britten and performed by the symphony orchestra of the Royal Air Force under Wing Commander R. P. O'Donnell. The author directed.

Atmospheric disturbances garbled short-wave transmission during the period of the original broadcast, and although the program was heard in Britain at that time, it was not heard in the United States until December 15, when it was produced as part of the extended home-based series. The role of Betty was performed by Edna Best in the American production, and the music was by Lyn Murray.

# AN ANGLO-AMERICAN ANGLE

JOE. Hmmm? What'd you say?

AMERICAN. Uh—could I speak with you for a moment?

JOE (*slightly puzzled*). Why, sure.

AMERICAN. You're an American, aren't you?

JOE. That's right.

AMERICAN. So am I. How long have you been here in England?

JOE. Few months.

AMERICAN (*as though seeking confirmation of an impression*). Tell me, how does America look to *you* from here?

JOE. You mean, from an English angle?

AMERICAN. Well, you might say from an *Anglo-American* angle.

JOE. Mmm. (*Considering.*) Well—

Music: *A crisp introductory cue, backing the opening announcement, credits, etc.*

JOE. Well—I didn't give that fellow a very good answer, to be perfectly frank about it. You see, I'd been so busy gathering impressions of England that it never occurred to me to stop and get a bearing on my own country from the angle of one of our Allies. And that was too bad, because by then I had only one more week left in England.

Anyway, I decided to think about it and try to get a line on how the U. S. A. looks to the native tribes of

199

the United Kingdom. I didn't have long to wait, because next morning at the hotel . . .

*A knock on the door.*

JOE.  Yes?

*Door opens.*

GEORGE.  Did you ring, sir?

JOE.  Yes, come in, George. (*Down.*) It was George, the fifth-floor valet. Wore a campaign ribbon on his vest and a frosted lens over his right eye—both from the last war.

GEORGE (*cheerily*).  What can I do you for?

JOE.  George, I'm going to clear out at the end of the week; so will you get my suit back from the cleaner's?

GEORGE.  Yessir. Going up north, sir?

JOE.  No, back to the States.

GEORGE (*big take*).  Going *home,* eh? (*Sincerely.*) Well, now, isn't that nice! Bet you'll be glad to get home, eh? You know, *I'd* like to go to the States some day. I really would.

JOE.  Why would you?

GEORGE.  Well, it's always seemed to me such a *democratic* country.

JOE.  More democratic than here?

GEORGE.  From all I've been told. No class distinction there, for one thing.

JOE.  No?

GEORGE.  And a freer educational system, too. State universities and such. Believe me, I wish *my* boy could go to college.

JOE (*slowly—after some thought*).  George, there are a lot of wonderful things that make an American very proud of his country, but there are also some shabby things, and I don't think it's especially patriotic to keep quiet about them. For example, you admire us for being democratic. But in some of our States a man has to *pay* before he can vote. Did you know that?

GEORGE.  You mean if he hasn't got the price he can't vote?

JOE.  Yes. Has Britain anything like a poll tax?

GEORGE.  No, sir. Nobody pays to vote here. But what about this: Britain hasn't had a general *election* in seven years.[1]

JOE.  Well, I think *that's* bad. We in the States find it's possible to hold elections and fight a war too.

GEORGE.  By the way, sir, speaking of elections—would you explain something to me about your last elections? Now I understand that certain members of your Parliament—

JOE.  Congress, we call it—

GEORGE.  Yes, well, now, how did it happen that—certain *Congressmen*[2] . . .

JOE  (*down*).  I had a little trouble and embarrassment answering George's question, but I did; and he seemed satisfied with the answer. And then, as he was about to go, George noticed a pile of magazines on my desk. . . .

GEORGE.  Er—might I ask—if you're not doing anything with the magazines—

JOE.  Take them if you like.

GEORGE.  Very kind of you, sir. . . .

JOE.  He went over to pick them up, but paused for a second to browse.

*Sound of pages turning.*

[1] The numbered notes will be found on page 222.

GEORGE (*admiringly*). My, what pretty bathing girls!

JOE. Ah, yes, an old American custom. That's where we get the S. A. in U. S. A.

GEORGE (*awestruck*). Certainly have beautiful legs, don't they?

JOE. Yes, certainly do.

GEORGE. Certainly have the best of *everything* in America, don't you? . . .

JOE. He turned the pages in a trance. Not a word came out of him until he struck an ad a dozen pages along.

GEORGE (*quoting; enviously*). "Skinless frankfurters! Send for free booklet of tempting recipes!" (*Chuckles.*) When your sausages have been sixty per cent *bread* for some time, as ours have, skinlessness must be an interesting improvement, eh?

JOE. Yeah.

*George turns a page.*

GEORGE. Look at this perfume ad: "Irresistible, piquant, saucy, vivacious, conjuring charm as fresh as the first spring flower—" I'll bet *that* stinks nice. . . .

JOE. He turned more pages—pages crowded with magnificent color advertisements of hosiery and furniture and electric kitchens—and to George it was all Arabian Nights. He wasn't really reading *Life* but a series of illustrated fairy tales having to do with a legendary country where *oranges* grow on *trees*—where the enchanted pig turns into a beautiful side of Virginia ham —a never-never land flowing with milk and honey and canned tomato juice. . . .

GEORGE. Er—is there any *rationing* in the States?

JOE. Oh, yes. Coffee, sugar, gas—

GEORGE. But you can still get all the butter and eggs and cream you want? And meat?

JOE. Yes, I believe you can.[3] We have meatless days, but—

*Another page is turned.*

GEORGE. Look at *this!* "Do you have trouble sleeping? Try the improved Beauty Rest mattress . . . for health and comfort. The royal road to sleep."

JOE (*down*). It was an ad showing a healthy, comfortable American, in four colors, snoozing away on the royal road. . . .

GEORGE. Just think, never having an alert wake you up at three in the morning! A whole country without a single bomb ruin! Isn't that *grand?*

*The sound of a buzzer, off.*

JOE. What's that?

GEORGE. Somebody ringing for me. My private alert, I call it. (*Big joke; laughs.*) You say I can take these?

JOE. Sure, go ahead.

GEORGE. Thank you. (*Going off.*) My wife will appreciate these ever so much, sir. Good day.

*The door closes.*

JOE (*after a pause*). That night I dropped into a newsreel theater . . .

*Music: Fade in background of a decadent waltz tune, circa the era of the first big musical films.*

JOE. . . . to see pictures of the RAF's thousand-bomber raid on Bremen.[4] On the bill was a series of shorts, mostly American, mostly very good. One was a collection of tremendous production numbers taken from lavish musical films of the past. Hundreds of girls and boys dancing on staircases, swimming and diving in formation, appearing and disappearing in mirrors. The most stupendous and titanic waltz in man's history! Those were the days of two cars in every garage and a beautiful chicken in every plot. When these films were made, it required a cast of thousands to impress Britons with the might and majesty of America. Today it takes a mess of skinless frankfurters and a pair of nylon stockings.

On came the newsreel, in the usual quiet fashion, with elfin music over the titles.

*Music: A terrific prolonged fanfare that flattens your ears.*

JOE. Elfin like an elephant. First it showed a picture of American Rangers and parachutists in training, and I was glad to see them looking so hard and fit. The voice on the sound track said categorically these boys were *the best fighters in the world*—and at that point I looked out of the corner of my eye to see how the natives in the audience were taking it. These people, I knew, remembered the Spitfire pilots in the Battle of Britain, and the crew of the Jervis Bay, and Paddy Finucane; and they were reading every day about Timoshenko's men at Stalingrad—all of which fighting men did pretty well for second-raters. I hoped and trusted the commentator was right, but still the extremity of his claim made me feel uneasy.

Next came an entertaining American comedy, and the audience enjoyed all except one scene—a scene in which an inexperienced housewife dropped eggs all over the floor and ruined a big cake. Nobody laughed

at that. It wasn't funny to an audience whose **allow-**
ance was one egg per month.

*Music: The waltz in again.*

JOE. The dancing girls and the mirrors returned **to the**
screen, and that's where I came in; **so** I got up and
strolled out.

*Music: Drops in perspective, but sustains behind:*

JOE. On the way I ran into the manager of the house and
chatted with him in the lobby for a while. About
movies. He said he liked American pictures. . . .

MANAGER. Curiously enough, you know, you Americans do
better by us than we do by ourselves.

JOE. In what way?

MANAGER. Well, I mean your pictures glorifying the British
Empire—you know—*Bengal Lancers, Lloyds of London, Disraeli, A Yank in the RAF*—all that sort of
thing. Very good, too.

JOE. What about cowboys and Indians and gangsters?

MANAGER. What about them?

JOE. Do you think they give a false impression of America?

MANAGER. No, not seriously—not enough to matter. The
impression most of us draw from your pictures is that
the United States is a country of great power and
energy—of unlimited enterprise and opportunity.
That's why you'll find so many English people want
to *visit* the States.

JOE. Mm-hm. What was the reaction here to a picture like
*The Grapes of Wrath?* (*Down.*) He didn't know.
Anyway, at that moment a customer came along with
some question or other, and I went out into the London night.

*Music: Out.*

JOE. Outside the theater it was darker than inside. A very black blackout, with no moon. Occasionally in the distance there was a bright blue flash like summer lightning. When I first got to London, I thought those were bomb bursts, but I found out later they were made by switches in the electric railways in the suburbs. I was hurrying because . . .

*Big Ben strikes ten, distantly.*

JOE. . . . I was on my way to meet my friend Betty at the theater, to walk her home; and I was late. Big Ben was already sounding curfew for the night life of the world's greatest city. Theaters throughout Britain must close down by ten P.M.—and there are no midnight shows on Saturdays, either. I met Betty . . .

BETTY. Hello. Glad you found your way.

JOE. . . . and walked her home along the Strand, down the Mall, by St. James's Park. She seemed low in spirits, and I asked her what was the matter. (*Up.*) You feeling depressed tonight, Betty?

BETTY. Oh, I don't know. I guess I miss the good old days.

JOE. Before the war, you mean?

BETTY. No, no, no. I mean the blitz days—when we were getting bombed every night.

JOE. You kidding?

BETTY. Not at all. There was *spirit* then. We were in the thick of the fight. Everything we did took on a kind of importance, because it might well have been the last time we did it. But this—this business of the war settling down to be a *normal* condition!

JOE. I don't get it—I should think you'd be grateful for

quiet nights and the fact that you can wake up in the morning without congratulating yourself on having lived through the night.

BETTY (*not unkindly*). Well, it's natural for *you* to think so, because you're an American, and your country so far is only knee-deep in the war. The things that happen to people when they're up to their *eyebrows* in it, expecting bombs in their living room or incendiaries in their haystacks—they're bad, all right, but they're not so terrifying as you might imagine. In fact, being up to one's eyebrows in war can be *inspiring*.

JOE. You mean the idea of crisis—the sense of danger—

BETTY. No, not that so much as a sense of values becoming clear. The trivial and petty things don't seem to matter so much any more. You stop quarreling with your neighbor; you don't worry about what might happen two days from now. The main thing is to get at the enemy, and the question of survival becomes— (*A little scream, not so much of fright as of surprise, as:*)

*Joe and Betty fall plunko into a trench—we hear the effect of bodies falling, breaking twigs, etc.*

JOE (*muffled tone*). What the heck's happened?

BETTY (*laughing*). We've fallen into a trench.

JOE. Are you hurt?

BETTY. I'm all right. What about you?

JOE. If you'll take your foot off my face, I'll help you out.

BETTY. (*Her laughter increases.*)

JOE (*over it*). Here, give me your hand. There! (*Good-naturedly.*) A fine thing! So that's your idea of a short cut to Buckingham Palace Road, is it?

BETTY. Isn't that the silliest thing you ever—

JOE. Leading me into pitfalls! I'll tell the Embassy about this!

BETTY. I should have remembered there are trenches near the sidewalk at this end of the Mall!

JOE. Don't tell me you've *memorized* the layout of all London's shelters and trenches?

BETTY. A good many of them. Might be useful if you're caught in a sudden raid. . . .

JOE. I hadn't thought of that—in fact I hadn't thought of many things, and after I saw Betty to her door, I walked all the way back from Chelsea to the West End, thinking about what she had said.

*Music: A midnight in the strings, taking on the mood of the following:*

JOE. It was midnight by now, and for some reason searchlights were probing the sky. There had been gunfire and raiders overhead a few nights ago, and maybe there was going to be trouble tonight.

Midnight in warring London; the streets deserted; the city sleeping; only the night watch astir; the fire watch; the home guard; the silent and ceaseless vigil of the rooftops.

Overhead the stars looked down noncommittally—the same stars that were burning when a Pharaoh was the master of Egypt, when Caesar was the master of Rome. The Afro-European midnight—drunken, mystic, and brutal. Midnight over London, Berlin, Mersa, Matruh, Copenhagen, Oslo, Malta, Dieppe. But in New York, dinnertime; in Chicago, dusk; in Hollywood, the afternoon sun. But no lights in London. Black, eastward across the English Channel. Black over Europe, black across six thousand miles of Russia,

China, and the far-off archipelagoes of the Pacific. Not a light in that direction. Not a light. Just black.

When I got to the hotel . . .

*Music: Out.*

JOE. . . . the lobby was deserted except for a couple of soldiers talking quietly off in a corner. I went over to the news ticker and looked at the teletype report of the day's events. Nothing much had happened.

The elevator man, stooped, gray, in his late fifties, had the usual pleasantries to offer. . . .

ELEVATOR MAN. Good evening, sir.

JOE. Good evening.

ELEVATOR MAN. Nice to have good weather for a change.

JOE. Yes. (*Pause.*) Not much news lately, is there?

ELEVATOR MAN. No.

JOE. Seem to have bogged down in the desert.

ELEVATOR MAN. Yes.

JOE. What's the matter? You look a little glum tonight. You bogged down too?

ELEVATOR MAN. Well, sir— (*Pause.*) I got word this morning that my youngest son is missing in Egypt.

JOE (*shocked*). Oh. I'm—sorry.

ELEVATOR MAN. Thank you, sir. . . .

JOE (*down*). I got off the elevator, slightly petrified. That was two trenches I'd fallen into in one night.

*Music: Epilogue to midnight passage.*

JOE. I had an appointment at the London office of a great American radio network.[5] I took a taxi through a badly bombed section, pulled up outside a plain apartment building. Across the street was a bombed synagogue; only its walls remained. Next to the shattered entrance stood an inscription:

INSCRIPTION. Blessed is he whose conscience hath not condemned him and who is not fallen from his hope in the Lord.

JOE. I got into a rickety lift, went up four flights, rang a bell, was ushered into a modest apartment—good, solid, middle-class living quarters. The walls were cracked and the woodwork warped from bomb blast. I asked the girl about this. . . .

GIRL. Oh, yes. They dropped a stick right along here. The one that hit the synagogue did this damage.

JOE. Did you always have your offices here?

GIRL. Oh, no. These are our fourth since the war.

JOE. What happened to the other three?

GIRL (*casually*). Blitzed out.

JOE. Were you in any of them at the time?

GIRL. I was in this one. Threw me right across the room. It took me a day to get the plaster out of my hair. . . .

JOE. Ed Murrow came in, and he took me along with him to the main building of the BBC, where he was going to make a broadcast.

The building was battle-scarred and wore war paint. Protective blast walls blocked the entrance. Policemen stood guard inside and out. We showed our passes, then went down to the cellar, the subcellar, the sub-subcellar, and deeper still. There were cots in some of the studios. Murrow said a good many of the staff of the BBC slept there.

There were no murals around this place. No conducted studio tours. Nothing for the eye. It was grim, almost military; had special chambers in case of gas attack.

Murrow prepared to broadcast. He put on head phones and gave me a pair, and then I listened in on transatlantic shop talk. . . .

NEW YORK (*filter*). Hello, CBS London. . . .

JOE. Murrow answered: "Hello, New York. Hi, Paul." [6]

NEW YORK (*filter*). Hello, Ed. Got you down from 42:30 to 44:00. . . .

JOE. That was the time he was to be on the air. Minute and a half, all told. Then Murrow asked New York where he should send the program when he was through with it. . . .

NEW YORK (*filter*). Cairo. Wait a minute. Hello, Cairo?

CAIRO (*filter*). Good evening, old man.

NEW YORK (*filter*). Who is it tonight? Burdette or Morrison?

CAIRO (*filter*). Morrison tonight.

NEW YORK (*filter*). Thank you. Get that, Ed? . . .

JOE. Ed said he got it. He pushed his chair back from the microphone and waited for the cue.

The preceding program came through from America. There was music and then the voice of David Ross. It sounded far away, as London sounds to listeners at home; it had an unreal quality—again the Arabia of one thousand and one nights. This time it was Sahib Ross announcing a tooth-paste program from the top of a radio minaret.

And then out of a London cellar Murrow spoke to the rooftops of America. When he was through he called in Cairo, and the capsule world was there for Kansas and Missouri and the shores of Lake Michigan. In the bowels of the British earth I listened to programs coming from the States. There was a song-stress singing "We Did It Before and We Can Do It Again" and "Johnny Doughboy Found a Rose in Ireland." Impatiently I swung the dial to another point and heard an American short-wave program to Europe, with its signature of "Yankee Doodle."

*Music: The OWI's arrangement of "Yankee Doodle," as heard over an ocean of static.*

JOE. It was good to hear.

*Music: A restatement of the "Yankee Doodle" refrain in an arrangement for strings legato, serving as transitional effect and segueing into a general innocuous background of an anemic restaurant orchestra.*

JOE. At the ritzy Savoy grill I found on the dinner menu an item reading:

MENU. La tasse de consommé à la Watrousky Stalin.

JOE. They were honoring Stalin on the menu at the Savoy, and that amounted to another blow to Hitler, because next to separating the United States and Great Britain his greatest hope had been to separate Russia and Great Britain. I pointed out the item to a friend. . . .

FRIEND. Ha! I wonder if it's red soup?

JOE. Wait a minute. Maybe I can find a consommé in honor of an American.

FRIEND (*looking*). Not that I can see.

JOE. That's disappointing.

FRIEND. When the Americans begin killing as many Nazis as the Reds, maybe they will get a place on the menu.

JOE. Give us a chance. We will.

FRIEND. Tell me, are there any quarters in America still hostile to Russia?

JOE. Yes, I dare say there are—scattered, of course, but there. Tory press, mostly.

FRIEND. You know, that's something I can't understand.

JOE. What is?

FRIEND. We consider it extremely bad tactics, both from a military as well as from a moral angle, to criticize an ally or cast suspicion on him, especially if he happens to be doing most of the fighting.

JOE (*fencing*). Are there no attacks on Russia here?

FRIEND. Now and then some blimp—the kind who used to admire Mussolini because he made the trains run on time.

JOE. Would you say Britain was going Red?

FRIEND. No more than Russia is going British. The people here simply admire the fighting qualities of the Soviets and suspect that they were misled about Russia before the war—they feel Russia has got something they were never told about.

JOE (*down*). The meat dish arrived. It was lamb on a skewer. . . .

FRIEND. Waiter.

WAITER. Yes, sir.

FRIEND. Will you ask the chef to include on the menu tomorrow a fricassée de poularde aux pommes à la Franklin Delano Roosevelt?

*The restaurant background cross-fades into:*

*Music: An ingratiating old English folk tune, lilting and not too rapid. It sustains under:*

JOE. I was listening to the British radio for the last time before turning in my set. In an hour I was leaving for home.

*Music: Alone for a moment.*

JOE.  It was a pleasant sound in my ears, this old folk tune, and it made me think of the England I fancied when I was a kid, just learning who was who among the nations. It was the England of September sunlight and the sonnets of Shakespeare that I learned in high school; and down to Kew in lilac time, and the nightingale singing his head off in the Surrey woods, and the gorse and heather in the hills—it was the old romantic English of the green farms and the thatched cottages on the moors.

*Music: Alone again.*

JOE.  I shut off the radio . . .

*A switch clicks.*

*Music: Out.*

JOE.  . . . before the song was finished. It was wrong to leave England with that tune in my ears. For there is no song yet written that conveys the England of a moonless blackout, or the England of raiders machine-gunning village folk in front of the market place—the England of the munitions worker who gets up before it's light and works all day and comes home after dark to a rationed meal and then takes his turn at fire-guard duty. The England I saw was no tea shoppe. It was a grim, crowded, shabby, busy country, with guns in the gardens and trenches in the parks and drilling down at Kew in lilac time. The romance there was the romance of Commandos blowing up guns at Dieppe and then strolling back to the beach eating apples; the romance of Stirlings taking off at dusk to raid Wilhelmshaven; the romance of powerful trade unions waiving their hard-won rights for the duration, and the government guaranteeing that they get them back; the romance of an excess profits tax with teeth in it; the romance of price control and rationing and conscripted women, and workers who aren't allowed to quit a job or be absent from it or late for it; the . . .

GEORGE. Ah, there you are! I was looking for you. Your bags are all packed, sir.

JOE. That's fine, George.

GEORGE. What time is your train?

JOE. Paddington at seven.

GEORGE. You haven't too much time, sir. I'd hurry it if I were you. Where's the porter? . . .

JOE. Just then the porter showed up—and I was on my way.

*Music: Anticipation of the journey. The passage segues to:*

*A train figure, which sustains at intervals, crossing back and forth at the proper moments to realistic effects of wheel noises as they sound inside a coach.*

JOE. West we went, west in the direction of the Irish Sea and the Atlantic Ocean, due west to the fairyland where the milkman delivers eggs and butter in the morning and nobody has to stand in line for a head of cabbage—the place where blackouts are practice and a man can pay his income tax and still have enough left over to buy a cigar. . . .

WOMAN. I beg your pardon—are there any first-class carriages on this train?

JOE. There are, but I'm afraid they're all full.

WOMAN. It does seem a shame to have to sit in a third when you have a first-class ticket.

JOE. Anyway the scenery is first-class.

(*Down.*) That got a smile. I sat, chin in hand, watching the first-class scenery go by; and I thought of the faces, smiling and unsmiling, that I'd met on the island of our ally in four months of wandering. I think an American would settle for those faces any time. Because they're no different from American faces. Anybody who can tell them apart is psychic and ought to be reading tea leaves.

The man sitting next to me opened a package of cigarettes. . . .

PASSENGER. Have a cigarette?

JOE. Oh—thank you very much. Er—what brand is this?

PASSENGER. Fifth Avenue.

JOE. Well, now, that's funny—the other day I bought some cigarettes called Bronx. Must be a series named after sections of New York City.

PASSENGER. Is Astoria part of New York?

JOE. Sure, right across from Manhattan.

PASSENGER. Well, there's an Astoria brand made by the same outfit.

JOE. It's a small world, all right.

BOTH. (*Chuckle.*)

JOE. He was a nice fellow—typical of the kind of guy who strikes up a conversation with you any place in England.

I took a deep drag of Fifth Avenue. And with it I inhaled a solemn thought: There are a lot of typical nice guys on this planet. How does it happen they don't get together? Is it beyond reason, I asked myself, that common people can strike up a lasting friendship—

something more permanent than a military alliance? Are the people going to let diplomats decide whether they shall be the same fast friends in peace as they are in war? That would be a pity, because it isn't the diplomats who are going to pull this war out of the fire. They may help with the arrangements—but you know who's going to win it? The little guy with the third-class ticket sitting opposite—the guy with the dirt under his fingernails and the fatigue of a twelve-hour day in his face. He's won things before in this war. It was he and his wife and his kid brother in the RAF who saved Britain—not a roomful of cabinet ministers. . . .

CONDUCTOR (*calling*). Reading! Reading! Train stops here five minutes. . . .

JOE (*musingly*). Reading, England; Reading, Massachusetts; Reading, Pennsylvania. All three in this war. It was a long way from Reading, England, to the one in Pennsylvania, but if you took a man from the main street of each town and put them together in a neutral pub, within five minutes they'd be toasting each other's health and pledging the common victory.

I decided that the little guy of America and the little guy of Britain talk the same language in more ways than one; they know what side their future is buttered on; and although one of them's been taking it a lot harder and longer than the other, when it comes to dish it out, they'll do the dishing.

The Britons I had met were proud people, and they asked no quarter, and they asked no pity. They'd been through fire, and they'd been tempered by it. And I thought: Americans are proud people too, asking nothing but the time and place to meet the enemy.

We're a good deal farther from the flame, and therefore we temper slower, but that's not our fault. Fire's fire, and *this* one's spreading. And whether it's to be the funeral pyre of all freedom or the forge in which is shaped the hopeful new world of the common man was what good common men were dying for that night.

The train sped on. England slipped past me in the dusk. I was leaving a strong and valiant people to return to one.

*Music: Conclusion.*

# AN ANGLO-AMERICAN ANGLE

Since the end of the war I have been viewing world events in the perspective of a line from the closing moments of the script to which this is appended: "Are the people going to let diplomats decide whether they shall be the same fast friends in peace as they are in war?"

The answer, up to the end of 1946, was yes. Or wasn't it? In how many countries of the world were the people consulted on policies which may lead to another war—or to anything? Were they consulted in England concerning a policy toward Java, at the time of the fighting in Indonesia? Or the people of the United States permitted to vote for or against OPA? Or the people of Russia invited to hold a plebiscite on any question of transcendent importance?

The nations are big boys now, and they know how to poll a referendum if they want one. Of course it is always argued that the masses are not yet sufficiently educated or informed to be trusted with fuller participation in the complexities of government. Very well, then, educate them further; inform them; let all nations address themselves immediately to the development of proper techniques so to do. Certainly the people are quickly educated on how to fight complex wars; how to compute complex taxes; how to tell subtle differences between brands of cigarettes.

I cannot see how it is possible for democracy to advance in the world, if the leading powers do not make increasing use of the referendum and plebiscite, with the object of granting voters an increasingly direct and immediate influence on matters dealing with their bread, freedom, and safety. Indeed one of the factors which have retarded democracy as a world force has been the static condition in which it has been permitted to remain for some years. Surely American democracy, for example, could be vitalized to the point where the electorate enjoys some choice in the actual nomination of its presidential candidates. Or to the point where it takes more than a half-interest in biennial elections. Democracy should never bore its beneficiaries. Too many good men have died in its name, for that to happen.

Never take your eye off a leader who does not trust his own electorate. History is full of them, and Britain has had its share. Much as I admired the wartime leadership of Winston Churchill, I could never forgive him for postponing a general election. To me, in England at the time, it was patent as early as 1942 that the electorate, though supporting the government's prosecution of the war, was weary of Churchill and would sweep him out of office at the first chance. Churchill knew it too, and so did the fifth-floor valet, when he complained about the long hiatus in general elections.

The overwhelming victory of the Labor Party in 1945 was accomplished by "the little guy with the third-class ticket." By "little guy" I mean no mawkish, sentimental, milquetoast figure—not the near-sighted, puny little fellow who symbolizes John Public in the cartoons—but a man who is literally little in income, property, investments, social standing, influence and renown. He is the individual feature of the featureless mass, and he is by nature peaceful, uncomplaining, good-hearted. He no more wants to kill Indonesians in Soerabaja or Jews in Palestine than he wants to kill Americans in Cheyenne. That's what makes him little, and that's why I'm for him.

In the four months I spent in England, I did not once in-

terview a high government official. The main objective of
the series (see notes on "London by Clipper") was to establish the character of the British *people,* and not to obtain the views or disseminate the handouts of the Ministry
of Information. The people were soldiers, sailors, workers,
miners, the theater manager, the elevator man, Police Officer Gilbert, the Everingtons, the Westerbys, Betty Hardy
the actress, Henry Blogg the lifesaver, Mary Seaton the
newspaperwoman, the RAF officer who handed me a dish in
the mess and explained, "This sausage is made of two ingredients—paper and sawdust"; the navigator, just returned from raiding Wilhelmshaven, who said wistfully,
"Somehow we're always first in over the target"; the
woman in Swansea who went to the Guildhall one morning
following a severe blitz and turned in two suits of clothes,
both nearly new, saying she had bought them for her two
boys, killed in the raid; the seven magistrates of the Court
of Petty Sessions, Cranbrook, Kent, on the morning of
5 October, 1942, hearing the application "in respect of a
child in need of care and protection" and four cases of
"riding bicycles without lights" and three cases of "stealing
growing fruit"; the advertising executive who sneered,
"The Russians have run away from the Germans with the
greatest gallantry" (this was while the battle of Stalingrad
was still at issue); Farmer T. R. C. Blofeld telling a meeting of an agricultural committee at Docking, Norfolk,
"What this item boils down to is that the British public,
which is what we are interested in, is not getting enough
milk from L——'s farm"; the Medical Officer of Health
of the town of Cromer, R. C. M. Colvin-Smith, who had,
following his name, the initials M.B., B.C., B.A., M.R.C.S.,
L.R.C.P., F.S.M.O.H.; the retired hairdresser who had
barbered for thirty years on luxury liners and was a mem-

ber of the Liverpool Volunteer Auto Corps: "I spend all my time polishing and petting my car. I've nothing else to do"; the fighter pilot in Paddy Finucane's squadron: "You don't want to hang around the flak at Calais or Dunkirk. People catch diseases there"; the Dover housewife, commenting on her evacuation from the coast: "I lost four stone, I did, in Wales. I was that homesick."

Of hundreds of people whom I met or watched or listened to in my wanderings, there were not more than two or three who would have embarrassed Flying Officer Smith of the Bristol-London train. The more I saw of them, the better I liked them, and I only regret that the brevity of my stay in the Isles kept me from traveling farther, and knowing them better, and learning more about an Ally at war.

*Additional Notes*. 1. The lapse stretched to ten years before Churchill, in an effort to stave off defeat by a maneuver that would leave the Laborites little time to campaign, ordered an election on July 5, 1945.

2. I could not well have developed this, but George was of course referring to our louder disruptionists—of and from whom he had heard so much. Such men were hard for our Allies to understand.

3. This was before the OPA really got down to fundamentals. Within a year Americans were living on greatly reduced rations, but we never approached the severity of the British system.

4. One of the first heavy raids on Germany.

5. CBS, of course. The office was in a flat at 49 Hallam Street, near the BBC's Broadcasting House.

6. Paul White, then director of news broadcasts.

# CLIPPER HOME

Last of the "American in England" series, this program of December 22, 1942, was based on the author's ten-thousand-mile homeward flight via West Africa and Brazil. The score was composed and conducted by Lyn Murray. The author directed.

# CLIPPER HOME

CLERK (*British*). Are you taking the Clipper to New York?

JOE. Yes.

CLERK. Has your passport been okayed by the American Embassy?

JOE. Yes, it has.

CLERK. You've been inoculated for smallpox and yellow fever?

JOE. Yes.

CLERK. Did you turn in your food ration, clothing coupons, sweets ration?

JOE. Yes, they're all turned in.

CLERK. Alien registration, national identity card, all your passes?

JOE. Turned in.

CLERK. Are you carrying any firearms, ammunition, or cameras?

JOE. No.

CLERK. Are you in possession of more than ten pounds in British currency?

JOE. Yes, I've got a little over thirteen pounds.

CLERK. Well, everything over ten will have to be left here. You can send it wherever you like in Britain. We'll give you a receipt for it.

JOE. Okay, fine.

CLERK. Are you carrying any letters or papers on your person?

JOE. No.

CLERK. Very well, thank you very much. That's all I need to know.

JOE. Now may I ask *you* something?

CLERK. Yes, certainly.

JOE. How long does the Clipper take to get to New York?

CLERK. Can't tell you that.

JOE. Well, *about* how long?

CLERK. Not less than five days. Might be longer.

JOE. Are there any sleeping accommodations aboard?

CLERK. No, sir.

JOE. You mean to say we sit up all the way from England to New York?

CLERK. I'm afraid so.

JOE. Where do we stop en route? I mean, besides Lisbon.

CLERK. Can't tell you that. Sorry.

JOE. Are we likely to be held up on the way?

CLERK. I'm sorry, I can't tell you that either.

JOE. Well, how about this: Will I be loaded off the Clipper in the middle of nowhere if somebody else comes along with a priority?

CLERK. I couldn't answer that, sir. There are no guarantees. About anything.

JOE. Mm. There's a war on, eh?

CLERK. Yessir, and you're traveling in it.

*Music: Introductory passage, dipping behind:*

*The putt-putt of an idling motorboat. This sustains as background.*

PASSENGERS. (*Ad libs as of passengers in a tender, mingling with sound effect:*)

SAILOR. Step down, please, and move forward! Watch your step, please! Watch your step! . . .

JOE. There was good reason for watching your step, because a slip would either break your neck or drop you into the Atlantic, or both. I stepped watchfully from the earth of the British Isles into the tender that was taking us to the Clipper. . . .

SAILOR. All right, cast away!

*The putt-putt accelerates, and over it:*

JOE. One of my fellow passengers pulled off his hat and made a circle with it over his head. . . .

PASSENGER (*calling*). Good-by, Elsie! Good-by! Take care of yourself! . . . 'By, Elsie! . . .

JOE. He waved at Elsie, and Elsie waved at him, and the shore fell back, and we swung around toward the Clipper. She loomed up big and gray, her wings spreading over half the ocean, her nose tilted up sassy and proud. . . .

SECOND PASSENGER. *Big* basket,[1] isn't she?

THIRD PASSENGER. Yeah, big ship.

*The motorboat slows down, idles, comes to a stop under:*

JOE. There was an American flag painted on her side, and in the thin light of late afternoon, with white clouds loafing along in the west wind, and the bay shining, and the wooded hills darkening, and the water very much impressed and full of reflections, the Clipper looked very beautiful. Her name was NC109652 or something like that, and I shall always love her.

*The passengers leave the tender, and we hear their steps on the hollow metal of the pontoon buttress as*

---

[1] The numbered notes will be found on pages 248-250.

*they board the ship and enter the cabin. This effect
continues as background.*

PASSENGERS. (*Ad libs.*)

JOE. We boarded and took our seats and waited. It was
the biggest plane I'd ever seen—had a lounge and a
long ascending passageway with stairs to each section.
I looked out of a window at the quiet shore town that
the war had made into a junction to be reckoned with
on the air maps. The place was minding its own business. Nobody stood around gawking at a Clipper on
the front porch.

　　I knew only one passenger aboard—Steve Laird,
correspondent for *Time*.[2] He had some dope on the
itinerary, and he leaned over and whispered to
me. . . .

LAIRD. Buzz buzz buzz Lisbon buzz buzz around two
walla walla gabble gobble hotel bizz bazz next afternoon.

JOE. Aha. Thanks. (*Down.*) Steve said we'd reach Lisbon
next morning and stay overnight at a hotel and probably leave the next afternoon. . . .

STEWARD (*advancing*). Fasten your belts, please. Belts
fastened, please. (*To Joe.*) Your belt in place?

JOE. Yuh. (*Down.*) I had no Elsie to say good-by to. Just
a country and a kindly people, and guns in the parks,
and moonlight on the blacked-out Thames, and a lot
of unimportant little guys, all friends and allies of
ours, who one day maybe will add up to something
very big for you and me and the rest of the world.
Those were my Elsies, and I could wave good-by to
them without wiggling a finger. . . .

LAIRD. Well, here we go. ´ . . .

JOE. The ship taxied out for its run, and when everything was in order the motors roared, and we took off like an important event.

*Music: A take-off that sounds like an important event. After a few moments the music settles into a steady horsepower growl, which then leads imperceptibly into:*

*The steady beat and vibration of four engines as they sound to passengers inside the cabin. This continues under:*

JOE. NC109652 zoomed along at a steady speed, manufacturing her own private hurricane. We were somewhere around the Bay of Biscay, where Nazi and British planes often get tangled up.

We'd been in the air six hours; blackout curtains had been up for five and a half; the passengers had gone through *Life, Time, Click, Pic, The New Yorker, Punch, Munch, Hunch, The London Illustrated Weekly,* and *Crunch.* We were all fatigued and drooping, not from the mags, but from having been up and traveling since five that morning. I knew that Lisbon lay some six hundred miles to the south of England, and that its climate was warm, but I didn't think it was as warm as the plane was getting. I peeled off my coat and vest and loosened my collar and sat quietly roasting; and when the steward came by, I opened one eye and said: (*Up.*) Hey!

STEWARD. Yes, sir.

JOE. Are we in the tropics already?

STEWARD. In the tropics? No. We're still several hours out of Lisbon. Why?

JOE. Sure gets hot in this part of the world, doesn't it?

STEWARD. Oh, that. (*Casually.*) Something's gone screwy with the heating system, that's all. Don't mind it. (*Going away.*) Matter of fact, it's freezing outside.

JOE (*up*). That's a great help. (*Down.*) And as I contemplated my headache and stiff neck and sore back, it occurred to me that no man has a right to expect anything about this war to suit his comfort or convenience. A fight against barbarism isn't a vacation cruise, and many a better man than I has done his ocean traveling on a raft, without magazines or thermostats, or upholstery, or even food or water. This war is the least de luxe of all wars. There are no featherbeds on the destroyers; no steam heat in the trenches or mint juleps in the desert; no air-conditioning in the jungles. What the fighting men of the United Nations are up against on a hundred fronts in terms of sheer physical discomfort is enough to cast the deepest shame on any complaining civilian.

Having put myself in my place, I felt better, and apparently I dozed off, because the next thing I knew was:

*Sound of steps.*

STEWARD (*as he goes up and down*). Twenty minutes to Lisbon! Be in Lisbon in twenty minutes! Take your overnight bags and passports with you. Don't forget your passports, now. . . .

JOE. The river Tagus was below us, faint in the pearly light of the Portuguese night. The Clipper banked, and suddenly there were the lights of Lisbon, bejeweled and twinkling. One of the passengers was all wrapped up in a window. . . .

MOVED. *Lights!* Look at that! Good Christopher,[3] what a stack of them! Aren't they *bright*, though! Isn't that perfectly grand? Have you ever in your life seen a sight like that?

JOE (*chiding*). Wait a minute, now—it's not as wonderful as all that, is it?

MOVED. Well, I don't know about you, but these are the first lights *I've* seen in more than three years!

JOE (*down*). I'd forgotten. Of course. Europe *had* been fighting longer than we. More than two years longer. And just a hundred miles east of those twinkling lights, over the mountains, the people of Spain were fighting the fight six years ago. The Axis won that round, and that's one of the reasons there aren't so many street lamps burning in Europe tonight.

We landed smoothly on the neutral Tagus.

*Music: Happy landing. It goes immediately into:*

*Auto horn, which blows irritatingly at intervals throughout:*

JOE. The automobile that took us from the Portuguese customs to the hotel seemed arrogant in its size, speed, the brightness of its headlights, and the raucousness of its horn.

*Horn.*

JOE. That was because we'd just come from England, where nights are quiet and dark, and head lamps show only a slit of light.

*Horn.*

JOE. Our driver tooted his horn like a man possessed.

*Horn.*

JOE. At visions, apparently, because . . .

*Horn.*

JOE. . . . nobody was in the streets at that hour.

*Horn.*

JOE. Apparently the motorists of Lisbon blow their horns at everything standing, including statues and monuments.[4]

Even though I'd experienced only four months of blackout, the unshielded window of my room at the hotel seemed like a shocking oversight, and my first impulse . . .

VOICE. (*Drunken singing in the street.*)

JOE. . . . was to snap off the light and pull down the shades. A couple of high-spirited Lisbonians started singing in the street below, and albeit the weather was mild and the air sweet, I shut the window.

*The window goes down.*

JOE. It didn't help much. But I slept anyway.

VOICE. (*Singing fades.*)

*A moment of silence. Then quickly fade in city noises, chiefly auto horns.*

JOE. I awoke late and hurried through breakfast, ordering food at the suggestion of the hotel waiter.

WAITER. Quer ovos, pão, manteiga e geleia, cafe com leite e alguma fruta?

JOE. Si si, or something. Yes.

*Noises of breakfast.*

JOE. There were *two* eggs—at one meal! Seemed obscene. And real cream, too. Coffee tasted no better than the British variety—but *three* cubes of butter! It was a banquet. . . .

WAITER. The car is ready to leave, senhor. They are waiting for you. . . .

JOE. I was late and had to rush to the Clipper. We tore through the city, seeing little of it beyond a blur of color, and a fleeting sense of antiquity and dignity and unbombed beauty.

And we got in the NC109652 and took off.

*Music: The take-off again.*

*Flight sounds behind:*

JOE. The coast of Portugal retreated quickly, and Lisbon, with all its refugees and spies and agents and nice Portuguese people, was lost in a mist behind a cape.

The air started to get floppy, and in no time we were in a rainstorm, with visibility nil. But to make sure of the nil part of it the blackout curtains came down anyway.

From Portugal to West Africa involves about as much flying as from New York to Los Angeles. And West Africa was where we were going; so we settled down for a long haul. After dinner the steward spread cushions on the floor for sleeping, and I dragged some back to the tail and made me a bed under a coat rack.

The vibration back there is greater because the tail is not insulated against sound and wasn't built to sleep in. But you don't notice squeaks and rattles when you're flying through the African night, with your head full of Canary Islands and Sahara Desert and Gold

Coast and Senegal and all the romantic names of your early geography class.

*Music: Atmospherics, as sound goes out.*

JOE. And while you sleep, unknown to anybody aboard, somewhere down there on the dark ocean, plowing eastward in a great armada, are thousands of your countrymen, on their way to invade North Africa.[5] The night is deep and the ocean wide, and between them they keep the secret. Meanwhile the stars look down, all mum; the motors stay at pitch; coats swing on the coat rack; the Clipper burns more space, the air foams in her wake; the planet turns toward morning. You sleep on. Around you, ranging outward to all compass points, men are dying as you sleep.

*Music: Up into morning. The conclusion discovers:*

*The sound of motors as before, under:*

JOE. Morning over the coast of West Africa, the sun higher and brighter at eight A.M. than it is over London at noon. Outside the windows, which two nights ago framed an Irish village and last night the cliffs of Portugal, lay now the westward fringes of a massive continent, five thousand miles across the middle.

*Motors fade under:*

JOE. We landed at a port called Censored,[6] all the physical features of the place bearing the same name. Ashore we ate a hearty breakfast and roamed around while the Clipper was having a snack of gas and oil, seeing . . .

CENSOR. Four words censored here.

JOE. And also the pretty . . .

CENSOR. Six words censored here.

JOE. And we stood on the banks of the . . .

CENSOR. Three words.

JOE. Watching the . . .

CENSOR. Two words.

JOE. . . . until it was time to go. And we flew to another port in West Africa,[7] also bearing a name unmentionable for good and sufficient reasons; and here, under a golden equatorial sky, with tropical trees swaying in a warm African wind, I came upon a curious item tacked to the wall of a house. It read simply:

SCORES. Scores of Saturday's leading games as follows:

> Yale 17,   Dartmouth 7
> Princeton 32,   Brown 13
> Notre Dame 21,   Illinois 14
> Minnesota 16,   Michigan 14

JOE. Inside the house there was a juke box, playing Bing Crosby, and a ping-pong table, to the use of which Steve Laird challenged me. Final score, Laird 21, me 17. It was too hot to play a return match; so we bought some soda pop and sat.

While the Clipper waited for cover of darkness to take off, I roamed the area, and every now and then a native would stop and look wonderingly at the strange white man who arrived that afternoon in the Thunderbird. What went through that tribal mind would be worth knowing, and I wondered whether it might be something like this:

NATIVE. Poor man. Belongs to the restless white civilization, which is always fighting. They say it's pretty terrible, too—worse than the cannibals. This lad looks harmless enough, though. Wonder what his tribe is fighting for this time. Something very obscure and intangible, as usual, I suppose. . . .

JOE. If that's what was in his mind, he probably would have a hard time understanding that the great commotion going on is something directly affecting the price he gets for coconuts, and also his chances of continuing to live the life he wants to live. Had it not been for some fighting between white folks seventy years ago, he might be up for auction in a slave market today. This fellow probably wouldn't get the drift immediately if you told him many millions of the white race and the yellow race and his race, too, are fighting this time for such intangible matters as the sovereign rights of common men and for such tangible things as a steady job and some good grub.

Was I being chauvinistic to wonder whether my West African would understand right off the bat?[8] But then, of course, not all the natives of even North America understand this war yet.

My day-dreaming ended when a fellow passenger came up to ask:

PASSENGER. Say, didja hear the latest?

JOE. What?

PASSENGER. We're leaving in twenty minutes. And we're flying a different ship. Better start for the landing pretty soon.

JOE. Thanks, I will. (*Down.*) Turned out he was right. We left at dusk, but in another ship. I didn't like it as much as the NC109652, but it took off just as gracefully, plowing through the warm waters of Censored[9] and rising into the trade wind with its nose pointed straight at the bulge of South America.

*Music: Take-off, leading into:*

*Motors, over:*

JOE. The passenger list had grown. It now included two Canadian officers, home on leave from a station in Arabia. . . .

CANADIAN. Listen, friend, you don't know what heat is until you've spent a summer in the Gulf of Aden. Sizzles your eyebrows. . . .

JOE. And a man and wife from our own Midwest. In the midst of World War II she was worrying about the evil of drink spreading throughout Christian civilization. . . .

WOMAN (*plaintively*). And when we got there in the morning, they served us a cold drink—and there was *rum* in it. *Rum!* . . .

JOE. And a British gentleman who was on his way to China through the States. . . .

BRITON. Actually Chinese is a simple language to learn. It hasn't any grammar in the sense we employ it. Very often you have to use circumlocutions to express an image. For example . . .

JOE. And a diplomatic mail courier, American. . . .

COURIER. How'd you like a game of Michigan rummy? . . .

JOE. And assorted Frenchmen, Poles, Britons, Czechs, and Americans. (*Pause.*) We crossed the equator southward in the middle of a night of strange time and came down in the Western Hemisphere.

*Music: Descent, somewhat briefer than when we arrived at Lisbon; at the finish we discover:*

*Effect of an air-pressure spray, which stops and starts ad lib while the passengers cough under:*

JOE. Brazil doesn't take any chances when it comes to catching African plant diseases or any other kind of disease; so before anybody could get off the Clipper after crossing the South Atlantic, the health authorities brought aboard a spray of foul-smelling insecticide and filled the ship with a heavy vapor.

*Fade spray.*

JOE. Our allies, the people of the city of Natal, were genial, as who wouldn't be in such a sunny climate. When I went to buy the local newspaper, hoping to understand enough Portuguese to see how the British Eighth Army was making out in Libya, an old native standing near by beat me to it.

BRAZILIAN. Permita-me, cavalheiro. Meus comprimentos.

JOE. Why, thank you very much. Grassyass.[10] (*Down.*) There was no reason for him to spend money on a paper for a North American he'd never seen before. Just felt kindly, that's all. There isn't much I can tell you about that Brazilian port and our allies there, because of the long ears of the Axis, but I *can* say I met an American Army flier there, and that he was carrying an odd-looking box under his arm, and odd noises were coming from it. When I asked him what he had in it:

FLIER. Oh, this? That's my mascot. Tiger.

JOE. He opened the box, and a gray kitten pounced out. . . .

FLIER. I took him with me from New Hampshire when I was home on leave. He's been flying with me ever since.

JOE. Does he like it?

FLIER. Loves it. Has eighty-six hours to his credit. Never a dull moment, eh, Tiger? . . .

JOE. Tiger was obviously an air-minded kitten. In a moment he was climbing over the pilot's cap. (*Pause.*)

We waited at the dock for a third change of ships. So far we had traveled seven thousand miles since we left London, and now we were farther from New York than when we started. Such are routine distances in a global war. (*Pause.*)

In due course, when everything was ready . . .

*Music: Another take-off, trailing into the clouds. It fades for:*

*Motors, which hold under:*

JOE. All night we flew north by west, streaking along like an apprentice meteor. We crossed the mouths of the Amazon, recrossed the equator, flew over Devil's Island, up past the steaming Guianas [11]—and then, having made a censored stop between the South and North Americas,[12] we set out over still another sea, for the United States. By now the passengers were real chummy, and it was like a flying country club. I played cards all morning with the courier, and the China-bound Briton filled in a steward with the lore of Hispaniola, and Steve Laird told a couple of spell-bound Frenchmen about the time he went through a black fever zone in Manchuria.

The war was somewhere else at the moment—Europe, Africa, Asia, Australia. Behind us, blackouts and one-egg-a-month and raiders coming in low over the coast; below us, the unruffled blue waters of the Caribbean; ahead, Miami.

By sundown we were home.

*Music: Home.*

JOE. Home is always the best land, because that's where you park your heart when you cross the border outbound. From the moment you leave, all the roads, rails, ship lanes, and skyways of the world point back to your own country. A number of times previously I had come home to the States from a foreign place, and each return was happy, as a homecoming should be. But somehow this time, when we tied up at Miami and I put my feet on Florida, there was a feeling I had never known before. It was a feeling of having reached home long before this—the feeling of having already arrived, not just once, but two or three times. Maybe it was the sensation of lights and two-eggs-at-one-meal in Lisbon—that seemed like home; or the football scores and juke box in West Africa; or the kitten from New Hampshire in Brazil. . . .

CLERK. You surrender your passports here, please. Customs is down the hall.[13]

JOE (*still talking to himself*). No, *that* wasn't it at all. It was the fact that *England* had seemed so much like home to me—the language, the people, the American soldiers crowding the place. . . .

CUSTOMS. Thank you, your baggage is okay. Exit to the terminal is on the left. . . .

JOE. Yes, that certainly was a big part of it. But also, I think, it must have been a vague realization, deep down, that the world has shrunk; that the world will never be the same. . . .

NEWSBOY. Evening paper, mister? Evening paper?

JOE. What's the headline?

NEWSBOY. Nolan to plead insanity tomorrow.

JOE. Let me have one.

NEWSBOY. Here y'are.

*Sound of papers.*

JOE. A local murderer was pleading insanity, and that took the main headline away from Egypt, where there was considerable killing going on, and from Russia, where the murder was terrific. I had to search page one for news of El Alamein and Stalingrad. After the four-page papers of London, this thirty-six-page home edition seemed mighty like a blue-plate special. (*Pause.*)

On the streets of Miami I met a boy I used to know in New York. He was a sallow, mousy kid when I saw him last, but now he was wearing the uniform of a private of the United States Army, and he was wearing it quietly and proudly. He was married, and his wife was with him, and they were spending his leave in Miami. . . .

PRIVATE. I'd like you to meet my wife. We got married just before I was inducted.

JOE. How do you do.

WIFE. How do you do. . . .

JOE. His eyes were clear and confident; he stood straight without trying; he had become a soldier since I saw him last—a man. Before very long he'd be shooting Fascists somewhere.

I asked him the usual questions—how he liked being in the army, what had happened to our mutual friends. . . .

PRIVATE. Well, you know, Perry Lafferty's in the Air Force, and Charlie—he's up in Alaska, I believe. Do you remember Allan Meltzer's brother?

JOE. Younger brother?

PRIVATE. Yeah. He's in India.

JOE. Be darned.

PRIVATE. Jerry Ricco's in the navy; last time I saw him he'd just come back from Murmansk. Let's see what else . . .

JOE. We went into a drugstore and bought ice-cream sodas, which I had missed in England, although I rarely drink them; and we talked some more. I asked why he felt he was in this war, and his answer was impressive. He never once mentioned freedom or democracy or the Bill of Rights. . . .

PRIVATE. Well, I'm fighting for home, I guess. I mean, I want to get there and get it over with and get home again, and go back to work. (*Groping.*) I—I don't mean exactly I'm fighting *just* for home. I mean it wouldn't really *be* home, would it, if we lost? Wouldn't be the same thing any more. There wouldn't be such a thing as home if we got licked, would there? That is, the kind of home and home life we're accustomed to. You understand what I mean? . . .

JOE. His wife covered his hand with hers and smiled at him. I said I understood what he meant and offered to buy them another soda, but they had to leave.

I wandered down to the railroad station to inquire about trains to New York, and I found you couldn't get reservations as easily as when I left the States;[14] I'd have to wait a couple of days. So I walked over to the airlines office. I could see that traffic in the streets was far below normal; a cop explained to me that gas rationing was getting stricter, and the tire situation was very tough. Food, too. We were sending so much abroad. At the airlines office . . .

AIRLINES GIRL. Nothing today or tonight or tomorrow. But there's been a cancellation on the 9:30 plane Thursday morning, and I could put you down for that. . . .

JOE. She put me down for that. I went out and walked down to the ocean front. Four nights ago, Bay of Biscay. Today, Biscayne Bay. I found that while I had been away America had gone abroad. There was a boy from almost every family either in a foreign land or almost ready to go. And the hearts of the home folks were in every zone of time and every latitude from one pole to the other. Our men and materials and energies were going out around the globe, over all the oceans, to all the continents. Yes, the world *has* shrunk, I told myself. America was not just forty-eight united states and her territories; America today was every country where free men were fighting, wherever men were working for progress in our time and for a life still better in times beyond our time.

(*After a pause.*) I slept on that. Came Thursday morning, and I took the plane. . . .

P. A. VOICE. Nine-thirty express to Jacksonville, Savannah, Charleston, Washington, and New York. Passengers will please board at Gate 4. . . .

JOE. All the way home I thought about England and the Clipper and the grace of the country unrolling beneath the plane. Over Georgia I looked hard, trying to locate the army camp where my brother Al was stationed, but we didn't fly close enough to it; over Washington I noticed the new war buildings were nearly finished; and when I got to New York . . .

P. A. VOICE. Passengers taking the bus into town will find it outside Gate 4 on the lower level. . . .

JOE. . . . I was deep in a reverie, wondering whether, having now completed my journey, it would be possible to compress into one sentence the sum total of my observations; whether I could state simply, in few words, what hopes I had for the future of our earth— something that would add together the great British people whom I'd been among, and the lights of Lisbon, and the curious natives of West Africa, and the Canadians on leave from Arabia, and the soldier in Miami, and the map of the world at the terminal in New York.

And I decided after a tussle that you couldn't say it in one sentence; so I gave up trying.

But a couple of nights later, in the middle of rediscovering possessions that had been packed away in mothballs, I came across some old miscellany in a closet, and among it was a quote from Benjamin Franklin, all framed and pretty and full of dust. And I found that Ben had said what I was trying to say, a hundred fifty years ago.

FRANKLIN. God grant that not only the Love of Liberty but a thorough knowledge of the rights of man may pervade all the nations of the earth, so that a philosopher may set his foot anywhere on its surface and say, "This is my country."

JOE. I dusted that off and searched for a hammer and some nails and whacked it up on the wall, thinking it was as good now as when Ben wrote it.

*Hammer strokes. They continue as punctuation in:*

JOE (*repeating as he hammers home*). "God grant . . . that not only the Love of Liberty but a thorough

knowledge of the rights of man . . . may pervade
all the nations of the earth . . . so that a philosopher
may set his foot anywhere on its surface . . . and
say, 'This . . . is my country.' "

*Final hammer strokes, going into:*

*Music: Finale.*

# CLIPPER HOME

Next to radio, the airplane is the greatest single force on the side of internationalism. Radio carries your voice abroad instantaneously; the airplane takes a little longer, but it has the virtue of hauling your body at the same time. Though we need communicate no faster, it's a cinch we shall be flying faster, and thus the countries of the world will be brought even closer together in time and space. As this develops, there will be less and less use for excessive nationalism. The isolationists and divisionists are perfectly aware of the trend and are therefore fighting harder than ever to block World Government. What with the atom bomb and all, theirs is something of a last-ditch stand.

It would be a happy ending for man's long quest if he were to realize the dream of One World while there are still a few people alive to enjoy it. But if any instruments of our wildly ingenious civilization are going to be of help, certainly radio and the airplane are chief among them. Properly used (which it hasn't been on any large scale), radio can do more for international relations than ambassadors, visiting generals, Olympic teams, and exchange professors. The airplane, as quite a few observers have realized before Joe, can do for the world what the automobile has done for this country—make it all one piece.

"Clipper Home" was a testimony of Oneness, based first on a predisposed opinion but backed up by an immediate personal experience. If there had been any doubts left in my mind about the shrinkage of the globe, NC109652 and her sisters would have dispelled them. I never traveled so far so fast and with such ease. Between Foynes and Miami there was nary a bump. It was more comfortable sleeping on floors aboard those Clippers than in the pillowed berths of swaying, rattling, and thumping Pullmans. The whole trip had a sleight-of-hand air about it; it was quiet, clean, uncluttered. From the casualness with which our crews took off, flew vast distances, alighted, refueled, and took off again, I was convinced that airplanes could do anything expected of them and go anywhere. In the three years since then, the *Gloster* has zoomed along at 606 m.p.h.; a B-29 has flown 8198 miles nonstop.

Of the nine scripts that made up "An American in England," this was the only one that did not concern itself directly with England, nor justify its title. But it seemed to me that any series dealing with the people of an Ally could make sense only if viewed in the perspective of the future, of a working world order, an ultimate supergovernment that would make war impossible. Otherwise one might as well write a sheer travelogue. The gist of this script was that America had infused itself with the world outside her borders, that the U.S. existed "wherever men were working for progress in our time and for a life still better in times beyond our time."

Franklin's internationalism was philosophic and was arrived at without benefit of the industrial and scientific revolutions and the political cataclysms which have since made it clear that as a *practical* (as against purely philosophic) concern, the world must get together or perish. To my knowledge, the quote from Franklin had not been given wide currency until Carl Van Doren in 1938 placed it in the magnificent setting of his biography. Some weeks after the broadcast, I was delighted to see the *Saturday Evening Post* make a cover of the same quote. A few more magazine covers, a couple of murals, a postage stamp, a good House of Representatives, and the future is safe.

*Additional Notes.* 1. What he actually said was "big *bastard*," but this is no kind of language to be overheard by the 4-H Clubs of America. "Big basket" sounds close enough to the original, anyway.

2. Since then Laird left *Time* for work in films and radio.

3. Another bowdlerism. The man said "Good Christ." Radio's vocabulary of epithets is that of the Girl Scouts of America.

4. Later I found out the reason. In Lisbon's streets the right of way at an intersection goes to the motorist who first blares his horn.

5. The attack on French Morocco began on November 7, not long after the period covered by this flight.

6. Bolama, the Bissagos island capital of Portuguese Guinea. A hellish spot, humid, women bare above the waist, beggars, a bedlam of a market place. In the midst of tropical appurtenances and vegetation, smack in the center of the village's little area of quays, stood an imposing granite monument, very modern in design, commemorating the 1933 flight of Balbo and an Italian squadron from Rome to Chicago. The fliers had put down at Bolama, en route to Natal, and Mussolini wished the island to remember it, and him, forever. The Pan American Airways representative in Bolama arranged a stupendous breakfast for us, including five or six kinds of exotic fruits and African delicacies. To men who had but two days before been living on English rations, this was a banquet of rare delight.

7. Fisherman's Lake, a beautiful body of water near Monrovia, Liberia, and the site of a U.S. Army outpost. The "house" referred to in this speech was an Army recreation building.

8. My treatment of the native here came under criticism from a few American listeners who felt I was not being cordial to the Liberians. I am still trying to figure out what they meant.

9. Again, Fisherman's Lake. The only scare I got on the entire flight was when our ship had trouble lifting on this takeoff. She was heavily loaded with passengers, freight, and fuel and had to fight to leave the water. We were heading straight for the west bank of the lake and seemed only a few feet from crashing when the ship shook off enough gravity to skim over palm trees and cross the adjacent beaches of the Liberian coast.

10. Joe's pronunciation of *gracias,* or "thank you," in his best Sunday Portuguese—and his best Sunday Portuguese was none too good, because the word is Spanish.

11. A few months afterward, the writer Eric Knight and a planeload of government and military officials crashed to their deaths in this vicinity. They were bound for the conference at Casablanca.

12. Trinidad.

13. It was a part of the customs and inspection routine to take the temperature of each passenger. We all stood around while a sad-faced health officer glumly popped clinical thermometers in our mouths. It was the only time I had seen this done at a point of debarkation, and the spectacle of a ring of thirty passengers, each silently biting a thermometer, was genuinely comical.

14. This allusion was to become grimly humorous in the

light of later developments. Whereas train space between Miami and New York at this time was sold out *days* ahead, it soon tightened so much that bookings were made *months* in advance, and people waited in all-night queues for coach space.

# YOU CAN DREAM, INC.

Produced as the sixth of the "Columbia Presents Corwin" series, on April 11, 1944. John Griggs performed as the Vice-president in charge of sales; Ralph Bell played the Esthete; Minerva Pious was Minnie; Samuel Raskyn was Dad, the Keats fancier. Joseph Julian and Ruth Gilbert did the elevator scene, and Robert Trout and Harry Marble played themselves. Alexander Semmler composed and conducted the score. The author directed.

# YOU CAN DREAM, INC.

VICE-PRESIDENT. I'm Vice-president in charge of sales of a new public utility—a service dealing in dreams of all varieties for every purse. Now let me explain.

You Can Dream, Inc., specializes in furnishing daydreams to people who are bored with what they're doing and would like to get away from routine. Simply apply in person or by letter, stating the nature of your work and the extent of service desired; that is, whether you wish for daydreams on a daily, weekly, or monthly basis.

For instance, take the case of Miss W., a young stenographer who applied for one of our moderate-priced dreams. She came to us with this story. . . .

STENOGRAPHER. Gentlemen, I am a stenographer. I work in a law office typing contracts. Puddefath, Hunnebun, Smigley & Dorset. It gets very monotonous. I guess I type about ten thousand words a day, not counting dictation and answering the phone.

*Symbolically her typing fades in.*

STENOGRAPHER. It seems as though I'm forever typing. . . .

*The typing comes up in the clear and goes along briskly for a few seconds.*

*Then a phone rings, and our girl answers it.*

STENOGRAPHER. Puddefath, Hunnebun, Smigley & Dorset. Mr. Puddefath? Just a moment. . . .

253

*Buzzer.*

STENOGRAPHER. And the dictation I have to take. . . .

DORSET (*dryly*). The owner agrees to duly execute, acknowledge, and deliver or procure the due execution, acknowledgment and delivery . . . to the purchaser of any and all further assignments and other instruments . . . in any form approved by counsel for purchaser . . . that may be necessary or expedient . . .

STENOGRAPHER. And then I have to type it up and make six copies of it.

*Typing up big, ending on a sharp carriage return.*

STENOGRAPHER. Do you get what I mean?

VICE-PRESIDENT. Madam, we not only get what you mean, but we have the very thing for you. Daydream Number 8. Here it is.

*Music: As though by the pressing of a button the mechanism of a prefabricated daydream is set in motion. The orchestra conveys this in a passage that is later to become a motif—a mildly mystic abracadagio-type theme.*

VICE-PRESIDENT (*setting the stage*). You come to work in the morning and there is a new partner in the law firm. He is Mackinlay Smigley, young cousin of Uriah Smigley, and a graduate of Yale. He is handsome. . . .

SMIGLEY. Will you take a contract?

STENOGRAPHER. Yes, sir.

SMIGLEY. I hereby grant, assign, transfer, and set over unto you, exclusively and forever, my love, my entire love. . . . Moreover, I warrant and represent to you that

nothing herein contained shall be interpreted or construed as pertaining to the contrary notwithstanding.
. . . Have you got that?

STENOGRAPHER. Yes, sir.

SMIGLEY. That will be all. (*Significantly.*) For now.

STENOGRAPHER. Yes, sir. . . .

VICE-PRESIDENT. Then you go to your desk to type it, pushing aside the flowers that have been left there since you were last at your machine, and you begin to type.

*The typing begins as before. But this time—*

VICE-PRESIDENT. And now you are no longer knocking out a contract. You are at the keyboard of a musical instrument.

*Music: Cream off the top of Kostelanetz.*

VICE-PRESIDENT. And you float with the floating shift; and when you press the margin release . . .

*Music: Ethereal celeste effect; shimmering strings under:*

VIC-PRESIDENT. . . . you are released. You touch the space bar and drift in space among asteroids and asterisks; the ampersands of time run through your fingers. The crescent moon closes a parenthesis. . . .

*Music: The orchestra glimmers like a spray of sequins as the typewriter takes over.*

VICE-PRESIDENT. Contract? Ha! The keys strike sparks against a platen of platinum! The carriage is drawn by six white minks!

*The carriage returns sharply. Silence.*

VICE-PRESIDENT (*hushed, like Frank Gallop at Carnegie Hall*). You are in a concert hall at the console of the great Corona. Around the vast hall are busts in marble of the great composers—(*picking them out as he looks around*) Beethoven, Brahms, Bach, Puddefath, Hunnebun, Schubert, Smigley, Dorset. The audience is quieting, hushed and expectant. The conductor comes out, bows, turns to you. . . .

CONDUCTOR. The following, when performed by you and by us, will constitute a complete and binding concerto between us.

VICE-PRESIDENT. You nod your head. The baton is raised.

> *Music: Concerto for typewriter. It begins importantly, but soon retards and diminishes to make way for the entrance of the typewriter.*
>
> *Our L. C. Smith starts with a bold, strong, even rhythm, but soon gets into antiphonal passages with the orchestra. The space bar, the carriage return, and the bell punctuate with effect. At length the concerto, being of one movement (and that brief), ends with a great flourish.*[1]

VICE-PRESIDENT (*no longer addressing the stenographer; to the radio audience*). Well, that, ladies and gentlemen, was Daydream Number 8, and it will give you a rough idea of the kind of precision work we do. For example, our Concerto for Typewriter comes in several sizes, including those in two, three, or four movements; also we are planning, for fall release, a cantata for a comptometer.

Very well now, is there someone else with a problem who is interested in our high-quality dreams?

[1] The numbered notes will be found on pages 273-275.

ESTHETE. My name is Humphrey Bromfield. I am a cultured and sensitive young man, deeply interested in the arts, and for some time now I have been worried about the fact that my fiancée seems less and less to care about sharing my enthusiasms. She prefers to think and talk about movies and crooners and sensational murder trials.

VICE-PRESIDENT. Please go on.

ESTHETE. I think she inherits her questionable values from her father, a very gross and opinionated man with no cultural background whatever.

VICE-PRESIDENT. Yes, well, what is your problem, Mr. B?

ESTHETE. Well, I would like to apply for an intellectual-type daydream in which the girl of my daydreams would be completely versed in the seven lively arts. Have you got anything like that around?

VICE-PRESIDENT. You bet we have. There's a very fine esthetic daydream, the 24D—which we'd be very glad to have you try out. It's fully equipped with a cultured father and, if required or desired, two spare cultured brothers.

ESTHETE. Do you mind if I try it out?

VICE-PRESIDENT. Glad to have you. That's what we're here for. No obligation to buy.

*Music: Spell motif.*

VICE-PRESIDENT. You have just brought your girl home from a symphony concert, where you heard the Brahms Variations on a Theme by Semmler, and (*fading*) you are sitting in the living room. . . .

ESTHETE. The Brahms piece was charming, of course, but my favorite of all his works remains the First Symphony. Don't you agree, Minerva?

MINNIE. Aah, I tell ya, most of the time he's abstruse and sophisticated, and that gets me down. I grant ya his stuff is magnificent in outline and elaborate in detail, all right, but gimme the beautiful sorrows of Chopin or the mighty harmonies of Beethoven.

ESTHETE. Yes, my dear, but after all, Chopin—

MINNIE. Brahms is too reticent for my dough, y'get what I mean? I concede to ya he has a great fecundity in melodic invention. That I'll give 'im. Now take Beethoven. If you was to make analogies wit some of the other artists, you could say there's a synonymity between his woiks and the thunderin' luxuriance of literary power which ya find in Shakespeare. . . . Hand me another one of them bom-bons, cookie.

ESTHETE. But, my dear, such a comparison—

MINNIE. Now take Sophocles. Sophocles—there was a guy who saw life steady and saw it whole. He had a high sardonic humor, so to speak, whereas the comedy of Voltaire was different. As An'tole France says, "In Voltaire's fingers the pen runs and laffs." Ain't that high-class corn for ya? Huh? And while there's a kind of tumultuous splendor and glowin' purity in some of Brahms's passages, he still ain't got that *thing*— that blend of impressionism wit sentiment which you find in the woiks of Wagner, for instance. D'ya know what I mean?

ESTHETE. Yes, Minerva, but you can hardly compare—

MINNIE. Why not? You know what Aristophanes had to say about comparisons, doncha? Well, okay. Besides, it ain't enough that the creative artist should be merely aflame wit a sense of life. He's got to know how to *control* it and *synthesize* the whole damn thing, and the more premonition, the better. Ain't that right, Dad?

DAD (*from across the room*). What's that, Minerva?

MINNIE. Why don't you pay attention, Colonel, instead of sittin' there wit that mint julep?

DAD (*coming on mike*). Ah'm sorry. Ah was busy readin' an early edition of the essays of Montaigne, as told to Mahvin Lowenthal.[2]

ESTHETE. But, Minerva—

MINNIE. Pop, tell Hump here your thesis about premonition as relative to the libido—

DAD. Ah'd ruther illustrate mah point by quotin' the great poet, John Keats.

MINNIE. Go ahead, quote.

DAD. Quote:

> "When ah have fears that ah may cease tuh be [3]
> 　　Befo' mah pen has gleaned mah teemin' brain,
> Befo' hah-pilèd books in charact'ry
> 　　Hold like rich gahners the full-ripened grain;
> When ah behold, upon the night's stah'd face,
> 　　Huge cloudy symbols of a great romance . . ."

MINNIE (*correcting him*). "*High* romance"—not *great* romance, you dope.

ESTHETE. But what has this to do with—

MINNIE. Your point is well taken, bub, but as Shakespeare said in that immortal passage from *Julius Caesar:* "The evil that men do lives after them."

DAD AND MINNIE (*begin to quote simultaneously*).

> "The good is oft interred with their bones;
> 　So let it be with Caesar. The noble Brutus
> 　Hath told you Caesar was ambitious;
> 　If it were so—"

*Music: Spell motif takes it away socko, and when the dream is through being taken away, we are again in the salesroom.*

VICE-PRESIDENT (*tentatively*). Do you think that's anything you could use, Mr. Bromfield?

ESTHETE. No. And if that's a sample of the kind of day-dreams you're carrying, I don't want any part of them. Why, it's insulting and ridiculous, and furthermore—

VICE-PRESIDENT. But, my dear man, that's only one of several.

ESTHETE. I'm not interested! Good day!

*Bromfield goes out and slams the door.*

*Our vice-president picks up a telephone and dials three numbers. He is fit to be tied, as we see when he reaches G.W.:*

VICE-PRESIDENT. Hello, G.W. Say, what are you trying to do with that 24D item? . . . Well, no! We just lost a sale! Well, have you *heard* it? . . . Well, it's *terrible!* How did the casting get *away* from you like that? . . . No, I *didn't* see the memo . . . Yes—well, whose fault is *that?* . . . Bill, the very first thing that you people should look into is the compatibility angle. Well, it's too late for that *now.* Well, if this happens again, we're just going to have to look around for somebody who *won't* make mistakes . . . Well, all right—yes, get rid of the whole line—I don't know, maybe Mammoth Studios [4] . . . okay . . . yeah . . . yes, I saw the report . . . No—yeah—okay. Good-by.

*Buzzer.*

SECRETARY (*through dictograph*). Yes, sir.

VICE-PRESIDENT. All right, Miss Siegelaub. Send in the next customer.

SECRETARY. Right away.

VICE-PRESIDENT (*talking to himself*). You build a business up from a wishbone. You work night and day. You put in overtime and Sundays and holidays, and then your nephew has to mess it up.

*A door opens.*

VICE-PRESIDENT (*professionally cheerful once again*). Oh, come right in, sir, and be comfortable. What can we do for you?

STEVE. My name is Steve Chartoc, and I run a local elevator up and down all day long. This can get very dull, as I only go to the fourteenth floor; and after you've been operating the car for a while you learn how to do it automatically, so you could practically stop it in your sleep. The elevator is always crowded, too; so you don't get to meet people, and consequently you make very few contacts that can do you any good.

VICE-PRESIDENT. Yes, Mr. C., and I take it you would like an occupational daydream?

STEVE. Yeah. I've tried making up my own daydreams, but whenever I do, I miss a floor and get hell from some passenger.

VICE-PRESIDENT. We have just the thing for you.

STEVE. Good.

VICE-PRESIDENT. It is known as the 32 Jumbo. Would you like to try it?

STEVE. I sure would.

*Music: The spell motif, with automatic door control.*

VICE-PRESIDENT. You take over the elevator on the late shift. It looks the same as it has always looked, but you know there are subtle differences. The elevator is crowded as usual, and you make all the stops up to the fourteenth floor. The last passenger to get off is a willowy blonde with very dark eyes. She is about to leave the car when something makes her hesitate. . . .

BLONDE. Do you go higher?

STEVE. Not as a rule, ma'am. This is the last local stop. You have to catch the express car if you want to go higher.

BLONDE. I would like to go to the top floor.

STEVE. Yes, ma'am. Express is just across the hall.

BLONDE (*going away*). Thank you very much.

STEVE (*calling her back*). Just a minute, miss. I'll take you.

BLONDE. Oh, thank you.

*Steve slides shut the elevator door and starts the car upward. We hear the floors whisk by.*

BLONDE (*with a note of alarm*). But you've gone *past* the twenty-fifth floor!

STEVE. Yes, I know, madam. At any moment we will go through the roof.

BLONDE (*terrified*). No, no, you mustn't!

STEVE. Be calm, madam, and brace yourself.

*There is a terrific crash. After the reverberations subside, we hear the pitch of the continuing elevator. It has shaken loose of plaster and beams and is heaven-bent.*

BLONDE. We are rising! We are going very fast!

STEVE. Yes, ma'am. There isn't so much friction now.

BLONDE. But what will happen to us?

STEVE. Trust in me, madam. I shall see you through.

BLONDE. Through *what?* Ooh—(*with growing alarm*) see how far we are above the city!

STEVE. I am afraid that is to be expected.

BLONDE. Oh, dear.

*A swooshing sound as the car continues to ascend.*

BLONDE. What's that?

STEVE. We are merely passing through a series of cumulo-cirro-stratus clouds.[5] Be steady.

BLONDE. And we're above them now?

STEVE. Yes, ma'am. We are accelerating.

BLONDE. What's that coming toward us?

STEVE. Have no fears. It's a PBY patrol plane.

*The sound of an airplane motor in and out quickly as a PBY flicks by.*

STEVE. Small wonder they are puzzled.

BLONDE. But what if he decides to attack us?

STEVE. Don't worry, we'll soon be out of range.

BLONDE. It's getting very cold.[6]

STEVE. I came prepared for this.

*Click.*

STEVE. The automatic heater.

BLONDE. And my ears feel funny.

STEVE. I shall turn on the pressure stabilizer.

*Click.*

BLONDE (*now beginning to admire him for his foresight and calmness*). You are a wonderful man.

STEVE. Not at all. I do my job, and I try to do it well. You see, all my life I have tried to rise above my environment and reach heights never before attained by any other elevator operator, living or dead.

BLONDE. That's a noble ambition.

STEVE. In other words, I've hitched my wagon to a star, and I have often thought that—

BLONDE (*off mike*). I get terribly dizzy when I look out of this window.

STEVE (*who does not like her inattention*). Please face the front of the car.

BLONDE. You are so strong, so good, so wise.

STEVE. You are beautiful.

BLONDE. Oh, please.

STEVE. Do you think you could learn to care?

BLONDE. I might.

STEVE. Will you kiss me?

BLONDE. Don't you think this is rather sudden?

STEVE (*chagrined*). I—I don't want to take advantage of our position. Perhaps you are right.

*Buzzer.*

BLONDE. What's that?

STEVE. The starter. He wants me to come back.

BLONDE. Are you going to?

STEVE. Never!

BLONDE. But what kind of future is there in just keeping on climbing?

STEVE. Madam, I am in heaven when I am with you.

BLONDE. You say the loveliest things.

*A terrific swoosh as of an express train going by in nothing flat.*[7]

BLONDE. Was that an asteroid by any chance?

STEVE. Indubitably.

BLONDE. That was close, wasn't it?

STEVE. Trust in me. I shall see you through.

BLONDE. But to where?

STEVE. What does it matter? I love you.

BLONDE. Oh, Stephen—I love *you*. I loved you from the minute that large woman stepped off at the fourth floor and I saw you for the first time.

STEVE. I felt it. May I kiss you?

BLONDE. Please do.

*Music: Tag.*

STEVE. Well, then what happens?

VICE-PRESIDENT. Then you wake up on the fourteenth floor.

STEVE (*disappointed*). Oh.

VICE-PRESIDENT. However, if you would like daydream Number 60A, we can carry you further along.

STEVE. I would like that.

VICE-PRESIDENT. Well, send in your application, and please mention the Columbia Broadcasting System when you send it in.[8]

STEVE. Yes, sir.

VICE-PRESIDENT. Next?

ANNOUNCER. I'm an announcer named Harry Marble.[9]

VICE-PRESIDENT. Yes, Mr. Marble. What is your problem?

MARBLE. Well, I'm an announcer.

VICE-PRESIDENT. I see. And what kind of dream can we service you with?

MARBLE. Well, I have always felt it's a pity announcers are relegated [10] to opening and closing routines with little chance at self-expression, and I—

VICE-PRESIDENT. Do you mean you want to dream about being an actor?

MARBLE. Oh, no, no, no. I'd just like to be featured in a daydream whereby I could still announce, but with style and dash.

VICE-PRESIDENT. Style and dash?

MARBLE. Yes, something by which the listener could remember me—by which there would be no mistaking
me for Frank Gallop or Ken Roberts or Tony Marvin.

VICE-PRESIDENT. You'd want them to make no mistake
about the fact that it was *Harry Marble* announcing—
right?

MARBLE. Yes.

VICE-PRESIDENT. Easy! What you want is Closing Routine
Daydream 29-30.

*Music: Spell motif, continuing briefly under:*

VICE-PRESIDENT. The program is nearing an end. The
studio is tense. The distinguished audience sits with its
eyes fixed on a door through which is expected, momen-
tarily, a high personage. At a CBS microphone in a
press box high above the studio sits Robert Trout,
the famous radio reporter. He is describing the
event. . . .

TROUT. Ladies and gentlemen, I believe Harry Marble has
just entered the studio at the west portal. Yes, it *is*
Marble. He's tanned and healthy, and he's nodding
to the company as he strides briskly toward his microphone. The musicians in the orchestra have risen to
greet him.

*The orchestra rises.*

TROUT. The conductor has stepped off the podium to shake
his hand. Mr. Marble has graciously accepted the
baton that has been proffered to him, and he is now
breaking it over his knee and handing back the narrow
end—it's an old Chinese custom, I believe, but the sig-
nificance escapes me at the moment.

The conductor is bowing, and now Marble has *turned* and is heading this way. He has just waved to several justices of the United States Supreme Court who are sitting in the audience, and they have waved back. *The justices waved right back at him!* There is an air of festivity and gaiety such as I have never *seen* in a studio! *My!* Now four actors have stepped up and are presenting Mr. Marble with gifts appropriate to the occasion. From left to right they are a bouquet of flowers, a bronze plaque, a loving cup, and a marble urn.

STUDIO AUDIENCE. (*Laughter, off.*)

TROUT (*with forced gaiety*). Mr. Marble has just pulled a *nifty,* ladies and gentlemen! In accepting the marble urn he said he hoped to make it a receptacle for "Marble earnings." You can see why he is a great favorite here.

Now he is continuing his progress toward the microphone, carrying his gifts in one hand and his script in the other. He's a dashing picture with his coattails flapping in the air-conditioning system.

He is very happy. We can see that from here, and as he—*oh-oh*—he nearly tripped over a microphone cable! But nothing ruffles his composure. No, *sir!* Good old Harry! And here he is, abreast of the microphone, ready to make the important announcement for which you have all been waiting. The next voice you hear will be that of Harry Marble. (*A pause. Then hushed and reverent.*) A great hush has fallen on the assembly. At any moment now you will hear the long-awaited voice of Harry Marble. (*A long pause.*) I don't know what's delaying him. His eyes are closed. He is about to speak. . . .

MARBLE (*after another pause*). This . . .

> *Music: A great fanfare. The orchestra, trigger-happy, has jumped the cue.*

MARBLE. . . . is Harry Marble.

> *Music: Another great fanfare.*

MARBLE. It is my privilege to tell you that you have been listening to "You Can Dream, Inc.," a presentation of the Columbia Broadcasting System.

> *Music: The curtain, this time in earnest.*

# YOU CAN DREAM, INC.

I am not the first to treat of dreams as an industry. The whole science of psychoanalysis is geared to the assembly line of the subconscious. Daniel, as far back as Babylon, made a good living, by appointment to the king, out of interpretive analysis. The standard lightweight dreams of today are dispensed like Chiclets through popular songs, magazine fiction, movies. Dreaming is the oldest, most economical and trustworthy form of escape currently in use, and it is only a question of time before some enterprising outfit, with headquarters in a plexiglass tower, will set up the kind of business suggested in this script. It's got to come.

I have had my share of daydreams, and I can't complain. Dreams of Chimborazo and of the Far Nientes, of dignified and talented women with faces like Helen of T. and bosoms like Lana of H., who cook magnificently and solve script problems; of flashy and killing remarks I could have made in last Tuesday's encounter with a salon wit; of free evenings with nothing to do but catch up on reading or see a movie. Much of my waking childhood was given over to Steigian dreams of glory, mostly involving home runs with the bases full and blazing touchdowns. I used to rescue beautiful women from holocausts, too. I confess this merely to indicate I am not making sport of Miss W., or Messrs. Bromfield, Chartoc, or Marble. I'm all for them, and I only wish my prefabricated daydreams were more stable and practical and that I could have done better by each customer.

I suppose if there ever *were* a firm like You Can Dream, Inc., it would find that the dreams most in demand would not be novelty fantasies or bargain-priced megalomaniac visions, but simple quality dreams designed along the most realistic lines. It is historical and tragic that illusions of grandeur have always come cheap, whereas the humblest dreams of the masses—dreams of peace and profitable labor, security, and freedom—should be the highest-priced and hardest to obtain. Few sensible people waste much time dreaming of an idle and luxurious life. They set about to realize modest and plausible dreams through the agency of sheer hard work.

"You Can Dream" was one of the few light scripts among the twenty-two produced in the 1944 series and was certainly nothing to write your boy on Saipan about. Its structure is so loose that scenes can be removed and substituted like the suspended rooms in Paul Nelson's marvelous modern house. In my first draft I included a dentist who was bored with his work. "Although I have a very nice clientele," he complained, "I find that after a while mouths get to look very much alike." He was provided with a dream in which Adolf Hitler turned up as a patient. No time was lost. "Who did this work for you?" asked the dentist, examining Der Führer's mouth. "Gesund gestalt Scharnhorst," replied Adolf, through considerable hardware in his mouth. "Hm," said our man. "First thing we've got to do is rip out all those gold inlays. Miss Callaway, the reverse hammer, please." The script then called for assorted terrifying noises of a clinical nature, after which came the cold water syringe, the Number 6 Wedelstedt chisel, the Number 8 round burr coarse drill, and the Number 39 inverted cone burr. Between operations there were chatty shafts of one-way conversation, such as: "This is going to be a little sensitive, I'm afraid. . . . Of course I could never understand how you sold the German people such a bill of goods. . . . Mm. Quite a lot of decay up there. . . . Now if you'll just hold the back of his head, Miss Callaway, we can get this over with in a very short time. (*Activity.*) . . . There! You look a little pale, Mr. Hitler. Would you like to rest for a moment? . . . Now just a little more drilling, and then we'll be ready to take the nerve out. (*More drilling.*) Now we're just about ready for that little old nerve, aren't we? May I have the root canal reamer and the pulp broach, Miss Callaway? And will you wipe the perspiration off the patient's nose? We don't want to get any moisture in the cavity."

This went on, with savage detail, until the dentist called Miss Callaway aside.

"Am I seeing things?"

"Why, what's wrong?"

"Was his mustache white when he came in here?"

This particular daydream was frankly an exercise in sadism and much too graphic and tasteless to broadcast, but it felt good to write. Some of my friends who loathed Hitler as religiously as I did read the scene and laughed till they nearly died, but others who hated with equal intensity and steadiness were offended and outraged by it. They said it caused them to wince and shudder. One reported that the whole business made his gums hurt.

*Acting.* The vice-president is a graduate of the College of Commerce and Business Administration of the University of Illinois and is all that you would expect of such a character. He is calm and suave throughout, except when his nephew fouls up the casting on dream 24D.

Miss W., while not exactly written to be played straight, should not be caricatured. If there is any criticism implicit in the routine of the law office, it is directed at said routine, not at the party of the first part. Should it come to Miss W. versus Puddefath, Hunnebun, Smigley & Dorset, I am all for the lass. The typewriter, on the level of stenography, is a beastly machine, and legal language the most boring of all. The Underwood is the final stage in the degeneration of the feathered quill, and the legal document stands at the antipode to rhetoric. Poetry's best exhibits are those whose words are most incautious; the pride of the law office, on the other hand, is the roundly categoric supercautious contract that says the same thing a hundred different ways, in order to avoid loopholes.

Mackinlay Smigley, the Yale man, is a suave, purring baritone of the commercial announcer school, and his avowal of love is intended to be just as ridiculous in the setting as Dad's quotation of Keats in a Southern accent later on.

The episode of the esthete was written with Minerva Pious in mind. Minnie's tough girl is the funniest in the world, and the absurdity and implausibilty of this sequence made it the best listening of the script. Samuel Raskyn, who performed the julep-drinking colonel, is a phenomenon of dialects. He has more variations of Southern speech than are likely to be found in the South itself.

The affair of Steve and the Blonde was conceived as a sort of animated tintype, and the vignette involving Harry Marble was played perfectly dead pan by Robert Trout and Marble himself. The danger of a scene like this is that it may be a greater joke to the radio trade than to a public at large unfamiliar with studio procedure.

*Music.* Alexander Semmler composes in the romantic tradition and is happiest in the boundless acres of fantasy. His scores for "The Odyssey of Runyon Jones" and "Psalm for a Dark Year" are excellent cases in point. So charming are his miniatures for orchestra that on several occasions I have asked him to compose quickies, lasting from a minute to three minutes, which could be played in the clear and in their entirety. His overture to "Between Americans" was later arranged as a suite and performed by symphony orchestras. The Concerto for Typewriter No. 1 in D was another such. The typewriter, a tubby-sounding Royal, was used as a percussion instrument and miked separately to give it due prominence. Semmler made full use of the seven basic percussive sounds of the machine: key against platen, space bar, shift key, back spacer, carriage return, line-space lever, and bell.

*Sound.* The sound crew must rise to the occasion in the elevator daydream. The crash of the ascending car as it plows through the roof of the office building requires a judicious blend of live and recorded effects. In the stage where the elevator is passing through a layer of cumulo-stratus clouds the actors spoke through a flutter box—a device that breaks up the voice and makes it sound ripply or, as the name of the gadget implies, fluttery. Certain sounds that the layman might consider routine, such as those made by an elevator moving normally in a shaft, are among the subtlest to convey, and whenever you see the bare direction "swoosh" or "crash," you are looking at a symbol of hard labor on the rock pile for soundmen, engineers, and directors.

*Additional Notes.* 1. Five minutes before this program went on the air I dashed from the control room to demonstrate to Harry Baker, drummer in the CBS orchestra, what I thought was lacking in his reading of the final passage involving the carriage return of the Royal. Nobody laughed when I sat down to the typewriter, but the enjoyment was general when, in a final flourish intended to show just what emphasis I wanted placed on the last chordlike effect, I slammed the return so hard that the tension spring broke. The machine was useless, and an emergency posse was sent out to hunt down a typewriter to replace the one I had smashed. The nearest office was several floors away, and of course all Columbia's desk typewriters are fastened to permanent supports. The program went on the air, and still no typewriter. Finally, a minute and a half before the concerto was due, two porters rushed in with a replacement. It was an adding machine. I screamed through an intercom to the soundman, "For God's sake, get a *typewriter*, not a comptometer! Do you know the difference?" He nodded, whipped off his earphones, tore out, was back in a minute with an old broken-down machine that had no doubt typed a letter congratulating Buchanan on his election to the presidency. Baker, the typewriter virtuoso, was thoroughly shaken by the time the machine was set before him, a bare three seconds ahead of his entrance in the score.

2. An allusion to Marvin Lowenthal, an authority on the essayist, whose *The Autobiography of Montaigne* (a compilation of biographical material from the essays) is delightful reading.

3. From the sonnet whose first line is its title.

4. Mammoth buys anything.

5. The trade name for mackerel sky.

6. The blonde is not here obliquely inviting Steve to put his arm around her. It *does* get cold at this altitude.

7. By this time, the elevator scene may seem too long in the playing. If so, the sound of the passing asteroid and the allusions to it can be cut without any loss.

8. Reminds me of the story told by Robert Colwell, who served in Luxemburg as radio chief of the Psychological

Warfare Detachment, 12th Army Group, for the OWI. During the last days of the war, Radio Luxemburg broadcast invitations to German soldiers to surrender. The advantages of prison life in Allied camps was made clear, and the prospective client was requested, "Please mention Radio Luxemburg when you are surrendering."

9. In your own production change Marble's name to that of your local announcer. But in this case you will also have to change or eliminate Trout's reference, later on, to the gag about Marble earnings.

10. True, true. Announcing, with few exceptions, and from the standpoint of artistic accomplishment, is about the most unrewarding job in a studio.

# THE MOAT FARM MURDER

## *The True Confession of Herbert Dougal*

Adapted from English court records expressly for Charles Laughton, who took the role of Dougal, and Elsa Lanchester, who played Cecile, in a production directed by the author on July 18, 1944. It was the eighteenth program of the "Columbia Presents Corwin" series. Music was composed and conducted by Bernard Herrmann.

# THE MOAT FARM MURDER
## The True Confession of Herbert Dougal

OFFICER. And now, if the stenographer is ready, we will proceed with Mr. Dougal's confession from where we left off in our last session. Go ahead, Mr. Dougal.

DOUGAL. I did not find Miss Holland as generous as I expected; in fact, until we actually went to the Moat Farm she drew but very little money out of the bank. I didn't have very much money, but what I did have I soon got through, and that was why I suggested that we should buy a farm. I told her that my father would not live long, and that upon his death I was entitled to a large sum of money, and I further showed her a claim I had against the War Office for arrears of pay due to me. . . . (*We are flashing back to the incident. Cecile is Miss Holland.*)

CECILE. When will the payment on this claim be made, do you have any idea?

DOUGAL. Oh, when they get around to it, I suppose. You know how they are at the War Office.

CECILE (*busy reading*). Yes, well . . . (*Pause.*) No, no; don't take it back. I want to read it a bit more closely. . . .

DOUGAL. Everything went all right up to the time that the farm was purchased, and I certainly did intend that the deeds should be made out in my name, but to this Miss Holland would not consent, nor would she pay the deposit in my name, and therefore all the visions

I had had of getting hold of the farm, turning her out, and selling it melted away. I could see she intended to be master, and that she had been so in the habit, during her life, of doing her own business that even if we did make any profit it would be she who would be handling the money.

Finding she was so tight-fisted, I began to think of various schemes to put her out of the way, but I thought I would wait a little while and see if she altered. I think she was naturally very mean. It was strange to find a woman so close,[1] because otherwise she was not so bad, and she would often try, when I was miserable or down in the dumps, to cheer me up by playing or singing to me.

She was old-fashioned in a lot of her ways, and when I suggested that she should buy herself new dresses and wear more fashionable clothes, she said she would wear what she liked. . . .

CECILE. I will wear what I like, is that clear? I don't *want* to be in the fashion; and in my view, if two people were fond of each other, it doesn't matter what they wear, does it? . . .

DOUGAL. She had a lot of clothing belonging to her aunt, and she was always twisting, mending, and altering a lot of old dresses that I wouldn't have given house room to. She was rather snappy at times, and if I didn't quite agree with everything she said she would bounce out of the room. . . .

CECILE (*in a huff*). Very well, if that's how you feel!

*Slams the door.*

---

[1] The numbered notes will be found on pages 307-308.

DOUGAL. Perhaps toward the evening she would get over her temper, and then she would come downstairs and plead for forgiveness. . . .

CECILE (*approaching*). Herbert!

DOUGAL (*coldly*). What is it?

CECILE. I'm sorry about losing my temper.

DOUGAL. Oh, are you now?

CECILE. Yes, I'm afraid I was sharper than I need have been. (*Pause.*) Do you forgive me?

DOUGAL. Why, yes, Cecile, so long as you realize that I was right in the matter.

CECILE. I suppose you were, Herbert.

DOUGAL. Then let's forget it.

CECILE. It's only my state of nerves, really, that makes me give way to such temper. . . .

DOUGAL. I didn't mind these fits of temper, because they gave me an opportunity of clearing out and having a good day and a game or two of billiards. I was drinking very heavily then, because I had made up my mind by this time to either get a lump sum out of her and clear out, or put her out of the way and have the lot. I made up my mind at last to put her out of the way.

*Music: Murder motif comes in and winds under narration.*

DOUGAL. I used to sit and think about it for hours, because, although I had done a lot of things during my life, I couldn't quite make up my mind to go so far as to murder her. I thought once that I would have a bit of an accident, and that I would contrive to get her out of the house in her nightdress so that she might be found drowned in the moat, and that at the inquest I could say she was in the habit of walking in her sleep and had no doubt fallen into the moat. But when I came to examine the water I found it was only about a foot or so deep. Once I almost decided to let her shoot herself, only she had such a horror of firearms that she would not let me even keep them in the house. I tried to get her to make a will, leaving everything to me, while I made one also, leaving everything to her.

*Music: Out.*

CECILE. But why do that?

DOUGAL. It only seems to me the right and proper thing to do.

CECILE (*not interested*). Well, I've already made my will.

DOUGAL. You have?

CECILE. Yes, and I don't intend to alter it.

*Music: In.*

DOUGAL. All this caused me a lot of trouble, and I used to sit for hours and hours conjuring up all kinds of schemes to get rid of her. At this time I got positively to hate her, and when we actually moved into the farm I had definitely decided what I should do. I thought that a very good place to bury her would be the ditch, and that was why the very first week we were at the farm I gave orders for it to be filled in. Although she knew nothing about it, she came out of the house and stood by the side of the ditch whilst I and Pilgrim, the laborer, were discussing the best way to fill it up. The elder tree stood by the side, and I can see her there now, holding one of the boughs, and arguing against the ditch being filled in until proper arrangements had been made for draining it another way.

*Music: Cross-fades to:*

*Digging. The sound continues under:*

CECILE. I don't think you know what you're about, Herbert.

DOUGAL. Cecile, my dear, I know very well what I'm doing.

CECILE (*bristling*). But I have a right to my opinion and more than a right to discuss what is being done on this farm. This laborer here knows more than you do about it.

DOUGAL. I prefer that we leave him out of this.

CECILE (*calling*). Pilgrim! Pilgrim!

PILGRIM (*off*). Yes, ma'am.

CECILE. How do you think this should be done?

PILGRIM (*advancing*). Well, ma'am, I think the proper way to do the job is to make the new drain first and *then* fill in the ditch.

CECILE. There—you see, Herbert?

DOUGAL. I see nothing of the sort. (*Down.*) I had made up my mind what I was going to do with her; so it did not suit my purpose to accept his advice, and I insisted on the work being commenced at once, although I did not want the filling in completed.

*Music: The murder motif.*

DOUGAL. I don't think I should have done it had I not been drinking heavily, but the more drink I had, the more determined I became and the easier it looked. I wanted money very badly then, and I made one final appeal to Miss Holland to let me have some money until I got my dispute with the War Office settled, but she refused. . . .

CECILE. I know very well what you want that money for. To spend it in drink! Well, you can't have it! . . .

DOUGAL. She was so close that she would not trust me with even the wages to pay the farm hands, and at last I was pushed in such a corner that I determined to finish the matter that week.

*Music: Up sharply and then down, muttering, behind:*

DOUGAL. Of course I know all about firearms, and when the wind was in a certain direction I fired the revolver off several times in the coach house, in order to see if anyone heard it while they were in the back of the house.[2]

I was very glad to find that nobody heard any report, and I placed the revolver, fully loaded, and some cartridges on a shelf in the coach house, ready for me when I wanted it.

*He places revolver and cartridges on wooden shelf.*

DOUGAL. It was there seven or eight days before I finally used it, and now and then I would have a shot or two just to see if I still had my old skill of being able to make sure of hitting anything at twenty yards.

*Music: Suddenly out, when:*

OFFICER. Just a moment, Mr. Dougal. What about the testimony of the servant girl that you made advances to her late one night?

DOUGAL. What that servant girl says about going to her door is about right, although I think she exaggerates a little. I had had a skinful of brandy that night, Miss Holland and I had quite a row, and she accused me of a lot of things. Of course I declared that the servant's story was a lie from top to bottom, but she stood up for the girl, and she made herself so ill that she cried very nearly the whole of one day. On Friday morning we had made it up. I got around her by lunch time, and we made up our quarrel and she had forgiven me, and that was why we thought of going for a drive. As it was a beautiful night we let the horse walk slowly home,[3] and I should think it was about a quarter past eight when we got back to the farm. When I had taken the horse out I thought she would go in the house, but instead of that she made some remark about its being a beautiful moonlight night.

*Music: Tremolando passage beginning quietly under:*

DOUGAL.  I had pushed the trap into the coach house by this time. I stepped up on the side of the trap . . .

*Hollow step.*

DOUGAL.  . . . reached down the revolver . . .

*Takes revolver off the shelf.*

DOUGAL.  . . . and as Miss Holland stood just near the door looking at the moon, I shot her.

*Pistol shot.*

DOUGAL.  She dropped just like a log . . .

*The body falls.*

DOUGAL.  . . . and then I pulled her into the coach house.

*He drags the body along a wooden floor.*

*Music: Out, damned spot, under:*

DOUGAL. If I live to be a thousand years old I shall never forget the feeling as I caught hold of both her hands and drew her along until I got her into the coach house. All kinds of things came into my mind, and my heart seemed almost to stand still as I put my hand inside her dress to feel if her heart was beating.

*Music: A surge.*

DOUGAL. Of course I knew that she was dead, and yet—I don't know what made me do it—but I knelt down on one knee and pulled her head and asked her to speak if she could.

(*Up.*) Cecile! Cecile! Speak to me! Cecile, do you see me? Cecile!

(*Resuming narration.*) I didn't think this was of much use, and why I did it I can't tell even now, but I thought for a moment that she might come to, because there was no blood about, and I wasn't quite certain where the bullet had struck her.

Great beads of perspiration began to run down my back, and when I left the coach house I had a most peculiar sensation as if someone was following me. I thought the doors of the coach house had opened and she was walking out after me; I could almost feel her touch me, and as true as there is a God in heaven, I was ready to drop.

*Music: The mood.*

DOUGAL. I must have stood there some seconds, and then I put my hand into my pocket and drew out the revolver and turned round and looked straight at the coach house. I could not quite get out of my mind, nor get rid of the feeling, that something or someone besides myself stood between me and the coach house. I still had an impression that someone would come toward me; so I leveled up the revolver and stood there with it in my hand.

*Music: Suddenly cuts out, leaving:*

*Night sounds only.*

DOUGAL.  I don't think I could have uttered a word to save my life; my tongue was like a great ball of fire, and I quite hurt myself trying to get some saliva to moisten my mouth and my parched tongue. Then I remembered how silly it was; of course there was no one, and I put the revolver back into my pocket and walked into the house.

*Steps, on wooden floor.*

DOUGAL.  We usually kept some brandy in a decanter in the sitting room; so I pushed the door open . . .

*The door opening.*

DOUGAL.  . . . and I picked up the decanter . . .

*The decanter clinks.*

DOUGAL.  . . . without waiting for a glass. (*Feverish gulping.*) I think I must have gulped down half of its contents. This seemed to steady me, but not for long.

*Music: The first curdlings of conscience.*

DOUGAL.  Every few minutes I broke into a violent perspiration, and then my tongue would become so hot and my lips so dry that I had to rub them with my fingers to get some feeling into them. I seized the brandy bottle again, and I had another good swig at it, and then, I don't know why, but I thought it might be all a mistake —that perhaps, after all, the bullet hadn't struck her, and that she had only fainted, and she might come to if I gave her some brandy. So I caught hold of the decanter and walked across with it in my hand to the coach house; but I couldn't make up my mind for a second or two to go inside. I called out—

*Music: Drops away.*

DOUGAL (*calling*). Cecile, Cecile!

(*Down.*) And then I thought what a fool I was, because everything had gone just as I had planned it, and there was not a living soul near, and I had nothing to fear.

*Music: Out.*

DOUGAL. Then I went into the coach house, but it was dark, and I pushed the door farther open so that some of the light from the moon would come in.

*The door creaks.*

DOUGAL. She was in exactly the same position as I had left her; so I knelt down and poured some of the brandy over her face, thinking perhaps it might revive her . . .

*Pouring from the decanter, the brandy splashing over her face.*

DOUGAL. . . . but really I knew this was impossible, because she was dead. I tried to sit her up, but she fell back, and I knew all was over then.

Of course I had arranged everything, and I had mapped out days before where I was going to bury her; but I sat down and began thinking over new schemes, and every few minutes I kept touching her and feeling her pulse and speaking to her.

I went back to the house and had another good drink of brandy, but although it was neat, it seemed to have no impression upon me. I could not get rid of the burning sensation in my throat, and I kept on walking backward and forward outside the coach house.

I tried to smoke a cigar, but I had to light it a dozen times, because I forgot all about it, and it went out.

I made up my mind that it would be best not to put her in the ditch, but to take her away and bury her somewhere else; so I took off her hat and her veil and the jacket she was wearing, and I picked her up in my arms and walked down by the side of the little moat.

*Music: The grim procession behind:*

DOUGAL. Her head was leaning over my shoulder, and as I carried her along I wished there was a great big furnace there that I could put her in and watch her burn. I thought of cutting her up into pieces and putting her into the moat, but I thought of the time it would take me, and I was afraid of being interrupted.

She seemed so heavy, and when I got up into the fields I sat her down and put her head against a bank. I could not make up my mind what to do with her; so I laid her flat on her back and went back to the house again to get some more brandy, for I was shaking from head to foot. I kept burying my nails into my flesh as I walked along, and I had to close my mouth to prevent my teeth from chattering.

*Music: Out.*

DOUGAL. Somehow I wanted to bury her out of sight, and yet I wanted to keep her by the side of me; so I went back to the field and picked her up again and carried her back to the coach house.

*A cold wind under:*

DOUGAL. I found that she was getting cold and stiff, for there was a strong breeze blowing, and it was rather a cold night. It was a horrible sight to see her lying on the ground, and before I picked her up the last time I wished that she was alive again, because I thought, after all, she hadn't done me any harm; so I knelt down and kissed her once or twice. All the good times we had seemed to come back to me, and I remembered once or twice how when I had been queer through the drink she had nursed me and tried to get me well, and that, after all, it was a bit hard to do her in.

But then I began to think what would happen to me if she was found. I thought I would hide her in the haystack for a few days, but finally I made up my mind that I would get rid of her once and for all.

I went and got the fork, and I carried some straw and laid it down at the bottom of the ditch. I think the brandy then began to have some effect upon me, and I grew more brutal, and I began to think of the way she had nagged me, and the difficulty I had in getting money from her; so I went back to the coach house again and caught hold of her hand and pulled the ring off her finger.

*Music: A brutal, strident effect; bassoons mutter beneath:*

DOUGAL. She was very fond of this ring; it had belonged to the only man I really believe she ever loved. I asked her to tell me the story one day, and she did.

*Music: Fading now.*

DOUGAL. She said that while her aunt kept a ladies' school at Liverpool, she used to help her in the management; and whilst doing so (*his words overlapping Cecile's*) she grew very fond of the brother of one of the pupils —a midshipman, who . . .

CECILE (*speaking simultaneously with Dougal*). . . . and whilst doing so I became very fond of the brother of one of the pupils—a midshipman, who had returned home from a voyage. This young man and I fell in love with each other almost at first sight, and he vowed that he would make his fortune abroad and return to marry me. He had some relatives in the West Indies, and he went out there shortly afterward and took some kind of post. He used to write letters to me, but just when everything looked bright, he was drowned through the upsetting of a yacht, and his body was not recovered for some days. When it was found, the ring that he wore on his finger was taken off and sent home to his parents, who gave it to me. . . .

*Music: Now the morbid motif returns. It follows the contour of the narration:*

DOUGAL. Well, I took that ring off her finger . . . and just as I did so a stray moonbeam came through one of the cracks of the door and played about her face. It made me quite shudder. Also I put my hand down and caught hold of the gold cross that was round her neck and wrenched it off . . .

*The chain breaks with a small, sharp sound, simultaneously with:*

*Music: A nasty percussive effect in the strings.*

DOUGAL (*goes right on*). . . . snapping the chain on which it used to hang round her neck. I had another drop of brandy then, and I turned her over, put my hand in her pocket, and took her purse. I don't think I knew what I was doing then.

I picked her up in my arms, and just as you would carry a baby, I carried her out of the coach house and laid her on the straw that I had put in the ditch. Then a change came over me. The more brandy I drank, the more brutal and wicked I seemed to get. One minute I wanted to kiss her, and the next minute I wanted to pitch a lot of mold over her; but at last I made up my mind that I would bury her and get her out of sight.

I thought of what had happened but a few days before, when she stood by the side of the ditch talking to Pilgrim and myself about filling in the ditch. . . .

CECILE (*a ghostly voice*).[4] I don't think you know what you're about, Herbert. . . .

DOUGAL (*resuming narration*). I thought perhaps, unless I covered her over, the fowls would scratch away the straw; so I got some brambles and twigs, and pieces of wood, and I stretched them over her body. And I went back into the house and had some more brandy, and then I went to bed.

*Music: Insomnia motif under:*

DOUGAL. I couldn't sleep, and I got up and walked round the farm and down to the road and back again. I couldn't keep my eyes off the ditch, and I kept thinking that perhaps the fowls would get loose and they would scratch the mold away; so I got down into the ditch and kicked some more earth over her until it was about a foot deep. Once or twice I was tempted to pull the straw away and have another look at her face, but I tore myself away and walked about the farm.

I am sure I aged that night twenty years. I never closed my eyes the whole night long, and I could not keep still or rest for even a quarter of an hour. I tried to read, I tried to write, I tried to sleep; but it was all in vain. Not one single moment's peace did I have, and I am sure that if I went once to the ditch I went twenty times.

I now began to wish that all traces of this night were obliterated, and I was tempted once or twice to pitch the ring and the cross into the moat, but somehow I could not do it.

One of the first things I did was to open her desk . . .

*The desk drawer opening.*

DOUGAL. . . . and go through a lot of her papers, in order to find out, if possible, how much money she had. She kept her accounts very neatly, but I was very disappointed when I found that she was not worth more than six or seven thousand pounds. I thought perhaps she had some more cash concealed about the place somewhere; so I turned over her trunks and boxes . . .

*Rummaging through trunks and boxes.*

DOUGAL. . . . but I could not find any, and I certainly did feel somewhat disappointed.

*Music: Insomnia motif.*

DOUGAL. I used to have terrible dreams at night, and as I went about the house I used to fancy I could hear her voice. I think if I went once to look at the ditch I went a hundred times a day, and I am sure if anyone had watched me, they would have grown suspicious and thought that there must be something under that ditch.

*Music: Out.*

OFFICER (*after a pause*). Yes—go on, Mr. Dougal.

DOUGAL. I come now to a terrible part of my life, because, however clever one may be and however well one's plans have been carried out, there always is the suspicion lurking at the back of your head that you may have made one little blunder that will lead to the truth coming out.

It's all very well to try and drown your thoughts in drink, and as sure as I am alive on this earth, no one tried harder than I did to banish entirely from my mind all recollections of that terrible night, but I found that it was physically impossible. . . .

CECILE. What a beautiful moonlight night . . .

DOUGAL. It did not matter where I was or who was with me, the moment there was a lull in the conversation, the moment my attention was taken from anything, away back to the farm went my thoughts, and again and again the whole of the incidents of the three weeks Cecile lived there came before me. Sometimes I would walk about the farm by myself, and if I did there was always that feeling that she was going to step out of the grave and touch me on the shoulder. There was always the feeling, wherever I went, that something was near me, that there was someone present besides myself; and yet I knew that there was not. I never could really make up my mind that she was dead; and yet I knew she was. As sure as I stand here, I can swear that I have gone into the coach house hundreds of times, expecting to see her lying on her back as I dragged her in there; but nothing would make me believe she wasn't until I had gone in and seen for myself. . . .

CECILE. Herbert . . .

DOUGAL. I did this two or three times a day sometimes, and all the time I knew that I had buried her in the ditch and that she was still there. I have tried to reason with myself times out of number, but it was no good—I had to go into that coach house and see for myself that she was not there.

*Music: Insomnia motif under:*

DOUGAL. Sometimes, when I have been walking along or sitting in a railway carriage, I have closed my eyes and tried to make myself believe that it was all a dream and that she wasn't dead, and it was some foolish thought that I had got into my mind. I have got up and said to myself: "You are not a murderer, old man, whatever else you may be," and then I have sat down again, and I have felt much better and more satisfied; but unfortunately this didn't last very long. . . .

CECILE. Herbert! . . .

*Music: Darker color.*

DOUGAL. A few minutes later my mind traveled back to
May nineteenth, and there I could see myself loading
the revolver in the morning, putting it on the shelf,
and then taking the pony out of the trap . . .

CECILE. What a beautiful moonlight night . . .

DOUGAL. . . . and standing on the step and shooting her.

*A loud but ghostly hollow and reverberating gunshot.*

*Music: Ends.*

DOUGAL. Why, even after she had been dead three years
I could close my eyes and still feel that I had her in
my arms; I could still feel her head hanging over my
shoulder, and I could still see her face as I laid her in
the ditch.

At one time drink would send me to sleep, and perhaps for a few hours I would forget all about the
Moat Farm; but as time went on I found it impossible
to get a night's rest, and then I took to walking in my
sleep, and I thought I should have gone mad when I
found out I was a *somnambulist!* [5]

I remember one night I returned from London, and
I don't think I was quite sober, and after having a
good look round I went to bed, I should think about
eleven o'clock. I remember quite well taking off my
clothes and getting into bed, but just before daybreak
I suddenly came to myself, and I found that I was
standing by the side of the ditch . . .

*Night sounds and light wind.*

DOUGAL. . . . and that a spade was in my hand. I was in
my nightshirt, and I had got out of the bedroom,
walked down the stairs, opened the door, crossed over
the moat bridge, gone into the coach house, and then

gone to the grave with the spade in my hand. I think
I must have been standing there a long time, because
I was very cold and my nightshirt was wet with dew.
I shook from head to foot, and my teeth chattered and
I was aching in every limb when I awoke; so I pitched
the spade back into the coach house and went back to
bed . . .

*The outdoor night sounds and wind fade.*

DOUGAL. . . . and there I lay awake, counting the hours.

*The clock strikes four.*

*Music: Insidious, under:*

DOUGAL. I was really afraid of myself, and I thought that
one of these mornings the laborers would come in and
find me standing there, and I thought of all kinds of
methods to prevent myself being found there. The
only way that I could prevent myself walking out to
the ditch in my sleep was locking the gate at the entrance of the moat bridge. I put a bit of chain around
it . . .

*The chain clatters against the gate post.*

DOUGAL. . . . and before I went to bed I used to see that
it was padlocked.

*The padlock snaps.*

DOUGAL. Although this did not prevent my walking in my
sleep, it stopped me going out to the ditch, because I
used to go right up to the gate, and as it was locked
I feel certain I used to turn round and go back to bed.
I know I did this, because one day the gate was painted
white, and when I woke up next morning I found my

hands covered with white paint, which showed that I had been down to the gate and tried to open it.

*Music: Horror and insinuations of insanity; then out.*

DOUGAL. I got very ill about this time, and I felt certain that I should go mad if I did not do something to distract my thoughts. I thought I would go to Paris, and at last I made up my mind to get one big check cashed and go away for good.

I packed my bag, putting all the things I wanted in it, and I caught an early train to Newport Station. At Liverpool Street I met some people I knew, and got on the drink again, but I managed to catch the midnight mail to Paris.

As I was going away I felt quite happy, and I thought I would leave everything and not a soul should know where I was; but when I landed in Paris a strange feeling came over me, and I began wondering what was happening at the Moat Farm. It was no good—I was obliged to go back, and after I had been in Paris a couple of days I started for home.

*Train wheels rumble, under:*

DOUGAL. I had some extraordinary fancy that someone belonging to Cecile had come to the farm and, not finding her there, was making inquiries, and that if I didn't get back at once the ditch would be opened and the secret of her disappearance solved. Although I caught an express at Liverpool Street, the train did not go fast enough. . . .

POLICE OFFICER. Tell me, Mr. Dougal, when did you first begin to sense danger—before or after the investigation of your forgery was started?

DOUGAL. When the Superintendent called at the farm I began to see danger, and I thought it best to leave the farm once and forever. I didn't know where I was going when I left it, and sometimes I didn't seem to care whether they found me out or whether they didn't. I was so tired of it all, and yet the moment I thought of a hand being placed on my shoulder I conjured up all kinds of pictures. I have seen myself tried; I have heard myself sentenced; and I have felt myself standing on the scaffold with the rope round my neck.

*Music: Curtain sneaks in under:*

DOUGAL. But at times as I sat in my cell I often thought that, after all, I was only living a life of misery, and it would be better to end it.

*Music: Conclusion.*

# THE MOAT FARM MURDER

Charles Laughton has the youngest spirit of any actor I know, and I know hundreds of them. He is an experimentalist at heart, a curious and inquisitive craftsman; a mixture of erudition and naïveté; a genius who, like all geniuses, has a good healthy ballast of ham.

It is not accidental that the Laughton who could brilliantly re-create such characters as Henry VIII and Captain Bligh, Rembrandt and Javert, should be interested in performing for the radio a role that films would never let him do: John Brown. Late in 1939, I made a short adaptation of the section of Benét's *John Brown's Body* that treats of Brown's trial and execution. It was intended for a series which I was then directing called "Pursuit of Happiness." Laughton, whom I had never met, happened to be in New York the week this was to be done, and I brought the script to him. He was excited about the experimental nature of the adaptation and went to work with a zeal that astonished me. It was a kind of expression that was new to him, as it was to myself (and, come to think of it, as it was to radio), and Laughton was as fascinated as a bird dog on the trail of a pheasant. He rehearsed endlessly, and worried and argued and conjectured and debated until he, an Englishman, finally licked the problem of projecting a Kansan to Americans.

The Brown spot succeeded, and the taste of blood had Laughton licking his ample chops. Within two weeks he was back on "Pursuit" as Thomas Wolfe. In succeeding years he was to perform other daring and unsafe roles for me—

as Job (straight from the Bible), Carl Sandburg, Walt Whitman, and an expanded Wolfe.

Most top film actors won't go near anything on the radio that bears the slightest suspicion of being fresh and original. They are afraid they may be heard at a disadvantage in a medium other than their accustomed one, and they have been conditioned by long practice at movie studios to beware of anything except safe and proven formulas. Notable exceptions to this conservatism are Fredric March, Franchot Tone, Robert Montgomery, Ronald Colman, Bette Davis (in the plays of Oboler), Groucho Marx, Robert Young, and Laughton. But of them all, none is happier than Laughton to tackle the really tough job, to work like a draught horse.

This is the only script in this collection that was not my idea and that I did not write. It was Laughton's idea, as it was his discovery. The story is that he was riding home in a London subway one night in 1928 and started to read a magazine he had picked up at a kiosk. It was an issue (Vol. I, No. 3) of *Life and Letters,* one shilling net, containing an article on tendencies in Persian poetry, an essay on "The Theatre and Jean Cocteau," and a bibliography of court life in the reign of Louis XIV. But it was the work of a nonwriter, the account of an elderly, bungling souse, that gripped Laughton and held him transfixed until he had gone three stations past his stop. The article, entitled "A Murderer's Confession," consisted of the verbatim confession of Samuel Herbert Dougal, who in 1899 murdered Camille Cecile Holland, a crime for which he was hanged four years later. The editor, in an introduction to the transcript, wrote: "It is not only a very curious human document, but it has as a story the vivid convincing power more often found in good fiction than in confessions."

At his home one night Laughton pulled the magazine out of a bookshelf and showed me the piece. He said he thought it would make a good program. I adapted the confession (which was long enough even in its abbreviated form in *Life and Letters* to have made an hour's broadcast) and asked Bernard Herrmann to compose a score for it. The result was something that sizzled the snoods and curled the whiskers of many a lady and gentleman in the radio audience.

Dougal's original confession, the editor tells us, began with the story of his isolation of the fifty-six-year-old Miss Holland by

intercepting her correspondence with her nephew, always going himself to meet the postman . . . and when she answered, inserting her letter in an envelope addressed to himself in London. . . . Their life together lasted about six months, of which three weeks only were spent at the Moat Farm. Dougal, who had been a soldier and twice married, was then fifty-three.

For purposes of compression, I cut a great deal of Dougal's description of how he prepared for the crime, and I eliminated almost all references to the servant girl who worked and boarded at the farm. Actually, the girl was there the night Dougal shot his wife, and a large part of the confession concerns Dougal's fright lest she had overheard the shot. He crept to her quarters to see:

She was still going on with her work, and I looked at her to see if I could read in her face whether she knew what had happened outside. Thank God, her first words were "Where's the mistress?" and I was just able to jerk out she has gone to London. I really believe that at that moment if I had even a suspicion that she knew anything about what had occurred, I should have shot her, and I knew that would not do, because she had written to her mother to come and fetch her away, and I knew the mother would be sure to be there, so I need hardly tell you how thankful I was when the girl went back to the kitchen, making some remark about she thought it was very unkind of "Mrs. Dougal" to go to London and leave her in the house after what had happened. As I walked away into the front of the house I stopped and listened once or twice, because I fancied she might follow me and watch what I was doing, but she went on with her work just as if nothing unusual had happened, and I could see she really believed what I said, viz. that her mistress had gone to London.

Three times that night and once the next morning he went back to the girl's quarters to make additional excuses for Miss Holland's absence. Even then he continued to be jittery about the girl. Of her departure from the farm that day, he says:

I was very anxious to see the back of the servant girl, and, therefore, I was pleased when her mother came and took her away. I knew the girl had not the slightest suspicion as to what had happened the previous night, because I felt certain that she would have raised an alarm when her mother came, and would have accused me to my face. When I got back to the farm I walked into the house, and I was quite pleased to find I had it all to myself; but I had some strange feeling that, somehow or other, that servant girl would do me some harm. It was a strange presentiment, and as the day went on I kept fancying she would come back and demand to know where her mistress was.

The horror of Dougal's story is his own, and I invented nothing save devices of production to heighten peaks and dredge depths. The Officer is on the scene merely to serve as a frame of reference: the somebody to whom Dougal must tell his story. Both here and in the case of Pilgrim, the laborer, I carried out indications contained clearly in the confession. All dialogue between Dougal and Miss Holland, including the pitiful story of how she came by her ring, are as nearly as possible in Dougal's own words.

Wherever the murderer is quoted as speaking for himself, no liberty has been taken beyond the changing of a word, at rare intervals, to clarify matters for the listener.

Certain situations that seem almost corny are only further proof that truth dramatizes every bit as well as and often better than fiction. The cruel irony of Cecile's standing by and watching her own grave being prepared—even arguing about it; Dougal's agonized relenting and his "kissing her once or twice"; the pulling of the ring from her finger; the stray moonbeam playing on her dead face; Dougal's awakening to find white paint on his hands—all these are right out of the record.

*Acting.* Dougal's narration must steer a cautious course between monotony on the one hand and emotionalization on the other. This is a confession, not a soliloquy: a statement, not a stream-of-consciousness. Once or twice, at certain turns in the story (especially when Dougal says, "I come now to a terrible part of my life"), our murderer may sag, may show the terrible strain at the seams of sanity. Even then the indication must be brief. Dougal has the innate stoicism of the British. The emotional repression and control that pulled him through the long, haunted years between crime and discovery also enabled him to tell his story graphically enough to give us the willies. Laughton's performance was a model of sublety and shading. At times he would brace himself, within a passage, to keep command of what he was saying. At other times he sounded almost apologetic, almost ashamed of certain details of his story—and he conveyed all of this by the most delicate kind of inflection and trimming.

The role of Miss Holland is far less demanding than that of Dougal, which is not to say it's a pushover. Elsa Lanchester, whose range of characterization is almost as

wide as her husband's, made the woman completely understandable, therefore deeply tragic. She was irascible and
determined; she wore the pants in the household. At times
she was scornful, as she had a right to be with a crook and
a drunkard like Dougal. But the essential softness of the
woman was there too—the quality that made even the cal-
lous Dougal say "otherwise she was not so bad"; the thing
in her that made her cry "very nearly the whole of one day"
over the incident of the servant girl; the impulse that made
her stop (in what to me is one of the most terribly poignant
moments of the story) to admire the beauty of the moon-
lit night, just a few seconds before she was to be murdered.
It seems plain that she never recovered from the death of
her lover in the boating accident; at least it is significant
that she never married.

*Sound.* When I was adapting this grisly business, I
thought to use sound not only for atmosphere, but punctuationally, to help relieve long stretches of narration. In rehearsal, I found to my surprise that sound was not necessary
at all times; that instead of helping to create mood, it sometimes surfeited our scene. This sort of thing is likely to
happen whenever speech is dynamically self-contained; that
is, whenever its images are so clear and provocative that no
help is needed from outside. Laughton's performance, trans-
cending as it did the written word, made it possible for
me to dispense with much of the sound. But since future
producers, especially in Wilkes-Barre and Mamaroneck, are
unlikely to be able to engage a Laughton, I have left the
sound directions as they were in the original working script.

Certain effects, often seemingly simple ones, are hell to
bring off. At the point where Dougal tries to revive Cecile
by splashing brandy over her face, we tried a dozen combinations of faces, microphones, and perspectives, without

success. Using a grapefruit for Cecile's face made too dull a sound; wooden objects were also dead (no jokes, please); I tried the soundman's own face, and poor Berne Surrey was almost drowned before I turned from him to a cocoanut wrapped in oilcloth. Here is where visualization has it all over unsupported sound: almost any halfway adequate splash would have been okay for a movie or television image, but the ear alone is not to be satisfied easily. There wasn't time enough to spend perfecting this detail; so I did what I am most reluctant ever to do in such circumstances: I gave up the search. Usually I allow enough time for sound rehearsals to take care of such matters, but we were in a jam for time that night, and the listener had to take Dougal's word that he poured brandy over Cecile's face.

Another effect that gave us trouble was the wrenching of the gold cross and chain from Cecile's neck. The snapping of a metal chain sounded like anything but the snapping of a metal chain. We finally worked it out by breaking a thin chicken bone close to the mike.

Now and then a grand piano can be of great help as an acoustical chamber, and I used it as such to create the ghostliest possible auspices for the return of Cecile's voice to the imagination of Dougal. The effect was produced by inviting Miss Lanchester to stick her head under the raised top of a Steinway and having her speak into a dynamic microphone placed against the sounding board. The sostenuto pedal was kept depressed, so that the voice, touching off a free mass vibration of piano strings, twanged and echoed and rang and throbbed. In the studio proper, the effect seems like nothing at all, but by proper amplification in the control room it can be made to sound most unpleasantly like the dead voice of that tax collector you murdered back of the barn last year.

The soundman had a triumph in this show, at the point where Dougal relives the shooting ("I could see myself . . . standing on the step and shooting her"). Here we put a pistol, instead of Miss Lanchester's talented head, under the piano top, and the impact and vibration of the report would have jolted a sleeping listener out of both sleep and a year's growth.

*Music.* Bernard Herrmann has written more great dramatic scores for radio than any other composer, and this was one of them. It was morbid as a morgue, and whatever in Dougal's narration did not raise goose pimples was taken over by the orchestra. The score was done in the same month as Herrmann's magnificent work for the Laughton broadcasts of Whitman and Wolfe and helped make the period one of the most prolific and successful in his career. Listeners and musicians who heard the shows will not soon forget Herrmann's contribution, nor will a grateful writer and director.

*Additional Notes.* 1. Here, in the original confession, Dougal repeated the adjective "mean." Laughton believed the word would be misunderstood by American listeners; that Dougal meant close, penurious, miserly, as the English use it. I argued that Dougal may well have used it in the American sense; so we split the difference, and used both adjectives.

2. There was a temptation to score this spot for sound, and at first I thought the effect of Dougal's practicing for the murder might convey something sinister, but I tried it in rehearsal and decided against it. It is best to keep the shot for a more dramatic entrance; to contain your thunder.

3. I had thought of accompanying this allusion with the sound of horse and buggy, but the reference is too brief, and the pattern would only collide with effects soon to follow.

This seems to me a good example of where to leave sound out of things. In a way the question is related to the abuse of the function of music in pictures—the kind that underscores every action. Music should not be cheapened by having to run upstairs or downstairs, to sit, stand, whirl, slide, step, bow, toss, and turn with every movement of an actor on the screen.

4. This is the first entrance of Cecile as a ghost. She is not a spirit bidden to a séance and does not speak balefully, with consciousness of ghosthood. She is a photographic image, wired for sound, in Dougal's imagination; therefore her speech and inflection are just as sharp in this reading as when she first spoke the line in the scene with the laborer.

5. This has great shock value and should be played with that in mind. Several correspondents said it was the high point of the play for them.

# NEW YORK: A TAPESTRY FOR RADIO

First produced on May 16, 1944, as the eleventh of the "Columbia Presents Corwin" series. Martin Gabel narrated. The musical score was composed by Frederick Steiner and conducted by Lyn Murray. The author directed.

It was repeated on July 24, 1945, with Orson Welles as Narrator.

# NEW YORK: A TAPESTRY FOR RADIO

*Music: An introduction descriptive of the annoyance of Fifth Avenue at having to cross Broadway in full view of Twenty-third Street.*

NARRATOR. The time on the four-faced Paramount clock says in quadruplicate that it is ten o'clock.

And so good evening to you, Queen of the Hemisphere—

Four times good evening—

And by this time tomorrow, may the enemies of all free men's metropolises be more desperate and damned than ever!—

End of salutation.

*Music: City motif, strong, heroic, like the façade of a well-made public building.*

NARRATOR. Let us acknowledge that you have a handsome profile, City of New York, and get that over with.

Long ago you were voted the most likely to succeed, and tonight the twelfth generation of Americans salutes you with the usual references to your size, industry, accomplishments, glitter, and grandeur; also with special reference to the populace that takes you for its lawful address: the Manhattanese, Brooklynites, Astorians,

311

Jamaicans, Bronxites, who think the rest
of the world is all right to visit, but who
wouldn't want to live anyplace but here.

This tapestry, being dimensioned by a half-
hour of your time and the arbitrary limits
of the city,
Has for its warp the Avenues and for its weft
the crosstown Streets
(The shuttle traveling back and forth, as
you'd expect, between Grand Central and
Times Square) ;
As for loom, that's what ships do on the horizons of the city practically continuously
(In which connection God bless our navy and
the ships of the merchant marine, as well
as the Port of New York Authority, and
sailors of the National Maritime Union,
346 West Seventeenth Street).

So much for bobbin, shuttle, loom, and weft.
Regarding individual threads, you will have to
follow them by listening acutely,
For there will be excursions and motifs,
snatches of native song and speech, time
signals, bulletins, reflections, and footsteps,
To say nothing of the retirement of batters at
first base and of ballerinas from ballet at
the age of forty.

However, the main design is in the middle
And will be clear enough when you stand back
and see the whole.

The people of the city are the main design—
The names in the directories, but for the grace
  of whom the place becomes an empty
  mesa and a pincushion of stone,
A petrified island of forgotten dividends and
  cobwebs in the elevator shafts.
What that design is, you citizens of sister
  cities, you hearers on the plains and up-
  lands,
Sit still and listen.
It well may be a special hope, a pattern of
  felicity to and to your kids,
To fetuses conceived this month and next and
  ever after.
That, as I say, comes later.
But it's in the weave, if you will stay and look
  it over with us in a certain light.

*Music: Jollity in the park in the month of May.*

MILLIE. Hey, Peggy, look who just come outa that store—
Robert Montgomery, in a *uniform!*
BERTHA. So what do you want me to do, break a leg?
NARRATOR. Pick any street in the city from First to Two
  Hundred Forty-first and take it over to
  the laboratory for an X ray.
  You will find, on developing both the film and
  yourself,
  That the corpus wears a top hat though its
  toes stick out;
  That there are present all the elemental back-
  bone virtues of the species (being neither
  better nor worse in this regard than
  Keokuk cross-sectioned);

That sin and sickness appear as shadows on
the plate—nothing extraordinary about
that, is there, Doctor?—

And that all the typical figurations of love,
hate, fear, passion, tribulation, joy, grief,
are clearly marked and evident.

SAM. Hello, Shorty. What's cookin'?

SHORTY. What's cookin'? Nothin's cookin'.

SAM. What do you hear from your boy?

SHORTY. Who, Manny?

SAM. Yeah, Manny.

SHORTY. What I hear from Manny? He's in the South
Pacific, that's what I hear from Manny.

SAM. Is he been in any fightin'?

SHORTY. Is he been in any *fightin'?* You see this handkerchief?

SAM. Yeah.

SHORTY. So I'm blowin' my nose in it.

SAM. So what?

SHORTY. So it comes from a dead Jap officer, that's what.

NARRATOR. Do not underestimate these people, for they
are you.

Do not hate them because the Yankees keep on
winning forever. There will come a team
out of Cleveland, one day, or Boston.

Do not mistrust them because of their accent,
for we ourselves might be incomprehensible in Oxford.

LULU. So I says to him: "Sure, I'll miss you. Like poison
I'll miss you," I says to him. "If you want to see how
much I'll miss you, just stick your finger in the pond
at Central Park and then pull it out and look at the
hole."

NARRATOR. One feature you will notice, straightaway, is
the congestion.

From German Yorkville to outlying Latin
Quarters, lebensraum is nil.

This is true as well of the areas of ritz and
pâté de foie gras,

For even on those avenues where fingerbowls
with lilies in them must precede the
coffee . . .

HOST. Have a spot of brandy, Edgar?

NARRATOR. . . . the next-door neighbor breathes down
your incinerator shaft.

You can't get the real truth about it in an al-
manac.

The guidebooks can go only so far.

They're candid enough about how the local
girl made good. But just where in the
index is the guy who jumped out of a
window because he couldn't take it?

SUICIDE. Take somebody your size, New York!

NARRATOR. The wind off the river may be an authority on
conditions in New Jersey or even in Ohio,

But what does it know about a meeting of
stockholders at 1 Wall Street at three
this afternoon?

TREASURER. . . . total surplus and capital stock, gentlemen . . .

NARRATOR. What knowledge of the shish kebab, stuffed
grape and cabbage leaves, baklava, halva
available in the Syrian district?

How can the Congressional Limited, which
goes only as far as Penn Station, know
about the beauty of the women, about

the current exhibition of Cuban art, about the politics of Williamsburgh?

CITIZEN. Go fight City Hall. That's what I says to him. He got no answer.

NARRATOR. How can you tell, from Seat No. 5 on the plane from Pittsburgh, what goes on here?

*Plane sounds in, under last phrase.*

NARRATOR. Put your nose to the cold window and look out over the starboard wing. Already you're within the city, though it's still ten minutes to LaGuardia. There's the harbor, crinkled under the influences of a bland wind; the statue of Our Lady of the Freedoms a green speck in the blue bay; and the downtown cluster of real estate standing cool and reasonable above the vapors. . . .

*Fade motors under:*

NARRATOR. What can you tell, from such an altitude, of the clip joints and the subway jams and clinics?

Of cabbage in wholesale markets and of kings in exile? [1]

Of time and of the river?

Of star performances at the Hayden Planetarium?

Dost know anything of the historic import of these parts?

HISTORIAN. George Gershwin slept here.

NARRATOR. Of flower salesmen brightening the night?

[1] The numbered notes will be found on pages 335-338.

SALESMAN. Get your gar-denias. Get your fresh gar-
denias![2]

NARRATOR. Of exports and imports of the port (aside
from ammunition for our Allies, and reverse lend-
lease)?[3]

DELLA CIOPPA. If you wisha very fina caciotella, latticini,
mozzarella, ricotta, provola affumicata—justa come to
B. Della Cioppa,[4] 1275 Bleecker Streeta, inna Village.

NARRATOR. Of the telephone exchanges—the Indians with
feathers?

AL. ALgonquin 4 . . .

NARRATOR. And fat old Dutchmen.

STYE. STuyvesant 9-9598?[5]

NARRATOR. And Spanish gold.

EL. ELdorado 5, please.

NARRATOR. And Englishmen at play?

BO. I'm calling Bowling Green 9-2291.

NARRATOR. Salut au monde!

O Whitman! Whitman! Of Manhattan the
son! Where are you tonight, Walt Whitman? We ask of you a sentiment about
this place. A line that we can quote for our
broadcast.

WHITMAN. A great city is that which has the greatest men
and women.[6]

NARRATOR. We thank you; we thank you in behalf of the
conjoined creeds—the Jew, the Christian, the Moham-
medan, the speakers of the foreign and the ancient
tongues. . . .

*Music: Under the Narrator is faded in a cathedral
organ, which comes up full and then sustains behind:*

PRIEST (*chanting*). Exaudi quaesumus Domine, supplicum preces, et confitentium tibi parce pecoatis: ut pariter nobis indulgentiam tribuas benignus et pacem. Ineffabilem nobis, Domine, misericordiam tuam clementer ostende: (*fading*) ut simul nos et a peccatis omnibus exuas, et a poenis, quas pro his meremur, eripias. . . .[7]

*Music: Comes down as voice fades; out, behind the Narrator.*

NARRATOR. Lord God of Hosts, there are very many voters in this town.

Your angels would be doing well to know the names of half of them.

It is beyond the power of certified public accountants to follow all the comings and goings of the people to and fro and up and down, especially on week ends and around October first.

Only the Lord Himself could tell just what a man from Harlem thinks this moment, riding downtown on the Eighth Avenue express.

Only a surpassing and great Omniscience could keep close track of things in all five boroughs, including Richmond.

Yea, even the hushed transepts of the church itself might confuse any but the Highest,

What with the differences in ritual between the Seventh-Day Adventist Ephesians (West One Hundred Twenty-third Street), the Abyssinian Baptists (One Hundred

Thirty-eighth), and the Chinese First
Presbyterians (Thirty-first Street, East).[8]

*Music: Love on brownstone stoop at three in the
morning after an evening at the RKO Proctor Theater*[9] *and a long walk in the park. It sustains, behind:*

GIRL. Good night, darling. Will you call me in the
morning?

BOY. You mean I can't come in for a while?

GIRL. No, my mother's sleeping in the front room.

BOY. Well, let's stay here on the steps a while, huh?

GIRL. But I have to punch a clock on Canal Street at nine
in the morning.

BOY. Well, how about me? I hafta be back at camp.

GIRL. Well, all right, Ted. Just for a little while.

BOY. Bess— (*Pause.*)

GIRL. But you'll get lipstick all over you.

BOY. I'll take that chance. (*Pause.*)

NARRATOR. The season of spring has returned from a
winter in South America

And has already had certain intimacies with
the trees of the public and private parks,
as well as with the flowers and grasses
thereof.[10]

It has also appeared in various guises, mostly
beguiling, but occasionally overcast, with
prevailing northeasterly winds.

However, on sunny days—somewhat hazy in
the morning, clear by noon—

It stands leering outside office windows;

It consorts with all manner of washing hung on
all manner of lines;

It fishes for pennies in the gratings of subways
And is generally pleased with itself, all the way
from the Canarsie marshes to the Yonkers line.

*Music: Hurdy-gurdy has begun to fade in under the last [11] line. It comes up, establishes, and sustains briefly behind:*

BARD.    Go down to Kew Gardens in lilac time, in lilac time, in lilac time; [12]
Go down to Kew Gardens in lilac time (it isn't far from Manhattan!) and it can be reached easily by taking an E train on the Independent Fifty-third Street line, or a BMT from Times Square, or if you want to spend more than a nickel, you can take the Long Island Railroad from Penn Station.

*Music: Hurdy-gurdy fades.*

EDNA. Well, I finally told him.

BLANCHE. What do you mean, you finally told him?

EDNA. He says I only develop an interest in an individual if he happens to be socially conscious.

BLANCHE. Believe me, that's some nerve!

EDNA. Personally, I think it's a compliment. It's a privilege to be socially conscious.

BLANCHE. Certainly, after all, it's a very important time in history.

EDNA. Why, sure, history's being *made!*

BLANCHE. Every day.

EDNA. So I said to him, I told him, "Harry, you should *read* more!"

*Music: Sudden upsweep.*

NARRATOR. Oh, Charlie, what's the score, and who's in
there pitching?
Come on, Charlie, give us a flash from the ball
park . . .

*Fade in background of a ball game. Hold it behind:*

NARRATOR. . . . where the crowd is cheering a base hit to
right by Mahool,
Sending Buxton home with the tying run.

Ah, yes, Charlie, it is well to relax
And a fellow needs to get out,
But will you not turn to the young Jew beside
you,
He being a flier of the Bronx, home on con-
valescent leave,
And cheer him for making a base hit too—
The base being in Germany, and the hit being
right down the alley?
Did he not send a bombing run across the
plate?
How can you tell the players without a score
card, Charlie?
Look at the ribbons on his chest, and drop that
subscription to the Brooklyn Fascist
paper [13] you've been reading!
The game is almost over, Bud, and the All
Stars are ahead.

*Music: In praise of the All Stars—a fine and meaning-
ful flourish for nations united.*

SPANIARD (*with importance; an announcement*). La Flor
  del Bagio—Bodega y Carneceria!

NARRATOR. Groceries and meats, to you, in Spanish
  Harlem.

SPANIARD. Dulces y refrescos tropicales . . .

NARRATOR. Little Spain, out of islands Caribbean, and
              southerly from there—
        Nicaragua, Colombia, Bolivia, the Argen-
          tine. . . .
        A hundred thousand people speaking Spanish,
        A city Pan-American within a city.
        And further up the line?

HARLEM. (*Street cry, faded on.*)

NARRATOR. Negro Harlem listens to a street cry and it
              hears a boogie-woogie piano playing a
              little 'riginal composition down there in
              the Ace of Clubs. . . .

  *Music: Boogie-woogie piano, like he say, retarding
  under:*

NARRATOR. But it ain't just song and honeysuckle, neigh-
              bor:
        It's a place of homes and shops, and it contains
          the biggest Negro concentration in the
          world.
        And if you take the trouble to go down and
          interview the older docks and slips along
          the island,
        They will point out the ghosts of rusty, weath-
          ered piers where once fat, crowded slave
          ships put in from profitable hunting
          grounds of Africa—

> How many wars ago?
> Well, off these same Manhattan shores to-
> night, the warships of the reunited states
> ride at anchor,
> And men of Harlem are aboard.

*Music: A sock cue.*

WOMAN. I got a V-letter from my boy in India yesterday, and he says he visited the Taj Mahal, but for his money it don't come up anyway near to the Empire State Building.

NARRATOR. In three-quarters of a million New York win-
> dows of all sizes and conditions,
> The service star gives notice to the passer-by
> That each has sent a delegate to the conven-
> tion of the nations
> With instructions to shoot on sight.
> Fire and blood are first on the agenda;
> And, participating in the various contests
> (East Side, West Side, all around the
> world)
> Is the Swede from Bruckner Avenue.

SWEDE. Hey, will ya tell Hulda to send me a picture of the baby? Here I got a kid two years old, and I ain't seen him yet!

NARRATOR. And the muscular Greek corporal from Twenty-fifth Street.

GREEK. Look, when you go back, will you tell 'em what we'd like is Crosby records and a transcription of a Fred Allen show? [14] Personally I'd appreciate a couple of snappy pin-up girls and a good hot dish of stafádo.

NARRATOR. And Captain O'Mahoney of Flatbush, moral stockholder of the Brooklyn Dodgers.

O'MAHONEY (*singing, to the tune of "Kathleen"*):
    We'll bomb you once again, Ber-leen,
    You'll wish you had of stood in bed,
    We'll give it to you on the bean,
    Two-ton shillelahs on your head. . . .

NARRATOR. O G.I. Joe, of Manhattan the son,
    Your father came to the city on a big white
        ship, or a dirty tramp, or a cattle boat,
        and the ship had a name;
    But you have slipped down the Hudson in the
        night on a gray ship, nameless, the hour
        likewise anonymous, the compass-bearing
        sealed inside an envelope.

    The city of immigrants has emigrated to the
        wars,
    The borscht and the pastrami, the feinkuchen
        and smörgåsbord,
    Patiently await the last communiqué.
    Meanwhile Nostrand Avenue is deeply inter-
        ested in the eastward course of landing
        barges,
    And a Staten Island ferryful absorbs the eve-
        ning paper for the latest dope from
        Wewak.[15]

    *Music: A cue of hopeful green stuff woven. It comes
in softly and backs the Narrator's next speech.*

NARRATOR. Americans on this wave length:
    Can you make out the bright green threads
        among the lesser colors in this tapestry?
    The interwoven hopes of those who turn the
        turnstiles?

The dreams held by commuters to the well-
kept lawns of Scarsdale and of Greenwich?

Tune in on Sunnyside, canvass the gashouse
and the garment districts,

Take a poll of visions on Park Avenue, Hell's
Kitchen, and the Bowery.

You will see they're not so far apart.

Just hold the hopes up to a light, one at a
time—

From Lenox Avenue, for instance.

MOTHER. I just want my boy to come home, that's all, on
his own two feet—and with the war won so's it'll stay
won.

NARRATOR. From Talman Street, near Jay.

FATHER. I'd like to see my way clear to be able to afford
a bathtub in this house.

NARRATOR. From West New Brighton.

EXECUTIVE. Won't it be grand to be able to fly in from
Westport every morning in a helicopter?

NARRATOR. From Ninth Street and Avenue D, above the
garage.

GIRL. The whole city—if it could only look like the park
along Riverside Drive, huh? Rollerskating, and
handball and tennis courts, and grass and trees? All
new houses instead of these old tenements—boy, won't
that be something?

NARRATOR. From Sutton Place south, by the whistling
tugs.

BIG SHOT. Just think, Paul—your branch office in Shanghai,
thirty-six hours across the north pole—Pelham Bay to
Liverpool in twelve!

NARRATOR. Can a song of hope be sung by the graduating
class of P.S. 186?
Arranged for symphonic orchestra and choir,
and performed at Carnegie?
Danced to at Roseland?
Given the works by Melchior at the Met?
Could be, gentlemen. Could be. Many a hit
tune has come from Broadway!
Uptown on the down beat, lads,
And take it away!

*Music: The hope theme up with a flourish, and out
precipitously.*

NARRATOR. City of Ginsberg and Garibaldi, Koslowski and
López,
What are you doing on St. Patrick's Day?
Marching, of course, down Fifth Avenue.
And what are you doing on San Gennaro's
day?
Dancing, of course . . .

*Music: Neapolitan folksong in, and behind:*

NARRATOR. . . . along Mulberry Street
(The rumor being there are more Italians in
New York than in Napoli,
Or Roma, or Firenze),
And the candles on this day (this year) burn
brightly for the martyred saint;
And though the sweetmeats would be sweeter
far if Frankie and Pasquale were home
from Anzio,
They taste pretty good as they are, blessed
be the Virgin Mary.

*Music: The folksong is alone for a while, and then it segues to a French tune. This holds under two lines, then cross-fades to a solo guitar.*

NARRATOR. And on Bastille Day,
    The French Republic's Independence Day,
        hardly a fortnight further into summer
        than our own,
    The tricolor is flown beside the flag that La-
        fayette, a lend-lease general, helped us to
        get started,
    Whereas Hungarians and Czechs, and Ger-
        mans, Hindus, Balkans, Portuguese and
        Danes,
    They have their little cities-within-the-city,
        too:
    Their churches and their restaurants and gift
        shops, movie houses, newspapers, and
        foreign-language programs on the
        radio. . . .

*Music: By this time the guitar has prepared us for some good flamenco vocalizing, which we hear in the clear, as though through the courtesy of Manische-witz's matzoth, over WBNX.*

NARRATOR. Is there by any chance on the island tonight
    A visiting fireman from Kansas City who
        knows somebody in Washington with con-
        nections in London?
    If so, would he kindly take a message to the
        next peace conference—
    The one that G.I. Joseph of Eighty-second
        Street is at the moment fighting to ar-
        range—

And see that there is smuggled in among the
    representatives

The mere hint of the barest memorandum of a
    notion?

Something for their scratch pads, to be
    scrawled upon and doodled over during
    deepest thought?

A mark, a democratic imprint, a U. S. figura-
    tion, a Yankee doodle?

This is what it is:

Here in the tall city with the British name,

The people of all nations checkering the num-
    bered streets,

Having come from Warsaw, having come from
    Plymouth, Kleinvardine, and Chungking,

Having come from Africa and Oslo and
    Caracas,

Having worked and played and voted, loved
    and listened to the radio,

Fought in the wars and paid for them as well,

Having kept their customs and their languages,
    played their own sweet music on the fiddle
    and accordion—

Did nevertheless find time to rear and populate
    the greatest city in the world

And make of it a symbol celebrated up and
    down the longitudes.

You see, it can be done!

Yea, make a note of that: it can be done.

You have it on the solemn word and deed of all
    five boroughs, gentlemen,

That nothing is impossible.

Do but consult the main design and see, in
     miniature,
The nations living side by side so effortlessly,
     no one calls it peace;
Yea, block to block and house to house and
     door to door
They get along—
With scraps betimes, a little botheration such
     as happens in the best of families,
But never anything a court or free election
     can't take care of.

Now, then:
You want to buy a rug?
Very fine, a bargain, genuine American?
Then take a look at this:
Oriental in parts, but all the compass points
     come into it;
And see: the main design—is that a hope, or
     isn't it?
A hope that out of little people, greatnesses?
And towering accomplishments?
Rapid transits to tomorrow morning?
And fraternity along the Grand Concourse?

Ahoy, the century ahead!
Announce it in lights above Broadway,
And post it in the Public Library!

Workers, lovers, kids and patriots near and
     far along the main stream and lesser
     eddies of the network,
Greetings from the city!
Greetings, greetings!

*Music: Finale.*

# NEW YORK: A TAPESTRY FOR RADIO

You are expected in the city, if you have not already been there. The day of the American who has lived all his life in Oklahoma, or who has never been to New York, is in its twilight. The war took millions of men who had never been outside their own counties and shuffled them about the country and the world. Planes, trains, ships, buses, and parkways converge on New York from the damnedest places, from blessed places, from indifferent places.

When I began writing this script in the spring of 1944, using Central Park as my office, I thought of approaching the subject as a traveler approaches the city—on a bus, perhaps, resting his head against an antimacassar, reviewing the smelly meadows of Elizabeth (a city in New Jersey) as the telephone poles whoosh by; and the bus, gross as a hippopotamus but painted to look streamlined as a raindrop, bears on down U.S. 1, past Newark airport. Suddenly it scoots up a ramp with a flutter of exhaust and buzzes along the Pulaski Skyway toward the Holland Tunnel.

Or else the visitor would approach by rail, gliding southward along a bank of the Hudson—wondering, as he takes the big curve at Bear Mountain, what such handsome Rhenish scenery is doing so close to his destination. Or northward from Baltimore, he would see the panoramic backsides of Philadelphia and Trenton and count the creeks and rivers crossed in flight. Or he would descend through Bridgeport on the Sound—riding a noon express out of

Boston. And if he were to approach by ship . . . et cetera, et cetera.

I toyed with these thoughts for a while and finally gave them up. Then I walked many a mile around the duck pond, and watched seals being fed at the Zoo (there's one that would make a better shortstop than some I've seen at the Polo Grounds), and tramped over hill and dale and circled the site of the razed pagoda and sat on the rocks and admired the pretty girls and basked in the spring sun and cursed my time and medium and dodged bicycles and fed squirrels and suddenly hit on the tapestry idea. After that I felt better.

There are a thousand approaches to the subject of New York, and all have been thoroughly explored. My choice of the tapestry concept was dictated, as so many of my pieces have been, by considerations of the moment. The advocates of world unity were having tough sledding (as they have always had; as they have this very day), and I was convinced that every kind word said in their behalf, every argument advanced, was to the good of all except those who are happiest only when hotly sniffing for a war. The columnists and commentators who were later to pull for the failure of the San Francisco Conference were then busy sniping at Washington and our Allies and labor and the Atlantic Charter and everything else that was constructive and hopeful. It almost seemed that to believe in Victory was a subversion; that Unity was a Communist concept financed by Moscow gold. They were ready to skin Roosevelt and Willkie alive, not to mention Stalin and Churchill. But how did they feel about the seditionists on trial in Washington? "Elderly male defendants of the 'Village Atheist' stripe," wrote one of them. The same man who had attacked Roosevelt as a "double-crosser . . .

a somewhat shabby and tricky gent, with a broad streak of hypocrisy and mouthing the noble drool of a charlatan," went on to uphold Liz Dilling, Winrod, and other indicted Fascists for "insisting on their native-born privilege as free white Americans to raise hell with upholders of accepted traditions, and, out of pure deviltry, to be different or at least have the fun of indulging a martyr complex."

Against such mass-circulated poison it was important for every writer and artist of good will to offer antidotes. Though I did not write "New York" as an *answer* to any columnist or newspaper, nor even think of it primarily as a crusading piece, I certainly had the local enemy in mind.

The choice of the tapestry theme—a tapestry of peoples —in one way narrowed the compass of the script; in another, widened it. It helped me to winnow and discard, as inconsequential, hundreds of notes I had written when I was compressing what I knew and felt about the city into three or four pages of memoranda. And at the same time I was able to broaden the implications well beyond the city's limits.

I shall resist the temptation here to compare New York with other cities or to spring into a general essay. Just take it from me, if you have not already taken it from somebody else or from your own observation: there is nothing like New York anywhere in the world. It is not only the particular symbol of a heterogenial population, but the symbol as well of everything and anything else by which a city gets to be a metropolis.

*Acting.* Martin Gabel, of whom more is said in the notes to "On a Note of Triumph," narrated the original production. A year later, I repeated the program from Hollywood, with Orson Welles in the role. Recordings of the two broadcasts would make an interesting study in techniques

and styles for students of acting and direction. Both inter-
pretations were affirmative and challenging. Gabel gave it a
youthful impetuousness; Welles, a mature and philosophic
quality. Gabel shaped scenes, Welles concentrated on lines.
From a standpoint of virtuosity it would be like comparing
Horowitz with Rubinstein—each of them a master, each
going his own way, each eminently listenable.

Some of the incidental characters beg to be caricatured,
but I urge you to deny them this. Millie and Bertha and
Lulu are from the Bronx and Brooklyn, and they talk the
way they are written. But there is no need to out-Kober
Kober. Those who remember Katherine Locke's incom-
parable Teddy in *Having Wonderful Time* know that the
true portrait of a borough belle lies considerably this side
of all-out comedy. There was depth and poignance in Miss
Locke's portrait, as well as a brilliant humor.

Sam and Shorty are a couple of tough cab drivers, the
kind who, if they get into an argument with another cabbie
or a truck driver, think nothing of stopping traffic to hop
out and slug one another in the middle of Third Avenue.
The Boy and Girl on the brownstone stoop are any boy
and girl, and you don't need to go looking for an accent.
Not everybody in New York says goil and berl and soit'ny
and pernt.

*Sound*. This is an easy night for the soundman, and he
can pick his teeth or read the basic writings of Sigmund
Freud throughout the rehearsal and air show, except when
he is flying us in from Pittsburgh or giving the narrator a
background of a cheering crowd at the ball game. We used
the actual effect of a baseball crowd, because it sounds unlike any other. The disc had on it the clear crack of a bat
hitting a ball, and it was a simple matter to goose the volume of the crowd to bear out the Narrator's report that

the crowd cheered a base hit by Mahool, sending Buxton home with the tying run.

*Music.* Frederick Steiner composed a warm and indigenous score, which leaned toward the blues and had rich Gershwinesque color. Lest anybody worry about the literalness of my direction for the introductory passage, that is only my way of torturing composers.

For the Neapolitan song indicated in the passage beginning "City of Ginsberg and Garibaldi," Steiner arranged "Funiculi, Funicula," and, as a prelude to the French allusion ("And on Bastille Day"), segued from the lively Italian tune to a pensive and autumnal variation on "Il y Avait une Petite Bergère."

The hurdy-gurdy effect swimming up out of the passage on spring in New York was one that involved half of Manhattan before we were through with it. In the world's greatest city, my secret operatives cruised for hours trying to find a hurdy-gurdy man. Finally, two days before the broadcast, they located one and brought him to the studio. He spoke no English, and I spoke no Italian. I phoned Columbia's short-wave department for an emergency Italian interpreter, and among us we spent an hour auditioning for the right song, going over matters of compensation, rehearsal time, transportation to the studio, and other such sordid details, which come under the heading of radio production. Our talent nodded and approved and understood everything we said, but never showed up for rehearsal. Richard Sanville, whose relationship to my control room was that of the Canadian Mounted Police to the Dominion of Canada, took the hurdy-gurdy as his responsibility. He combed the hurdy-gurdy belt of lower Manhattan, and although he never found the original *man,* he did find a hurdy-gurdy. Somehow the Theater Guild was mixed up in it. Sanville knew that John Wildberg of the Guild knew a man who knew an actor who knew where to get in touch with a hurdy-gurdy player who had once appeared in a Guild play, and the chase was on. All I know is that a wheezy and off-key hurdy-gurdy appeared out of the great nowhere of New York ten minutes before the program went on the air. The effect lasted fifteen seconds, and I will thank you not to ask whether it was worth the trouble.

In the New York broadcast, the guitar and voice of Tana de Gamez performed the flamenco music leading into the peroration, but in the Hollywood production, Charles Lewin, on reconnaissance patrol, could locate nothing resembling a flamenco singer; so we settled for a cantillating Arab. The script's direction for this spot is unnecessarily bizarre, inasmuch as Manischewitz's matzoth would have few customers among the Spanish-speaking or flamenco-singing population. But WBNX (BNX for Bronx) *is* one of the stations in Greater New York that specialize in foreign-language broadcasts. I sometimes tune them in for the amusement of hearing commercials I can't understand.

*Additional Notes.* 1. During the war the city was host to many European refugees, some of them members of the nobility. But most of the counts and princes sought the more temperate climate of Hollywood, and that was all very fine, except that it annoyed antiroyalists like myself to be dining or working somewhere and hear a public-address loudspeaker paging "Prince Mufti—you are wanted on the telephone. Prince Mufti. Telephone." Can't they leave off titles in deference to our democratic tastes? How would it be if we, visiting in their courts, were paged as "Citizen Jones" or "Republican Smith"? A small prejudice, perhaps, but when the prince is called to the telephone seven times in a half-hour, it does get to be a bore.

2. This is an actual character who sells gardenias in the Times Square district. He was discovered by Edward Mayehoff and gathered into the rich catalogue of Broadway types that Mayehoff, in documentary and vastly entertaining fashion, collected between Fortieth and Fiftieth Streets. The line is sung in a loud growl, and the "gar" of "gardenias" has the value of a whole note. The delivery should sound almost as though the salesman were swearing, and indeed the prototype himself often shocks passers-by when he makes his "gar" sound as if it were on its way to being "gahdamn."

3. A topical allusion. About this time, the isolationist press was taking pot-shots at lend-lease, and the Administration was reminding us that, aside from giving us blood and victories, some of the Allies were actually sending "reverse lend-lease." The later reference to LaFayette as a lend-lease general was meant to be another cartridge in the same clip.

4. Pronounced "Choppa," as in the name of the distinguished Guy Della-Cioppa of CBS.

5. There is a rule that no real telephone number may be used fictionally on the air. The Stuyvesant and Bowling Green numbers were furnished us by the telephone company. You'll get a sweet voice on the telephone if you dial either one, but it will be a special operator asking you who do you think you're calling.

6. From "Song of Myself" in *Leaves of Grass*.

7. Part of the Litany of the Saints appearing in *A Manual of Prayers for the Use of the Catholic Laity*. It translates:

Graciously hear, we beseech Thee, O Lord, the prayers of Thy humble servants, and forgive the sins of those who confess to Thee; that, in Thy bounty, Thou mayest grant us both pardon and peace.

Show forth upon us, O Lord, in Thy mercy, Thine unspeakable pity; that Thou mayest both loose us from all our sins, and deliver us from the punishments which we deserve for the same.

8. There are many colorful and exotic church names in New York, of which these three are fair examples. Others: Church of the Most Precious Blood, Church of St. Benedict the Moor, St. Illuminator's Armenian Apostolic Church, Iglesia Metodista Episcopal Church, New Dorp Moravian Church, L'Église Française du Saint-Esprit, St. Ann's Church for Deaf-Mutes, St. Mark's-in-the-Bouwerie, Memorial Church of the Huguenots.

9. The RKO Proctor Theater was on my mind at the time this script was written, because three or four times a week, without fail, I would be awakened by a ringing telephone early in the morning (after working until 4 A.M.) by middle-aged housewives asking what time the feature went on. My number was one digit away from the theater's number. I fought it out with the New York Telephone Company until they changed my listing.

10. The spring of 1944 in New York was the kind that would make a poet of a traffic cop. It burst upon the burg like an inspiration. Day after day of bright, sunny skies, and balm in the air, and impatient buds busting out all over. April, usually cold and rainy and disagreeable, was full of sparkle and flash. Something went wrong as a result of this magnificence, because the following summer was the most unrelenting and terrible since the Indians.

11. Better isolate the hurdy-gurdy, because it makes a penetrating sound and cannot be faded on and off physically with relation to the Narrator.

12. A glancing parody of Alfred Noyes's poem, "The Barrel Organ," whose refrain is, "Go down to Kew in lilac time." Kew Gardens is a pleasant suburb, in the Middle

Queens (Long Island), within subway reach of Manhattan. It was actually named after the Royal Botanical Gardens at Kew in England. If you intend to broadcast the passage over a network, you had better clear it with Noyes's American agent, who at the time of this writing was David Lloyd. That's what I had to do. Go on, you need the exercise.

13. Namely, the *Brooklyn Tablet*.

14. The allusion was not haphazard. I based it on official reports of the requests of soldiers overseas.

15. Wewak was in the news at the time this was written. The Pacific war moved so fast between the first and second broadcasts that the reference was changed to read "Tokyo" in the 1945 version.

# TEL AVIV

GUS. Nice break for Doug Adams, huh?

ED. Who's he?

GUS. He's that young country editor picked by a syndicate to go around the world.

ED. Never heard of him.

GUS. Well, you will tonight.

ED. Howzat?

GUS. By listening to the radio.

ED. Listening to what on the radio?

ANNOUNCER. To this program. It seems that one afternoon (*fading*) at an airport in Cairo, Egypt, two American newspapermen . . .[1]

*Music: An introduction, which takes you there.*

QUIZ. Hey, Doug, get a load of the leftenant.

ADAMS. What about the leftenant?

QUIZ. Pretty cute, ain't she?

ADAMS. Yes, pretty cute. Now let me finish writing this cable, will you?

QUIZ. I wonder if she's taking the plane to Tel Aviv with us?

ADAMS (*abstractedly*). Could be.

QUIZ. Doug—how long is the flight from here to Tel Aviv? . . . Doug? Dja hear me?

ADAMS (*looking at a schedule*). Lessee—timetable—Cairo to Lydda—that's the airport for Tel Aviv—(*mumbling*) Jerusalem . . . Haifa . . . Beirut . . . here

---

[1] The numbered notes will be found on pages 371-373.

it is. Flight 21, Cairo-Lydda, two hours and twenty-five minutes.

QUIZ. I wouldn't mind if it was two hours and twenty-five *days* as long as that babe's in the party. *There's* my idea of a beautiful dame!

ADAMS. Don't you ever think of anything else but beautiful dames?

QUIZ. Sure. Passable dames.

ADAMS. Just a wolf in wolf's clothing, that's all you are. Why don't you fall in love with a girl sometime?

QUIZ. My dear Adams, can I help it if my interests are purely—

AIRPORT LOUDSPEAKER. Attention, passengers on Flight 21 for Lydda, Haifa, and Beirut: Departure has been delayed one hour. Flight 21 will leave at approximately 13:30.

QUIZ (*getting up to go*). Well, an hour to kill, eh? In that case I think I'll lose no further time striking up an acquaintance with that—

ADAMS. Hey, wait a minute, Romeo. C'mere. Sit down.

QUIZ. Leave us not pull my coat tail, willya?

ADAMS (*sitting Quiz down*). Why don't you spend this hour striking up an acquaintance with the Hebrew language, seeing as how we're going to a Jewish city? You'll get along better with Tel Aviv if you take some time with this handbook.

QUIZ (*grumbling*). Aagh—I know plennya Hebrew: aleph, baze, vaze, gimbel, dullard, kibitz, schlemiel, guniff, kosher, gefilte fish, Yehudi Menuhin. . . .

ADAMS. Splendid. You have a remarkable command of pidgin Yiddish . . .

QUIZ. Thank you.

ADAMS. . . . which has so little to do with the Hebrew

language, it wouldn't do you any harm to spend an hour with this booklet.

QUIZ. Why can't I read it later?

ADAMS. Won't do you any harm to get a general idea of the city before you get in trouble there, as you undoubtedly will.

QUIZ. Oh, well, all right, if it'll make you happy I'll *read* the thing. (*Grumbling.*) Gotta do homework yet— good pictures ain't enough, gotta be a linguist. . . .

ADAMS (*reading cable*). Lessee now—lemme count the words in this cable. (*Mumbling cablese to himself.*) "Forster Consolsyndic USA filing 3000 extelaviv Wednite thence Moscow via Teheran . . ." [2]

QUIZ (*his nose in the handbook*). Hey, Doug?

ADAMS. Yuh?

QUIZ. Ain't the Jews supposed to be one of the oldest peoples in the world, if not *the* oldest?

ADAMS. Yes, why?

QUIZ. Then how does it happen the biggest all-Jewish city in the world is just thirty-five years old?

ADAMS. Well—that's a long story, Quiz. (*He ponders for a moment; then:*) Y'see, it's like this . . .

*Music: We assume Adams will have brought Quiz up to date on the saga of the Jews before the plane leaves, and the music at this point covers up not only an excursion into history but the flight to Lydda. In any case, our correspondents are now in a hotel room in Tel Aviv, as we discover in the following scene:*

ADAMS. What's the matter, are you in a daze?

QUIZ (*very much so*). Huh? Oh—oh, no, I'm fine.

ADAMS. Then put down your bag and take off your hat. You're *here*. You've arrived.

QUIZ. I was just thinking about something.

ADAMS. Well, I hope you're out of the trances before Christmas.[3]

QUIZ. Nice room, ain't it?

DOUG (*off*). Yeah. Pull the blinds, will ya, while I hang up these coats?

QUIZ. Okay.

*Up with the Venetian blinds.*

QUIZ. Hey, lookit *this,* Doug!

ADAMS (*still off*). What is it?

QUIZ. Practically all of Tel Aviv from this window.

ADAMS (*coming on*). Hey, this *is* a swell view! Did you ever see bluer water than that?

QUIZ. And looka that white beach, will ya? Blue and white!

ADAMS. You don't have to fall out of the window, son.

QUIZ. But looka them white houses against that blue sky! Doug, if you saw that in a painting you wouldn't believe it.

ADAMS (*going off*). I might. Depends on the painter.

QUIZ. Like a technicolor picture! Pantachrome B 101.[4] Everything blue and white! Primitive colors!

ADAMS (*amused*). Saay—I've never seen *you* in such a froth, Quiz—what's come over you?

QUIZ. Huh? Why? Whatsa matter?

ADAMS (*in a kidding tone*). There's a different look in your eyes ever since we landed at Lydda. What's going on here?

QUIZ. Well—I—uh—nothing. Why?

ADAMS. Out with it, Quisinberry.

QUIZ. Out with what?

ADAMS. Did you fall for that girl officer on the plane or something?

QUIZ (*a little quivery*). Fall for the girl officer on the plane?

ADAMS. You sat next to her all the way up from Cairo, looking at her like a lovesick calf. What's her name?

QUIZ. Aviva Hashahav.

ADAMS. Egyptian?

QUIZ. No, Jewish. She's a member of the British ATS. Sort of a British Wac.

ADAMS. Aviva, hm? Nice name.

QUIZ. Same like Aviv. Means spring. You know, Tel Aviv means Hill of the Spring. Well, you see, her name—

ADAMS. What was she doing on the plane?

QUIZ. She lives in this burg—born here. She's home on furlough. Lives on a farm with a funny name—which I forget. Why you so curious all of a sudden?

ADAMS (*vastly amused*). Quiz—look at me!

QUIZ. Whatsa matter?

ADAMS. (*Breaks into laughter.*)

QUIZ (*miffed*). Well, what's so funny?

ADAMS. I really believe you're smitten!

QUIZ. Aah, don't be crazy. I just *met* the girl—she's pretty all right, and we had a fine talk and all that—

ADAMS. What did you talk about?

QUIZ. Oh—how she used to work on the corrective farm here . . .

ADAMS. *Collective* farm!

QUIZ. . . . and about how they dance the Hora on the Sabbath—thatsa kind of a Jewish jitterbug dance, I guess.

ADAMS. Happens to be the national dance.

QUIZ. And how she used to come in from the farm at night with her family and go to the concerts of the Tel Aviv orchestra. Guess it's a kinda local swing band, but *classy,* you know—like Mark Warnow.

ADAMS. Yes, a man named Toscanini was its first conductor.

QUIZ. That's right, she said that too.

ADAMS. You really got hit between the eyes, didn't ya, Junior?

QUIZ. Aah, you're dizzy with the heat, Adams. We just had an interesting chat for a couple of hours, that's all. You don't have to make a big thing of it.

ADAMS. Okay, okay. Relax.

QUIZ. Okay. You too.

ADAMS. Let's unpack this stuff and then go down and eat, huh? Then we can go around town and talk to all kinds of people. Like to get a good cross-section of this town. Lots of colorful people here—sort of a meeting of East and West.

QUIZ. I thought the twain never met.

ADAMS. Well, they do. They say there are more different languages spoken here than any city its size in the world.

QUIZ. Well, I speak three myself.

ADAMS. That so?

QUIZ. English, American, and double-talk.

ADAMS. C'mon, stop dreaming and unpack.

*For a few seconds we hear the ad lib sounds of unpacking and walking about the room. Quiz is thinking hard, and at length he stops to ask:*

QUIZ. Hey, Doug—

ADAMS (*off*). What?

QUIZ. Can I ask you something?

ADAMS. Sure.

QUIZ. Uh— (*He pauses; gulps.*) Did you fall in love with your wife the first time you met her?

*Music: A gay commentary on Quisinberry's dilemma; when it fades we hear:*

*A pattern of construction noises, as in the building of a house. Adams is interviewing a hod-carrier named Shameer. They have been talking for some time.*

SHAMEER. Yes, eighty generations, Mr. Adams. Think of it—eighty generations!

ADAMS. Certainly is a long time for a people to be without a home.

QUIZ. By the way, Mr. Shameer—did you ever hear of a girl named Aviva Hashahav?

SHAMEER. No, I'm sorry.

ADAMS. You were saying, Mr. Shameer, that your work—

SHAMEER. Yes. You see, I work with a pick and shovel. I carry bricks on these construction jobs.

ADAMS. Uh-huh.

SHAMEER. It's not easy work—certainly nothing like practicing law, as I once did in Germany. But something happens to you here. You see things *grow*.

QUIZ. Just how do you mean?

SHAMEER. Well, this Rechow Allenby, this fine broad street with palm trees and these modern buildings—this was a sand dune when you were still a child. This whole place was *desert* thirty-five years ago.

QUIZ. No kidding?

SHAMEER. *Now* it's the biggest city in Palestine, and the happiest in the Middle East.

ADAMS. And you feel you've been a part of its growth, is that it?

SHAMEER. *Feel?* I can look around me in the city and see the very bricks I've carried—see them standing in place, doing their job. Why, the Bet-Haam—the House of the People—stands on ground I helped to *dig.*

QUIZ. Pardon me—do you mind lifting the hod, Mr. Shameer? I'd like to get a picture of—

ADAMS (*annoyed*). Hold it, willya, Quiz? We're talking.

QUIZ. Aw, I'm just tryin' to get a picture, thassall.

SHAMEER. Mr. Adams, I suppose I'm romantic and sentimental about it, but after all, the work of a bricklayer *does* sometimes outlast the conquests of kings. I often think about the people who were locked up in the miserable ghettos of Poland and Rumania and other countries just a few years ago and now have shelter and peace and clean air and sunshine in the houses we've helped to build. Sure I'm happy. Why shouldn't I be happy?

*Music: For transitional effect, an old Hebrew melody, arranged and tapered so that it goes lightly into:*

*Light street noises.*

NEWSBOY (*fades on under music*). *Davar Iton Erev! Davar Iton Erev!*

QUIZ. Did I hear straight? Is that guy selling papers or singing opera?

ADAMS. He's selling papers.

NEWSBOY (*calling and fading on*). *Davar Iton Erev! Davar Iton Erev! Davar Iton Erev! Davar Iton Erev!*

ADAMS. Here, boy, let's have a paper.

NEWSBOY. Toda Raba.[5] (*Fades off, still hawking.*)

ADAMS. It's the *Davar—Palestine Labor Daily*. (*He stops to read it appraisingly.*) Good makeup on this front page.

QUIZ. Printed all in Hebrew?

*Pages turning.*

ADAMS. Sure, what do you expect? Look—pictures of the fighting in Italy.[6]

QUIZ. No Li'l Abner or Joe Palooka?

ADAMS. No, not even Dick Tracy. Let's see—guess this is the editorial page, and this would be the sport . . . (*Suddenly stunned.*) Hey!

QUIZ. What is it? (*Sees what Doug has stopped at; starts laughing.*) Hah! What the heck is a picture of *you* doin' in there?

ADAMS. Why—why, this must be one of my pieces for Consolidated!

QUIZ (*excited*). Look—and there's my pictures of Liberia [7]—with Hebrew captions! Hey—we're international celebrities, you know that?

ADAMS. They certainly get around with that syndicate. (*Marveling.*) Of all the unexpected—

QUIZ. Hold on, chum—do you see what I see across the street, or is that a desert mirage?

ADAMS. What?

QUIZ. A soda fountain selling cold orangeade and frosted milk shakes!

ADAMS. Well, so it is! First thing like that since we left the States.

QUIZ. Tel Aviv, I *love* you!

*Music: Another transitional effect with local color in the right places. It cross-fades to:*

*Pattern of heavy machine-shop noises, which, after establishing in the listener's ear, comes down behind:*

GIRL. Would you like to go out to where it's less noisy? A tank shop isn't exactly the best place for a quiet interview, is it?

ADAMS. No, I guess not.

QUIZ. And besides, my nerves are on edge! I almost got run over by a jeep on my way here.

ADAMS. Always beefing.

QUIZ. If I knew any Hebrew swear words, I'd of told the monkey driving that thing—

ADAMS. But that was an American soldier. He'd never have understood Hebrew cuss words.

QUIZ. That's just the point. He was bigger'n me.

GIRL. Well, here we are. Let's step inside the office.

*A door opens and closes, and the sounds of the tank shop are almost entirely shut out.*

GIRL. Much better. Now you were asking about these shops, Mr. Adams?

ADAMS. Yes, how does it happen there's so much military equipment here?

GIRL. It's all war material. You see, this was the chief repair depot for the British Eighth Army in the African campaign.

ADAMS. That so?

GIRL. Many a tank we patched up here in Tel Aviv went back and gave the Nazis hell, if you'll pardon the expression. We're pretty proud of our contribution.

ADAMS. But I understand under British mandate there's no conscription in Palestine?

GIRL. That's right.

ADAMS. Are there many Jewish volunteers from here in the armed forces?

GIRL. Over twenty-five thousand, and growing all the time.

QUIZ (*still on the lookout*). By the way, miss, did you ever hear of a girl named Hashahav in the A.T.S.?

GIRL. Well, there are several families in the city by that name. It's Hebrew for Goldberg, you know.

QUIZ. Her first name's Aviva. Lives on a farm somewhere, but I forgot the name. Wish I knew how to find her.

GIRL. Well, she might be in town for the Histadruth Neshev.

QUIZ. What's that?

GIRL. Neshev is our word for party. They hold it on the Sabbath.

QUIZ. Sabbath? When does the Sabbath start?

GIRL. Friday at sundown. See a lot of folk-dancing there.

QUIZ. Mm. This Neshev sounds like it ought to be plenty photogenic, huh, Doug? Doncha think we ought to cover it, come the Sabbath?

ADAMS (*to set him at rest*). Okay, Quiz, okay. (*Turning to the girl.*) Tell me, Miss Kritinsky, what's the feeling in Tel Aviv about the war in general? I mean about the basic issues—Atlantic Charter—the movement toward world collaboration—

GIRL. Well . . . (*Considering.*) Mr. Adams, you say you're stopping at the Gatrimon?

ADAMS. Yes.

GIRL. Did you notice the name of the street that's on?

ADAMS. Well, I don't believe I noticed it, no.

GIRL. It used to be called Hayarkon Street. But the name was officially changed some time ago to Rechow Umot Hameuchadot.

ADAMS. Which means?

GIRL (*proudly*). Street of the United Nations.

> *Music: A prideful passage. At its end:*

> *Café background—dishes, ad libs, etc. Adams and Quisinberry are sitting at a table with an American flier. Café sounds drop behind for:*

ADAMS. What did you say your name was, Sergeant?

O'SHAUGHNESSY. O'Shaughnessy. Patrick X. O'Shaughnessy. South Chicago, Illinois.

ADAMS. And I take it you're with the air forces?

O'SHAUGHNESSY. Yeah. We got an airdrome out near the Lowenthal farm. Matter of fact, our mess hall is in Lowenthal's old barn.[8]

QUIZ. Ever meet a farmer named Hashahav?

O'SHAUGHNESSY. Can't say I did.

WAITER. Shalom, gentlemen. Yes, sir, what'll it be, gentlemen?

ADAMS. We already ordered. Gave it to the other waiter.

WAITER. Oh, all right, fine.

QUIZ (*calling after the Waiter*). And tell him to step on it, willya? I'm starved!

ADAMS. Tell me, Sergeant—how do you like it here?

O'SHAUGHNESSY. I like it fine.

ADAMS. You like the people?

O'SHAUGHNESSY. Yeah. Not many Irish here, but I like the Jewish people fine. There's a nondenominational church they put up here for all the different soldiers. (*Low; confidentially.*) And you wanna know something?

ADAMS. What?

O'SHAUGHNESSY. There's no anti-Semitism here! (*Great laugh.*)

ADAMS (*not joining in the laughter*). What about anti-gentilism? Any of that?

O'SHAUGHNESSY (*sobering quickly*). Hey—as a matter of fact, you know, I wondered about that the first week I was here. But they ain't no such thing.

ADAMS. No signs saying "White Semites Only"?

O'SHAUGHNESSY. Nuttin' like that.

QUIZ. What about people saying, "Some of my best friends are gentiles"?

ADAMS. Or Jewish newspaper ads saying "restricted clientele"?

O'SHAUGHNESSY. Never seen such a thing. And wanna hear something else?

QUIZ. What?

O'SHAUGHNESSY. There's a concentration camp for Nazis out in Sarona—that's just outside of town—and these Nazis were the worst kind of fifth columnists before the war—they were stoogin' around to stir up trouble amongst the Ayrabs and all like that, and when the war came they were chucked into the clink, see? And you know what?

ADAMS. What?

O'SHAUGHNESSY. There's a *Jewish watchman* guarding those Nazis! (*Laughs.*) Ain't that poetic justice for ya?

ADAMS. I take it the Nazi prisoners are not whipped and tortured by the Jews?

O'SHAUGHNESSY. Naw, I seen them. If anything, I think they're gettin' off too easy.

ADAMS. They don't have to wear a swastika on their clothes or the word "Deutsche" pinned on their back?

O'SHAUGHNESSY. Nope.

QUIZ. Ya mean they don't have to scrub the streets while people stand around laffing and insulting them?

O'SHAUGHNESSY. Naw, waddya think? This is a civilized country.

QUIZ. Aah, if I was these Jews in Tel Aviv I'd shoot them Nazis down like dogs, every one of them!

ADAMS. That's what twenty-five thousand of these Jews *are* doing, Quiz—shooting down Nazis. But where it counts the most—on the field of battle.

*Down the street outside the café a trumpet has been blowing at irregular intervals.*[9] *It advances in perspective as the scene progresses. None of our people takes notice of it until later.*

O'SHAUGHNESSY (*there having been no pause in the discussion*). Y'know something I find out, bein' here six months? That anti-Semitism stuff you run across in some places back home in the States is nuttin' but a racket. Ignorant people get sucked in just the way they did in Germany when they fell for Hitler.

ADAMS. That's right. It's one of the oldest rackets in the world—making a scapegoat out of a minority. There was a time when Christians were a minority, too, and they were scapegoated right into the arena to be mangled by lions.

O'SHAUGHNESSY. You said it, brother.

QUIZ. Whozat, Harry James [10] making with the trumpet?

O'SHAUGHNESSY. That's the old guy comes around every Friday night to blow the horn announcing the Sabbath. They observe Sunday on Saturday here, you know.

ADAMS. Or maybe it's we who observe Saturday on Sunday,

considering the Hebrews had their Sabbath in practice
a long time before we did.

QUIZ. Ya mean it's the Sabbath right *now?*

O'SHAUGHNESSY. Sure, it begins sundown Friday—all the
shops hafta close now.

QUIZ (*remembering that Aviva is likely to be at the Sabbath party*). Well—uh—this is the night they got that
big Neshev on, ain't it?

O'SHAUGHNESSY. That's right, Mac.

QUIZ (*galvanized*). Well, so long, you guys. (*Going off.*)
I ain't very hungry—I'm on my way to a folk dance.

ADAMS (*laughing*). Hey, Quiz—come *back* here!

*Music: A bright passage to wipe out the scene. But at
the precise point where you expect the transition to
end, the orchestra sweeps with full energy into the
Hora, an infectiously gay and rhythmic dance.
Through it we hear:*

*Some hand-clapping in time to the music, and at inter-
vals:*

DANCERS. Yehoo!

*Through all this Quiz is wandering lonely as a cloud,
looking for Aviva. Doug has been helping him scout
the floor.*

ADAMS. Well, did you find her, Quiz?

QUIZ. No. I'm still searching for her. She's about my
height.

ADAMS. I'll keep on looking on this side of the crowd.

QUIZ. Well, if you spot her, Doug, whistle with two fingers
in your mouth, willya?

ADAMS. Okay.

*Music: We hear the Hora alone for about ten seconds.*

*Then, suddenly, up from behind Quiz:*

AVIVA. Mr. Quinceberry!

QUIZ. *Aviva*—say, I'm glad to see you! I been looking . . .

AVIVA (*who has been dancing and is under the sway of the music*). Come on, Mr. Quinceberry, let's join the dance.

QUIZ (*meekly*). Quisinberry.

AVIVA. Come on, you'll like it, you really will!

QUIZ. But I can't dance this dance—it's too strenuous!

AVIVA (*taking him firmly in hand*). That's all right, you'll learn!

QUIZ (*protesting*). But wait a minute—but I— (*As Aviva yanks him into the dance.*) Hey!

*Music: The Hora swallows up his protest and comes to a peak; then it gradually diminishes and retards in the spirit of transition. It fades away under:*

ADAMS. It was terribly good of your daughter to ask us to visit you here on the farm, Mr. Hashahav. I always wanted to see a collective farm.

HASHAHAV (*about forty-five*). It's been a great pleasure to show you around, Mr. Adams. Not often do we have a privilege of this sort. Why don't you take your coat off and be comfortable?

MRS. HASHAHAV. Yes, please do, Mr. Adams.

ADAMS. Thank you, Mrs. Hashahav, I will if you don't mind.

MRS. HASHAHAV. Would you care for a drink of wine from Jewish grapes grown at Yegia Kapayim?

ADAMS. I would indeed.

*Sound of Hashahav moving about the room.*

ADAMS. Is Yegia Kapayim another collective like this?

MRS. HASHAHAV. It's a new garden suburb of Jerusalem. The name in Hebrew means Labor of Thine Hands— after one of the Psalms of David.

ADAMS. Very beautiful name.

HASHAHAV. Here y'are, Mr. Adams.

ADAMS. Thank you very much. Where's Quiz gone?

HASHAHAV. He's sitting on the porch with Aviva. I'll bring some wine out to them.

MRS. HASHAHAV. I'll do it, darling. (*Going off.*) It won't be long before dinner, Mr. Adams. I hope you won't mind waiting.

ADAMS. Oh, no, don't worry about that.

*Hashahav pours, and we hear the sounds of clinking glasses.*

HASHAHAV. We have three hundred for dinner every night, you know.

ADAMS. As many of you as that, eh?

HASHAHAV. Yes, and after dinner tonight there's a general meeting, which all but the children attend. They go to bed.

ADAMS. I hope you have better luck getting yours to bed than I have with mine.

HASHAHAV. Oh, you have children, have you?

ADAMS. Two. Boy and a girl.[11] Uh—would you—would you like to see their pictures?

HASHAHAV. Very much indeed.

MRS. HASHAHAV (*returning*). Did I hear you say you had pictures of your children? I'd love to see them.

ADAMS. Oh, dear. I find I've left them at the hotel.

MRS. HASHAHAV. Oh, that's too bad. How old are they?

ADAMS. Five and eight. But don't get me started talking about my kids—I'm the typical father, you know.

ALL. (*An amiable chuckle.*)

ADAMS (*deciding to take a serious tack*). Mr. Hashahav— do I understand that this was completely barren soil when your collective started?

HASHAHAV. My friend, when we came here there was nothing but wasteland—not even water. Sometimes only a bucket a day for fifty people—and we had to fetch that bucket of water from miles away and pay dearly for it. But we dug our own wells, and we built roads—

ADAMS (*incredulously*). You mean the fine roads we came out on were built by you people?

HASHAHAV. Entirely. Everything you see here is the work of bare hands, Mr. Adams. These houses, roads, the new reservoir—orchards, vineyards, the gardens—all the work of free Jewish men and women, many of them people who were hounded and persecuted in some of the so-called enlightened countries of Europe. They came here, bought their way here, almost as your Pilgrims went to America—for independence and a chance to make their own life out of a wilderness.

ADAMS. I don't suppose it's been easy.

HASHAHAV. Ah, yes—we could tell you some stories. But what good thing *isn't* hard to come by? Do you know of any?

ADAMS. No, I guess not—I—

*Off mike, a community bell sounds the call for dinner.*

MRS. HASHAHAV. That's the dinner bell, Mr. Adams. Arya, will you get Mr. Adams' coat from the closet?

HASHAHAV. Another sip of wine before we go to the mess hall, Mr. Adams?

ADAMS. No, thanks, this is fine, thanks.

AVIVA (*coming in from the porch, with Quiz in tow*). Are we all ready to go to dinner, Mother?

MRS. HASHAHAV. Yes, Aviva.

ADAMS. Well, Miss Hashahav, has Quiz been telling you all about America?

AVIVA. No, as a matter of fact we were discussing poetry mainly, and he—

QUIZ (*quickly*). Doug, didja know they have holidays here to celebrate the birthdays of poets?

ADAMS. Yes. (*To Aviva.*) Did Quiz tell you about the great American poets—Whitman and Sandburg, and the—

AVIVA. No, but he *read* me some poetry.

ADAMS. Oh. Longfellow?

QUIZ (*embarrassed*). Uh . . . no. Quisinberry.

*Music: A sprightly cue before dinner. When it ends, we hear:*

CAST. (*Ad libs, as of a dinner just ending.*)

*The chairman of the meeting, rising, raps for attention. His gavel quiets the room.*

HAKVUZA (*in Hebrew*). Shalom, khaverim.[12] Instead of the meeting we had planned for tonight, we are going to dispense with business at hand to extend a welcome to our guests of honor, Messrs. Adams and Quisinberg of the Consolidated Syndicate of the United States. Here's Khaver Ishar Hame Iri, Mnaheg Hakvuza, who will introduce our guests.[13]

MNAHEG. Shalom, khaverim. I know you will forgive my speaking English tonight, but this is in order that our friends from the United States, Mr. Douglas Adams and Mr. Perry Quisinberg, may understand all that is being said.

As our good secretary has just told you, we are going to dispense with the business at hand to welcome Messrs. Adams and Quisinberg to your farm. However, I would just like to announce at this time that the Red Mogen David—which, I should explain to our guests, is the Jewish Red Cross—will on Thursday night begin another course in first aid and that on Monday, May twenty-ninth, there will be an important meeting of the Histadrut—the General Labor Federation—to discuss the program of collaborating with the Jewish Agency in the training of pilots and mechanics for the RAF, also the providing of medical care, food and clothing, for families of soldiers and pioneers.

And now I am going to extend the privilege of introducing our guests to Khaver Arya Hashahav, who has been host to them since they arrived earlier in the day.

HASHAHAV. Toda Raba, Menahale. Khaverim and Khaverot:[14] Mr. Adams is an American newspaper editor on an assignment to visit the Allied countries to tell his own readers back home how he finds the people of the United Nations. All of you have read his articles, which by a most happy coincidence have been running in the *Davar,* and I know that you have as many questions to ask of Khaverim Adams and Quisinberry as they have been asking Tel Aviv the past week.

But with his leave I should like to call upon Mr. Adams to speak to us now for as long as he wishes and to say anything that is in his mind to say, whether about what he has seen in his voyaging, or what he's seen here, or what he hopes to see.

Mr. Douglas Adams of Centerville, United States of America!

CAST. (*Applause.*)

ADAMS (*rather haltingly*). I'm afraid I'm no speechmaker, ladies and gentlemen. I have enough trouble expressing myself in writing, where I can at least use an eraser and go back and begin again . . . and this is a pretty unusual situation for me. But if you don't mind, why, I guess I—I won't mind, either.

CAST. (*Amiable reaction.*)

ADAMS. Mr. Quisinberry and I have been in Tel Aviv and its vicinity for about a week now, and I can tell you that we have been much impressed by both big things and little things. Maybe those are one and the same . . . I guess they are.

It may seem a little thing that although Tel Aviv is not a rich city, one rarely sees a beggar here, in contrast to other cities I have seen. It may seem a little thing that there are no ragged children with sore eyes nor hungry-looking people on your streets. I don't mean that everybody's well off here in a material sense —I've seen otherwise.

But all the good *little* impressions do add up; and when you put 'em together with the big things like the pride and industry of your people, your fine cultural life—we attended the Habime and Ohel theaters, for instance—and your excellent agriculture—I guess *you* know about that . . .

CAST. (*Amiable laughter.*)

ADAMS. . . . all in all, the picture becomes one of infinite *hope,* and I begin to understand why the people here are so happy—happy in spite of the war being close to you here, in spite of bombs having been dropped on your city and of your having lost many of your friends [15]—in spite of large, depressing political problems, which I know are going to take patience and hard work to straighten out.

But above all, this city seems to me a living example of what can happen when the human spirit—which, believe me, is the same in Centerville as it is in Tel Aviv—is just given a chance to flourish like any other of God's living things. When people can live the way they were intended to live, in a home of their own, by the labor of their hands, and raising children to be useful citizens of the better world that we all hope is in the making. Uh— (*Pause.*) Thank you for everything.

CAST. (*Warm applause, which is washed out by:*)

*Music: A penultimate passage of Hebraic flavor. It fades before:*

*The background of an airport. Adams and Quiz are leaving for their next destination, and Aviva and her father have come to see them off.*

QUIZ. I'd like you to hear another poem, which I wrote last night, Aviva.

AVIVA. But your plane leaves in five minutes, Perry.

QUIZ. Well, then, I'll leave it with you. It's entitled "Viva Aviva," and it's—it's kind of a love poem. I'd like you to remember me by it, and write me when you—

ADAMS (*coming on*). So here you are, kids! I've been looking for you. Got your duffel bag, Quiz? We leave in a couple of minutes.

QUIZ. Yuh, yuh, I'm all set.

HASHAHAV. Here, let me help you with the grip.

ADAMS. No, that's all right, thanks, Mr. Hashahav. Well, sir—you're terribly good to've come to the airdrome with us, and I appreciate more than I can say all you've done.

HASHAHAV. Not at all, Mr. Adams. It was *our* pleasure. I wish we could see more of you.

ADAMS. Well—uh—I'd just like to say one thing before I leave.

HASHAHAV. What's that, Mr. Adams?

ADAMS. I think you people have a wonderful word that you use for greeting—the word shalom.

HASHAHAV. Shalom . . . yes . . . meaning peace.

ADAMS (*slowly—not glibly—almost gropingly*). I—I just hope that if and when we meet again, in a future not too distant, that word will be—well—that word will have a new meaning and a more lasting one than we have ever known.

HASHAHAV (*quietly*). I hope so too, my friend. Shalom.

ADAMS (*with feeling*). Shalom.

*Music: Finale.*

# TEL AVIV

Smack in the middle of the war, the Office of War Information asked CBS whether it could develop a "good-will" series about an itinerant newspaper editor sent by a syndicate to tour the world. The idea was for the traveler to meet our Allies—to give his readers back home (meaning our listeners) a line on the kind of people they were and the kind of war they were fighting.

Columbia asked me to direct and produce the series and to write the opening program. Ranald MacDougall, whose "The Man behind the Gun" had just won the Peabody Award, was invited to write the rest of the shows. We accepted, and the series went on the air from Hollywood on August 17, 1943. Within a month MacDougall was snapped up by Warner Brothers, and I was left holding the baggage of Douglas Adams and Perry Quisinberry.

MacDougall had taken the pair as far as Cairo (via programs on Belém, Monrovia, and Marrakesh), and the next scheduled stop was Tel Aviv. I sent out an SOS for research and technical advice and was answered by Max Lipin, formerly a Reuters correspondent in Palestine. I naturally wanted all place names, descriptions, facts, attitudes, and the general milieu to be authentic. We had a single long-dinner conference; I took notes between courses and was off on the script. I was fascinated by what Lipin told me of the city and its people and impressed by the Hebrew language, which I had never really encountered before then. (If there is a more beautiful name than Aviva, send it to me and I will name my first daughter after your suggestion.)

The theme, objective, and principal characters of the "Passport" series had been pretty well established by the introductory broadcast, wherein the Consolidated Syndicate invited Adams to New York to talk over the project. Ralph Forster, managing editor for Consolidated, met him and they talked:

DOUG. But with all the great war correspondents there are, why do you want a small-town editor like *me* to go around the world?

FORSTER. The very fact that you're a country editor who's never done big-league reporting is exactly why we're interested in you.

DOUG. How do you mean?

FORSTER. Adams, there's something few of us realize—most of the people of the world are small-town people. In this country *70 per cent* of the population lives in towns and villages—did you know that? (*He pauses for a reply; there is none.*) We want a man who knows the feel of an American town—who knows the color and flavor of Centerville and Greenfield—we want him to travel around the world in this war and tell us in his own language how it looks to *him*. Does that make sense to you?

DOUG. Well, what exactly would you expect in the way of reporting?

FORSTER. We'd want you to tell this country about other countries just as you've been telling Centerville about Centerville.

DOUG. What about front-line stuff—wouldn't you want that?

FORSTER. We don't want you to write about big military actions. That's being done wonderfully well right now. We want you to write about the people—how they live, what the war's done to them—are they pulling together or scrapping among themselves. . . .

DOUG. I see.

FORSTER. For example, how do American boys get along with them? What do our soldiers and sailors and marines do when they're on leave? Are they making friends for the United States? What kind of people are fighting on our side? Are they like us? *Do* they like us? (*Pause.*) Get the picture?

Doug got the picture, and then Forster rang for Quisinberry. It was no case of admiration at first sight. Quiz,
the Weegee of the international scene, considered Adams
a hayseed and was rude to him in their first meeting. "With
all due respect to Mr. Adams," Quiz said, "he never been
out of the country before. He don't know his way around.
Why, me, I been all over the place—London, Paris, Vienna,
Berlin—I've photographed *kings!* I covered some of the
finest coronations and assassinations you ever hope to see.
You ask Quent Reynolds what he thinks about me."

When Forster explained that this trip did not happen
to include Paris or Vienna and that Adams had been engaged to write about commoners, not kings, Quiz persisted:
"Chief, you don't seem to realize you're sending me out
around the world with a guy edits the Dingville *Bugle*. Now
I'm a professional photographer of years' standing, and
with all due respect to you, you're gonna hurt my reputa-
tion if you couple me up with an Eagle Scout. You know, I
covered wars before this one."

The relationship improved as soon as writer and photographer got to know each other, but throughout the series
Quiz remained a foil for Adams. He was essentially as
good an egg as he was a cameraman, but his general ignorance about worldly matters and some of the prejudices
growing out of that ignorance gave Adams a handy anvil
against which to hammer points intended for the instruction or edification of the listener.

As a subject, Tel Aviv presented many tough problems
of policy. Jews themselves were (and are) sorely divided
on questions affecting Palestine. The British were (and
are) playing hokey-pokey with Jewish-Arabian relations,
and the situation presented a political problem as difficult
as India's. Obviously a program about Tel Aviv would have

to do several inside loops to avoid offending Zionists, anti-Zionists, or the British. (Not that I am against offending —I've done it now and then, and love it—but this was a good-will series.)

I had only one policy yardstick, and it was in the shape of a memorandum I wrote before the series went on the air. It is just as important to understand objectives before work is undertaken on a radio series as it is to draft blueprints before starting to build a house. Readers interested in the way groundwork is laid for a job of this sort may find the text of that memorandum informative. I quote it here because I believe it a fair basis for some such series in the future:

1. Adams will have definite, clear, articulate reactions to the things he sees and hears. He will have political and economic opinions. He will express them. But his statements will never be presented as, nor have the sense of, an official American point of view; nor will they necessarily be representative of public opinion now current in the United States. His reactions will stem from his own character as we shall establish it: an enlightened, fair, internationally-minded American who hopes for and believes in a better world after victory.

2. Adams will see much that disturbs and shocks him. He will realize that the world today, even on our side of the fence, doesn't by a long shot measure up to the standard set by the Four Freedoms and the Atlantic Charter. Where human conditions are substandard, Adams will see them; the substandard peoples will often talk of their own plight and their own hopes.

3. Adams will see vividly the mistakes of the past. He will recognize their stupidity and inhumanity. He will realize, wherever he goes among our Allies, that people are fighting with us because they believed our leaders when they enunciated the Atlantic Charter; because they believe now that Americans will help to translate them into reality.

4. We know, of course, that among the United Nations there are governments that have practiced democracy well and others that have practiced it not at all. Adams will be talking to people who

suffered long and hard at the hands of undemocratic governments who now fight with us for common objectives. In these cases, we will not directly criticize the established governments of any of the United Nations, nor will we cast aspersions specifically upon any of their official representatives. Our approach will always be constructive. We will not harp upon what people have lost or suffered in the past at the hands of men who still govern them. Rather, we will emphasize what they now have to gain through victory, by the application of the democratic principles to which their governments have now publicly subscribed and to which they are now committed before the world.

5. In casting his eye to the future and the postwar world, Adams will always express himself broadly and in generalities. He will not have bright ideas about future boundaries; he will not speculate about the political or economic systems of the future; he will not try to sell any concrete plan for world collaboration.

6. Adams may often see things abroad that suggest similar problems at home. If he were at home at this moment, running his paper, he'd be writing editorials about these home-front problems. He will be thinking in these terms too in his travels. He will often use his home town—Centerville—as a point of reference and comparison in his conversations with people abroad.

Admittedly the series, by pursuing the policies laid down in this prospectus, attempted to inspire. The idea was to pull for unity and victory. Was that bad? The omission of ugly details concerning certain aspects of the recent history of our Allies was quite beside the point. To have dwelt upon them would have been to play exactly the same tune as Goebbels, who was constantly reminding the world that the British, in their time, were dreadful imperialists. It would be like saying, "Fight for Your Country, Buy Bonds, Keep 'Em Flying—But Don't Forget There's an Occasional Lynching in the South, and a Bad Political Machine in Jersey City." The sins of the United States in the Spanish-American War had nothing to do with this one, and if the Soviets once chose to liquidate a great many kulaks, this was hardly the time to argue about it.

*Acting.* Film stars doing radio work can be put roughly into two categories: those who are interested primarily in the publicity of big shows, plus the fees incumbent to them; and those who want to do good or useful work, even though the rewards may not be great. It is characteristic of the former that they exercise little taste in the selection of material, permit themselves to be miscast, work indifferently in the studio, and manage somehow never to have their names connected with memorable broadcasts. Robert Young is definitely one of the second group—an extremely conscientious worker, concerned about what he is doing and why. The gift of great talent does not necessarily go along with intelligence, decency, or amiability, but when it does, it creates its own happy auspices, and its influence spreads far. When "Passport" stopped after eight weeks to make way for prior commitments, there were loud squawks from listeners around the country, but nobody took it harder than Young himself. Confronted by more work than he could handle, he had given "Passport" priority because he believed it could accomplish some good in helping us to understand our Allies. Young was the happiest possible choice for the role of Doug Adams. He was young, without being a Mr. Deeds; informed, without being a know-it-all; sincere; fully aware of the seriousness of his mission. Within the compass of this single script Young went through a typical range of qualities: he was the big brother in the airport scene; he kidded Quiz at the hotel; became very much the reporter in scenes with Shameer and Miss Kritinsky; was incisive when questioning O'Shaughnessy on the subject of anti-Semitism; was the warm, friendly guest at the home of the Hashahavs.

Dane Clark, who performed as Quiz, was then beginning a movie career which has since advanced brilliantly. He made the photographer sufficiently annoying to Adams and the listener to be astringent in a warm and amusing way. In Brazil, French Morocco, and Egypt, Quiz, then being written by MacDougall, gave Adams plenty to worry about. He flirted with a native woman in Marrakesh (an offense that has cost broken bones to many an infidel before Quiz), and Adams had to save him from being mobbed. In Cairo, Quiz disappeared on a three-day toot while Adams searched the bars and bistros and, in alarm, phoned the army, navy, and police. The incident gave Adams an opportunity to lecture Quiz on the responsibilities of an American when visiting in a foreign land. I decided to make Quiz a nicer guy when I took him over, not because MacDougall's version was not valid and entertaining—he was a real pleasure to have around—but because I didn't want Quiz to be running afoul of the law in places like Moscow and Chungking. There was already enough trouble in both countries without our boy chipping in.

Joan Loring, who had yet to make her exciting entrance to the nation's movie houses as Bessie Watty in *The Corn Is Green,* forthrightly portrayed Aviva. She made the girl bright and twinkling, endowed her with an irresistible and gay energy capable of sweeping Quiz off his feet and into the Hora before he knew what had hit him.

Aviva's father, Arya Hashahav, is a pleasant man who speaks with a Continental accent just as slight as Aviva's accent is British (Aviva picked up a little of it in the ATS). Hans Conreid, than whom there is no more versatile radio actor all the way from Tel Aviv to Timbuktu (via Topeka), gave Hashahav the dignity and likeableness which is his due.

*Sound.* No special problems. The watchman's trumpet announcing the sabbath during the café scene is not a sound, but a musical effect.

*Music.* Contrary to the impression existing in some quarters that ought to know better, Hebrew music is not all "Eli Eli" or "Kol Nidre." It can be as amiable, lively, and infectious as our own jive. Lud Gluskin and Lucien Moraweck, who frequently collaborate in such matters, adapted and composed a right smart score. Gluskin can be reached in care of KNX, Hollywood.

*Additional Notes.* 1. This prefatory exchange between Gus and Ed is simply a device to avoid the necessity for an announcer's saying, "Tonight's broadcast tells the story of two newspapermen," et cetera. In these slight lines of dialogue we have shortened by two-thirds the usual exposition required to get into a scene such as that at the airport. The story tells itself. Why beat it to the punch?

2. Cablese is not difficult at worst, once you have been exposed to it even briefly. This is a mild specimen, translating as follows: "Forster, Consolidated Syndicate, USA: Filing 3000 words out of Tel Aviv Wednesday night, then proceeding to Moscow via Teheran."

3. Please note that Quiz does not groan at Doug's pun. He accepts it as one of the facts of life, having made his adjustment to punning at an early age. I strongly suspect the humor of people who moan, groan, and make as if to strangle the perpetrator of a pun. Why? A good pun, though small of scope, can be as much a thing of beauty as a well-turned ankle. Real nice to have around.

4. An invented name. We don't usually like to advertise real products on the air. Quiz here would have been thinking of Kodachrome or Ansco Color as he rhapsodized over the scene before him.

5. Means "thank you."

6. The Italian campaign was still being fought at the time of the original broadcast. We were bombing Benevento, Capua, and Leghorn around then, and our armies were just north of Salerno.

7. Two weeks earlier, Adams and Quiz had visited Liberia. The script was one that gave MacDougall and me considerable trouble, because we felt that little of a constructive nature could honestly be said about a country whose administration was harsh and corrupt.

8. True, as are other details in the script. Lowenthal *did* have a farm, and his barn *did* serve as the mess hall for an American air base near by.

9. A loud, rasping flutter note. The watchman blowing this trumpet is not, as Quiz later intimates, to be mistaken for Harry James.

10. Husband of Betty Grable, and a genius at getting results from a trumpet.

11. This was a running motif in the series. Adams, like so many young fathers you know, was forever showing victims snapshots of his children. It was one of the devices by which we kept him bound to home and reminded the listener from time to time that Adams was a married man. None of these details was accidental, for at the inception of the series, Davidson Taylor (for CBS) and I went over the character of our hero most carefully. We decided that Doug should be married and a father, in order to present the point of view of a man with family responsibilities, a man to whom the future meant not only his own welfare but that of his kids.

12. Meaning "Greetings, comrades."

13. Lipin assured me that this sort of courtesy is exactly what the collective would extend to Adams and Quisin-

berry. He had often seen this happen in similar circumstances.

14. Translation: "Thank you very much, Mr. Chairman. Ladies and gentlemen."

15. Tel Aviv took its share of bombing. The Italians on September 11, 1940, destroyed a block of houses, killing 150 people, of whom fifty-five were children. A mass funeral was held, and the Arabs as well as the Jews mourned the tragedy.

# MOSCOW

First produced in Hollywood on September 28, 1943, as the seventh of the "Passport for Adams" series, starring Robert Young as Douglas Adams. (See "Tel Aviv," which precedes this play.)

Most of the data and many of the incidents in this script were based on material cabled from Moscow in the week preceding the broadcast by Bill Downs, then CBS Moscow correspondent. The author directed.

# MOSCOW

QUIZ. Well, when do we get to see Joe? Hm, Doug? Have you made an appointment with him yet? . . . *Hey, I'm talking to ya!*

ADAMS. Sorry, I was writing. What'd you want to know?

QUIZ. When do we see Joe?

ADAMS. Joe who?

QUIZ. Who d'ya think? If we're only gonna be here ten days and you want me to get a ·picture of him, you better—

ADAMS. Quiz, we're *not* going to see Stalin.

QUIZ. Why not?

ADAMS. Well, he's kinda busy. Y'see, it's like this—

*Music: Introductory theme, flavored Russian. It fades to discover:*

*General background of street. Adams, Quiz, and an official government interpreter, Ludmilla Kozlova, are walking together in the blackout.*

QUIZ (*who has an eye for passable dames*). Tell me, Ludmilla, are all official interpreters assigned to foreign correspondents as good-looking as you?

KOZLOVA. Well, not exactly. One or two of them have beards. (*Amiably.*) Are all American photographers as fresh as you?

ADAMS. Don't mind him, Miss Kozlova—he fell in love with a girl in Palestine a couple of weeks ago, and he's been off balance ever since.

377

KOZLOVA (*laughing*). Oh, I see.

ADAMS. What's the name of this street?

KOZLOVA. Gorky Street.

ADAMS. After Maxim Gorky?

KOZLOVA. Yes, that's right.

QUIZ. Gorky—wasn't he a sports writer? Seems to me I heard his name somewhere—

ADAMS (*patiently*). No, Quiz, he was a very great nov— (*Scuffle.*) *Ouch!* Hey! Keep off my feet, will you?

QUIZ. Oh, I'm sorry. Didn't see where I was going. Unaccustomed as I am to public blackouts.

ADAMS. I'll buy you a compass.

LOUDSPEAKER (*with sudden and startling effect*). Vnimaniye, tovarishchi, cherez piat minut budyet peredano vazhnoye soobshcheniye!

Attention, comrades. There will be a special announcement in a moment. Please stand by. Stand by.

ADAMS. Where's that coming from, Miss Kozlova?

KOZLOVA. Loudspeakers at the corner. That's our radio system for the duration.

QUIZ. What did he say just then?

KOZLOVA. He said there would be a—

LOUDSPEAKER. . . . Peredano vazhnoye soobshcheniye!

Stand by for a special announcement. Stand by.

KOZLOVA. Said there'd be a special announcement in a moment and asked everybody to stand by. They'll probably play some music now until it's time for the announcement.

ADAMS. I take it the government called in all privately owned radio sets at the outbreak of the war?

KOZLOVA. Yes, that's correct.

QUIZ. If you don't mind my saying so, that seems to me a heck of a thing to do.

KOZLOVA. Why?

QUIZ. Frankly, because I think the motive for taking radios away was that they didn't want people to hear news from the outside. And if I—

ADAMS. Look, bright boy—do you ever read the newspapers that you take pictures for?

QUIZ. Sure.

ADAMS. All right. Who's occupying Odessa?[1]

QUIZ. Odessa? The Nazis.

ADAMS. Who's in control of Kiev?

QUIZ. The Nazis.

ADAMS. Who's been in Smolensk for two years now?

QUIZ. The Nazis, Daddy. Now ask me the sixty-four-dollar question.

ADAMS. Who controls the radio transmitters in those cities?

QUIZ. *The Nazis!* So what's that got to do with it?

ADAMS. How would it be if the Nazis were able to countermand every government order just by broadcasting over the radio to listeners in their homes, and get everything so confused that—

QUIZ. Oh, I see. I get it. You mean like what happened in France when the Germans captured—

ADAMS. Yes. You're catching on, Junior.

QUIZ. Uh-huh. Well, uh, my apologies, Ludmilla.

KOZLOVA. Not at all. Quite all right.

QUIZ. Misunderstood your motive.

KOZLOVA (*amiably*). We're used to that, my friend.[2]

ADAMS. Er—where are all these *people* coming from, Miss Kozlova?

KOZLOVA. Oh, apartment buildings in the neighborhood. They're gathering to hear the announcement.

---

[1] The numbered notes will be found on pages 405-406.

QUIZ. Boy, this is the blackest blackout I ever want to get lost in a strange city in!

KOZLOVA (*chuckling*). Worker right behind us just bet another man ten rubles they're going to announce the fall of Kiev.

ADAMS. How's the other fellow betting?

KOZLOVA. On Dnepropetrovsk.

ADAMS. Well, we can't lose either way.

*Music: A loud, metallic fanfare on the loudspeaker system.*

KOZLOVA (*over this*). Here it comes.

VOICES. (*Hushed now. There is a little rustling and whispering at first, but soon the silence is spread evenly.*)

QUIZ (*hushed*). Gee, it's so silent all of a sudden! What does that mean?

KOZLOVA. Just tension, I guess.

ADAMS (*also hushed*). Almost like the quiet in a courtroom before the reading of a verdict, isn't it?

LOUDSPEAKER. Nashi voiska na zapadnom fronte prodolzhayut uspeshnoye nastupleniye. Oni forsirovali reku Dnepr i posle upornykh boyev sevodnia 25-vo sentiabria, zanyali neskolko naselyonnykh punktov v raione Smolenska.

Our troops on the Western front continue their successful advance. They have crossed the river Dnieper and today, September 25th, after stubborn fighting, they have occupied several inhabited places in the region of Smolensk.

VOICES. (*Tremendous, tumultuous cheering.*)

LOUDSPEAKER. Nami vziat obratno Smolensk, kotoryi yavliaetsia samym silnym strategicheskim punktom na zapadnom fronte.

We have retaken Smolensk, which is the strongest strategic point on the Western front.

VOICES. (*More cheering.*)

LOUDSPEAKER. Sevodnia posle dvukhdnevnovo boya nashi voiska slomili upornoye soprotivlieniye vraga i zaniali strategicheski vazhnyi punkt; etot punkt nakhoditsia v napravlenii Gomelia. My zaniali Roslavl.

Smert nemetskim zakhvatchikam!

Today after a two-day engagement our troops have broken the stubborn resistance of the enemy, and have occupied a strategically important point; this point is in the direction of Gomel. We have occupied Roslavl. Death to the German aggressors!

VOICES. (*The crowd cheers, and so do Adams, Quiz, and Kozlova. After a couple of healthy whoops the cheering dies down in a buzz of ad libs.*) [3]

ADAMS. How does it happen there's so little cheering, Miss Kozlova? This is a pretty important victory.

QUIZ. Yeah, I should think everybody'd go to town on *this* one.

KOZLOVA. I don't know. (*Sighs.*) I guess we've been fighting too long. I guess it's that we can't think of big, joyous celebrations while the enemy still occupies *any* Soviet soil. (*Brightening.*) But you'll see a victory salute, though.

ADAMS. What kind of victory salute?

KOZLOVA. Siege guns in the suburbs and rocket guns here in the city—probably start in a minute or two. They time it on the hour or half-hour following the announcement. Be a little while yet.

QUIZ. I'd sure like to be here the night you guys push over the border.

KOZLOVA. That'll be a little while yet, too.

ADAMS. Think maybe before next spring, Miss Kozlova?

QUIZ (*excitedly*). Hey, look! Look! What are them flashes on the horizon?

KOZLOVA. Those are the siege guns. You'll hear them in a moment. Takes time for the sound to reach us.

*Firing of rockets—a fairly close effect, resembling the sound of corks coming out of bottles.*

KOZLOVA. There go the rockets.

ADAMS. Looks like a Fourth of July celebration back in Centerville.

QUIZ. Say, you could read a newspaper in this light, you know it?

VOICES. (*Occasional cries of "Khorosho," "Krasivo," "Ochen krasivo," continuing in the background until:*)

*Big guns—a heavy, rolling sound like concentrated thunder.*

ADAMS. Well, Quiz—that's the sound a war makes when it's in your suburbs.

KOZLOVA. This one was in our suburbs, all right. Nazis were five miles from where we're *standing* before we turned them back.

RUSSIAN (*one of the crowd, to Ludmilla*). Prostitye tovarishch, eti grazhdane Americantzy?

KOZLOVA (*to Adams*). Pardon me, Mr. Adams, this man wants to talk to me. (*To man.*) Da, oni Americantzy. A chto?

RUSSIAN. Ya srazy uznal ikh po obuvi i odezhde. Ya khochu privetstvovat ikh, Da zdravstvuyut soyedinyonnye shtaty Ameriki.

KOZLOVA (*to Adams*). This man says he could tell from your new-looking clothes and shoes that you're an American, and he wants to say something to you.

ADAMS. Tell him to go ahead.

KOZLOVA. Pozhaluista.

RUSSIAN (*to Adams*). Da zdravstvuyut soyedinyonnye shtaty Ameriki!

ADAMS. What's he saying?

KOZLOVA. He's saying: "Long live the United States of America."

ADAMS (*pleased*). Well, that's very nice of him. How do you say: "Long live the Soviet Union"?

KOZLOVA (*in a low tone*). Da zdravstvuyet Sovietskii soyuz!

ADAMS (*repeats aloud*). Da zdravstvuyet Sovietskii soyuz!

QUIZ. Yeah. That goes for me, too. (*He attempts to repeat the phrase but bogs down.*)

CROWD. (*Delighted and appreciative, they cheer him on. The toast-swapping and viva's reach a peak, when the scene is wiped out by:*)

*Music: A passage combining well-known American and Russian themes, such as "Yankee Doodle" and the Internationale.⁴ This is a loud orchestral punctuation, and when it diminishes we hear faintly in the background:*

*The effect of soldiers on the march, singing a Red Army song. Under the first part of the following scene the effect rises in perspective, as though the troops were passing beneath the window of Adams' and Quisinberry's hotel room. It comes to a peak about a minute along, but never does it get very loud or dominate the dialogue.*

*Quiz has been asleep. He awakens, turns over in bed, looks around:*

QUIZ (*awakening*). Hey, Doug—you awake?

ADAMS (*off*). Yep.

QUIZ. What's that singing going on?

ADAMS. Red Army men marching in the street. You can see them from the window here. It's barely getting light.

QUIZ. What are you doing up at *this* hour?

ADAMS. I've been working.

QUIZ (*incredulously*). Working?

ADAMS. I promised Forster to file a story Wednesday, and I figured the wrong way on that nine-hour difference between here and New York. Been pounding away all night to get it finished.

QUIZ. Well, whyncha hit the hay? You look pooped.

ADAMS. No, I've got to finish it. Want to hear what I've written so far?

QUIZ. Sure. Wait a minute, I'll get a cigarette.

SOLDIERS. (*Their singing is now directly under the window, then moves off.*)

ADAMS. Starts off like this. (*Reading.*) "Moscow, U.S.S.R. —I have been in the Soviet capital ten days, and that's long enough to make a man realize there's a very big thing going on here—bigger than any book that's been written about it—bigger, certainly, than anything Adolf Hitler expected to run into."

QUIZ. I like that.

ADAMS. "I am frank to say I cannot begin to grasp the enormity of this young and powerful and amazing country. I can't speak its language. I don't know my way around the city. I don't pretend to know much about Communism in theory or practice. Nor am I able to report on the battles that at this very moment are raging a few hundred miles north, south, and west of here. You already know the main thing about them, anyway—that the Red Army is winning and that the civilized world has reason to rejoice."

QUIZ. Couldn't of written it better myself.

ADAMS. "I'm a reporter from a little town named Center-ville, U. S. A. Maybe I don't know what to look for in a city like this. All I can tell you about with author-ity and conviction is the few people I have met in the few days I've been here. They are kind and friendly and terribly determined people. I like them. I know you too would get along with people like little Olga, and Miss Kozlova, and the legless tank driver, Utenko, and Doctor Kagan, and the soldier Androni-kov, and all the others we met.

"Now take Utenko.[5] (*Fading.*) He was a tank driver in the Red Army until he was wounded in the bitter fighting around Smolensk before it fell to the Nazis early in the war. (*Fading further, in prepara-tion for a flashback.*) He came in the other day carry-ing a bottle of vodka."

*Effect of the wooden-legged Utenko faded in.*

UTENKO. Tovarishch Adams! Tovarishch Quisinberry! I wish for you please to have drink with me!

QUIZ. Well, thanks, Mr. Utenko, but bein' as how your vodka is strictly rationed, and—

ADAMS. Yes, we mustn't be drinking up your—

UTENKO. Aaah, no—you must drink! How could I put my last bottle to better use than this? Here, let me fill your glass.

*Clink and ad lib bottle noises.*

QUIZ. Well, what'll we drink to, pal? You name it.

UTENKO. Let us drink to my leg.

QUIZ. Your *leg,* you say?

UTENKO. Two years ago I lost my leg at Smolensk. But now—my leg is once again among *friends! (Laughs, fading.)*

ADAMS *(back to his manuscript).* "Or the incident of the boy and the sea captain.[6] It happened while I was walking along Red Square with a captain in the American merchant marine *(fading)* whom I'd met at a luncheon of Anglo-American correspondents at the Hotel Metropole. He was saying to me:"

CAPTAIN. . . . and so when we got to Murmansk we laid in for repairs, see?—both me and the ship. I got out of the hospital in six days, but the damn ship is still— *(Pause.)* Say, what are those kids following us for?

ADAMS. I dunno. Maybe they're curious about your uniform.

CAPTAIN. Well, they don't have to tag after me as though I was a circus.

ADAMS. Maybe they're a sort of junior Dick Tracy society.

CAPTAIN. Yeah. Well, anyway. You know, I never saw anybody unload ships as fast as them dockhands at Murmansk. Most of them women, too. They certainly appreciate the stuff we're giving them.

ADAMS. *Giving* them?

CAPTAIN. Yeah. Why?

ADAMS. I wouldn't say giving. We're getting something in return, aren't we? We give them tanks and jeeps and airplanes, and they give us military victories. Now do you call that—

CAPTAIN. Take it easy, Adams, I was just saying they appreciate the stuff we're *bringing* them. . . . Does it make you feel better if I say "bring" instead of "give"?

ADAMS. Yes, it does.

CAPTAIN. Matter of fact, up in Murmansk the Russians gave a gift of a bonus to every member of the crew in that convoy—gave 'em a bonus equal to what they got paid for the whole trip. And you know what the head guy at the port says to me? He says, "Tovarishch Harrison," he says, "I would like to say that ever—" (*Pause; his eye falls on the kids again.*) Well, now it looks like *we're* following *them.* Why do these kids keep circling around us like a pack of wolves?

ADAMS. Don't ask me. Let's stop and see what they do.

CAPTAIN. Yeah. (*Growling.*) Gives you the creeps, having small fry at your heels tagging along for six blocks.

ADAMS. Looks like a spokesman has made up his mind to come over.

CAPTAIN. What's he got behind his back? I don't like this.

ADAMS (*up, to the children*). Hullo, there. What do you want?

BOY. Pozhaluista, moriak, vozmitye tsvetochki v znak blagodarnosti. Vy pomogayete nam pobedit vraga.

ADAMS. I think he wants you to take these flowers, Captain. You better take 'em.

CAPTAIN (*abashed; snorting*). Flowers! I can't take flowers. What am I gonna do with flowers?

BOY. Vozmitye eti tzveti!

ADAMS. Can you understand what he's saying?

CAPTAIN. He says to take these flowers because I help them to win the war. (*To boy—mixed Russian and English.*) Go away. . . . Ne mogu! Ne mogu! Go away.

*The boy goes away.*

ADAMS. I'm afraid you've hurt his feelings, Captain.

CAPTAIN. Huh? You think so? (*Up.*) Hey, come back

here. (*As the boy returns; low, to Doug.*) I suppose
I *could* carry them a little way. (*Up.*) Spasibo!
Blagodaryu vas! Thank you.

BOY. Pozhaluista.

CAPTAIN. Okay, bud.

*The kid goes back to his comrades.*

CAPTAIN (*to Doug*). I'd hate to be seen by the first mate
carrying two roses and a daisy across Red Square.
(*Fading.*) Look here, Adams, why don't you take one
for your coat lapel? Looks better on you than
me. . . .

ADAMS (*reading again from his article*). "A couple of
nights later, in the middle of dinner with Bill Downs—
he's the CBS Moscow correspondent whom I used to
hear back home in the States—a filling in one of my
back teeth fell out. I asked Bill what to do about that;
so he got on the phone with somebody who got in
touch with somebody else, and the next day I went
down to a dental clinic. I found the dentist was a
woman, and when I told her I'd never been treated
by a woman dentist before, she was amused. . . ."

DENTIST. Aah, yes, dentistry has been women's profession
in Soviet Union for many years. Not in America same
way?

ADAMS. Well, not very many, I don't think. But then you
people go big for women in all the professions, don't
you?

DENTIST. Ah, yes. Locomotive engineers, sea captains, even
fly fighting planes. They have given to the Hitlerites
much pain in this war. Open, please.

*A little drilling.*

DENTIST. Mmmm. Who did this work on your gold inlay?

ADAMS (*with a mouthful of equipment*). Dennis bag oam in Cennawill.

DENTIST. Dentist in Centerwille, hm?

ADAMS. You like it?

DENTIST (*patronizingly*). Is good. Is all right. Tell me, Mr. Adams, Centerwille is on the steppes in America?

ADAMS. Well, we doan call 'em shtepsh inna Midda Wesh; we callem grade plainssh.

DENTIST. Great plains—ah, yes. And (*fading*)—tell me, in America why do you permit some newspapers to attack war effort and friendly Allied nations, hm? Why is permitted to attack British and Soviet . . .

ADAMS (*reading*). "And then there was the afternoon we visited the prison camp just outside Moscow.[7] My photographer, who hates Nazis with a kind of holy zeal, was disappointed to find them so well taken care of and living in clean quarters. Most of the prisoners we talked to were quiet and respectful. . . ."

FIRST PRISONER. I reached military age during the war and was called up. I was fifteen when war began.

ADAMS. Any other members of your family in the army?

FIRST PRISONER. No. I have two brothers of ten and twelve in school.

ADAMS. Your brothers probably won't have to fight in the war?

FIRST PRISONER. I hope not.

QUIZ. Do you think Germany will win?

FIRST PRISONER. No, not now.

ADAMS. But formerly you did?

FIRST PRISONER. Bitte?

ADAMS. Previously? You once thought they would?

FIRST PRISONER. Oh, yes. I thought we would win until we were defeated at Stalingrad.

ADAMS. And then?

FIRST PRISONER. Then I began to doubt it. . . .

ADAMS (*reading*). "Another prisoner said he had been working in a factory until four months ago, when his class was called up. I asked him who does the work now. . . ."

SECOND PRISONER. Oh, I suppose women. Or French prisoners.

ADAMS. Many French prisoners in your plant?

SECOND PRISONER. A great many, yes.

ADAMS. Do they work well?

SECOND PRISONER (*fading*). Some do, some don't. . . .

ADAMS (*reading*). "But what led to our meeting Major Balkanov was our interview with a real die-hard Hitler boy—a tall, arrogant flier who had bombed Rotterdam, London, Coventry, and Leningrad. . . ."

NAZI (*contemptuously*). Oh, Americans, are you?

QUIZ. Yeah.

NAZI. I see. What a pity you have to come all the way to Russia to find German prisoners!

ADAMS. We have a few of our own German prisoners.

NAZI. Well, not for long you won't have.

ADAMS. No?

NAZI. You Bolshevik democrats will never win. We will smash New York like we did to Rotterdam and Warsaw.

QUIZ. Zat so? With what, f'rinstance?

NAZI. The Luftwaffe. It is being withheld at the moment, but when—

QUIZ. Withheld! You said it, brother! (*Laughs.*)

NAZI (*angrily*). Do not call me *brother!*

QUIZ. Take it easy, chum. It's just an American expression.

NAZI. There is only one expression for Americans—*dirty swine!* You and everyone in your filthy—

QUIZ (*at white heat*). Listen, you dog, I don't take that from *nobody!* Put up your dukes, you—

*They clash, and there are blows. Adams and a Russian guard intervene.*

ADAMS. Hey, come away, Quiz. Break it up! *Stop* it, Quiz!

QUIZ. Lemme go! Leggo! Lemme get at him. . . . Hit me over the head with a chair, will you, you Nazi scum!

ADAMS. Now take it easy, Quiz. Your head's bleeding.

GUARD (*in German*). Prisoner, come with me.

RUSSIAN. You should not do this, Mr. Quisinberry. This must be reported immediately. You shall have to come with me to the commandant.

QUIZ. Lissen, I'd do it all over again if I—

ADAMS (*sharply*). Shut up, Quiz. And do what the guard tells you.

QUIZ. Okay, okay. (*Grumbling and fading.*) That's the kind of yellow rat that oughta be strung up. Maybe he can get away with bombing women and children, but when he starts to . . .

ADAMS (*reading*). "We were ushered into the office of the prison commandant. He looked sternly at Quiz for a moment, then smiled and went over and put a hand on his shoulder. . . ."

BALKANOV. Mr. Quisinberry, I know how you feel. We hate them worse than you.

QUIZ. Then why dya treat 'em good?

BALKANOV. My friend, we treat German war prisoners well not because they are entitled to humane treatment. Actually they are accomplices in crimes without parallel in history. Things like branding and torturing prisoners—mass executions—all kinds of . . .

QUIZ. That's just what I'm *sayin'!* Then why do ya—

BALKANOV. We treat them humanely because we believe in human dignity, Mr. Quisinberry, and in international law. If we were to stoop to the atrocities—

QUIZ. Yeah, but whaddya gonna *do* with them monkeys? The only good Nazi is a dead Nazi, *I* always say.

ADAMS. Why don't you let the Major finish?

QUIZ. I'm sorry.

BALKANOV. I agree that the only good Fascist is a dead Fascist. But not all these men you have seen here are Hitlerites. Many Germans in the field have come over to our side and are actually fighting along with our partisans. Here in Moscow is a National Free German committee, made up entirely of Germans and including many war prisoners. They have called upon the German people at home to overthrow Hitler.

QUIZ. Well, the way I look at it, the German people had plennya time to overthrow Hitler before now. I think we oughta massacre every German man, woman, and child after this war.

BALKANOV (*laughing*). Personally, for humanity's sake, I am glad you will not have a seat at the peace table, Mr. Quisinberry.

ADAMS AND BALKANOV. (*Laugh.*)

QUIZ. (*Grunts. The scene fades into:*)

ADAMS (*reading*). "It developed that my photographer's personal war with the Axis was not without casualties. Next day Quisinberry's hand was badly swollen, and we took him to a hospital for an X ray. They found a fractured knuckle, and when Quiz complained of a severe headache, they took pictures of his skull and decided to keep him under observation for a few days just in case he might have suffered a concussion when the prisoner conked him over the head with a chair. I went to see him the day he was discharged, and I found he'd made friends with half the hospital. . . ."

QUIZ. Hey, Doug, I wantya to meet Dr. Kagan. . . . Dr. Kagan, this is my son, Douglas Adams.

ADAMS. How do you do, Doctor.

KAGAN. How do you do, Mr. Adams. It looks very much as though your father, Quisinberry, is going to live. The chair, however, may not recover.

ADAMS (*with mock gravity*). You don't think insanity will set in later on? You know, bump on the head and all that—

KAGAN. Insanity? In this case, how could you tell?

QUIZ (*laughing*). Great sense of humor Doc's got. Hey, Doc, tell Doug the one you told me about Goering and the pile of fertilizer [8]—

KAGAN. Ah, yes, I wish I had time, Mr. Adams, but it's a long story, and I've got to hurry down to the operating room for amputations. But you'll be here for a while yet?

ADAMS. Oh, sure.

KAGAN (*going off*). Then I'll be back. See you later. Make yourself at home.

ADAMS. Seems like a swell guy.

QUIZ. Sure is. Cheerful—wonderful sense of humor— keeps the whole ward in good spirits.

ADAMS. Seems rather young to be turning gray, though.

QUIZ. Well—lost two sons in this war. And he's had to amputate hands and legs and arms off an awful lot of kids in this hospital.

ADAMS (*sympathetically*). Is that right.

QUIZ. Yeah. Some of them even tortured by the Nazis. (*Fading.*) I tell ya, Doug, ya kinda get a different slant about this war when you go around and talk to some of these people. . . .

ADAMS (*reading*). "Quiz took me around to see some of the kids. There were several who had lost an eye or a hand. I stopped to talk to one little girl, Olga. She had seen her mother, father, and sister hanged for sheltering wounded Red soldiers. The nurse lifted the bed covers, and I saw that Olga had no feet. The Nazis had made the people of her village walk across a field to see if it were mined.[9] I thought of my Billy, at home, being ordered to walk across the common at Centerville and having his feet blown off while German officers and soldiers looked safely on. Yet I found no despair in that hospital. The wounded were returning to useful life even as they lay in their beds. Andronikov, for example, who had lost his right arm in a tank battle near Kursk. . . ."

ANDRONIKOV. What was I before the war? An accountant on a collective farm.

ADAMS. Do you want to continue at accounting after the war?

ANDRONIKOV. Naturally. In a month's time I will be writing as well with my left hand as I did with my right. I had my first lesson yesterday. . . .

ADAMS (*reading*). "When Dr. Kagan rejoined us later and we went the rounds, we saw many wounded soldiers studying agricultural and scientific books. The surgeon told us that studies are directed and examinations given at the bedsides. We fell to talking with another English-speaking Red soldier; when the doctor told him his operation had been set for tomorrow, he complained. . . ."

STUDENT. Couldn't you possibly postpone it, Doctor?

KAGAN (*surprised*). For what reason, Vasily?

STUDENT. Well, I have an examination in a week's time, and I don't want to fall behind. If you could only postpone the operation for ten days— (*Fading.*) Do you think that could be done, Doctor? If it could be arranged . . .

ADAMS (*reading*). "Dr. Kagan invited us to his apartment for dinner that night. We ate smoked salmon and wonderful black bread, but no butter, and some hot soup with cabbage leaves. There was some vodka, and we drank to the victory of the United Nations. I plied the doctor with questions about Russia and the war, and he plied me with questions about the United States and after the war. One thing he said in the course of the evening struck me as a vivid expression of the sacrifice the Soviets have had to make in order to throw the enemy back from the Volga to the Dnieper. . . ."

KAGAN. Mr. Adams, the fact is there's not a family in the Soviet Union that hasn't given somebody to the war— a son, brother, father.

ADAMS. You mean every family is represented in the armed forces?

KAGAN. No, sir. I mean every family is represented in a *grave*. We have lost *five million* fighting men.

QUIZ. Five million!

KAGAN. To say nothing of ten million civilian dead.

ADAMS. And to think some people back home have the nerve to say you're not keeping faith!

QUIZ. Not many like that, Doug. Not many.

ADAMS. That's a terrible lot of dead people.

KAGAN. Yes. (*A long sigh.*) Will you have a cigarette?

ADAMS. No, thanks.

KAGAN. You?

QUIZ. Thanks.

KAGAN. Not very good tobacco, sorry to say. We have the best subway; you have the best cigarettes.

ADAMS. Yes. That *is* a magnificent subway. I've seen art museums less attractive.

QUIZ. Are those pictures of your sons on the table, Doc?

KAGAN. Yes.

ADAMS. Fine-looking boys. One was an aviator, I take it?

KAGAN. Yes. Grischa. Flew a Stormovik. The younger, Yakov, was a machine-gunner. (*Pause.*) Yes, those are my boys. . . .

ADAMS (*reading*). "My photographer and I did two things before we left Moscow for Stalingrad. First, we brought a doll and a picture book to little Olga in the hospital. Quisinberry made a fool of himself with antics and general face-making, but I must say he succeeded in getting that little drawn, pale face to smiling and then laughing. The best picture Quiz took in Moscow was the picture of that laughing kid. (*Pause.*) The second thing we did was to take a bus over to the Bogdanov Institute and present ourselves to the blood donation center. I must say it was Quiz's idea, though I fell in with it enthusiastically.[10]

"Both of us had been blood donors back in the States; so there wasn't anything strange to us about the procedure, except that this time the nurse asked us:"

NURSE. Do you care to send the customary message along with the flask of your blood?

QUIZ. Message to who, sister?

NURSE. To the wounded man who receives your blood. We
always do that.

ADAMS. That's a wonderful idea. I'd love to.

NURSE. Here. Pen and ink for both of you.

QUIZ. Swell. Now lemme see—

NURSE. No, no, no—don't get up yet. You've got to keep
quiet. You can compose lying down as well as sitting
up.

QUIZ. Okay. Now lemme see, what'll I say . . . (*Pause.*)

ADAMS (*reading*). "Quiz finished his before I did. I'm not
very good at inscriptions. . . ."

QUIZ. Hey, wanna hear what I wrote?

ADAMS. Shoot.

QUIZ. It's a poem, sort of. Listen. (*Reading.*)

From a Yank who was born on the shores of Maine
Here's something to take in a serious vein.

Like it?

ADAMS. Well . . . it's pretty light, isn't it?

QUIZ. Sure. It's to cheer him up. Ain't that the idea?

ADAMS. But you weren't born in Maine, were you?

QUIZ. No, I was born in North Dakota. But I couldn't get
that to rhyme with anything. Still, it's a cute idea, ain't
it? "Something to be taken in a serious vein." (*Ex-
plaining.*) You know, blood—injected into the vein—

ADAMS. Yes, I know, I know. But by the time it's translated into Russian—

QUIZ. Oh, all right, all right—what've *you* written?

ADAMS. Well—uh—it's kind of serious. Uh. "Dear Red
Army fighter—I hope this gives you strength, as you
and your comrades have given strength to the common
cause of liberty. I am an American, and this blood is
from my very heart.

*Music: Sneaks in.*

ADAMS. I only hope that it may reach yours and make you feel something of the warmth that we, your Allies across the world, hold for you and for the heroic struggle of your people."

*Music: The passage comes up to a peak, then goes down behind:*

QUIZ (*having listened raptly to Doug's reading*). That's a pretty good piece there, Doug, all in all. Only one thing I'd like to—

ADAMS. But I—uh—I wasn't quite finished. Got another paragraph.

QUIZ. Oh, well, go ahead and read it.

ADAMS. Just thought I'd indicate where we were heading after Moscow.

QUIZ. Good idea. Go on, read it.

ADAMS. Okay. "Tomorrow we take a plane for Stalingrad,[11] the city that, though in ruins, stands among the noblest edifices of all time. I can hardly wait to walk the streets that a million Nazis could not hold, though they were told they were the mightiest army in the world." That's the end.

QUIZ. Mm. That's okay, kid. . . . I got one suggestion, though.

ADAMS. What's that?

QUIZ. In that part about my fight with the Nazi flier, you left out what I did to *him*.

*Music: Tag.*

# MOSCOW

No single area of international relations has been so cluttered with garbage as that standing between the Soviet Union and the West. No country, certainly not Germany or Japan, has been so vilified by the majority of the American press and by a large section of the church. No more bitter controversy has filled our bookshelves and forums than that over the U.S.S.R.'s record, its political morality, its intentions with respect to the rest of the world.

One can draw a line down through the middle of a fairly fat *Who's Who* and divide artists, scientists, statesmen into camps of anti- and pro-Soviet sympathy. Even the group of writers who set greatest store by their tradition of objectivity—the war correspondents—was hopelessly divided on the subject.

The ferocity, persistence, and gigantic dimension of twenty years of world-wide anti-Russian activity created a fear and hatred of Russia that became the No. 1 political and psychological factor leading to the war. This complex was very largely responsible for the attitude of the democracies toward the Spanish war—a war in which the republic's only material support came from the Soviet Union. It was also the dominant force leading to Munich and to the crowning insult of not inviting to that meeting the U.S.S.R. (then co-holder of a military treaty with France and Czechoslovakia).

Distrust and hatred of Russia was the triumph of a long and calculated propaganda of suspicion and wishful thinking. The Reds were inept, lackadaisical, unholy. They spent their time fornicating in a great, happy community of free love; they were thorough atheists; their air force was pitiful and their planes not much better than kites. The Bolsheviks (a term that by itself came to be synonymous with bomb-throwing and a dirty bearded rabble) were purgers, liquidators, unremitting enemies of the individual. Midway in the war, I remember reading an article by the *financial* editor of an American newspaper chain who had suddenly become an expert on Russia. He took for his theme the Decay of Excellence as typified by the Soviets. In Russia, he said, it was antisocial to excel in anything, hence punishable by exile or death. He went on for columns to nullify Russia's accomplishments in the arts and sciences, dismissing Shostakovich in a word, omitting Glière, Prokofiev, Simonov, Sholokhov, Pavlov, the country's scientists. As I read the piece, I realized that at some point he would have to account for the excellent showing of the Russian armies, which were even then sweeping the Germans back toward Berlin. The explanation was not long in coming: If the Russians had not killed off their best generals in the purge, he said, referring to the Moscow trials, *they would not have had to lose so many men turning back the Germans.* Italics are mine.

Such disgusting perversions, pumped daily into the homes of millions of Americans through the enormous pipelines of the reactionary press, could not fail after a period of years to affect public opinion. But all this ingenious propaganda was undermined and damaged as soon as the Russians tangled with the Nazis. It then became clear, through the military dispatches on page one, that the editorials that had been running inside were remarkably false. It turned out the Reds were not a peasant horde, ill equipped and of low morale. They were not straining to break free of a tyrannical government. They had a good enough air force to protect cities like Moscow and Leningrad from ever taking the beating that fell to Warsaw, Rotterdam, and Coventry. They counterattacked and defeated what was up to then the mightiest military machine that had ever been built in the history of the world.

I was never a cheerleader for the Russian system of doing things, as, for that matter, I have always had certain reservations about the way the British, Dutch, Swiss, and we Americans do things. I never subscribed to the belief, as did so many sympathizers in this country, that the Soviet Union could do no wrong. But it seemed to me, from where I was sitting, that the U.S.S.R. was doing things less wrong than was being charged by the kind of witch-hunters who pronounced Shirley Temple a Red. And I got to wondering about the Russia-haters. I thought it singular that the very people who were complaining about the liquidation of dissident kulaks and White Russians by the Reds were silent about the pogroms of Poland and Rumania and not interested in the liquidation of dissident Chinese elements in the boilers of locomotives (see Malraux's *Man's Fate*). Also odd was it that those protesting most about horrible living conditions in the Soviet Union were not disturbed by horrible living conditions in Marseilles and Yokohama and the slums of Harlem; that those objecting most to lack of religious freedom in Russia were unconcerned about discrimination against religious groups in India. There was rather a disproportion between the number of American editorials attacking the Kremlin and the number attacking the Ku Klux Klan and Hirohito. And of course it was nothing to get exercised about when Hitler clapped Jews and Reds and Catholics into concentration camps back in the early 1930's. The Russia-baiters could do business with Hitler, because he was a gentleman standing in the graces of Krupp and Thyssen and Lord Londonderry and the Cliveden set. When it came to sending a United States delegation to the Olympic Games in Berlin, it mattered nothing that Hitler had crushed democracy like a cockroach.

One could almost admire Russia for those who hated her, just as one could almost depreciate Russia for those who loved her unquestioningly. The latter were forced into fairly awkward public positions when Russia made sudden and unpredicted moves; and the embarrassed stammering of the self-appointed interpreters on those occasions was hardly constructive. But the Bolsheviki, one gathered, could not be so terrible after all, if their worst enemies were the same people who hated and actively worked against Negroes, Jews, Catholics, the Roosevelts, Willkie, organized labor, the United Nations, any and all liberal legislation, and even peace itself.

The years proved that one could be a capitalist (Joseph E. Davies) and still be friendly to Russia: one could be a Republican (Wendell Willkie, Bartley Crum, Russell Davenport) and still respect the Soviet government; a churchman (the Dean of Canterbury, Harry F. Ward) and still think tolerantly of the country; a newspaper publisher (Marshall Field) and not eat Stalin for breakfast every morning. Throughout the war the government of the United States was well aware of the score on Russia, and the men in Washington who were most intent on winning the war, and quickly, knew that the only way it could be accomplished was by unity among the United Nations. At this stage unity ceased to be a mere passive ideal and became a war *measure*.

It was with this understanding that enterprises such as "Passport for Adams" were undertaken: to serve as counterattack against Goebbels' campaign for splitting the Big Three; to combat, by the strategy of truth, propaganda lines originating both in Berlin and among isolationists here in the United States.

The script on Moscow was no more nor less euphemistic than any others in the series. It is not especially euphemistic to honor the good qualities of an ally. If Adams' report on his ten days in the Soviet capital happened to be vastly unlike the story told by W. L. White (*Report on the Russians*), it was because Bill Downs, CBS Moscow correspondent, reported things differently. A week ahead of the broadcast, Downs sent me a yard-long cablegram that served as source of most of the background of the script. I cannot vouch personally for the accuracy of Downs's information, because I was not in Moscow at the time; but his report was distinguished from White's in at least one important aspect: no group of American correspondents later repudiated Downs, as they did White, for distorted and irresponsible reporting of the Russian scene.

The blackout in Moscow, the celebration of the Red Army victory, the toast-swapping, the story of the tankman Utenko and other details came from Downs. The incident of the boy and the sea captain was transplanted from the locale of Baku, where it actually happened, to Moscow, as a matter of dramatic license. The source for this was an article by W. W. Chaplin, entitled "Stopover at Baku," in the *New Yorker* of April 10, 1943. The business of the blood transfusion was suggested by the experience of Larry Lesueur, who had preceded Downs as CBS representative in Moscow. Lesueur had himself given his blood in the manner of Adams and had written a note to go along with it. The only material taken directly from Russian sources was that dealing with the hospital and the German prison camp. Most of this came from the official Soviet *News Bulletin* and from an article by Ilya Ehrenburg.

Several months after the broadcast Downs, back in this country, listened to a recording of the program. He said he found it accurate in outline and detail, except for what he believed an exaggerated sweetness and light in the Soviet attitude toward German prisoners. The Russians, he said, hated the Nazis so deeply that Balkanov's "We treat them humanely" was a little hard to accept all the way. Not that the Reds committed atrocities on the Nazis, but neither did they sit around a hot stove together, swapping funny stories and pledging each other's health in vodka.

*Acting.* The prison scene was the only one in the whole series in which physical violence occurred—although Quiz came close to it in Marrakesh. Ludwig Donath, a magnificent character actor whose Nazis were unsurpassed in all radio, made Quiz's antagonist everything there is worthy of hanging in an SS man. Dane Clark's explosion into anger and fisticuffs was sharply acted, and the scene raised the hackles of listeners accustomed by then to the orderliness of our odyssey.

Robert Young's performance made due allowance for variation between direct address and narration. It must be remembered that Doug, in telling this story, is not narrating to an audience, but reading something to Quiz. The approach is much simpler and more relaxed than ordinary narration, and it was in order to keep this fixed in the mind of both actor and listener that I interposed occasional responses from Quiz, such as his gratuitous "Couldn't of written it better myself."

*Additional Notes.* 1. Seven months later the Germans were thrown out of Odessa in the offensive that carried through to the Rumanian border.

2. So used to it, in fact, that the Russians, in return, became the most suspicious and untrusting nation in the world.

3. A difficult moment of production. The cheering cannot be cut precipitously, nor can it be faded too long, or it will sound like a Greek Orthodox chorus taking cues from a control room. The complications are many and involve size of cast, studio acoustics, the quality of crowd sound effects, hard work, prayer, and luck.

4. The "Internationale" has since been superseded by an anthem that I think is musically lukewarm and unsatisfactory. For *my* pitchpipe the best (or at least the most stirring) of all national anthems continues to be the "Marseillaise."

5. None of the names of characters, living, dead, or one-legged, was actual, even though most were drawn, as was Utenko, from real people whom Downs and Lesueur met and knew.

6. In Chaplin's story in the *New Yorker* the sea captain was the author himself. The dope about the bonuses paid American sailors was quite true.

7. There was particular interest in the Russian treatment of prisoners at this time because of the then newly organized Free German Committee made up of anti-Nazi elements among the captured German armies.

8. There *was* a joke beginning this way, but the phrase "pile of fertilizer" was obviously metonymous. The story could not be told on the air, nor should it be told here.

9. This actually happened. No atrocity you can imagine was left undone by the Nazis before they were through.

10. See Larry Lesueur's *Twelve Months That Changed the World*, wherein he describes the transfusion on which the scene is based.

11. Doug and Quiz flew to Stalingrad for the script of the following week, which closed the series.

# THERE WILL BE TIME LATER

Produced on August 15, 1944, as the last of the "Columbia Presents Corwin" series. House Jameson was the Soliloquist; Hester Sondergaard, the Teacher. Bernard Herrmann composed and conducted an original score. The author directed.

# THERE WILL BE TIME LATER

SOLILOQUIST. This is the moment to dig in.

There will be time later for the dish that
takes two days to make
And the collection of stamps from occupied
countries,
And the novel in seven volumes that will be
finished, if all goes well, by the turn of
the decade;
There will, of course, be many a pretty
actress on the cover of *Life;*
And it's conceivable that fishing in the High
Sierras will range from good to wonderful, indefinitely.
Meanwhile your son and your neighbor's
awake ten thousand miles apart to the
alarums of one war.
The robomb drops in Aldwych, and the girl
in the white dress to whom you were
talking a minute ago is inside out, and
bloody, and hardly to be salvaged for
a decent burial.

It is certain that medicine will sooner or later
turn up with a low-priced cure for sinus-
itis
And that postwar horses will run well at Suf-
folk Downs and Hialeah
And the ballet will develop a six-day wonder

with matinées on Wednesday and Saturday;

But today three continents and archipelagoes unnumbered crawl with armor

And patriots listen through a blacked-out night for sounds of vengeance in the suburbs.

There will be a time later when assorted airplanes, having retired,

Having pigeoned home from the Balkans to the plains of Texas, from the atolls of green Pacific seas to the formal hangars of March Field,

Having flown, aquiver with triumph, straight through layers of war and weather to the designated ports,

Will, duly upon arrival, and after reasonable interval, be shuffled and assembled for the victory parade.

*We hear, fading in under the Soliloquist (who continues without interruption), the sound of three thousand planes, stretching from Forty-second Street to the outskirts of Baltimore. The effect builds slowly to an immense peak under the following:*

SOLILOQUIST. The advance notices will not exaggerate:

Hundreds of miles long, mind you, and taking hours to pass a given bleacher seating the Committee on Arrangements.

It will be a fair day in summer, ceiling unlimited, with a smicker of wind and a cloud or two;

And in proud ships named Dopey, Easy Ace,
and Jack the Giant Killer

Will be borne beribboned airmen, flak-free,
rudder-steady, kidding on the intercom,

Aircraft (friendly) sighted at eleven, seven,
six, three, four, and twelve o'clock.

The county sky will beat with a terrible biblical noise

And you will run up to your roof with your
firstborn, and he will blink at the sun
and sneeze, and you will point upward
an index finger—

See the pretty airplanes, Tommy?—

And his mouth will be open and his eyes behold the eclipse of a million square
miles of firmament,

But nothing of it will he understand, although he be told and told again.

Yet when he is old and we are gone and the
planes long junked,

He will still remember the sunny morning
and the roar that frightened him at
first, and how that afternoon his father
took him to a movie, first one he'd ever
seen.

*The twelve thousand motors of three thousand bombers rise to a terrible biblical noise. Then the effect cross-fades, at first almost imperceptibly, to:*

*Music: Entering on a level, tutti, it ups, downs, softens, and becomes a reverent commentary behind the following passage:*

SOLILOQUIST. It is permissible for us to crow for twenty minutes and be happy,
    To enjoy the late communiqués at dinner this fine evening in this brightening world,
    But neither you nor I must overdo it.
    For only this fine morning over picturesque terrain, a soldier, with the glory of Cherbourg well behind him,
    With Italy in his back pocket and republics in his debt,
    Inched forward on his belly confidently, as he had done successfully before, and drew a bead.
    He was unaware, at the time, of the optimistic tone of the Associated Press war summary,
    And likewise witless of the firm closing of stocks last evening (steel had a notably good day).
    By night he was beyond receiving range of the dream of the radio writer published on the unjammed air of America,
    For he was clipped by a bullet at 9:45 on the nose . . .

*Sound of a whining bullet under "bullet."*

SOLILOQUIST. . . . And henceforward must be numbered among the grand total of casualties (thirty per cent below expectations, up to Aachen).
    As he is dead, no one can speak for him concerning love and death and politics and taxes:

Yet it is reasonably safe to assume that he
would be amazed to hear the war is
won, that the whole thing's over, and
that from here on in it's a breeze.

It didn't seem that way to him this morning
when he was clipped, as I say, by a hostile bullet as he crawled on assignment
toward the German border.

So if we're crowing, thanks to him, because
the news is good, is wonderful, is getting
better,

Let us crow for twenty minutes only,

And get back to work.

*Music: Comes up sternly, then cross-fades to:*

*Effect of hoofbeats on soft ground. Four horsemen
are advancing slowly toward us, their horses almost
at a walk. They stop after a moment. . . .*

SOLILOQUIST. There will be time later when the horsemen
of the Apocalypse ride in from the
quadrants of the earth

And pull up by a misty woods back of an
old battleground;

And the one whose name is Conquest will dis-
mount, and he will break his bow under
his knee and trample it;

He will wipe blood from both hands on the
hide of his snow-white horse, and turn,
and fade into the mists.

And the one whose name is War will grasp
his great sword by the hilt and circle it
round his head

And fling it far, and it will shatter on the crosses of fallen soldiers.

And the dead young men will hear the sound, though their thoughts be distant and their bones be intersticed with grass.

And the saddle of the red horse shall be empty.

And the one called Famine will drop his balances, remembering the look of the rich wheat fields upon the way, and he too will alight, and skulk into the darkest shadows of the woods, taking care to avoid the barest touch of the seed of the meanest fruit;

And only the rider by the name of Death will sit still on the pale horse, and listen for sounds in the wind, and turn away in the direction of the west . . . (*Hoofbeats going off.*[1])

Leaving the riderless horses to graze forever on substances of night.

*Music: A comment on the foregoing, fading out behind:*

SOLILOQUIST. Now a compound fracture is a wicked thing, and so is a missing part.

For Nature, in all her wisdom and notwithstanding her proven generosity,

Made no allowances for blast.

Shrapnel, too, was outside the reckoning of sperm and ovum,

[1] The numbered notes will be found on pages 436-437.

And the misfortunes of this oversight may
be read in the charts of men on the ambulance trains.

You must admit that however tomorrow
may be planned,
Whether the barn is to be converted to a
studio,
Whether the lecture season of the women's
club will extend to June and will include
a two-piano recital (as it did last year),
Whether Liberia will subscribe to the inter-
allied monetary plan
And Pan American be given the polar route
to Moscow,
There will be a noticeable limp always, in
certain of our company;
And a sharp twinge in the vicinity of the
scar, come rainy weather;
And the boy with the clear blue eyes who was
valedictorian of his high school class
And who wanted to marry Selma as soon as
he got back
Will look out at the world from a mateless
bed,
Trying to recall his name and the outline
of an image hidden deep down in a
tangle of debris.

Naturally there will be opportunity later for
adjustment of the tax rates,
But in the meantime the medicine stands on
the white tray and is taken every two
hours, night and day:

> And the tattered face is built up, cartilage by
>    cartilage:
> And the bone knits slowly.

DOCTOR. How's the old back feel today, Johnny?

SOLILOQUIST. And the brisk and busy nurse comes with the
>    clean sheets to the speechless psycho
>    case, and talks a good line even though
>    he cannot answer.

NURSE. Well, you look happier this morning, Solly. Did
you have a good night's sleep? . . . Here, let me
freshen this bed for you. Tha-at's right. Easy, now.

SOLILOQUIST. And Solly grins without reference or connec-
>    tion to the facts of his case,
> His intellect having been destroyed by a land
>    mine below Avranches,
> And while the nurse lifts him . . .

NURSE. That's it, Solly. Tha-at's a good boy.

SOLILOQUIST. . . . He smiles as an infant smiles, not be-
>    cause the world is happy or a neat joke
>    has been made,
> But because our kind are born benign, with
>    goodness in them.
> And even before the senses grow to any
>    shape, or after they are sprung apart
>    with age, or idiocy, or hard knocks, still
>    the germ-plasm of our species has a
>    smile for you.

*Music: A gentle, poignant phrase, transitional to:*

SOLILOQUIST. This is the very moment to dig in.
> There will be time later for the solemn com-
>    memoration of the great event

And the cantata sung by massed choirs over
the combined networks.
The outstanding poet of the war will emerge
and be honored by the Poetry Society.
The fall catalogue of a leading publisher will
announce a striking new history of the
military strategy of World War II,
Telling, among other things, how the Fox
was foxed,[2] and how the intuition of the
Supreme Aryan was frustrated by a
Jewish general in the direction of East
Prussia.
The Museum of Modern Art will find ex-
hibitable matter in the films and ar-
chives, maps and camouflage of battle;
And in the classroom the children (not yet
here this evening, but awaiting the return of fathers from the sundry fronts,
thence presently to be conceived)
Will take their seats quietly, and listen.
TEACHER. What you are about to hear, boys and girls, are
records of the sounds of war, made during the great
blitz in the Battle of Britain. First of all you'll hear
the sound of a warden's patrol going about its duty
on a London street in the blackout, during an air raid.
Now this record was made on the night of September
27, 1940, and is absolutely authentic. By this I mean
it is not faked; it is the real thing.

*We hear the sound of a phonograph needle being
placed on an actual recording of the effect the teacher
has described. Such a record was made by the British
Broadcasting Corporation and appears in their catalogue as NPH 764. In it is the sound of hobnailed*

*shoes scuffing the sidewalk; of bombs falling distantly;
of near-by antiaircraft guns in operation. At intervals
in the course of this effect, the Soliloquist comments:*

SOLILOQUIST. In the long view backward shall not the hobnail of the home guard, scuffing the side-
walk,

Make as loud a ringing as a clash of swords
against Achilles' shield?

Who shall bookkeep the glory of this war?

And is the farmer boy who dove his trainer
straight into the earth from fifteen thousand feet (a mistake, mark you, but it
was at night, and his first try at flight
by instrument alone [3])—is he so far beneath a hero?

Hallowed be the anti-Fascist hobnail on ce-
ment, the privy-cleaner, the button-
polisher, the cook who scrambled eggs
digested by the pilot who sank the
cruiser in midmorning!

TEACHER. And now we shall hear the various types of guns
used in World War II. First, the Sten gun, a small
automatic weapon made at low cost, but very effective.
It was often dropped to the brave men of the under-
ground and to partisan fighters, about whom you will
learn more later.

*We hear the angry spitting sound of this gun, with its
waspish ricochet.[4]*

SOLILOQUIST. And the sun will stream through the classroom windows, and the leaves of the
trees tremble, and the birds stop singing
and cock their heads and wonder what

sort of thing has overtaken the young
bipeds inside the schoolhouse. . . .

TEACHER.  And here is the sound of the trench mortar used
so successfully by our great Russian allies when they
turned back the Nazis and gave us time to get ready
to strike from the west.

*The guttural bullfrog croak of the trench mortar.*[5]

SOLILOQUIST.  O little bullfrog who scattered panzers in the
          dead of winter,
          The city of Lenin and the Kremlin walls shall
          remember you!
          Also the banks of the Don and the Volga,
          the Thames and Mississippi.

TEACHER.  Here now is the sound of a seventy-five-milli-
meter field gun being fired by a British gun crew in the
first Battle of France.

*A close-up of the firing of a seventy-five. Through it:*

GUN CREW.  (*Shouted commands.*)

*We hear the locking of the breech, the detonation, and
finally the shell whooshing off toward the enemy.*[6]

SOLILOQUIST.  It will all be there in the classroom: the
          muffled command and the detonation,
          the shudder of ravaged air as the shell
          makes way.
          It will be there, ageless and accurate and re-
          peatable—
          Just lift the needle and put it down again;
          the moment will obligingly recur.
          Not contained on the same side of the disc,
          however, for a class so young, is the

color of the French valley that fall
morning, and the posture, name, and
former occupation of the dead Tommy
fifteen feet away;

Also the smell of powder in the burnt nostril;
sweat under the honest armpits; the
letter in the gunner's breast pocket, concerning how a Fascist mission twelve
days ago destroyed two streets of workers' homes in Swansea.

Later to be explained to the advanced classes
will be how the seventy-five's had to
take over when petitions failed;

How in the first place the valley was be-
trayed by sharpies, their home offices in
unexpected places, high and low, including Whitehall and the Quai d'Orsay.[7]

*Music: Sneaks in under:*

SOLILOQUIST. The teacher will gather up the records and
examine them for flaws, inasmuch as
they're to be played again tomorrow.

Meanwhile, as of the instant, anti-Fascist
hobnails scuff along in Kensington, and
the patrols of Glasgow swing into their
fifth year.[8]

The stuttering Sten has stitched another German gut in a hedgerow of the district
Orne,

And the bullfrog croaks nightlong in the bogs
of Lithuania.

*Music: Comes up transitionally.*

SOLILOQUIST. There will be time later for the staple things.
Love will occur again, between cool sheets,[9]
    and out of the way of the weathers;
Eyes will have license to glow in the light
    that slants through Venetian blinds,
And lips kissed in the secret hours will speak
    again the ancient felicities of lovers.

The heart of man has four chambers, and
    each shall be filled with tremors in the
    spring.
The season of summer shall insinuate with
    song and evidences of fertility,
Whereas the autumn, by incendiary meas-
    ures, shall inflame the woods and dem-
    onstrate how it is possible to grow old
    without loss of beauty.
Winter, with its stern outlook and its
    northern bearing, will merely under-
    score the warmth of the most ordinary
    bed, providing it is justly shared.
The earth can be relied upon to conspire and
    assist, performing as a mutual friend,
And the moon will once more be in character.

Thus will the planet, busy as it is between
    this solstice and the next, help out a
    man and woman; and the race, a staple
    always, will continue.

Meanwhile, the spleen of man is in command
    of him, and not his heart:
Your brother and your grocer's kid, one in
    the hellish heat of Aden and the other

in the clammy Pribilovs, have been a
year without a glimmer of a girl.

The word has gone among the vine-ropes of
New Guinea to the jungle fighters from
East Boston and Seattle, that a nurse,
a living female, uniformed, but of a
shape distinct and recognizable as that
of Woman,

Has arrived and may be gandered for a
short time only, before she flies on to
the Marianas;

And in the hothouse evening, through the
strangling green of tropic bush, the
hungry soldiers, bearded, sweaty, hike
for miles down to the airstrip

Just to gaze in silence from fifty feet away
upon the constellation of a single girl—
a flash of golden hair, a sparkle of
white teeth, and trim American ankles.

And in this shining symbol, conspicuous and
jeweled as a meteor in a moonless sky,

The G.I. sees his wife, his honey, and his
hope;

And she is all things ever said and done between the two:

The walking on the beach, the first kiss—in
the rumble seat;

Her profile, proud, across the dining room,
Hand held in church,
Dawn through the screen door,
Double features at the Palace—artificial
stars, but air-conditioned in the summer,

> Bridge at the Obers',
> Pregnancy—her mother was a great help
>     toward the end of it—
> Flowers, somehow, and a dim, lost evening
>     gown packed in a trunk in mothballs,
> Waiting for B-29's to finish off in Tokyo,
> Waiting for a thrust of Rokossovsky's army
>     on the Eastern Front,
> Waiting for the trapdoor under Hess's gal-
>     lows.

*Music: Comes up for a meditative moment, then sud-
denly darkens to an ominous quality. This builds to:*

*Thunder, which grumbles at intervals behind:*

SOLILOQUIST. War has the voice of a million muzzles,
> And where it speaks, dust hangs in the air
>     for weeks;
> Violence is consummate; the overtaken cow
>     lies with burst udder on the hummock;
>     no worm is safe;
> The bomb digs deeper than the mole.
>
> All creatures living in the earth and air, en-
>     tire censuses of seas, have felt the
>     shock:
> The twin screws of the dreadnought scatter
>     seaweed in luminous waters:
> Depth bombs blow up whole nations of
>     schooling fish,
> While in the heavens the eagle is outflown,
>     or mangled on the tail assembly; [10]
> And spores are liquidated in the vapor trails
>     of true Miltonic battle.

Every leaf and every frond knows all about
  it, and the humus in the ground is well
  informed;
Even neutral mountains are aware, a hemisphere distant,
For the crust of the globe is fairly resilient
  and will instantly transmit a jolt in
  China to the confidential seismographs
  of Colorado.

As I say, all fish and fowl have heard about
  it, but the pompous editor has not;
With malice aforethought he signals the
  pressroom and transforms anonymous
  wood pulp into a published lie.
The dancers of Bali can give eyewitness
  testimony and the children of Kam-
  chatka make report,
But from the unimpressed politico who has
  not heard the tidings, expect no more
  than local and continued mouthings.
Stale and immoderate, with increasing
  wind—
This is the year for it.[11]
When the candidate for district office runs
  against the dead and wounded, saying
  they died for exactly nothing,
Then the tactics call for you to take pins
  from the battle map of Germany and
  stick them in the county seat!

War has a voice of a million muzzles, which,
  though amplified by death and taxes,

Still is a whisper in the ear of him who tells
    you: "Take it easy, slow down, neigh-
    bor, take it easy. Whole thing's in the
    bag."
He's deafer than he's dumb, this man,
For though you shout to him in metal tubes:

VOICE. War! War! A war is on!

SOLILOQUIST. He'll be absorbed in the six-point landing of
    a mosquito, detectable by its faint high
    hum.
You can cry to him:

VOICE. Look to the East! Your countrymen die for the
cause and you!

SOLILOQUIST. And he will look at his navel, through which
    turns the axis of the earth.
You can admonish him:

VOICE. We are liberating Europe! We advance on all the
fronts! The armies of free people are driving to
Berlin!

SOLILOQUIST. And he will make tidy notes of the campaign,
    predict new landings, and point to total
    victory in the State of Maine;
    Instruct the army in techniques of warfare;
    Corner the market on Modiglianis;
    Buy up first editions, but no war bonds;
    Charge the foreign-born with being foreign-
    born.[12]
    And when you talk to him of postwar plans
    for employment, he will say:

FASCIST. Why should we bother with the Great Unwashed?

SOLILOQUIST. And when you tell him it's the Great Un-
    washed who wash away the stains of
    high corruption,

It's the common man, unmanicured, whose
hand prevails against the Elite Guard,
He will rejoin:

DIFFIDENT. You make me sick, you and your people with
a capital P.

SOLILOQUIST. At that point you can break the news to him:
The People shall remain in capitals, coming
before Princes in the alphabet of things,
And in the eyes of free men now and ever
hence
The unwashed shall be white as snow, even
if the dirt and smell of battle lingers on
them for a generation.

*Music: Old flags gathered in a place of honor.*

SOLILOQUIST. Some things can wait, and some things can't.
The paint job can hold over, but the blueprints'd better move along.
There will be time later for the dividend and
for further findings from a bathysphere.
The lot on the California hilltop can afford
to wait until after the cellars of Warsaw are cleaned out.
But in the meantime noncommittal mailmen
keep distributing familiar Greetings
from the President—Form 215, for
pre-induction physical—
And the boys who passed their physicals
some time ago die on a sand dune with
the sense of winning in them.

The while we talk about it, Truth, revised,
expanded, stirs from among the ashes
of burnt books;

The essence of dignity, last seen hurriedly
　　packing a bag in a hotel in Munich,
　　picks itself up from the gutter where
　　the old Jew lay beaten and bleeding.
The dream of hairy-chested amity flies on the
　　shuttle route from Oxfordshire to
　　Minsk.[13]
The key is heard turning in the concentration
　　camp amid the clamors of the box bar-
　　rage,
And Liberty, that dog-eared parchment
　　signed by Christ, the angels, and a most
　　impressive list of sponsors big and little,
Gets dusted off again.

*Music: Curtain.*

# THERE WILL BE TIME LATER

In the spring and summer of 1944 I produced twenty-two broadcasts for CBS, of which this was the last. All but five dealt with current issues and had to do, more or less, with the war. Previous to this series I had done about forty broadcasts dealing exclusively with such matters. During this period of several years people often asked me, some in a friendly, others in a hostile spirit, why I felt it necessary to plug so constantly at social and war themes. The answer was not that I was asked to do it, or ordered to do it, or paid to do it, or talked into doing it. It was a matter of my personal conscience—an apparatus that, for good or bad, would let me do nothing else.

You have all met representatives of the school that believes there is a dichotomy between what is loosely called Art and what is just as loosely called Propaganda. You may belong to the school yourself. I do not. But then, to me the equation is not one involving art and propaganda, but art and conscience—and I believe the latter pair mix as readily as gin and tonic.

Do you demand that I define what I mean by conscience? Artistic conscience? All right, find chairs for yourselves and listen to some facts about an artist named, let's say, Jack. He was any artist—he could have been a painter or a writer or a musician back around ten years ago.

One fine morning, the paper arrived on Jack's doorstep, and he let it in with the sunlight and the milk. He felt well, having just slept eight hours without benefit of ear stopples or phenobarbital: his health, his tone, his psyche were sound; his conscience rested easy as a pillowed cat. Then, between Wheaties and coffee, he read that a defenseless market town had been flattened by Fascists and that 12,000 miles away our best scrap-iron customer had anchored a battleship in a yacht basin and was pouring sixteen-inch shells into the native quarter.

None of Jack's cousins was in Spain, none of his holdings in China; yet, notwithstanding the distances between his table and those countries, notwithstanding the expected exchange of notes between foreign secretaries, notwithstanding the syndicated opinions of columnists or the prayers for peace constantly ascending from powerful churches, he was angered of his own accord, and slapped the paper down on the table.

Was Jack a prophet, foreseeing Prague, Rotterdam, Pearl Harbor, Lidice, lynched fliers, and the robomb? He need not have been, for it is no trick to prophesy lightning from a thundercloud. The point is that he was angry, that he wanted to do something about it, and he did. He entered the fight, rolling up his sleeves upon the summons of nothing but his conscience. Perhaps like John Lardner, like Ben Leider, like the Flying Tigers, Jack left love, friends, and possessions behind him, and, in violation of the codes of nonintervention, journeyed privately to meet the enemy, gunsight to gunsight; or perhaps he stayed at home and wrote a poem, spoke a piece, signed a resolution, danced a tap dance at a benefit for the wounded of Spain or China. In any case, his conscience was ahead of his time and was accordingly subject to investigation by Congressional committee.

Was Jack unique? Was he original? Hardly. There is nothing anomalous about an artist's slapping down the morning paper at an evil tiding, and slapping it hard. Any man with enough imagination to sense even fractionally the agonies of oppression can loathe a new tyranny long before the newsreel evidence arrives at the neighborhood movie house. A feeling man does not require the confirmation of a best seller or a declaration of war by his government before he takes a stand or participates in an "effort." Fascism, as I have said elsewhere, was our enemy before December 7, 1941, and those with the keenest consciences knew this best, cried the loudest warnings, and were at war with the Axis far in advance of most of their countrymen.

Shakespeare told but a half-truth when he wrote, "Conscience doth make cowards of us all." Only when we anticipate committing an evil or unkind act does our better self swerve us by intimidation. Whole peoples have gone forward bravely to dangers and to death when they were impelled by clear purpose and a just cause. In every spontaneous struggle for liberty in the history of the world, conscience has made tigers of the mildest men.

It should have surprised nobody that artists like Jack were ranged against Hitler, Mussolini, Hirohito (remember Gropper's cartoon in *Vanity Fair?*—the one that the Japanese Ambassador protested), and Franco long before the protocols of sovereign democratic states.

A good artist is governed by principles in his work. He is faced with considerations of integrity—integrity of style, structure, content. Unless he is a snob, a purist, an escapist, or an out-and-out traitor like Ezra Pound, he has an emotional concept of freedom, not a legalistic one. To him Justice transcends mere Law (law varying as it does from State to State and country to country) and becomes an abstract and shining quality—a quality to be sought not in the courts of a realm but in the heart of man. Moreover, the true artist has a feeling for his fellow, for the broad humanities; he understands something of the play and stress of outer forces upon himself, and upon you and me. Naturally, with this kind of moral radar equipment, he—Jack— can clearly see a betrayal of principle before it has turned the corner of a headline. In times of crisis and war he is able quickly to translate the bald report, the political maneuver, the communiqué, the arrow on the frozen map, into terms of blood and living pain, into terms of anger, hate, and the passions of struggle.

It is easy and it is old stuff to name names, to call the roster of the Jacks of this and other times who, because of their consciences, have fought with their wits and their art for freedom, for tolerance, for progress. Most often they fought with limited means against enormous odds, pitting their isolated talents against the enemy in whatever form, against public apathy, sometimes even against the hostility of those in whose interest they worked. This, as I say, is literally ancient history.

What is not so old is the concept of a world in which the artist no longer fights singly, but in league with fellow artists everywhere; in which his work is circulated wider than the decrees of kings. The dramatist no longer needs the combination of an angel, a Broadway theater, an advertising campaign, and a two-year run to make the impact of his ideas felt. Radio can do it for him overnight. The constructive influence of a constructive novel is multiplied a thousandfold by the constructive movie of that novel. Good magazines carry the good word into barber shops and dentists' waiting rooms, club lounges, living rooms. The architect who makes better homes for workers becomes, by the success of his handiwork, a propagandist for better light, air, sanitation, health. The painter whose conscience has been galvanized strikes off a mural, paints a slam-bang poster which six Allied countries reproduce. Shostakovich writes a symphony expressing triumph over the barbarian, and ambassadors assemble at its première. Toscanini, who would rather be slapped than play a Fascist anthem, programs Verdi's "Hymn to All Nations" along with a concerto by the Beethoven who once tore up a dedication to Napoleon. The conscientious film star refuses to appear in a role that degrades his or another's race or violates his ethics.

All in all, the conscience-controlled artists have done much better than the practical ministers, at least up to now. "Poets," wrote Shelley, "are the unacknowledged legislators of the world." The artist, learning long ago that the features of man's body and soul are identical everywhere he is born and lives and dies, became the first internationalist, the perennial interventionist, the tireless promoter of causes. He has since then surpassed the church as an advocate of the brotherhood of man, constantly creating new arguments for old dogmas. Half a century ago Tolstoi wrote:

Universal art, by uniting the most different people in one common feeling, by destroying separation, will educate people to union, will show them, not by reason but by life itself, the joy of universal union reaching beyond the bounds set by life. . . . In our time, the destiny of art is clear and definite. The task . . . is to establish brotherly union among men.

Today, at last, and for the first time in history, the world conscience of Art stands a better-than-fighting chance of being joined by a world conscience of nations. For the first time, at Teheran, the artist's abstract view of Justice was shared by the leaders of nations when they vowed to pursue to the ends of the earth the criminals of this war, to ferret them out of hiding and to punish them.

I believe it is important that all active consciences speak out. Ultimately the pen may assume again a power greater than the sword. In the meantime, let conscience mix freely with art, and don't ply Jack with questions about why he feels it necessary to plug so constantly at social and war themes.

"There Will Be Time Later," in its point of view, its emphasis, the specific nature of most of its allusions, is the most topical of the plays in this book. It mentions Aachen and Avranches, where fighting was current or recent, and it projects to the future the recapture of Warsaw. My main reason for including the script (aside from the possibility that it may interest you as radio writing) is my hope that it may serve as a point of reference and a commentary on the state of complacency of a too large minority in the nation during the last year of the war.

It was this minority that, while the world was convulsed in the agonies of a brutal and unremitting war, enabled movie theaters and night clubs to break all records; saw to it that horse racing rolled merrily on; helped the black market to corner meat, cigarettes, and train reservations. Because of it, the Treasury Department had to coax and wheedle the richest nation on earth into supporting bond drives; had to auction off gimmicks or sell kisses or throw together all-star radio clambakes; had to ask magazine publishers to reproduce likenesses of war bonds on front covers; finally had to step in and withhold taxes at the source. The complacent minority in Hollywood worried about whether it was making too many war pictures—whether escapist entertainment would sell better. (The important war documentaries such as the "Why We Fight" pictures, produced for the War Department by Frank

Capra and Anatole Litvak, went begging for civilian release.)

By and large, the people of the United States fought a magnificent war. In face of the moral disadvantage of being thousands of miles from the nearest front line, they turned the country into an arsenal and a powerhouse undreamed of by our enemies; they raised and equipped a superb Army and Navy; they beat the Germans at their own game of scientific accomplishment. But in doing all this they had to buck a complacency that sometimes hugged, like a mist, the ground of the forty-eight States. They fought the good fight in spite of the fact that isolationists were making harsh speeches in Congress, and the OPA was being incessantly harassed, and the administration was fending off constant Republican attacks—especially, and naturally, in election years.

It was in a mood kicked up by such considerations that I set to work on the script. I did not expect to be on the air again for a long while; hence the program was to be a sort of valedictory. If, consequently, it has moments of bitterness, if in places it has a valedictorian air, you know why.

It happened that around the time this program went on, the Allies were making rapid progress in the west. Thinking the war might end at any moment, I went to work immediately on a V-E script. In the weeks following, when German resistance stiffened and V-E Day was no longer imminent, I worked more leisurely on the preparation of the Victory show. In order that the published version of the script might be available simultaneously with the broadcast, I also prepared a book manuscript and used a number of passages from the piece at hand as parenthetical interpolations in the main text. Readers familiar with the Simon and Schuster (non-radio) edition of *On a Note of Triumph* may recognize certain of these passages. This is where they came from.

*Acting.* In his book, *Radio Drama in Action,* Erik Barnouw writes about House Jameson:

> Jameson's voice is a magnificently mellow instrument; he is a master of language cadences and has a fine gift for irony. Narrative roles written for him by Corwin tend toward an elaborate style, with an Olympian quality about them. In these Corwin seems to look on the human scene from somewhere else.

What Mr. Barnouw says about House Jameson is certainly unassailable; and I suppose that here, once again, I gave House a script tending toward an elaborate style and looking down on the human scene from somewhere else. In any case, when it comes to the use of the gifts Barnouw ascribes to him, Jameson continues to be without a peer in the medium. I know the comparison is rash, but somehow I think of Bach whenever I listen to House speaking verse (not necessarily *my* verse; so please put that gun down). He has a clean, cutting intellectual incisiveness; his emotion is reined and contained, just as is Johann Sebastian's. Jameson gave the script in point all the stuff that has been credited to him, and more.

The Teacher is the only other role of consequence in this piece, and she was played by Hester Sondergaard. Miss Sondergaard's realism is the sharpest I have heard from any mature actress in American radio. Indeed her only match that I know of is an excellent character actress named Gladys Smith, who, as late as 1943, was performing as a member of the BBC repertory company in London.

*Sound.* No special problems, beyond getting the particular sound discs I used in the original broadcast. I had been invited to pick these effects out of the BBC's excellent sound library, and I brought them back to this country in 1942. Until lately they were impossible to obtain on this side of the ocean, but now one may buy them either directly from the BBC in London or through their New York office, 630 Fifth Avenue.

*Music.* Bernard Herrmann does not always like my scripts, and who can blame him for that? He has mumbled and grumbled about some that he scored, but this one stood in his favor; he was pleased. And though most of his scores are glowing, even those attaching to scripts he thinks below par, the music he composed for yon soliloquy had an extra incandescence.

*Additional Notes.* 1. One of the points not understood by some listeners was why "the rider by the name of Death" remained while the other horsemen had dismounted and their horses gone wandering off. Simple enough. Conquest, War, and Famine may yet end, but Death will still be among us, unless (God forbid!) scientists find a way of keeping us all alive forever.

2. Twice foxed was Field Marshal Erwin Rommel, known as the Fox: once in North Africa, once in Europe. The second foxing led to his death, from wounds, on October 16, 1944.

3. I had in mind here a story told me by Lieutenant Roland Kibbee, who trained pilots during the war. At the training field in California where he was stationed, an irascible colonel one night was giving instructions by radio to a pilot in the air. The colonel stood on the ground while the student, flying only on instruments, followed orders. Suddenly the pilot made a wrong maneuver, and the colonel lost his temper. He screamed at the boy, and for minutes on end so nagged and nettled him via radio that, while others including Kibbee stood by helplessly on the ground,

the pilot in the air lost his nerve and control, and dove straight into the earth.

4. BBC disc No. PH 390, Cut J.

5. BBC disc No. PH 3903, Cut 6.

6. BBC disc No. PH 3903, Cut 5.

7. There was some objection to this around CBS, on the grounds that the phrase "Whitehall and the Quai d'Orsay" was grist to the mill of those who were busy trying to wreck the United Nations and who would be delighted over any suggestion that our Allies themselves were in a degree to blame for the war. The objection made sense to me; so for the air show I ended the passage with "high and low."

8. There were nine months yet to go before the patrols could be called off.

9. One may not suggest over the air that love occurs between cool sheets. I bowdlerized it to read "between four walls."

10. Don't think this hasn't happened. Eagles have been known to *attack* planes, the dopes.

11. It was the year of national elections, and the campaign was at the time just beginning to get grim.

12. A reference to the cynical "Clear it with Sydney" routine of Herbert Brownell and his Republican National Committee—a smear campaign with nonaccidental anti-Semitic overtones. The canard concerning Hillman had chiefly to do with the fact that he was foreign-born. Late in the campaign the Democratic National Committee ran a column on the *Daily News* "Battle Page" showing a picture of our French-made Statue of Liberty, under which ran the legend, "Foreign-born."

13. American bombers had just begun shuttling from bases in Britain to bases in the Soviet Union.

# ON A NOTE OF TRIUMPH

First produced on V-E Day, May 8, 1945, under the direction of the author. The public response was such that it was repeated five days later in its original form save for minor changes in casting and production made by the author. (The second broadcast was recorded by the Columbia Recording Corporation and released as an album for commercial sale. The catalogue number is M or MM575.)

Martin Gabel was narrator. The score was composed by Bernard Herrmann and conducted by Lud Gluskin. Berne Surrey was sound engineer and Gary Harris studio engineer. Charles Lewin and Lou Ashworth assisted in the production. William L. Shirer appeared as himself, speaking from San Francisco, though the body of the program originated in Hollywood.

The twin broadcasts set new records for response following any dramatic radio program, surpassing the previous high point set by the author's "We Hold These Truths" in 1941.

By command of General Brehon B. Somervell of the United States Army, a German translation of "On a Note of Triumph" was made mandatory listening for every German prisoner of war in this country. Transcriptions of a German production by the OWI were used for this purpose.

The program was produced over the network of the Australian Broadcasting Commission on October 31, 1945.

On November 24, 1945, the author received the first radio citation of the National Council of Teachers of English, and in December of the same year was given a Page One Award of the American Newspaper Guild for the same broadcast.

[To CAPTAIN ALFRED F. CORWIN, A.U.S.]

# ON A NOTE OF TRIUMPH

*Music: Broad introduction. It comes down behind:*

NARRATOR. So they've given up.
    They're finally done in, and the rat is dead in
        an alley back of the Wilhelmstrasse.

    Take a bow, G.I.,
    Take a bow, little guy.
    The superman of tomorrow lies at the feet of
        you common men of this afternoon.

    This is it, kid, this is The Day, all the way
        from Newburyport to Vladivostok.
    You had what it took and you gave it, and
        each of you has a hunk of rainbow round
        your helmet.

    Seems like free men have done it again!

*Music: Bells ring, horns blow, and we rejoice. After a
good strong tutti, the strings go down like a crowd
quieting, and they stay behind:*

NARRATOR. Is Victory a sweet dish or isn't it?
    And how do you think those lights look in
        Europe after five years of blackout, going
        on to six?
    Brother, pretty good. Pretty good, sister.
    The kids of Poland soon will know what an
        orange tastes like,
    And the smell of honest-to-God bread, freshly

441

made and sawdust-free, will create a stir
in the streets of Athens.
There's a hot time in the old town of Dnepropetrovsk tonight,
And it is reasonable to assume the same goes
for a thousand other cities, including some
Scandinavian.

It can at last be said without jinxing the campaign:
Somehow the decadent democracies, the bungling Bolsheviks, the saps and softies,
Were tougher in the end than the brown-shirt
bullyboys, and smarter too;
For without whipping a priest, burning a book
or slugging a Jew, without corraling a girl
in a brothel or bleeding a child for plasma,
Far-flung ordinary men, unspectacular but free,
rousing out of their habits and their
homes, got up early one morning, flexed
their muscles, learned (as amateurs) the
manual of arms, and set out across perilous plains and oceans to whop the be-
jesus out of the professionals.

This they did.
For confirmation, see the last communiqué
bearing the mark of the Allied high command.
Clip it out of the morning paper and hand it
over to your children for safekeeping.

*Music: Folksong, which has been fading on, comes up
full.*

SOLOIST. We're gonna tell the postman,
Next time he comes 'round,
That Mr. Hitler's new address
Is the Berlin buryin' ground.

CHORUS. Round and round Hitler's grave,
Round and round we go.
We're gonna lay that feller down
So he won't get up no mo'.

SOLOIST. Hitler went to the Russian front,
Where every bullet missed him,
But he caught a dose of Stalingrad
That spread all through his system.

CHORUS. (*Repeats.*)

SOLOIST. Adolf Hitler started hot,
He was mighty big and bold,
But the Allies slapped him down so hard
He caught his death of cold.

CHORUS. (*Repeats.*)

*Music: Behind the chorus we cross over into the orchestra, which fades down behind:*

NARRATOR. There are many variations on the foregoing—
many a different tongue and tune saying
the same thing.
The Serbs would refer to it as:

SERB. Obil osimo okolo naokolo
Hitlerovog groba, okolo naokolo.

NARRATOR. And the Danes:

DANE. Og saa gaar vi rundt om Hitler's Grav,
Hitler's Grav, Hitler's Grav.

NARRATOR. The Greeks have a word for it:

GREEK. Gyro sto mnima too
Hitler gyro gyro pername.

NARRATOR. Obviously the occasion calls for a round of
cheers and a toast with the very best you
have in the house,
And it is entirely appropriate to make a joke
and laugh at it.

But fix your eyes on the horizons; swing your
ears about.
Size up the day and date,
Look in on prayer and thanksgiving, song and
laughter dated Planet Earth, May 1945.
You mother in St. Louis on the Mississippi,
whose firstborn is a visitor in Magdeburg
on the Elbe . . .

MOTHER. Thank God I'll get my boy back instead of a
telegram.

NARRATOR. You patient wife of Bridgeport whose husband
sat it out inside a Nazi prison . . .

WIFE. Now he'll be home for longer than a furlough. Now
he can see our daughter for the first time—she's two
years old, and it's strange to think they've never met.

*Music: Sound of a small church organ coming in be-
hind:*

NARRATOR (*over the effect*). You minister and congregation in a wooden church, having come in from your
farms through the nippy night air of New Hampshire,
meeting together to thank the God of Wrath for justice done . . .

MINISTER. O sing unto the Lord a new song.

CONGREGATION. Let the congregation of saints praise him.

MINISTER. Let the praises of God be in their mouth,

CONGREGATION. And a two-edged sword in their hands,

MINISTER. To be avenged of the nations

CONGREGATION. And to rebuke the peoples;

MINISTER. To bind their kings in chains

CONGREGATION. And their nobles with links of iron;

MINISTER. To execute judgment upon them; as it is written,

CONGREGATION. Such honor have all his saints.

*Music: The scene has by now cross-faded to ritualistic Hebrew music under:*

NARRATOR. And you rabbi in the synagogue, by the light of the Menorah, by the light of the candelabra descended from the tabernacle in the wilderness, from Egypt to the Oklahoma prairie town . . .

You rabbi entering another Red Sea crossing in the ancient scroll . . .

RABBI (*over music*). No great tyranny has ever lasted. The empires of Pharaoh, Caesar, Philip, Napoleon, Hitler—each flourished, and held sway, and was destroyed. They were powerful, but all of them forgot one thing: that the only civilization that can endure is a free one.

*Music: Cross-fades into Catholic chant, behind:*

NARRATOR. And you bishop in the cathedral, singing Te Deums to Him Who has again delivered man . . .

BISHOP. Te Deum laudamus.

PRIESTS. Te Dominum confitemur.

BISHOP. Te aeternum Patrem,

PRIESTS. . . . omnis terra veneratur.

BISHOP. Tibi omnes angeli,

PRIESTS. . . . tibi coeli et universae potestates:

BISHOP. Tibi cherubim et seraphim (*fading*)

PRIESTS. . . . incessabili voce proclamant:

BISHOP. Sanctus, Sanctus, Sanctus. . . .

NARRATOR (*over fading effect*).

> Have you time right now, listener, to stop in
> at a hundred million homes?
> Some of them with plaster loose from the last
> bombing . . .
> Some in towns where townsmen's blood mixed
> lately with rainwater in the gutters . . .
> In farmhouses of steppe and upland, in mining
> villages with regimented chimneys . . .
> In apartments of executives, where décor is im-
> peccable and genuine Utrillos hang . . .
> In tenements where El trains go by every seven
> minutes with a rack and roar . . .
> In the rooming house where the young 4-F
> mechanic lives on the third floor rear,
> It's top of the evening, hip hip hooray, how
> about another drink, Alf?—and a very
> good time's being had by all.
> Meanwhile the crowds gather. . . .

*We hear, fading in, noises of tumultuous celebration.*
*The effect builds slowly under:*

NARRATOR. Crowds in Times Square, Piccadilly, Nevsky
Prospekt, crowds in the Loop, crowds on
the Boulevard—

> Gaiety and neon, laughter and the blare of
>     horns, headlines cheerful as a Christmas
>     poster—
> Noise and glitter. This is it, kid, this is The
>     Day—this is what we've been waiting for!

*Noise up full.*

NARRATOR. But through the din, the clamor, do you hear
>     a whisper?
> In your mind's good ear and in the hearing of
>     your conscience, don't you get a voice?
> Listen—

> Listen . . .

*We hear crowd noises only. They are beginning to
lessen.*

NARRATOR. Nothing yet—just crowd. But listen close.
> Take your good ear out of low range,
> Whisk it high, hoist it up to cirro-stratus
>     country, up to where a bird can hear it-
>     self think, where a B-29 has wing room.

*The crowd noises fade away, blending into atmos-
pheric sounds, under:*

NARRATOR. Flash across a dark Atlantic heaving under the
>     sway of a victor's moon.
> Listen for intimations of wind and water, and a
>     rush of fog eastward of the Grand Banks.

*The atmospherics cross to:*

*Music: Sea drift, under:*

NARRATOR. Below these waters, strewn beneath the lanes

of porpoise and whale, the bones of how
many good men lie?

How many hulks rot here, how many barrels
of blood and oil mix with the tides of free
connecting seas?

But never mind. Running as we are, eastward,
against the grain of time, we are over the
Isles in a hop and a jump; we are established now, on the continent.

So listen closely.

*Music: We hear music only. It is in the clear for a
moment, then fades out.*

NARRATOR. In just a moment now.

Don't expect to hear metallic speech from a
rosette of amplifying horns on the high
poles of the public address system,

But listen for a modest voice, as sensible and
intimate to you as the quiet turning of
your own considered judgment.

Now we are ready.

The voice you hear will be that of the conqueror—

The man of the hour, the man of the year, of
the past ten years and the next twenty.

*Music: A quiet passage behind:*

SOLDIER. I'm a private first class in an army of one of the
United Nations. If you don't mind, there are some
things I'd like to ask.

*Music: Fades under:*

NARRATOR. Just a guy in uniform you've met somewhere, or seen in the newsreels loading a truck or marching, or read about in the dispatches.

A fighting man—glad to be alive, a little tired, but in good shape, a dozen battles notched in his gunstock and dug in his memory.

Who is he?

His name and rank and nationality don't matter much; could be a Tommy or a Yugopartisan, a Red Army fighter; could be a G.I., your neighbor's brother—or your son.

Good. Now picture him where he may be to-night in Europe:

Perhaps in his cot in a barracks, his hands behind his head, thinking things over:

Perhaps he's standing on a village green before a monument to the dead of World War I;

Perhaps he's strolling in a history-weary valley under the same stars that twenty-five hundred years ago watched a Persian brand of Nazis take a beating in the hills of Marathon.

Close your eyes, and it could reasonably be this boy, that boy, any boy at all with war still thumping in his ears.

Close your eyes and concentrate and listen.

*Music: The soldier motif in the strings again.*

SOLDIER. If you don't mind, there are some things we guys would like to ask.

*Music: Poses the question:*

SOLDIER. First of all, who did we beat?

*Music: Surge.*

SECOND SOLDIER. How much did it cost to beat him?

*Music: Surge.*

THIRD SOLDIER. What have we learned? What do we know
now that we didn't know before?

*Music: Surge.*

FOURTH SOLDIER. What do we *do* now?

*Music: Surge.*

FIFTH SOLDIER. Is it all going to happen again?

*Music: Up full and then out behind:*

NARRATOR. Can it be?
    In the interim between the making of a toast
        and the drinking of it,
    Such questions on the lips of fighting men?
    Questions from areas of truce?
    Insistent, footnoting the surrender?

FIRST SOLDIER. Who've we beaten?

*Music: The motif proposes an answer:*

NARRATOR. Who've you beaten?
    Well, let's get hold of him and see.
    Lead him in and prop him up like a tomato
        plant before our microphone.

    Now! Look at this rubble of a man: ragged,
        broken, blond Nordic hair matted with
        pure Aryan blood, deaf from blast and

blind from smoke, chin down, tail between
   his legs.

   Pity the poor bastard?

GERMAN. I was ordered to do it.

NARRATOR. You hear? He was ordered to do it.

GERMAN. I'm a soldier. I'm a little man. I merely obeyed
   orders.

NARRATOR. Whose orders?

GERMAN. The party's.

NARRATOR. Who elected the party?

GERMAN. I did.

NARRATOR. Who supported the party?

GERMAN. I did.

NARRATOR. When you saw where the party was taking
   Germany, whose job was it to overthrow the party?

GERMAN. Mine.

NARRATOR. And did you?

GERMAN. No. I was a member of the party.

NARRATOR. He's meek now. He answers questions.

   He stands before you gun-reft, palms empty,
      steel whip confiscated;

   Wounded, defenseless, thrown upon your ten-
      der mercies,

   The quality of which, he trusts, shall not be
      strained.

   Observe him, note him well:

   Now . . .

   If you wait until we spin the mike about, so
      that it picks up the winter of a not long
      bygone year . . .

   It was the year Broker's Tip won the Kentucky
      Derby,

> And 3.2 per cent beer was proclaimed morally
> fit for Americans to drink.
> It was 1933.

> The mike, reversible, goes back to it:

*Music: Cold winter's morning in Berlin. A suggestion
of "Horst Wessel," overshot with Wagnerian brass.*

NARRATOR. Look at our German now:
> Fat and sassy, swastika on his arm band, cob-
> blestone in hand, ready to advance the
> cause.

*Tremendous shattering of a large glass window.*

NARRATOR. Another Jewish store window is broken, the
> stock will presently be looted, and the
> state is happy.
> Hey nonny-nonny, Achtung, and well-a-day.

> This has been a good week for the little man
> who obeys orders, and prosperity fills his
> jowls and biceps,
> For his Führer was appointed chancellor last
> Monday,
> And on Wednesday [1] . . .

*Peremptory knocking on a door. The door knob is
turned impatiently. Over this:*

NAZI. Open the door! Open!
NARRATOR. . . . raids on the homes of leaders of the op-
> position parties.
> And on Thursday . . .
NAZI (*snatching a paper*). This is what we think of your
newspaper!

---

[1] The numbered notes will be found on pages 495-496.

*Furious tearing apart of an edition as fat as a Sunday "Times."*

NAZI. You are forbidden by decree to publish any further editions as of today!

NARRATOR. . . . suppression of the opposition newspapers . . .

And on Sunday . . .

ANNOUNCER (*filter*). Attention! An official government decree. Henceforward it shall be deemed a crime against the state, punishable by law, to make any criticisms whatever of Reichschancellor Hitler.

Heil Hitler!

*Music: A metallic fanfare, as though from a loud-speaker.*

NARRATOR. All this in the first week they were in the saddle.

Every week thenafter, for twelve inbreeding years of fifty-two weeks each year, week in, week out—

The looking around carefully before speaking:

The leather heels on the doorstoop and the bell ringing insistently at three in the morning:

The storm trooper, authority dangling from the holster on his hip, smugness fitting him like tights: [2]

The new decree, even worse than the one published last week:

The dream of escape, the pillowful of border where Kind People wait just across, just beyond, on the other side, so near they see you and have pity for you; and then the awakening in the room in Düsseldorf. . . .

NAZI. You're under arrest. Put your clothes on and come with me.

NARRATOR. Violence beyond the fitful torsions of the straitjacketed maniac in the asylum . . .

NAZI. Tear his beard out by the roots. If his face comes off with it, all the better.

NARRATOR. Arrogance enough to dwarf an Alp . . .

DR. ENGELKE (*slight echo*). God has manifested himself not in Jesus Christ, but in Adolf Hitler!

NARRATOR. Last week, pillage; this week, murder; next week, burn the books, and don't forget the Bible.

Fourth week in April, trial of a thousand priests and nuns.

The men who were masterless but free now have a master but no freedom. However, they have discipline and a scapegoat, and one can go far on that.

Hunger and poverty and a couple of big contributions from a couple of big industrialists were enough to get them started,

And fancy treasons, foreign and domestic, kept them going:

Also, cruelties to make skin creep on the sweating scalp . . .

The fat and hairy fist against the fragile mouth . . .

*A harsh smash.*

NAZI. Now spit out your teeth, pretty one, and tell us— who else was in your trade union?

NARRATOR. The conscript children—putrescence in the classroom, scum injected in the growing arm . . .

CHILD.     My father last night said to my mother that he hates Der Führer.

NAZI. Good boy. Where do you live, Hans?

NARRATOR. Last week, purge; this week, Putsch; next week, break a treaty, form an Axis, give a hitch to Franco.

Meanwhile the small businessman who didn't kick in to the party is framed on a trumped-up charge of listening to the British radio and is thrust, protesting, on a table for the guillotine . . .

BUSINESSMAN (*terrified*). No, no! I'm innocent! I have no radio! I'm innocent, I tell you! No! I'm inn—

*The blade falls.*

NARRATOR. This week and every week the staggering lie: Nations stripped and tortured like a captive girl, while sidewalk superintendents stand by, around the world, and look on, fascinated. Even as they watch, of course, death warrants issue to themselves and to their sons.

Extra—double feature—Austria and Anschluss:

And the corpses of the suicides of gay Vienna are sanitarily disposed of.

Darkness rising: pageants and parades: drapes and flags and searchlights and the goose-step:

>Next week, umbrella dance at Munich—Salomé
>bearing the head of John the Czech.
>And coming soon, too soon, Lavish Spectacle—
>Millions in the Cast—Curtain Going Up—
>POLAND DEVOURED BY LIGHTNING AND LOCUSTS
>IN EIGHTEEN DAYS!

*Music: War!*

NARRATOR. Eastward, look, the land is bright! You can
read an occupational order by the flare of
the burning church.
>(Sixteen hundred of the townspeople are
locked in there, but their screams have
sizzled out, the children's being the first
to cease.)
>In the ruddy-complexioned evening of Byd-
goszcz, study, if you will, the reflected
glow on the face of the little man who
obeys orders.
>He hasn't had as much fun as this since the day
he split open the professor's head in the
well-planned scuffle on the Fröbelstrasse.

*Music: Punctuation.*

NARRATOR. Now if you will permit us to move the mike
along, being careful not to trip either over
the rubble of treaties or the ruins of Rotterdam,
>We will have a word with the same little man
who last month pasted Denmark and Norway in his scrapbook. . . .

GERMAN. Heil!

NARRATOR. Will you explain why Rotterdam was bombed

and thousands of its people killed *after* the city had surrendered?

GERMAN. Ya, sure. Schrecklichkeit.

NARRATOR. What is that?

GERMAN. Frightfulness, it means.

NARRATOR. Frightfulness?

GERMAN. Ya. That was our plan.

NARRATOR. You mean Schrecklichkeit is an official *policy* of the German high command?

GERMAN. Ya.

NARRATOR. Mm. (*Pause.*) You seem to be feeling pretty chipper.

GERMAN. Holland fell to us in four days, Denmark in one.

NARRATOR. And France?

GERMAN. We will be in Paris before the end of June.

*Music: Punctuation.*

NARRATOR. Scene: A clearing in the forest of Compiègne, before the end of June.

Occasion: unconditional surrender of Liberté, Egalité, Fraternité.

Cast, in order of appearance: Hitler, the sunshine boy; Goering, of the splendid Nordic belly; Brauchitsch, the man who looks like a rat; Ribbentrop, the rat who looks like a man; assorted admirals, generals, flunkies plenipotentiary.

Shirer, the reporter, stands at the edge of the clearing, watching the party advance to the armistice car. His eyes are on the face of the Führer, who the other day did a little dance for the newsreel cameras when

he learned the good news of the death of
France.

SHIRER. He glances slowly around the clearing, and now,
as his eyes meet ours, you grasp the depth of his hatred
—revengeful, triumphant hate. Suddenly, as though
his face were not giving quite complete expression to
his feelings, he throws his whole body into harmony
with his mood. He swiftly snaps his hands on his hips,
arches his shoulders, plants his feet wide apart. It is
a magnificent gesture of burning contempt of this
place.

NARRATOR. The gloating hour is to be remembered. File
it away in a bombproof corner, if such
there be, against a better time, if such can
possibly arrive.

Meanwhile, other gestures of contempt soon
fill the night skies over London.

The cocky pilot (little man with wings) smiles
in German, and the bombardier spits on
his punctual hands,

In forewarning of which, below, the news is
published on the blacked-out air.

*The London air-raid siren sounds an alert, which con-
tinues under:*

NARRATOR. And the workers of Britain, in bed with the
aches of a long day at the factory, overtime, no Sundays off, rouse now from their
body-warm blankets in the cold room,

Shuffle along to the damp shelter, bleary,
pooped out, hoping not to catch a direct
hit or a sore throat.

And inevitably, in some postal zone or other,
    the hit is a direct hit,
And the kid with the bright blond hair and the
    turned-up nose moans all night among the
    rubble because his left leg hangs in black-
    ened tatters, and he cries to his mother,
    who is dead.

*The siren comes up full. Then, under the following,
it cross-fades slowly to:*

*Music: A gay Strauss waltz, as coming from a café
orchestra on Unter den Linden.*

NARRATOR (*over the cross-fade*).
    The siren is a musician of no value,[8] knowing
        only one tune, which, each time played, is
        a disturbance of the peace.
    Oh, in the prime of the Luftwaffe, when there
        was nothing west of Dunkerque save pros-
        pects of disaster,
    The tenor of life in London was considerably
        beneath that of Berlin,
    For whereas the pubs of Westminster burned
        like books and synagogues and the waters
        of the estuary blazed with oil . . .

*Music: Up and steady under:*

NARRATOR. The warm cafés of Kurfürstendamm were
        busy and gay, and there was boating in the
        Tiergarten.
    The waltzes of J. Strauss of Austria (now
        part of the Reich) were especially lilting
        in the ballroom of the Adlon.

The dances of A. Dvořák of Bohemia (lately
absorbed by the Greater Germany) were
gay as could be,
And the contralto in the rathskeller, abrim
with charm, sang feelingly the lieder of
E. Grieg of Norway (Reich protecto-
rate). . . .

*Music: It comes up, enjoys itself, and goes down be-
hind:*

NARRATOR. And war was glorious,
And the best champagnes of France were
poured on the tables of the Schutzstaffel,
The finest grades of Danish bacon sputtered
in the skillets of loyal party workers,
Paintings from the Louvre hung tastefully on
the walls of Berchtesgaden,
And the iron ore of Sweden alloyed well with
the bauxite of Spain.

The music was but stimulating and the per-
formance but continuous,
With a minor fanfare for the pushovers in the
Balkans in the month of April . . .

*Music: Fanfare.*

NARRATOR. A flourish for the Isle of Crete in May . . .

*Music: Flourish.*

NARRATOR. And in June, sumer icumen in with the sound
of another broken treaty.

Yea, on the dawn of the second day of summer,
the little man who could be relied on to

take orders took yet another order,
proudly.

He advanced chin up, Stuka high, chest out,
tanks pointed east, into the Soviet Union,

And it was a great morning, and war was glorious, and it was exalting to kill and destroy
for Der Führer, as always;

And the fanfares soon came every hour on the
hour, on the Reichssender radio,

Smolensk, Kiev, and Orel falling to the accompaniment of pronouncements from Lord
Haw Haw.

LORD HAW HAW. It will be futile to hope that one day the
Soviets may rise again. They will never rise again.
They are being smashed, once and for all. When their
defeat is completed, Britain will stand alone, without
one single barrier between her and the foe.

NARRATOR. Bryansk, Odessa, Rostov, encirclement of
Leningrad, siege of Moscow, Russia staggering under the bulletins of D.N.B.

And the sale of Russian-German dictionaries
boomed in Leipzig, city of books and culture,

At about which time the little man took
another swig of captured vodka, stripped
another carload at Lublin, herded naked
men, women, and children into hot
showers to open their pores for the gas
chamber,

And then sat back in his barracks and listened
to waltzes on the loudspeaker in the
prison yard.

> Later, in conformity with the predictions of
> seasoned military observers, the Russians
> were crushed at Stalingrad, and that was
> the deciding blow.
> Hitler, the giver of orders, said so himself—
> said no power on earth could push the
> Wehrmacht back from Stalingrad—and
> who could doubt the word of him in whom
> God hath manifested Himself?
> What Hitler hath put asunder, no man could
> join.
> And that was that,
> And the wave of the future swept all before it,
> And the Century of the Uncommon Aryan
> opened up ahead,
> And Germany was promises.

*Music: The Nazi has arisen, and he shineth under:*

NARRATOR.  The little man no longer was a little man.
> He was a colossus who stood with one foot in
> Rhodes and the other in Finland.
> He clapped his hands, and a tanker went down
> off Atlantic City, aflame.
> He blinked his eyes, and there ensued mighty
> thunder, and Tobruk was his in a day.
> He inhaled, and a million slaves trembled in
> his galleys.
>
> Nothing like him ever was.
> He was organized from the womb (often
> illegitimate, with state approval) to the
> grave—of his enemy.
> His brand was on the soul of his victims,
> And the planet fitted in his palm.

*Music: Glory unto Hitler—but just for a moment. Then:*

NARRATOR. This is the man you have beaten.

*Music: A flourish for our side, leading into:*

SOLOIST.　The German Army General Staff,
　　　　　I guess they missed connections.
　　　　　They went a hundred miles a day,
　　　　　But in the wrong directions.

CHORUS.　Round and round Hitler's grave,
　　　　　Round and round we go.
　　　　　We're gonna lay that feller down
　　　　　So he won't get up no mo'.

SINGERS.　(*"Round and Round" trails off, cross-fading.*)

*Music: Orchestra gives out the Soldier's original question motif behind:*

NARRATOR. We return you to the conqueror,
　　　　　To the boy with the questions on his mind,
　　　　　To the man of the hour, the man of the year,
　　　　　　　the man of the next twenty years.

*Music: Preparation.*

SOLDIER. So that is the man we have beaten. How much did it cost to beat him?

*Music: The motif out after:*

NARRATOR. How much did it cost?

　　　　　Well, the gun, the halftrack, and the fuselage
　　　　　　come to a figure resembling mileages be-
　　　　　　tween two stars—

Impressive, but not to be grasped by any single imagination.

High octane is high, and K rations in the aggregate mount up; also mosquito netting and battleships.

But these costs are calculable, and have no nerve endings,

And will eventually be taken care of by the federal taxes on antiques, cigarettes, and excess profits.

However, in the matter of the kid who used to deliver folded newspapers to your doorstep, flipping them sideways from his bicycle,

And who died on a jeep in the Ruhr,

There is no fixed price, and no amount of taxes can restore him to his mother.

His mother sits in a room with a picture tonight, and listens to the clock ticking on the mantelpiece, and remembers, among other things, how he struggled with the barber when he was getting his first haircut, and how she tried to calm him.

And the upstairs tenant, in consideration of the news outdoors, says to his wife:

TENANT. Shall we invite Mrs. Frisch to come up? She's all alone tonight, and it seems sort of a shame.

WIFE. Well—I have a hunch she'd *rather* be alone tonight.

TENANT. Think so?

WIFE. I don't think she's in a mood to talk or carry on. She probably just wants to be with her thoughts.

TENANT. Maybe you're right.

NARRATOR. And the thoughts of the mother are tall, straight thoughts,
And they burn like candles, quietly and slowly—
And they trail into smoke and are lost in shadows.

And most of the fallen young leave mothers and fathers alive and awake tonight,
And if you wish to assess the cost of beating the Fascists you must multiply the number of closed files in Departments of War by the exchange value of sorrow, which is infinite and has no decimals.

Not to be overlooked, either, in such reckonings,
Is the international character of the love of human beings,
Since this phenomenon never has been bounded on the east by Eastport.
Elsewise,[4] what is a notice like this doing in the busy pages of the London *Times?*

NOTICE. To my dearly beloved boy, Donald H. Collins, Fighter Pilot R.A.F., on this, your twenty-first birthday, reported killed in action, September 6, 1941. Sadly missed. . . . Mother. . . .

NARRATOR. Elsewise, why the young mother in Baranovichi, Poland, writing to relatives in Orange, New Jersey:[5]

LETTER. My dear Moishkele and all my dear ones: On the twenty-fifth there was a massacre here as in all other places. People were thrown like dogs into privies, children were thrown alive down wells. We're still among those who have been able to survive, but for how long? We expect death every day. Now we are mourning the death of those closest and dearest to us. Your family is no more, Moishkele, not one of them was left alive. But I envy them. Must close this letter now. It is impossible to describe our torments. The one thing that you can do for us is to revenge yourselves on our murderers some day. Alas! Even a little revenge! . . . I kiss you all and bid you a last farewell before our death.

NARRATOR. And the reasons for mourning in Denmark are the same as they are in Ohio,
And the cost is not figured in kroner any more than it's measured in dollars.

There are, of course, the lesser entries in the book.
The amputated leg and the artificial eye have cost somebody something,
And the broken mind cannot be repaired by a pocketful of cash. Oh, no, no.
The deep red gouge across the inner calculations is the trail of hate,
And there is no accounting for the turns it will take, both sooner and later.
The slide rule, faced with this, is panicky and sterile,
And algebra goes home to die among the Arabs.

Shall the balance sheet be balanced?
By whom? How?
No combination of savants and learned cogs, holes punched in cards and electric motors,

No brow containing Euclid, not even the
serenest lores in consultation with each
other,
Could be else than baffled by the simplest problem of the cost of hunger in a baby's
bones.

Have you paid something of the cost, you
listener?
Well, you're not through paying and the bill's
not settled,
For in this way and that, for the rest of your
days,
The cost will appear—it will present itself in
the form of deductions from the pay
check,
In a surplus of widows and fatherless children,
In the remembering eyes of the sweetheart,
In the tubercular lung of the stunted girl,
In the stammering speech of the shell-shocked
boy,
In babies never to be conceived on love beds
never lain in. . . .

*Music: Up and into a solemn variation on "Round and
Round," segueing to the question motif, behind:*

NARRATOR. Again we return you to the conqueror,
Man of the textbooks of millenniums
ahead. . . .

*Music: The soldier motif.*

SOLDIER. But what do we know now that we didn't know
before? What have we *learned* out of this war?

*Music: Same treatment as in earlier pattern.*

NARRATOR. What have we learned?
>    For one thing, Evil is not always as insidious
>        as advertised,
>    But will, upon occasion, give fair warning, just
>        as smoke announces the intention of flame
>        to follow.
>    This is one due you must give the devil.
>    Satan, whose fine Italian hand is in the writing
>        of *Mein Kampf,* was, together with the
>        paperhanger, perfectly candid about the
>        blueprints.
>    Between them they announced they were going
>        to lie and plunder, and they kept their
>        word.
>
>    Never has disaster had so many heralds as this
>        war:
>    Cassandra spoke from every lecture platform,
>        and the notices were posted high and low.
>    A cabinet minister resigned at Downing Street,
>        protesting.
>    A President cried, "Quarantine!"
>    Moscow sent food and guns to Barcelona.
>    A housewife of Duluth boycotted German
>        goods.
>    An emperor of Ethiopia said in good French [6]
>        before the statesmen of Geneva:

SELASSIE. Je suis venu pour avertir l'Europe de la catastrophe qui l'attend.

INTERPRETER. I came to give Europe warning of the doom
that awaits it.

SELASSIE. Je suis venu pour défendre la cause de toutes les petites nations menacées d'agression.

INTERPRETER. I came defending the cause of all small peoples who are threatened with aggression.

SELASSIE. Aujourd'hui le problème a une portée beaucoup plus étendue que l'aggression italienne en elle-même. C'est la sécurité collective.

INTERPRETER. The problem today is much wider than merely a question of Italian aggression; it is collective security.

SELASSIE. La moralité internationale est en jeu.

INTERPRETER. It is international morality that is at stake.

SELASSIE. Dieu et l'histoire se rappelleront de votre jugement.

INTERPRETER. God and history will remember your judgment.

NARRATOR. Signs and portents!

> It was no furtive tapping on the window sill
>     at night,
> But clamorous pounding in the public square,
> Blow after blow, like a monstrous drop forge,
> Beating into shape the time to come.
>
> And the time came, and the prophecies matured.
> The storm arrived, and was no surprise to the
>     barometer—
> The Jew who had cautioned . . .

JEW. The Nazis are not against the Jews alone—that's just a sham. If you let them carry on this way, they'll be the death of Christians, too.

NARRATOR. . . . he saw gentiles die as well, and sighed,

And foraged for bullets in the cellars of the
Warsaw ghetto.
Yea, and the time came, and it developed that
Cassandra and the Jew were right and
that the Cliveden set was wrong.
Fire and brimstone, dropping from the sky,
were educational:
There were tongues in torpedoes, sermons in
bombs, books in the running battles.
Whatever was learned was learned the hard
way,
Between blood transfusions and last rites.
Each lesson fell trip-hammer hard, with a bang
that killed a citizen or two somewhere.

*Music: A percussive pile-driver effect, which is used
punctuationally in the following sequence:*

KANSAN. We've learned out of World War II that we'd
learned nothing out of World War I.

*Music: Stroke.*

FRENCHMAN. We've learned that nations that don't know
what they want will get what they don't want.

*Music: Stroke.*

TEXAN. We've learned that our east coast is the west bank
of the Rhine and that the defenses of Seattle begin in
Shanghai.

*Music: Stroke.*

BRITISH. We learned at Munich that a soft answer doesn't
turn away wrath; that if you offer your other cheek
to a Nazi, you'll get your head blown off.

*Music: Stroke.*

NEW YORKER. We've learned that a newspaper with a big circulation right at home can lie with a straight face seven days a week and be as filthy and Fascist as a handout in Berlin.

*Music: Stroke.*

SENATOR. We've learned that those most concerned with saving the world from Communism usually turn up making it safe for Fascism.

*Music: Stroke.*

MAN. We've learned that women can work and fight, as well as look pretty and cook.

*Music: Stroke.*

COCKNEY. We've learned that the Germans came close to winning the first time, even closer the second time— and might bloody well win if we give 'em a third time.

*Music: Stroke.*

RUSSIAN. We've learned the value of allies in a world where any war is sooner or later a world war.

*Music: Stroke.*

GREEK. We've learned that some men will fight for power, but that most men will fight to be free.

*Music: Stroke.*

VERMONTER. We've learned that freedom isn't something to be won and then forgotten. It must be renewed, like soil after yielding good crops; must be rewound, like a faithful clock; exercised, like a healthy muscle.

*Music: Toward a resolution of the "stroke" motif, but not to a finish; instead, drop briefly behind:*

NARRATOR. These and many more—
These are the lessons our sons and brothers
have turned to dust to teach us:
And whether Victory will stick, and the dead
be not made fools of,
Depends on whether what we learn is held as
close and constant as a catechism,
Come summer and prosperity, come winter and
the wolf, come ebb tide and come flood.

*Music: Up now. At the peak of a crescendo, pare away the instrumentation and segue to the question motif.*

NARRATOR. Again the conqueror, where he patrols in Germany tonight under a street light.
Again G.I. Triumphant, by whose dint the
lamps are going on all over Europe!

We return you to the conqueror.

SOLDIER. Here's another thing I'd like to know: What do
we do now?

*Music: Motif pattern, as before.*

NARRATOR. What do we do now?

Why, the war goes on!
And you yourself, man of the hour, start out
upon new worlds to conquer.

For though the swastika comes down and is
trampled under shoes made in Massachusetts and Lancashire,

Though the ovens of Lublin are avenged,
The war goes on, and peace stands offstage
    waiting for a cue at the end of a Japanese
    drama—
The part where the mighty warrior lays down
    the Samurai sword before a grocery clerk
    from Baltimore.

Meanwhile—unfinished business in Asia,
Killing to be done among the archipelagoes.
The cruiser turns about and makes for wider
    waters.
Liberators rev up for the long flight westward.
The forests of Bataan awake and sing.
The garrisons of China check the hour on their
    watches.

Shall those of us who never quite believed that
    war could come
Now hasten to believe it over?
We here at home who safely tidied battles into
    books,
Spliced the counteroffensive into a feature film,
    and went to see it together with an Andy
    Hardy picture at the Orpheum?
Shall we who followed the bloody tracks on
    maps and took assurances from pins that
    tanks had gotten through—
Shall any of us celebrate beyond the compounds
    of a day?

Look here. We hoist our microphone again,
    fifty feet higher than Everest,
And reconnoiter the air for items blowing

toward us on the west wind over unpacific
oceans.

*Music: Atmospherics, as in the eastward passage, be-*
*hind:*

NARRATOR. Listen—do you hear it? The report of young
men from Nebraska, dying!
Word that Kentuckians are padding through
the jungle lands of Burma,
Sailors from Ohio navigating coral seas,
Texas rangers bombing in pagoda country!

*Music: Up slightly.*

NARRATOR. Run westward in pursuit of the sun,
Westward with the grain of time over an
afternoon of ocean,
Over humid isles where the situation is in
hand, and into tropic skies
To overtake a young American on vigil.

*We overtake a Thunderbolt fighter. After establish-*
*ing, drop away for:*

NARRATOR (*up, calling*). Ahoy, there!
PILOT. Hi!
NARRATOR. Have you heard the news?
PILOT. Yeah! Pretty wonderful, ain't it?

*The motors drop away.*

*Music: The space motif takes over where the motors*
*have left off, carrying under:*

NARRATOR. Let's run on among the Indies.
Look below you now—sunlight fretting the

surface of the sea, horizons tentative in
  haze,
Islands alee, and the smell of vegetation mix-
  ing with ocean air.
In a flicker, banks of cumulus ahead now fall
  behind;
Leagues rush past; noonday is caught up with.
Now in our mike sight, straight below, like
  beetles in a pond,
Warships out of Newport News, destroyers on
  patrol.
We plummet to the leader, avoiding the up-
  draft of its stacks,
And through a ventilator on the starboard deck
Lower our microphone until it touches bottom
  in the engine room.

*The sounds of an engine room have faded in under
the foregoing.*

NARRATOR. Ahoy, there, engineer!
ENGINEER. Hi!
NARRATOR. Have you heard the good news?
ENGINEER. We sure have.
NARRATOR. What do you think of it?
ENGINEER. Two down and one to go!

*Engine sounds cross-fade to:*

*Music: Bathyspheric passage under:*

NARRATOR. Now we hoist us up and overboard, and dive
      with our equipment well in hand,
    Into the sea and under it:

*Effect of sudden dunking at high speed. Flutter mechanism on for:*

NARRATOR. Five fathoms down we go, and steady now.
Look up. The roof of ocean lifts and settles
slowly,
Tufts of seaweed pinned against the ceiling.
This is the boundless green estate of upper
ocean, where the mine and the submersible
perform, and tin fish swim among the
fauna.
Unreel the cable of this mike and light your
head lamp, for we're diving deeper
Past schools of angler fish and sailfins, down
to zones where greenness goes to blue and
blue to black.
Careful, now! Look sharp; push hard against
the crushing water. Can you make it out?
A shape long and slender, lying on a hummock
of the bottom, almost covered by a drift
of mud.
Alas, it's not an ancient hulk—it is a submarine
made in Wisconsin; the Scorpion perhaps,
the Amberjack, the Argonaut—

We beat upon her hull.

*We clank on the hull with a hammer.*

NARRATOR. Ahoy, there! (*Silence.*) Have you heard the
news? (*A long silence.*)
Listen! Can you hear us? Listen!
(*Shouting.*) It's all over with the *Nazis!*
We've *beaten* them!
Can you make that out?

You who are these long months unreported,
You who have been out of touch of any but the
    deep-sea angels of the Lord's leviathan
    reserves—
You who are resting—rest assured of *this:*
Over your heads and above the sea, victory has
    risen like the sun
And moves west as we tell these things to
    you—
Your brothers, going down to sea in ships
    from San Francisco, Liverpool, and
    Alexandria,
Sail toward the settling of a score.

Here with you on this ocean bed lie scattered
    your fighting comrades—
Men of the Cisco and the Perch,
The Yorktown, the Chicago, and the Liscombe
    Bay.
Each shall be vindicated in the proper hour!
The names of Hornet and of Wasp have been
    fitted with new stingers,
And on trim battlewagons sailors from North-
    ampton, Houston, Helena, and Lexington
Set out to resurrect the glory of proud, sunken
    ships that bore those names.

The Japs in conference tonight may well con-
    sider the latest news from Europe,
And while they're at it, please to note the
    weather forecast for tomorrow:

Dawn coming up like thunder.

*Music: A flourish, leading into:*

SINGERS.　Let me tell you, Hirohito,
　　　　　　Now that Hitler's down,
　　　　　　Better buy a black kimono,
　　　　　　Cause you're on your last go-round.

　　　　　　Round and round Hitler's grave,
　　　　　　Round and round we go.
　　　　　　Gonna lay that fellow down
　　　　　　So he don't get up no mo'.

*Music: Orchestra; a conclusion to "Round and Round" and a segue into the question motif.*

NARRATOR.　We return you to the conqueror.

*Music: Motif.*

SOLDIER.　But when we've finished with the Japs and the whole thing's over—well, what *then?* Is it gonna happen again?

*Music: The pattern again.*

NARRATOR.　Soldier, when the sweet morning comes and you are mustered out,
　　　　　　When you get paid off and there's a ticket in your wallet that guarantees delivery to street and number and the faces you have dreamed about in foxholes,
　　　　　　You must not forget to take along your homework in the barracks bag.
　　　　　　For there is no discharge in the war.
　　　　　　You are on probation only—you and the faces you have dreamed about, and all the rest of us.

Henceforward we must do a little civil thinking
every day,
And not pass up the front page for the sports
page as we did before.
Vigilance pays interest and compounds into
peace,
Whereas bland unconcern and the appeasing
cheek draw blitzkrieg as a lightning rod
attracts a thunderbolt.
A little civil thinking every day, that is the
homework: yea, shooting your mouth off
against the bad appointment and the
shoddy referendum,
Storming the redoubts of the local Schickl-
gruber,
Voting in season, and demanding of your representative that he be representative.

Peace is never granted outright; it is lent and
leased.
You can win a war today and lose a peace tomorrow,
Win in the field and lose in the forum.

Peace has a mind of its own, and doesn't
follow victory around.
What is two-thirds finished in Germany
Won't be three-thirds finished in Japan.
There's a homely maxim out of London says it
better:
COCKNEY. The duration's goin' to be a lot longer than the
war, guv'nor.
NARRATOR. You can make war quickly, but you make peace
slowly;

It takes a second to break a globe, but a long
time to put it together again.

There are some records in Washington say it
better . . .

RECORDS. Congress took only eight minutes to declare war
on Germany; and in the same session it took only five
minutes to declare war on Japan, but between this
war and the last one, the world took twenty *years*
trying to declare peace, and then couldn't do it.

NARRATOR. Listen.

To win is great; to learn from winning,
greater—but to put the lessons learnt
from winning hard to work, that is the
neatest trick of all.

Shall we live alone this time and like it?

J. DOE. We tried that before, and it didn't work.

NARRATOR. Shall we sit with the rest of the world in
common council, or stand apart in splendid isolation?

W. DOE. We stood apart last time, and it didn't work.

NARRATOR. Shall we merely assume it will happen again
in the course of human nature

And make up our minds not to make up our
minds about anything really important?

M. DOE. We tried the ostrich routine last time, and it didn't
work.

NARRATOR. Soldier—don't you feel in your bones that it
doesn't have to happen again?

Don't you know, sure as you're a winner, that
the sovereign peoples of the world yearn
everlastingly for everlasting peace?

Don't you know *they* all know, and would tell
you if you asked them?

Don't you feel in your bones that we can keep
    it from happening again? That we're
    smarter now we've learned some les-
    sons and stronger now we've made some
    friends?
For has it not been shown what free *united*
    peoples can accomplish? Wonders stag-
    gering the naked mind!

CITIZENS.    We came from behind and we came up fast,
We got together and spotted 'em aces and
    spades and beat 'em at their own game,
Showed 'em how to pull off what Napoleon and
    Hitler never even dared to *try*—invasion
    across the Channel;
Showed 'em how to flank a flank and blitz a
    blitz;
Showed 'em that when you *get together* and
    conquer, it works out better than divide-
    and-conquer;
Showed 'em how to wage a war and work and
    plan and sing songs, all at once:

CHORUS.    Round and round Hitler's grave,
Round and round we go.
We're gonna lay that feller down
So he won't get up no mo'.

NARRATOR.    Let the singing fade, the celebrants go home;
The bowl is drained and emptied and the toasts
    are drunk,
The guns are still, the tanks garaged,
The plane rests in the hangar;
Only the night remains, and the armed camps.

The boy with questions on his mind turns on his cot in the barracks—stares at the ceiling, says to himself:

SOLDIER. I hope to God it won't happen again. I hope they plan better this time.

NARRATOR. Outside, the dew of morning glistens like a hope,
And light of day is just beyond the local curve of earth.

The Plan gets ready for Tomorrow; Tomorrow is ready for the Plan.

*Music: Preparation: a slow, quiet, reverent theme which builds, not too quickly or obviously, under the Petition:*

NARRATOR. Lord God of trajectory and blast,
Whose terrible sword has laid open the ser-
pent
So it withers in the sun for the just to see,
Sheathe now the swift avenging blade with
the names of nations writ on it,
And assist in the preparation of the plow-
share.

Lord God of fresh bread and tranquil morn-
ings,
Who walks in the circuit of heaven among
the worthy,
Deliver notice to the fallen young men
That tokens of orange juice and a whole egg
appear now before the hungry children;
That night again falls cooling on the earth as
quietly as when it leaves your hand;
That freedom has withstood the tyrant like a
Malta in a hostile sea,
And that the soul of man is surely a Sevasto-
pol that goes down hard and leaps from
ruin quickly.

Lord God of the topcoat and the living wage
Who has furred the fox against the time of
winter
And stored provender of bees in summer's
brightest places,
Do bring sweet influences to bear upon the
assembly line:
Accept the smoke of the milltown among the
accredited clouds of the sky:

Fend from the wind with a house and a hedge
     him whom you made in your image,
And permit him to pick of the tree and the
     flock
That he may eat today without fear of to-
     morrow
And clothe himself with dignity in December.

Lord God of test tube and blueprint,
Who jointed molecules of dust and shook
     them till their name was Adam,
Who taught worms and stars how they could
     live together,
Appear now among the parliaments of con-
     querors and give instruction to their
     schemes:
Measure out new liberties so none shall suffer
     for his father's color or the credo of his
     choice:
Post proofs that brotherhood is not so wild
     a dream as those who profit by post-
     poning it pretend:
Sit at the treaty table and convoy the hopes
     of little peoples through expected straits,
And press into the final seal a sign that peace
     will come for longer than posterities can
     see ahead,
That man unto his fellow man shall be a
     friend forever.

*Music: Man unto his fellow man, a friend forever.*

# ON A NOTE OF TRIUMPH

Poor Germany! All smashed up, ruined buildings, broken beer bottles, hungry, ragged, her excellent Krupp works a tangle of junk, her submarines divided among the Allies, her Valkyries disheveled, her land overrun by gauche Americans, effete British, and savage Russians, her Siegfrieds deloused and punished, some of them hanged—is it not too much for a people to bear? It would seem so, less than seven months after the Nazis called it another war and quit. Already the slobbering of the sympathetic has swelled to a mighty chorus, and big hearts are bleeding throughout our land. *Life* ran a section on German refugees that pitied them with a tender and searching pity, and there were sermons from many a pulpit calling forth Christian forgiveness and charity for the misdemeanors of a misled German people. The priests and ministers thus filled with the spirit of the Lord were for the most part undisturbed when, earlier in the brutal career of this century, ruin and famine, persecution and massacre fell on millions of Chinese and Armenians, Rumanian and Polish Jews, Spanish Loyalists, Nicaraguans, Bolivians, Paraguayans, Indians.

When I was a kid I bummed my way to Europe. On a train in France one day I had a long talk with a young Frenchwoman, a gentle, mild-spoken character with the face of an angel and the voice of a seraph. She told me that she hated the Germans with an unquenchable and violent hate; that too many of her people, her friends, her loved ones, had died under the Kaiser's juggernaut; that the score between France and Germany had gone back far beyond the first war; that the Hun was incorrigible, and that he could be expected to make trouble again. At the time I smiled patronizingly and told her she was too close to her own personal experience, and to Germany, to take a proper universal view of Europe. I spoke with the determination and fervor of a pacifist, which I then was. "We are beyond thinking of war as an instrument of political expediency," I said. "If we are really earnest about peace, there need never be another war." It was all so simple, and I was so cocksure about the new world. My friend turned her face away and looked sadly at the rolling green fields of her country. They were drenched in sun, peaceful under an August sky, calm and rich with harvest. Nine years later, Nazi tanks were rolling over them again.

I doubt whether that woman, if she is alive today, can hate the war-making German much more deeply than I. I hated him when he was on the way up, and at his zenith, and on the way down. I hate him now that he is on trial. I hate him because he is at once the embodiment and the symbol of hate itself; because he sums up all that is obnoxious and evil; because he is pompous, arrogant, cruel, treacherous, bullying, predatory; because he will stop at nothing, including sycophancy and perversion; because he is the antithesis of all that we mean, or think we mean, by Brotherhood. This combination of qualities is not indigenous to Germany, any more than Fascism was born in modern Rome; but it has recurred with remarkable frequency among the Prussian crowd, and Fascism has never come so close to succeeding on a world-wide scale as when it was engineered and piloted by Berlin.

I do not agree with those who believe every German is born a moral and political jackal and that the German people can never learn to govern themselves. That would be subscribing to the theory of "vile inheritance of blood." If a family named Schmidt has in the past fifty years produced a remarkable number of thieves, murderers, sadists, rapists, and maniacs, that does not damn their descendants down to the last generation. In fact if a Schmidt today has a clean record and seems to be a decent egg, I would give him every break possible, but at the same time keep an eye on him. I need not employ him as a bank teller or trust him with a gun, but I would certainly not write him off as a loss. Environment, as we well know by this time, breeds qualities in men. The contribution of the slum to crime and disease is all too familiar. You despise the criminal who comes out of it; you apprehend him and shoot it out with him and punish him; but you do not hate his children nor deny opportunity to his wife and brother. If you have any kind of practical foresight, your action does not end there. You seek to get rid of the source of crime by eliminating its breeding grounds, just as marshes are drained to get rid of mosquitoes.

For a long time Europe was a political slum. It is too early to say whether the slums have been cleared since the end of the war, but it is never too late to acknowledge that from a few of the so-called better neighborhoods, such as England and France, came some of the worst influences of political morality. If the Britain and France of 1931-9 had been healthy and alert, neither Germany nor Italy could have become so corrupt.

I have been intrigued, as an amateur poking among classic ruins, to find how often what I call "glass house politics" has operated to the disadvantage of mankind. By this phrase, I mean the kind of politics which, living in a glass house, throws stones in all directions. It is glass house politics for any country to speak of peace, democracy, unity, and freedom if any of those is conspicuously missing within that country. Or for a country to subscribe to the charter of the United Nations, if within its own charter there is contempt and discrimination for whole millions of its people, and never an opportunity to share in the benefits of society. It is glass politics to believe that the keeping of peace does not have important beginnings at home. Certainly the *reverse* of the keeping of peace—the making of war—begins there. It began at home in Germany and Japan and progressed under the stimulus and direction of local Fascism, until it made war for the world.

One more opinion before I get to the story of the script: The military defeat of the most obvious Fascists—that is, the ones who were directly threatening us—was by no means synonymous with the end of Fascism. There are several quiet Fascist governments left over from the war. Whether Fascism, with these as its nuclei, can ultimately regroup and contest democracy again, is a question which cannot be dismissed.

Now when CBS late in 1944 invited me to write a program to be broadcast on the day of Victory in Europe, I was sure of only three things: that I hated the guts of the Nazis; that on V-E Day they would not be entirely finished; and that in all probability we soft-hearted Americans would begin feeling sorry for the Germans as soon as their defenses started to crumble. But, being no seer, I could not anticipate the form our victory would take—whether the Nazis would fight to the last Bavarian mountain pass and hang on as guerrillas; whether the German people would rise and revolt (ho, ho!) against the Nazis; whether one of the neutral countries would step in to negotiate for the Reich; whether there would be any such *thing* as an official V-E Day. Nor could I do more than guess about the mood of the American listener on the day of Victory. It was obvious even then that war in the Pacific would outlast the European war and that hundreds of thousands of our men would still be fighting on that day and the day after. Constantly there were press reports to the effect that no celebrations would be held, that this city or that city would rejoice quietly and pray at its churches for a speedy finish to the rest of the war.

There was another handicapping factor in the way: since Pearl Harbor I had written and produced programs almost exclusively concerned with the war and its issues. There were, it seemed to me, a limited number of ways of saying the same thing over and over, and I felt I must surely have explored them all. I was conscious of dredging deep into what reserves I could still claim in the writing of "There Will Be Time Later." It was the last of twenty-two consecutive weekly programs, and by the time I delivered that program to the network I was fed up with writing and wanted nothing more than to pick up a gun and join in the fighting. That, however, was an old conflict within myself and was basically attached to my intermittent doubts as to whether my programs were in any way helpful to the war effort. In any case, it began to look as though I would have little time to prepare this culminating broadcast, because our armies were smashing ahead in France, and the experts were giving Germany only two or three weeks.

The script did not come, and I was in despair. Ten days I gnashed my teeth, paced the floor, walked the park, listened to music, did some reading that I hoped might switch on the ignition. My mind was a vacuum, abhorred by Nature and the Muses. It was not funny. I sorely wanted to be represented on the air when the day arrived and was most anxious to produce for CBS a program of which it would not be ashamed, a program that would *say* something. But the pressure was relieved suddenly by an event that I would just as soon not have benefited from: the costly December counteroffensive in the Ardennes. It was apparent, as the Battle of the Bulge developed, that there would be no Allied touchdown that year; that it would be well into spring before the Germans could possibly be beaten. So I dropped the script, took up other projects, and returned to the job weeks later. From then on it was not exactly a hay ride, but at least I was able to measure daily progress.

I finished "Triumph" at the end of January and put it on the shelf. Soon afterward I began working on a broadcast to be aired from San Francisco on the eve of the opening of the United Nations conference, and, to make sure I would not be caught empty-handed on the day of Victory, took the working script with me to San Francisco. In the meantime Bernard Herrmann had completed a score, which he was holding in readiness in New York, and had dispatched photostatic copies to the west coast. This was for whatever conductor would pinch-hit for him should the broadcast originate in California.

The pre-conference broadcast over, I went to Hollywood to await developments. Martin Gabel, whom I had long before invited to narrate the broadcast, flew out from New York when the news picked up. He was idle for a week after he reached Hollywood, until early on the morning of May 7. On that day I was aroused by a telephone call at 5 A.M. from the CBS watchdogs at KNX, and I hurried to the studio. A cast and orchestra were quickly assembled and had already been in rehearsal for two hours when the news came through that the Kennedy (Associated Press) victory was false and that the official victory would not be declared until the following day. I continued with the rehearsal as though we were going on the air that night and recorded a performance for study. Next day we went at it again and were in fairly good shape by the time broadcast took air at 7 P.M., Pacific War Time.

I was so hardened to the script by the time it hit the network that I had no sense of its potentials, if any. From the time I had put it aside in January to the day of the rehearsal, I had changed one word: from "And how do you think those lights look in London" to "Europe" (London's blackout had been lifted a month or two ahead of the German surrender). I had not lived as closely with the script in the days immediately ahead of broadcast as is customary in my operations, and I was therefore cold on it. Gabel was much more confident and enthusiastic than myself, and so was Bill Fineshriber, who had accompanied me to the west coast for the San Francisco and V-E broadcasts.

It is most pleasant for a writer's estimation of his work to be revised upward by others. Too often it works in exactly the reverse pattern. The response to this broadcast exceeded not only my expectations, but, I am told, all previous records for drama broadcasts. Whether it was the state of mind of the audience on the nights of the broadcasts (it was repeated within a week), or Gabel's towering performance, or Herrmann's virile music, or some intrinsic value in the script, I am not qualified to say; but the reaction of listeners and of most critics was, to coin a word, terrific—all of which is taken up in detail in Mr. Holt's index of Critical Reception.

*Acting.* Erik Barnouw says Gabel has "a brusque quality and a sort of smoldering anger in his voice . . . a voice of challenge." He has that, all right, along with an aggressive intelligence and a sense of the history of his time, a passion for justice, and a set of political convictions that enabled him to sound as though he were woven right into the texture of the script rather than attached to it by special arrangement with some casting office.

Gabel hated the Nazis with a fine upstanding hate, and the anger in his voice had been smoldering for a long while. There was a powerful thrust to his introductory passage ("So they've given up"); a quiet contempt in his interviews with the Little Man of the Reich; a controlled bitterness in the pages tracing the rise of Nazi power. He was neither too soft in the "cost" section nor too genuflective in the petition that closed the broadcast. His emotion was at all times reined, yet clearly and unmistakably felt—suggested, in the way that veins and musculature are suggested in fine marble sculpture. The Lord God to whom Gabel addressed himself in the apostrophic finale was a Jehovah who'd had His eye on the war and did not have to be wooed and flattered and praised and crawled after. Gabel stood up when addressing the God of Victory. His hat was in his hand, but his heart was not in his mouth.

It was a heavy assignment, and Gabel carried it off brilliantly. In 120 minutes of air time (counting both programs), he made one minor *lapsus linguae*. He kept the repeat performance at as high a pitch as the first, which was no mean trick; if anything, he improved on the original. Radio's second nights are never as exciting as their openings, and I very much dislike to produce repeats. But this one, thanks to Gabel's consistency and the solid virtues of my cast and music, was a pleasure to do.

The Soldier-Conquerors were plain, simple men, as they mostly are in real life. I permitted none to sound like the side-of-the-mouth, *mot*-making Joes of Class B films and radio. Nor were the Germans and Nazis too obviously heel-clicking. The whipped Nazi who is introduced as an exhibit under "Who've you beaten?" was made (by George Sorel) a resigned, depressed prisoner of war—a thoroughly deflated and defeated *Übermensch*. The cocky German of the *Schrecklichkeit* interview was coldly arrogant and most pleased with himself. Ludwig Donath gave him all the dimensions he required, and one or two extra.

The young mother of Baranovichi who writes a letter to Moishkele in Orange, New Jersey, is one of the more difficult of the minor parts. She must be grief-stricken, yet not wailing; despairing, yet still strong enough of spirit to call upon the world, through Moishkele, to avenge the torment and murder of her people. Lucille Kibbee performed the role and made it as moving as Herrmann's background music.

Selassie speaks with a high-pitched and well-cultivated voice, and his French is excellent. I believe there are newsreel shots extant of the Lion making this very speech before the League of Nations, and these, if accessible, should be used for reference. Otherwise Peter Witt's reading in the record album of the broadcast is a good model. The Interpreter (Joseph Worthy in the original) speaks at low key; he is in the far background.

The Jew who warns that Nazis will be the death of Christians too, speaks without accent.

The Kansan, Frenchman, Texan, New Yorker, and others who appear in the montage of "lessons learned" are indicated merely for purposes of identification in rehearsal. I much prefer this to marginal notations such as Voice 1, Voice 2, etc. If it is possible properly to cast the Greek and the Cockney *as* a Greek and Cockney, fine!—the speeches could well be said by those to whom they have been ascribed. But it is not a must.

The Citizen who exults, "We came from behind and we

came up fast," is joyous and slightly vaunting. He, together with the folksingers, adds up to a last fling, a last faint whoop of celebration, before we turn our minds gravely and hopefully toward tomorrow.

*Sound.* Neither a picnic nor an ordeal for the sound department. Four effects require special handling. The "atmospherics" indicated in the passage, "Listen for intimations of wind and water, and a rush of fog eastward of the Grand Banks," should be recordings of actual transoceanic static, the kind that plagues short-wave broadcasts from abroad, especially those from England at 02:00 to 02:30 G.M.T. any Wednesday morning.

The air-raid siren that cross-fades to a Strauss waltz in the passage on the tenor of life in London should be none other than that contained in the BBC sound disc, Master No. 4193 (Library No. 19-B-12). This had better not be faked, because too many Americans among those likely to hear your production are familiar with the real thing. A great many soldiers and civilians from this side spent time in England during the war, and they will accept no substitutes when it comes to the signal of an air-raid over Britain.

The "effect of sudden dunking at high speed," when the Narrator plunges into the sea and under it, was a product of blending and high magic from the hand of Berne Surrey. He put together a sequence of recorded sounds, a soupçon of manual splash tank with a huge paddle wheel, and one or two other gimmicks. The sound was most graphic, and reminiscent of diving the wrong way and hitting the water flat on one's belly. If you insist on the sordid technical details, the sound discs were *Masque* record No. 552B, *Standard* No. 55B, plus an acetate of a film soundtrack.

For the clanking on the hull of the sunken submarine Surrey used a large tank, a heavy hammer, and a far corner of the studio. This effect, incidentally, impressed a great many listeners, among them Lieutenant Commander Edward Steichen, whose Navy photographic unit was responsible for the magnificent documentary film *Fighting Lady*. Steichen told me that for some time before the broadcast he had been working on a film documenting U.S. submarine warfare and that the sequence had affected him powerfully.

*Music.* Elie Siegmeister, in *The Music Lover's Handbook*, refers to "the orchestral skill and knowledge of special sound effects" of Bernard Herrmann and of his "background music" for radio. Siegmeister is right about the skill and knowledge, but it is inaccurate to call Herrmann's scores "background music," for they play a far more active part in the productions for which he chooses to compose. They are foreground more often than not, and in the case of "Triumph" his contribution was such that Jack Gould wrote in the New York *Times:* "Herrmann's original score was a decided and distinguishing asset, complementing and strengthening the narrative in the best tradition of music written for a play."

The song, "Round and Round Hitler's Grave," sung on the program by Johnny Bond and a trio, was composed ad libitum by a group of folksingers, musicians, and lyric-minded writers including Millard Lampell, Woodie Guthrie, and Pete Seeger. Even I threw in a verse. The song, should you want to try it on your piano, is copyright, 1942, by Bob Miller, Inc.

*Additional Notes.* 1. This is no exercise in dramatic license. Between the appointment of Hitler to chancellorship on a Monday and the following Sunday, the events depicted actually occurred.

2. In the original script, unexpurgated for radio, this line read: "The fat-assed stormtrooper, authority dangling

from the holster on his hip, smugness fitting him like a jockstrap." It was printed this way in the Simon and Schuster edition of the script and offended remarkably few people. I thought the indelicate phrases had the value of conveying emotional revulsion with relation to the storm-trooper—one of the ugliest of all Nazi appurtenances.

3. A play on the famous phrase from Job 13:4. But I might have known the listener would be in no mood to notice that sort of thing.

4. The use of this word sorely offended one critic. A "discriminating mind," he wrote, "could not possibly have written 'elsewise.' " Ho hum.

5. No invention, this letter was printed in *PM* on September 15, 1944.

6. Not trusting my own French, at the time I was writing this script I sent an English translation of Selassie's speech to an expert in the short-wave section of one of the networks, to render into his native language. This he did, and I sent it along to the printer. Half a hundred readers have since pointed out four glaring errors in grammar, syntax, and language. It was corrected for this version. At least I *hope* it was corrected.

# 14 AUGUST

Broadcast over CBS on August 14, 1945, within three hours after the news of the Japanese surrender. Orson Welles was the soliloquist. The score was based on music written expressly for this production by Lucien Moraweck and Mario Castelnuovo-Tedesco, together with excerpts from the Passacaglia written by Georg Philipp Telemann and orchestrated by Anthony Collins. Lud Gluskin conducted.

On the following Sunday, designated by President Truman as national day of prayer, this script was expanded and repeated over CBS under the title of "God and Uranium." At this time Olivia de Havilland assisted Mr. Welles. The author directed both performances.

# 14 AUGUST

*The report of a cannon.*

*Music: Introduction.*[1]

Congratulations for being alive and listening.

Millions didn't make it.
They died before their time, and they are gone and gone,
  for the Fascists got them.
They are not here, but their acts are here,
And they are to be saluted from the lips and from the
  heart before the conversation drifts around to recon-
  version.
Fire a cannon to their memory!

*Cannon.*

God and uranium were on our side.
The wrath of the atom fell like a commandment,
And the very planet quivered with implications.
Tokyo Rose was hung over from the news next day [2]
And the Emperor, he of the august stupid face,[3] prayed
  to himself for succor.
Sound the gun for Achilles the Atom and the war workers:
  Newton and Galileo, Curie and Einstein, the Arch-
  angel Gabriel, and the community of Oak Ridge, Ten-
  nessee.

*Cannon.*

Ladies and gentlemen: The peoples have come a long way
  since the time of Cain.
Much has happened, and the upward path has been strewn

with dinosaurs, tigers, Caesars, slave-traders, and
Fascists.

In spite of which, as you have heard on the radio tonight,

The best in the way of flags is flying over the lands of the
enemy,

And free men are being born on schedule:

New free men, conceived December last, during a counteroffensive against their elders in the Ardennes, are tonight breathing and kicking and making fists:

Whereas the saber-toothed tiger is nicely arranged with
fish fossils in the museum

And Caesar is twice hacked to pieces by his countrymen,
the second time strung up by the heels to cure

The trader in slaves cannot buy back his name from the
contempt of the generations

And the Nazi is parted from his pomp and his Führer,
pending announcement of the hanging day.

The Jap who never lost a war has lost a world; learning,
at some cost, that crime does not pay.

This too is worth a cheer.

*Cannon.*

Fourteen August.

Fourteen August to the gun turret and the turret lathe

And both stand still, and their masters stop to wipe away
the sweat of winning.

Fourteen August to the tractor in the wheatfield, and the
farm hand who heard the news from Washington on
the local wave length a few hours back.

Fourteen August to the flag on Surabachi, and to Colin
Kelly's boy and Meyer Levin's mother.

The bones of the expendables of Corregidor stir imperceptibly on 14 August.

Fourteen August, Chinese time, to the bridge at Mukden,
where the Japanese crossed over into war some fourteen years ago.

Fourteen August to the blood-brothers of Stalingrad, their
armies lately a burning wind across the plains of
Manchuria.

Fourteen August to the mending wounds among the hospitals, and to barracks bags, and to bunks and flight
decks.

Now homecoming.

Now the dog-tag exchanged for the name again.

They will converge from outlandish zones of time, from
secret Somewheres known alone to postmasters;

The comrades will write letters to each other for a while,
and then drop out of touch.

The mess halls, where the meals were on the house, will be
forgotten soon enough between Jim's Diner and home
cooking.

Beaches without beachheads.

Jobs without sergeants.

The men who tilted guns of battleships and stoked them
in epic battle

Will ride the level ferries of bay and river.

The tank man will drive a powered lawnmower while his
father watches.

The pilot with many missions will do errands for some
civilian company.

The bombardier who crushed a city in a blinding instant
will help his wife dry dishes in the kitchen sink.

Listeners on 14 August, 1945—

Size up the latest news bulletins against the morbid yester-

days of Warsaw and Pearl Harbor, fallen Paris, and
the blitz on London.
Weigh Potsdam against Munich carefully, removing from
the balance the millions who shall walk no more.
Sketch in the dates and happenings from textbooks and
from memory; and draw your own conclusions.
Are we agreed that all is one?
That the world's a single continent?
That mountains made of faith are not to be moved?
That Freedom is an endless river, jealous of its tributaries,
fertilizing the country through which it flows?
Study the time we live in. It will do you good.
Effective 15 August, peace, its care and handling, becomes
our ward!

*Cannon, and:*

*Music: Punctuation.*

Say it tonight with saluting guns, with psalms, with cham-
pagne and with laughter, but also remember the fields
beyond, and the names and faces beyond.
It is worth noting and remembering that here in this
August the grass is hearty,
The sky friendly, the wind in the wind sock,
Birds are competitive, the hills of home are in their accus-
tomed places.
All is accounted for
Except the farmer's boy,
And the mill hand who lived near the canal,
And the young men from the city block where the gutters
fry in summer.

One lies with an ocean across his chest at the bottom of
an Arctic deep.

Another sleeps with sand in his eyes where he fell on a
    beach in Palau.
The bones of the fisherman rest in clay far from the rocks
    of Maine.
And the miner's kid is under the ground of China.

The cricket sings in the summer night, but the soda clerk
    says nothing.
The fawn leaps in the wolf-proof wood, but jungle roots
    twine the postman's feet.
The turtle is young at sixty-one, but the flier is dead at
    eighteen.

Remember them when July comes round
And the shimmer of noon excites the locusts,
When the pretty girls bounce as they walk in the park,
And the moth is in love with the fifty-watt bulb
And the tar on the road is blistered.

They've given their noons to their country,
They've trusted their girls to you.
They are face to face with an ally's earth
For a bunch of tomorrows.

Remember them in the fall of the year
When frost airbrushes the withering leaf,
And the silo is fat as a bearing woman,
And the cleats of the backfield dig up gains to the praise
    of the stadium,
When the number-one goose says it's time to go, and the
    flock points a V to the south.

They've given their seed to forty-eight states,
Their football tickets to you.
The shirt on their back is a worm-cut rag
For a bunch of tomorrows.

Remember them in the sleeting months
When the sap stands still in the veins of the tree,
And the bottle of milk on the frozen doorstep raises its
     cap to the morning;
When the skating girls eddy like snow on the rink,
And the storm window hooked on the prairie farmhouse
     mutters in the gale out of Idaho.

They're dead as clay for the rights of men,
For people the likes of you,
And they ask that we do not fail them again
Tomorrow, tomorrow.

*Music: Finale.*

## 14 AUGUST

Why should anybody be impressed by the speed, or slowness, with which a work is accomplished? I am often asked how long it took me to write such-and-such a script, as though that were a measure of its intrinsic value. When fellow writers ask the question, it is usually out of trade curiosity, and I give them a civil answer; but I hardly see what it matters to others. To give credit for speed and dispatch on an assembly line or in a communications office makes sense, but in the arts it is as silly as associating wealth with talent or with virtue. In Old Testament days, disease and poverty were considered the inevitable result of sinfulness, and riches the reward of piety—a naïve concept which the author of the magnificent book of Job knocked into a mess of sackcloth and ashes. But to be awed by a *chef d'œuvre* simply because it was created on the back of a laundry bill while waiting for Junior to get through with the bathroom—that, it strikes me, is equally absurd. The script that is ground out overnight deserves no special appreciation and is certainly no mark of genius on the part of the grinder. Most of the credit in such a case should go to strong coffee and benzedrine.

Neither is haste an excuse for poor or inadequate work. One simply cannot follow a broadcast with the explanation: "Ladies and gentlemen, this wasn't very good because the author had only a day's notice and went without sleep last night to write it." Radio is full of hasty projects, pieced together with scissors and glue, and that is to its shame, not to its credit.

"14 August" was written overnight, alas. Nobody except maybe the scientists of Oak Ridge, Tennessee, expected the Pacific war to end so soon, and when the atom bomb was dropped it caught more than the Japanese unprepared. I, for one, was in California at the time, working on a piece of fluff named *L'Affaire Gumpert,* and Fineshriber phoned from New York to ask how I was fixed for a little V-J commemoration. I was against doing it, especially on such short notice, but Fineshriber is a persuasive executive. I sat up all night hacking at the order and came up with a fistful of lines for a single voice, to be supported by a single sound effect. Next to a straight talk, this was about as simple as such a piece could be.

My approach was sober. I assumed that those who wanted to get drunk and tear up directories and blow horns and raise hell would not be listening to the radio anyway; that the legitimate news of the day would have been pretty much used up by the time this went on the air, and that most people remaining by their loudspeakers would by then be willing to glimpse 15 August and the responsibilities beyond that day.

During the suspenseful hours when Hirohito and his cabinet were weighing the Allied ultimatum, Orson Welles was one of the newscasters who kept the Los Angeles area informed via KFWB. He was a very tired man, thirty-six hours without sleep, when he rushed to KNX for a brief rehearsal of "14 August," but he attacked the script with an energy and gusto that shook amplifying tubes all over the network.

Lud Gluskin, steady and reliable in all storms, organized a battery of composers and arrangers and copyists and musicians, and the program was thrown together in what I would ordinarily consider obscene haste. It turned out, as I

had guessed, that the script *was* the first sobering note in
the evening's schedule for CBS on the night of the surrender. The program was repeated, with expansions, on the
following Sunday. It wasn't as good as the original.

*Additional Notes.* 1. Very rarely does a recording of
cannon fire, when close by, sound like what it is. The volume
or "load" of the actual noise is usually too great for the
vibrating mechanisms of either the recording or the repro-
ducing apparatus—or both. But there are devices that simu-
late gunfire or thunder and have the advantage of being
controllable. One of these is the "thunder screen"—an ordinary wire screen such as you kick holes through in your
screen door at home. The screen is attached to the sort of
"pickup" or needle head that is part of standard home
phonograph equipment, and the pickup is connected to an
amplifying system. When the screen is struck, or even
touched lightly, the resulting sound ranges anywhere from
a grumble to a Miltonic clap of thunder, all according to
how much energy has been put into the impact and the degree of amplification set by the engineer. For the cannon
that punctuated this broadcast, I used a modified thunder
screen—a gadget built on the same principle, but using a single coil of wire instead of a mesh. The impulse was fed to a
large standing speaker halfway down the empty auditorium
of Theater A at KNX. The distance from the sound
speaker to the overall microphone serving the orchestra permitted a tremendous wallop in the effect, an impact that
could not have been otherwise achieved.

2. American newsreels some time later showed a picture
of this girl, Iva Togori, alumnus of U.C.L.A., all full of
smiles and giggles. She was being interviewed by a most
deferential and respectful American who asked such foolish
questions as "Are you glad the war is over?" Whether the

interviewer or interviewee was more contemptible was hard for the newsreel audience to decide.

3. The Emperor's face appears no less stupid in the many photographs published since the surrender, showing him going about the islands being adored by his faithful subjects.

# SET YOUR CLOCK AT U235

Written at the invitation of the New York *Herald Tribune* Forum to open the fourteenth annual forum program at the Waldorf-Astoria on October 29, 1945. It was read by Paul Robeson.

# SET YOUR CLOCK AT U235

Now we are in it together:

The rich with their automatic comforts, and the family
bunking seven in a room:

The highly trained, who understand the poems and the
engines; and those whose culture measures five hundred words across the middle:

Old people tired of wars and winters, and children who do
not yet know they are made of matter:

The famous face in four colors, nationalized on the cover
of the magazine; and the crowd face, the background
face, gray, nameless, out of focus:

Now we are in it, in it together.

The secrets of the earth have been peeled, one by one, until
the core is bare:

The latest recipe is private, in a guarded book, but the stink
of death is public on the wind from Nagasaki:

The nations have heard of the fission of the atom and
have seen the photographs: skies aboil with interlocking fury, mushrooms of uranium smoke ascending to
where angels patrol uneasily.

There have been improvements since: the atom can be far
more sullen than has yet been shown.

Attack it with another thrust of algebraic symbols and the
cutting edge of an equation, and there will be the
grand reaction:

The first news of it will arrive in your precinct as a shudder-
ing in the sky:

A glow, far off, brightening: heat beating outward in con-
centric waves: the atmosphere a band of fire: the seas
themselves, the wet seas, tinder:

The hills that looked on Christ will heave and crackle, and
quarries vaporize as eagerly as the dust of Pharaohs:

The earth, the tamed and tonsured earth, with all its gardens and substances, its places, breeds, and patterns, its
letters and its airs, will plummet out of grace; will
fail its orbit,

And soon enough will be a blistered ash, its moon trailing
lonely and ungoverned, like a dog after his master's
corpse.

Do not smile, do not smile as though knowing better.
It could happen.
The model is any suicide.
The model is Samson, destroying the temple and himself.

We are all in the zone of danger: we are in it together:
Hang a red lantern on your pillow.
The crackpot prophet stands at last within reasonable
prospect when he picks a date and says: "On this day
the world will end. Selah. Repent ye, sinners, and prepare."

It could happen, for man's time will not outride another
war.

As for the latest war, what's to become of its victors and
their victory?

Their dear-bought, blood-begotten, towering, and grave
victory?

Need the laurel wither?

Need the sword go blunt again with the rusting disease of
men and metals?

Need the worker be lucky to work?

Need an epoch hang on the tailored charms of a diplomat?

Need there be guts and gore on every map again?

Do not search the broad-minded sky for answers to these and kindred questions,

Nor trust the editorials in picture weeklies. Tea leaves and ouija boards are more reliable.

The answers are in us together.

For only if we've learned that every multiple of one comes but to ONE in the arithmetic of nations,

Then only was the long trip back from Munich necessary.

Then only can it be explained to echelons of airmen who left their mark in air

And to Marines whose faces rubbed off on the cinders of Iwo;

Then only was it worth the concentration in the camps, and what it was that happened to the little and the lost and unremembered.

Unless we work at it together, at a single earth,

Then do not bother to lay wreaths for sailors who went down burning in winter seas,

Nor mourn privates anonymous, who bled their names and all they knew and were into the mud of Europe.

For there will be others out of the just-born and the not-yet-contracted-for who will die for our invisible daily mistakes.

There will be others, yes, but with this difference: Next time, the fighting heart shall be unemployed: shall be replaced by a coil of wire:

The secret weapons of the spirit rooted out by an ounce or two of restless elements.

Valor no more shall be the truss of armies.

The regimental banners, the order of the day, the skill of
killing drilled into the recruit, the encampments, the
massive embarkations—they have arranged themselves and withdrawn to the museum, they have retired next to pikes and arrows.
Now the control board and its buttons, the air-conditioned
laboratory, dustless and remote, by the waters of the
wired lake: these are the armed forces.

But alarm is easier than pride to point with:
We are in it together, and that, when held up to a proper
light, gleams good as much as ill.
Oneness is our destination: has long been: is far the best
of places to arrive at.
The signs along the way, at Galilee and Philadelphia and
Gettysburg, said:

ALL CREATED EQUAL

STRAIGHT AHEAD

KEEP GOING

STICK TOGETHER

ALL IS ONE

Beneath the loud and glooming auguries of doom are
modest noises of beginning, keenly awaited as the cry
of the newborn or the first cuckoo of spring.
It can well be an entrance, not an exit, that we made between pillars of flame arising from bombs one and
two.
The chemicking that could destroy us, together with our
pots and pans and allies, can also do as bidden by us:
outperform whole teams of genii: be servile to the
meek: reform our wayward systems peacefully.

The choice rests in the trusteeship of victory:
One or nothing; wealth, or laying waste:

Men, or Jew and gentile; men, or the color of men;
Jobs above profits, or profits above jobs:
These are the choices, and we make them daily.

What will it be, sir? Madam?
Make up your minds, please, and the sooner much the
      better.
Your children are growing.
They want to know.

# SET YOUR CLOCK AT U235

Hyperthyroidal, Lucid, rude, orthoëpic *Time* (rhymes with rhyme) called the *Herald Tribune* Forum "prestigious" (November 12, 1945). By this it meant to say that prestige, not jugglery, was attached to it. But they were righter than they knew, for the prestigiousness that goes into the blue-printing of such a forum is enough to qualify its master mind, Mrs. Ogden Reid, as a distinguished producer—a producer in the most literal sense.

I was one of more than forty people who were invited, many weeks in advance, to contribute to the fourteenth annual Forum. As I watched the planning develop, and when I saw the program actually come off, I was amazed at the calmness and precision with which Mrs. Reid juggled a thousand details—scheduling of speakers, timings, radio pickups, transcripts, staging—all with a quiet intensity, charm, and efficiency.

Mrs. Reid had asked me to dramatize the theme of the 1945 Forum, which was "The Responsibility of Victory." I decided against a formal "dramatization," for I have little faith in the effect of what is known as a "sketch" before a visible audience. A single person standing at a microphone can possibly create an illusion, but two or more actors at mikes are just so much baggage, and you might better listen to a transcription.

It was Mrs. Reid's idea that Paul Robeson should narrate the piece, and I was delighted to fall in with it. Robeson, fresh from a national success in Margaret Webster's production of *Othello,* readily consented, and his reading opened the Forum program on the night of October 29.

The only other time I had worked with Robeson was when, in 1939, he introduced the Robinson-LaTouche "Ballad for Americans" on a series I was directing. He had also appeared on a six-continent roundup in a CBS documentary called "Word from the People," but on this occasion his part of the program came from a dressing room in a Chicago theater, while I was in a Navy auditorium in San Francisco (both on the same continent). In neither instance had he performed any writing of mine, but after hearing him speak "Set Your Clock" I was sorry I had not written a dozen programs for him to narrate, and I resolved to make up for lost time at the first opportunity. It was an amazing performance—civilized, poised, clear, penetrating, neither emotionalized nor intellectualized, but communicated straight from the heart, or whatever chamber it is from which absolute conviction flows.

Robeson was followed immediately on the Forum program by General George C. Marshall, not yet retired as Chief of Staff. The General quickly contradicted my thesis that the regimental banners and the massive embarkations are all done with. "It is not hard to predict," he said, "that supersonic atomic rockets will have a profound influence on any war that ever again has to be fought. But, rather than decrease the necessity for our preparation both in manpower and matériel, this terrible new weapon will tremendously increase it." This amounted to a direct hit on the line "Now the control board and its buttons . . . are the armed forces." But I was morbidly reassured of the validity of my point when, later, scientist after scientist stated publicly, at various intervals, that the atomic bomb had made thoroughly obsolete the type of warfare that involves huge masses of men.

By this time there should be little doubt in anybody's mind that the possibility of exploding the earth is actual and active. I was taking no dramatic, or should I say scien-. tific, license in my speculations concerning the "grand re- action." *Time* reported on December 3, 1945:

When the scientists gathered in New Mexico to test the first atomic bomb, they weren't entirely sure just what would happen. A few suspected that the nuclear chain reaction might spread from the bomb's uranium, flash around the world in the air and burn every living thing to a crisp.

# CRITICAL RECEPTION

THE FOLLOWING SECTION has been prepared by the publishers for the instruction, guidance, or just plain curiosity of those interested in critical response to Mr. Corwin's programs. So many requests for such information have reached both our own offices and those of the Columbia Broadcasting System that for the necessary material we have jointly combed newspaper and magazine files, listener research organizations, and the Office of the Provost Marshal General of the United States Army.

We have tried to be as just as possible in our selection, separating neither the wheat from the chaff, nor the sheep from the goats. The business of radio criticism is a growing one and there are few important newspapers without departments relating to such activity. It seems to us high time that a group statement of this sort should be taken note of.

*The Publishers*

# THE UNDECIDED MOLECULE

This was one of three plays (the others: "Unity Fair" and "New York"—the latter appearing on page 309) concerning which *Time's* radio editor wrote:

> Corwin labored mightily on his favorite stock in trade: the supremacy of the common man. All he brought forth were tired platitudes, well-worn dramatic tricks, cacophonic sound effects.

The broadcast attracted no reviews and only two comments other than *Time's*:

> Barbara Kilby in the New York *Daily News:* "Four stars for Corwin again . . . delightful."
> Edwin Levin in *PM:* "Corwin can go his own way, for all of me, so long as he and Groucho deliver in such a monstrously merry manner."

The program drew heavy mail, a good deal of it from college students and instructors of chemistry and allied sciences. They said they enjoyed the ribbing.


## UNTITLED

Unlike other scripts in this collection that attracted widespread critical attention, this was not, to our knowledge, disliked by any reviewer. It drew about fifteen hundred letters, all but three of them friendly. Coolest reception was from extreme leftists, who thought it "defeatist" and "cynical." The primary audience of the broadcasts was expanded by wide printed circulation, as the script appeared in *Coronet* (November, 1944), *Reader's Scope, PM, Vogue, Scholastic,* and the Des Moines *Register.*

Highest praise for "Untitled" came not from radio but from a drama critic—Arthur Pollock, in the Brooklyn *Daily Eagle* of June 1, 1944. Arnold Blom in *PM* called it "an American masterpiece which should be heard over every station in the land." Jack Gould in the New York *Times* found it "haunting." *Liberty* called it "the radio classic of the war years."

A year after its original production, "Untitled" became one of the first major undertakings in televised drama when Ben Feiner adapted and directed the script for WCBW-CBS. Lou Frankel wrote in *Billboard*:

> With bated breath and every other platitude in the critic's kit, we waited to see this, television's first attempt at telecasting one of radio's classics. . . . Words carried the listener to emotional peaks which the video portion of the program did not match. . . . It was a tribute to Corwin's wizardry with words. The words lived and breathed; the speaking, playing and production were as irrelevant as the vapor exuded on a frosty morning. . . . There is, as most everyone knows, a sweep, a scope, a movement to Corwin's writing which, when the author does the producing on the air, at least stirs the listener, slowly at first, then faster and stronger until the audience gulps, cries or goes through the emotional wringer in some other fashion. In this television presentation, the words had the same effect to which the visual presentation neither added nor detracted. . . .
>
> Don't tackle anything as good as this unless television can add something.

*Variety* liked it better, crediting the production with "full impact" and praising Feiner's translation to the video medium:

> The force and eloquence of Corwin's writing and the punch of his message are still so rare a thing on the video scene as to make [the] program an event. . . . The first Corwin work to be presented on television, it demonstrated how well suited his writing and style is to the medium.

The script became the most widely performed of any of Corwin's work, especially by military and naval personnel. It was produced several times by the Army's School for Special Services in Lexington, Virginia, and at installations throughout the country and overseas. It even had the honor of being plagiarized and published under the title "I Was Hank Peters" as the work of "Private H. P." in an issue of *Yank,* on July 8, 1945. The matter was called to *Yank's* attention by Captain Jerome Morey, then in France, in the issue dated August 5. Captain Morey, with Major Alexander Wolf, had earlier produced the script at Maastricht, Holland, and at the U.S. Army's 108th Evacuation Hospital in that country.

Pollock's column in the Brooklyn *Eagle* was almost in the nature of an editorial:

What the theater needs is more of what the air gets from Norman Corwin. You listen to Corwin's programs and you tell yourself they are too good for the radio, that he ought to write for the theater. But that, no doubt, is only because you happen to be a partisan of the theater. Corwin might say that such stuff as he makes his programs of would be wasted on so small an audience as the theater's. At any rate he manages to say more with less apparent effort in a half hour than most playwrights say in an evening. . . . Take his program *Untitled.* Just a picture in words of a boy who died in this war. No story. No plot. But those who listened saw the boy and the life he had lived, and understood what kind of boy he was, what the war meant to him, and what his dying meant. . . . Nothing could be simpler. And yet Corwin pulled the whole world together in that broadcast . . . knitted together this war and the last and the future and all the people and their aspirations everywhere. All this he does in the simplest, plainest, unpretentious words, homely words with rhythmic and soft force and music in them, words that move more than the words and visible action of most plays or movies. He can find the right word, the specific, pictorial, telling word . . . and make the word count.

CBS received the 1945 Citation of Distinguished Merit of the National Conference of Christians and Jews for "Untitled." The Conference said it made the choice

because this program dramatically interpreted the achievements and feelings of the American service man at the front and thereby stimulated listeners at the home front to attain the same high loyalty and devotion.

## EL CAPITAN AND THE CORPORAL

Not reviewed as a play, but mentioned in passing in an article by Aiken Welch in *Liberty* (February 10, 1945):

To the listener [the stairway incident] was an unusually realistic station scene. To the radio professional it was a classic in the handling of microphones. . . . Nor is it unusual for a heroine of Corwin's to interrupt a glowing love scene to remind her lover of the Spanish Republican cause and its relation to the present war.

## SAVAGE ENCOUNTER

A survey made by CBS in 1944 claimed that "Savage Encounter" was the most popular single broadcast of the 1944 "Columbia Presents Corwin" series. The mail was favorable and fairly heavy, and the broadcast was well liked within the trade. Of press comments, all of them approving, the most forthright was Walter Winchell's. He wrote in his syndicated column:

The most moving and convincing story around the theme "What are we fighting for?" that I have ever heard. The setting was enchanting, the technique superb and the performance big time. It should be repeated over all networks at least once a day and night.

## LONDON BY CLIPPER

Listener ratings ranged from fairly good, in England, to fairly poor in the United States, where the entire series suffered from the opposition of Bob Hope, then the highest-rating show in radio. ("An American in England" was heard by a British audience through recordings played over the BBC's Home and Forces Services.)

Both "London by Clipper" and the series as a whole were favorably reviewed by critics in both countries, the British press treating the opener as a news story. "Evidence of new Anglo-American collaboration," wrote the *Daily Mail*. Fleet Street at that time rarely gave feature space to radio, preferring to leave that to the BBC's publications, *Radio Weekly* and *The Listener;* nevertheless, the *News-Chronicle* on July 28, 1942, considered "London by Clipper" sufficiently newsworthy to devote an eighth of its entire edition (newsprint shortage had reduced all daily papers to four pages) to a reprint of the script.

The austerity of the broadcast from a productional standpoint, a condition forced upon the author by the vagaries of short-wave atmospherics, turned out to be an advantage rather than a handicap—at least in the view of critics. Said *Variety:*

Short-wave limitations had the effect of stripping Corwin down to a calculated simplicity that is not contemptible as a model even when production limitations would not exist.

Gordon McConnel of the BBC called it

proof that the human voice and the written word, unhampered by pseudo-atmospheric background effects, can bring broadcasting to a lofty artistic level. . . . What a relief to have a conversation in a station buffet with no mechanical clattering of cups; another in a train, with no train noises . . . finest example of broadcast dramatic entertainment since Gielgud's production of Linklater's *Cornerstones.*

John K. Hutchens in the New York *Times* found in the program

a poet's vision, a good reporter's clarity and a technician's precise knowledge of his craft. . . . Everything done in little touches, but the cumulative effect is profoundly stirring . . . a distinguished program . . . major work in a minor key.

He went on to discuss the objectives of the broadcast, linking it with a variety series ("Britain to America") then being short-waved by the BBC for pickup by NBC:

The test of such programs is, of course, whether or not they bring you closer, in understanding and emotion, to the people they describe. *An American in England* and *Britain to America* do precisely that. . . . You will note, by the way, a curious thing about these programs that come by way of short-wave and then are rebroadcast here. The reception is sometimes shaky, fading in and out, like the sound of the sea across which they travel. In a domestic show that would merely be annoying. To these reports it adds a certain sense of wonder, a suggestion of places at once so far and so near.

The Glasgow *Herald,* writing after a later program in the series, found Joe's odyssey

keenly aware of the drama in quietness and simplicity, of the tremendous evocative power as well as artistic value of restraint rightly used.

Robert J. Landry in *Variety* thought that the large orchestra was

unnecessary, as a small unit would have sufficed and short-wave transmission is not the ideal medium for big orchestras. [But the program was] poignant, believable and rich in clear mental pictures, . . . it should add up to a net contribution to British-American understanding.

Mail on the series was slight in America, but there was a fair response from the British. No rating was taken in the states, but the BBC's "Listener Research" organization made a report on the series, which is summarized under "Clipper Home."

## Home Is Where You Hang Your Helmet

Not reviewed. Light mail.

## An Anglo-American Angle

*Variety,* September 9, 1942: "Despite unfavorable atmospheric conditions that blotted out more than half the program completely [it was] impressive and inspiring . . . philosophic in character . . . dignified, yet simple and moving."

Reaction to the program is further discussed under "Clipper Home."

## Clipper Home

Radio's critics generally review the opening program of a series and then neglect the remainder, unless some broadcast of exceptional power or merit attracts their ear. *Variety* alone among the trade publications has a "Followup" department. In the case of "An American in England," five of the nine broadcasts were reviewed by *Variety,* but beyond the opener, none was reviewed elsewhere.

Against Bob Hope on a rival network, Corwin's domestic rating was low. While the two programs were as far apart as they could be, Hope's had long been building up to the highest rating in radio, and the comedian unquestionably absorbed some potential Corwin audience.

The total impression of the "American in England" series was that it had done its job. "Cromer" was liked best, "London by Clipper" next best, and "An Anglo-American Angle" rated third. The clearest and most informative of the scripts was "Ration Island," which the author did not include here because of its restricted and narrow subject (food and clothing); the least effective was "London to Dover," and the general rating for "Women of Britain" and "The Yanks Are Here" was only fair. All of the three last named are described by Corwin as "taut, overbusy with reportage, and stylistically beneath the other scripts."

The BBC's Listener Research studied English audience reactions to the entire series and had this to report:

The programs were heard by 10.3 of the adult civilian population. The alternative program being broadcast at the same hour [Fridays, from 8 to 8.30 P.M.] was a mystery series called "Death in the Hand," and rated 8.4.

The Appreciation Index was 8.4, or seven points above the average for 80 feature programs which had been the subject of panel reports up to then . . . an extremely good figure.

In an attempt to gauge the reactions of listeners to the programs as a whole, they were invited to say to what extent they found it interesting, stimulating and penetrating. The following tabulation gives their answers:

| | Per cent | | Per cent | | Per cent |
|---|---|---|---|---|---|
| Very interesting | 65 | Very stimulat-ing | 47 | Very penetrat-ing | 19 |
| Mildly interest-ing | 31 | Mildly stimu-lating | 29 | Quite penetrat-ing | 51 |
| Rather boring | 3 | Rather obvious | 14 | Rather superfi-cial | 20 |
| Very boring | 1 | Very obvious | 5 | Very superficial | 2 |
| No reply | 0 | No reply | 5 | No reply | 8 |

Listener comments were also sampled. The majority, commenting on the American's views, said they agreed with him on most points. There was some disagreement on his placing of "the common guy on too high a pedestal." These are a few opinions:

"I thought the American's view rather eulogistic; he made us appear almost perfect in our war effort, and we are still a long way from that."

". . . If he is a typical American, then I like Americans."

". . . after all we only behave as all decent people should."

"Very practical and to the point, and with the usual American frankness. He certainly puts his finger on our weak spots as well as our strong points. These talks should break down the wall of prejudice and insularity we have built around ourselves."

"Laid on the heroism too thick."

"He seemed to express the very things we find going through our minds at the sight of the artificial glitter of American magazines."

"Use of music most effective. The whole technique focused attention on the *thoughts* of the American. The omission of background noises was original, pleasing, and greatly helped in concentration on words."

"I think the idea of the narrator merely speaking his thoughts aloud to himself was a good one. . . . It is a method particularly satisfactory for an American, there being no self-consciousness of any kind, just a serious intense interest in everything. . . ."

"It might have been me just looking around. . . ."

"Old stuff."

Others were struck by the general vigor of the script, which they called "full of pep," "punch," and American humor, others by the contrast between this "plain statement of facts without ballyhoo and propaganda," and the "over-rehearsed style," "bellowing," and "blasts of noise" which they associate with English propaganda features. Others mentioned the frank way in which criticism as well as praise was given where it was due, which they felt made the picture "healthy and natural," much better than the "usual sort of propaganda where no one speaks except to point out that everything in the garden is lovely."

Joseph Julian received enthusiastic praise. He was called "a great guy, hope to meet him again," and listeners said he "carried one along" with him. His characterization was apparently so convincing that many listeners were in doubt about whether he was an ordinary American making a report or an actor playing a part.

Most spontaneous comments were very favorable, and there was a demand from a tenth for more programs on similar lines. There was no unanimity among the few adverse comments [which came] from about 10 per cent of the listeners reporting [and] dealt almost entirely with the incidental music, about which the usual complaints were made. These were balanced by special praise from the same number of listeners, who were particularly struck by its descriptive appropriateness. One listener wrote it was "very definitely *right,* not just pretty-pretty," and another spoke of "Britten's little bits of musical humor."

Less than 12 per cent of the listeners reporting said they would have preferred to have listened to a straightforward talk on this subject. This question is asked fairly regularly about feature programs, and on the average a quarter of the listeners say they would have preferred a talk. The unusual smallness of the vote in this case can be taken as an additional tribute to the broadcast.

Summary: The series has been listened to by audiences of considerable but by no means exceptional size. But listeners who have heard them have rated them very highly. The Narrator, Joseph Julian, was very much liked and the technique of writing was appreciated, but it is possible to trace some sense of embarrassment on the part of British listeners at what they feel to have been rather extravagant praise of themselves.

The entire series was produced over the network of the Australian Broadcasting Commission with such success that it was repeated in full. Leslie Rees in the Australian radio publication *ABC Weekly* wrote (January 30, 1943):

Corwin was the ideal radio reporter to send to Britain. Not only because he is observant, can render conversations with easy charm, has "the bump of wonder" and can get vividly excited by all kinds of new things he sees, but because he also has a heart, the common touch.

## You Can Dream, Inc.

Not reviewed. Mail was light, and favorable with the exception of two or three correspondents who demanded to know what Corwin thought he was doing by writing such "unimportant trivia" during a time of war. Opinion within the trade was divided. William Fineshriber of CBS thought the script quite poor.

## The Moat Farm Murder

No known reviews. The mail was light. The show was generally liked, with Bernard Herrmann's score coming in for an unusual share of the honors.

## New York: A Tapestry for Radio

Not reviewed. It was one of the most popular of the 1944 series, drawing heavy and favorable mail both from New York and around the country. The Armed Forces Radio Service distributed the program to installations overseas, and for a long time letters trickled in from outposts, telling of the nostalgic pull it exerted upon its listeners. In 1945, the Museum of the City of New York asked for the original manuscript of the broadcast, and got it. CBS earlier presented a recording of the show to Mayor LaGuardia.

## Tel Aviv

A breakdown of mail on the eight programs that made up the "Passport for Adams" series showed "Tel Aviv" to be the second most popular broadcast. "Moscow" was the first. The program was not reviewed individually. Details on the reaction of public, press, and radio trade to the series as a whole are contained under "Moscow," below.

## Moscow

"Moscow" was generally received as the most popular broadcast in the series. The series itself, although a summer replacement of only eight weeks' duration, scored one of

with political life and social customs of foreign peoples"; 173 liked
the programs because they "help win the war" and "champion the
little fellow."

## There Will Be Time Later

Not reviewed. The program drew fairly light but enthusiastic mail.

Within radio itself the program was received indifferently, and the New York program department of CBS
itself was divided on its merits. The chief complaint was
that the script was "confused" and "difficult to understand."
For some reason, it made an especially strong impression
on the west coast and was later repeated, by transcription,
over stations in Hollywood in connection with bond drives.

## On A Note of Triumph

From the standpoint of listener and press reaction, "Triumph" hit a jackpot unlike any dramatic program in radio's
experience: 4278 letters, cards, and wires, of which seven
were disapproving; a thousand telephone calls at CBS in
New York, and upward of 1600 at CBS in Hollywood.
(No telephone statistics were received, or asked for, in
other cities.)

The broadcast, as a result of unusually wide circulation
(two network productions, a book, an album of records,
and a reprint in *Coronet*), attracted unusually wide critical
comment. Carl Sandburg, in an unsolicited letter, called it

a vast announcement, a terrific interrogatory, and certainly one of the all-time great American poems.

The press reaction, while not nearly as lopsided as 4271 to 7, was nonetheless most friendly and in some instances enthusiastic. Among national magazines the distribution was fairly even, with the *Saturday Review of Literature* leading the pro-"Triumph" camp. John Mason Brown, in a cover article distinguished (quite apart from its concern with "Triumph") for its searching commentary on the art of radio as a whole, wrote:

Mr. Corwin dares to raise . . . questions; dares to dramatize their answers, too. His poem, with its Whitmanesque cadences, is a newsreel in words of war emotions, battle reasons, and peace hopes. It is as ubiquitous in its world coverage, as only a radio news-roundup can be. It is more than a paean to victory, or a record of Nazi aggression . . . it is an important and stirring statement of the lessons we must have mastered, if you, and I, and all the little men and women in the grip of world events are to be free, happy and proud in the years ahead. Naturally [it is] even more effective when heard on the air . . . than when read. This is one measure of how superlatively right it is for the medium for which it was intended. But on the printed page it does more than hold up well. It provides its rich and exciting rewards. Mr. Corwin's mind, his style and his conscience all have muscles. It is hard to describe the power of his images, the variety of his rhythms, the driving conciseness of his phrases, and the happy mixture of the colloquial and the eloquent.

Of the emotional content of the script, concerning which there was to be some debate, Brown wrote that its author was

not recollecting emotions. He is feeling them. Their warmth and fury, their passion and sincerity blaze in his pages. Blessedly his spirit is not tranquil. Tranquillity and the age of Hitler do not go together.

Robert E. Sherwood in the New York *Herald Tribune* agreed with Brown about the emotional values:

A piece of writing possessed of great power and warmth and depth . . . worthy of a tremendous occasion.

But Mr. Sherwood objected to the swiftness of pace in certain sections:

The ability of the radio writer to transcend space and time in a flash fills old-timers who write for the theater with awe and envy. That is fine to read, because I can take my own good time about the journeys upon which Mr. Corwin commands me. But when I hear this shot out over the radio . . . I want to gasp: "Hey, wait a minute—I'm not out of those Grand Banks fogs yet."

Jack Gould in the New York *Times* disagreed with Brown, Sherwood, and others about the emotional power of the work. In a critique headed "A Minority Report," Gould found "Triumph"

woefully lacking in one element—heart. Every mood was projected with high efficiency, but without warmth, enthusiasm or a suggestion of participation. A day of days was slipping by and missing were the spontaneity of the moment, the buoyancy of spirit and the sense of the climactic. It was as if . . . a Park Avenue cocktail were being substituted for a good boilermaker over on Tenth Avenue. Mr. Corwin is for the people, passionately, vigorously and articulately, but *Triumph* was not of the people.

Howard Taylor in the Philadelphia *Record* found it

thrilling . . . moving and exciting, as well as historic . . . the radio play at its best.

An unsigned article in the same newspaper on the same day added:

one of the most moving literary documents of the war . . . something to hand down to your children along with the family silver.

The Milwaukee *Journal* was on Brown's side:

When *Triumph* was first heard on the radio some thought it lacked heart, was bogged down by sonorous words and phrases, or moved too swiftly or did not move at all. None of these criticisms holds true of the book . . . the power of Corwin's printed writing hits hard and convincingly. If anything, the celebrational piece gains in book form.

*Time* and *Newsweek* both believed that the broadcast came off better than the printed script. Gould took the opposite view. He wrote:

This department found the printed version immensely more stimulating than the radio production.

*Newsweek* found many faults:

At times . . . so involved in lush phraseology as to obscure meaning. At other times, guilty of radio's greatest fault: the cliché. Aside from these failings, a valiant idea, fervently expressed. Corwin's prose is frequently poetic, sometimes beautifully powerful . . . an exceptional radio program, but as a contribution to literature it is better propaganda than art.

*Time* said:

What makes the scalp tighten when backed by sound effects and Bernard Herrmann's excellent score and eloquent silences frequently looks tinselly in type. The eye sometimes misses the dramatic moment that Corwin skillfully devises for the ear. . . . *Triumph's* unrelieved pounding at its worthy message (internationalism) sometimes takes on the sound of an hour-long lecture; and occasionally, with the best intentions in the world, it is mawkishly patronizing about the little people to whom it is addressed. Yet the best of Corwin is a kind of poetry, and is U.S. radio at its best.

This was the Hollywood *Reporter's* view:

As powerfully lyrical in the reading as in the listening. A magnificent radio report which manages to put across its message with craftsmanlike ease . . . achieves the desired effect except for the almost unavoidable temptation to editorialize.

The critics of the trade were unanimous in their approval. George Rosen in *Variety* hailed it as "a milestone in radio." He reported:

The trade in general has not been stinting on adjectives, for the boys know well enough what it means to have a show that's the epitome of perfection on paper and yet to have it "play" just as well, if not better. Which is exactly what happened. . . . Without equivocation, chalk this up as one of the high-water marks in radio listening, a fitting, joyous climax to a memorable day in history. . . . Corwin is the first to prove that radio can inspire great works of art and, by the same token, he disproves the theory that writing for the medium fetters and binds creative talent. . . . *Triumph* should . . . take its place in the halls of fame. . . . [It] embodied all the hopes and lessons, all the entreaties and thanks into a climactic prayer that merits a repeat from every pulpit in the land.

*Billboard* carried its review as an editorial entitled "Corwin for Everyone." At the time the review appeared CBS had not yet completed arrangements with Columbia Records to issue the broadcast as a commercial album, and *Billboard's* chiding was based on the impatient assumption that CBS wasn't interested. The editorial said:

Once in a decade something comes down the pike that is so good it deserves to belong not to its creator or its sponsor but to the people. Last week radio had just such a something. . . . *Triumph* . . . the single greatest—and we use greatest in its full meaning—radio program we ever heard. It was, and is, great because it dealt, in simple yet specific words and thoughts, with the single most important event in the last hundred years, namely the rise and fall of Fascism. . . . *Triumph* was so good that CBS-New York piped it to every internal loudspeaker so those of its staff that had missed it could hear it . . . so fine a document of the whys and wherefores, the causes and effects, the results and cravings of this war that it should be played each morning for the delegates at the World Security Conference now conclaved at San Francisco . . . so important that it should be played by every radio station in every English-speaking country in the world. For literally *Triumph* is of the people—it comes from the heart and head of every G.I. in every uniform of every United Nation . . . everyone should hear it once every six months for the next decade. Then, maybe, we will not forget, and then, maybe, we'll have no more wars. But *Triumph,* unfortunately, belongs to CBS, and CBS says it will not release *Triumph* even after the repeat broadcast. . . . This program transcends the urgencies of purely competitive radio. It is in the public interest, necessity and convenience; it is of the people; it should be made available to the people.

Both script and broadcast were intensely disliked by Bernard De Voto in *Harper's Magazine:*

I had better offer this as personal opinion without trying to call it literary criticism. My colleagues who have reported so far disagree with me unanimously, and this is one that cannot be talked out at Joe's. If they are right, then I am not only wrong but irretrievably wrong. . . . I listened with a distaste that only occasionally yielded to satisfaction but frequently intensified to distress. . . . The factual broadcasts of CBS that preceded it on May 8—by John Daly, Bob Trout, Bill Henry, Major Eliot, and many others—had a professional cleanness and quality as well. Their reports roused and satisfied the very emotions that *Triumph* tried but failed to satisfy. They fertilized the listener's imagination as Mr. Corwin did not. The reportorial and editorial aspects of radio were superb. But when an acknowledged master of radio got to work on the same stuff he was dull, windy, opaque, pretentious, and in the end false . . . saccharine . . . preference for the unreal . . . inferior imagination and bad writing . . . tinny . . . counterfeit . . . bargain-counter jauntiness . . . too easily done . . . an essentially cheap achievement . . . semi-clever talkativeness . . . commonplace . . . vulgar . . . a rhetoric so flip that it degrades the emotions presumed to have created it . . . a mistake from the first line . . . bastard form of speech . . . spurious . . . pretentious failure.

De Voto likened "Triumph" to Pare Lorentz's film *The River,* which he then described as

shoddy . . . not substantial . . . in fact cheap . . . irritating . . .
Mr. Lorentz played a slight tune . . . no distinction came out of it
. . . Mr. Lorentz kept coming through clearly in *Triumph*.

Issue was taken with De Voto by the Cleveland *Press*,
whose Stanley Anderson wrote:

De Voto is alone in his attack. . . . [It is] remarkable that one
lone-wolf critic has taken it upon himself to slug.

The Toledo *Blade* called "Triumph"

a literary gem . . . as stately and magnificent as an ode, as realis-
tically disturbing as a bomb.

Josef Rosenberg in the Little Rock *Gazette* contrasted
the effect of the recording with that of the original broadcast:

Having heard the original, the effect was even more moving in its
recorded form. Possibly the stir of events at the time of the initial
broadcast was so overwhelming that its full impact could not be realized. Listening in the calmer atmosphere of the present, *Triumph*
impresses one as an enduring and historic work of art, befitting the
epic event it commemorates.

The Knoxville *News Sentinel* credited the program with

accomplishing the difficult, the near-impossible, to judge from much
of the V-E Day oratory which gave up without a struggle the problem of avoiding the trite. . . . [It] not only revitalizes the picture
of the pogrom, the firing squad, the arrogance of the Nazis, all grown
dim and almost meaningless through endless repetition of phrase . . .
but it does so in lines that are so concise, so telling that they are
highly quotable. . . . If a finer, more moving tribute to the years
just past and prayer for the years to come is written, probably Corwin
will write it.

The geographic extent of press comment was unprece-
dented for a radio drama and served as a measure of "Tri-

umph's" effect upon the country. An idea of the scope may be gathered from a few excerpts:

Raleigh (N.C.) *News Observer:* ". . . has captured the everlasting story which is the shadow and substance of the people, a living symbol of the fight for freedom."

Edmund Wilson in the *New Yorker:* "Putting most radio scripts into book form is a waste of ink, glue and paper, but this one . . . doesn't have to apologize for being in type. Although it's not one of the high-water marks in American literature, it is certainly on a par, as poetry, with some of the incantations composed for the radio by Archibald MacLeish."

The Hammond (Ind.) *Times:* "A compatible marriage of poetry and realistic dialog."

The Dallas *News:* "Charged with the emotions of the day . . . warm and close to the subject."

Stewart Matter in the Cleveland *Plain Dealer:* "Will stand as a monument to those who gave all for the cause of freedom . . . amazing force and intensity."

Frances Boardman in the St. Paul *Pioneer Press:* "Striking specimen of a new art form."

Oscar Smith in the Akron *Beacon Journal:* "Stirring, biting, at times beautiful . . . something for all of us to hear at frequent intervals, for our own good and for the good of the country."

C. B. Palmer, New York *Times Book Review:* "Has some of the qualities of universal truth . . . remarkably good reading . . . it comes out in eloquence, rhythm and idea . . . carrying the full force of simplicity . . . at times quick twists for irony seemed labored."

James Gray in the St. Paul *Dispatch:* "Corwin . . . likes to dally with his gift of words and sometimes he turns up with something pretty fancy in the way of an alliteration-laden line."

*Coronet:* "A magnificent, turbulent and beautiful piece of writing."

Walter Locke in the Atlanta *Journal:* "A lively exultation at the eradication of a rat."

Mary Little in the Des Moines *Tribune:* "Play of plays . . . a poetic, dynamic conception."

Fort Worth *Star Telegram:* "Its chief value even beyond its provocative emotional appeal, will be to keep before the mind's eye of the soft-hearted and proverbially forgiving American people the years of terror . . . approved by the German people as long as they thought they were winning. Those of our people who did not hear the broadcast should hear the recording, as a patriotic duty."

Norfolk (Va.) *Pilot:* "Deathless prose . . . deserves to be perpetuated . . . stands up under reading and re-reading."

William Juengst in the Brooklyn *Eagle:* "In deadly seriousness, yours truly remarks that he regards the prayer in *On a Note* as one of the finest bits of American writing."

Norman Rosten in *Book Find News:* ". . . the kind of radio you won't meet Monday through Friday . . . It has caught history on the run and brought it down . . . will make exciting reading long after V-E or V-J Day. The writing is powerful (though some may demur against the occasional over-poetic flourish). I do not know of a more conclusive summation in dramatic terms, of the heroism and meaning of the war, of why men fought to win and why their war must stay won. Corwin has paid a most eloquent tribute to the greatest cause of modern man."

Foreign reactions were not yet fully received at the time this section went to press, but the success of the Australian production was reflected by the Melbourne *Listener In,* which called the play

the most moving, exhilarating and inspiring piece of original work radio has yet given to the world.

There were no adverse criticisms of Bernard Herrmann's score, but a few critics disliked Martin Gabel's performance. In each of these instances the critic was hostile to the script as well. Gabel's majority of favorable notices, like that of the broadcast, was clear and wide.

An extraordinary set of reactions was that collated by the Office of the Provost Marshal General of the U.S. Army. German prisoners of war who listened to a translation of "Triumph" on OWI discs were invited to comment, and their voluntary responses, together with reports by American officers attached to P.O.W. camps, were released for this compendium. Some of them follow:

PW Camp, Atlanta, Nebraska (quotes of comments by several prisoners): "These records are telling the truth and each German PW should listen to them seriously—especially the die-hard Nazis." "Should such vilenesses really have taken place?" "The conditions in Germany were seen with the eyes of the American, as he saw them on V-E Day—and, of course, had to see them—impressed by the victory just achieved. The psychology of a German and the mentality of a German prisoner of war was not much respected, unfortunately." "Most PW's smiled when they heard of the German [sic] girls driven into brothels, or similar assertions. It was said: 'They tell us exaggerations; we are coming from Germany, we know that better!'" "In a propaganda program against Nazism it should be taken into consideration that a great part of the Germans only saw the glittering surface of the Nazi regime and admired the efficiency of dictatorship." "The telling of the atrocities under Nazism was very impressive for the PWs' minds. On the other hand several super-sentimental scenes had an disadvantageous result." "It is very hard to get an answer by a comrade, asking him what is your impression about the records. I have the feeling they are too fearful to say what they are thinking about. An older man told me, 'Indeed we know it now, it should be enough of this.' In general I observate that many men are getting more and more insuseptible. They are troubling themselves about the fate of their families. Several times during a discussion in the camp I got the answer: 'We need not words, we need help.'"

PW Camp, Ogden, Utah: "It is gratifying to be able to know the truth about what is going on in the world." "If we had only known the truth during the years of the war, we would certainly have done differently."

PW Camp, Blanding, Florida (report of the Assistant Executive Officer): "All [of the prisoners] listened silently throughout the playing. There was no audible reaction displayed during the playing, or immediately after. There was, however, some laughter when the 'Heil Hitler' oath was uttered, and at the singing of 'Round and Round Hitler's Grave.' . . . They enjoyed the sharp jeers at Hitler, Goering and Goebbels. . . . All of them took issue with the broadcast where it condemns the entire German people for supporting the ascendancy of Hitlerism and the brutal acts of the Nazi regime. Even our good anti-Nazis (from way back) felt that this blanket indictment was unfair."

PW Camp, Johnston, Florida (report of a prisoner of war): ". . . the audience [of prisoners] generally felt that the course of history could not have been intercepted under the prevailing circumstances. As the transition period at the time of Hitler's ascension to power did not exhibit the fatal disadvantages of a totalitarian government, the majority of the audience stated that it did not realize the momentous consequences involved. . . . The recording of this *Note of Triumph* accentuates the firm resolution of the American soldier not to let this ever happen again. This was the unanimous and vivid reaction of the prisoners of war at this camp: never to commit themselves to a totalitarian government again; to engage in a peaceful reconstruction of Germany under democratic principles; and to frustrate all movements which might lead to another atrocious war."

PW Camp, Chaffee, Arkansas (report of American officer): ". . . had a depressing effect upon the prisoners . . . left them with a feeling of uncertainty. . . . [Some] said it represented the unbiased and untainted truth . . . as only America is capable of presenting . . . they were all of the impression that it was a very true picture and were glad to have the opportunity to hear the broadcast."

On November 24, 1945, the National Council of Teachers of English gave its first radio award to "Triumph." The citation read, in part:

The most notable contribution of the year toward the development of new forms of artistic expression in the field of radio.

Earlier in the year the play had been cited by the Association of Teachers of Social Studies of New York City. On March 9, 1946, *Billboard* announced that "Triumph" had been voted "the outstanding broadcast of 1945" by a national poll of radio editors.

## 14 August

This was runner-up to "Triumph" and "Untitled" in listener reaction. It received over a thousand letters, none unfavorable. Critical response was sparse. Magee Adams in the Cincinnati *Enquirer* wrote:

In spite of five days for preparations, the studios came up with few victory programs worthy of yesterday's momentous event. The first couple of hours after the long-awaited announcement found the air jammed with man-on-the-street interviews, bits of coast-to-coast bedlam and statements by brass hats. It was not until 8 P.M. that a brief prayer struck a needed note of reverent thanksgiving. Tributes to those who fell in gaining the victory were conspicuous by their scarcity. Towering above the noisy improvisations was *14 August*. . . . The script gave voice in characteristic Corwin eloquence and imaginative sweep to the feelings of most adults on the light that seemed so long in coming.

George Rosen in *Variety* doubted whether the radio audience was prepared for the program:

As a paean of jubilation for victory achieved after years of bloodshed, and horrors, *14 August* may have embodied the feelings of a war-torn people. Yet the immediate response of the people by their unrestrained rejoicings makes it more probable that they were not ready as yet for any calculating appraisal, for any solemn appraisal or serious realizations. What the people wanted in those immediate post-victory moments were facts, substantiation—and more facts. That was enough, and everyone's pent-up emotions may have broken the barriers in different ways, yet the greatness of the occasion was personal to each one, and following so soon after the long-awaited announcement, Corwin's studied embodiment, in dramatic form, of his sequel to the V-E *Triumph* was ill-timed. No one was as yet ready to control sheer emotion or to harness joy to a narration, no

matter how simple its exposition or sincere its intent. Only simplicity
and dignity could be used in its projection, yet it may well be that no
commemoration could be simple enough.

## SET YOUR CLOCK AT U235

A number of civic, scientific, and political groups were
quick to embrace "Set Your Clock" as a statement of credo
with respect to the atomic age. Within a few weeks, ten
thousand copies of the poem were distributed by Americans United, a coalition of liberal and progressive organizations. The first mass meeting on the atomic bomb, at
New York's Madison Square Garden on December 4, 1945,
included a reading of the poem along with speeches by
Julian Huxley, Harold Urey, Harlow Shapley, and Henry
Wallace. It was performed on that occasion by Fredric
March.

J. Darling, editorial cartoonist for the New York *Herald
Tribune,* based two striking cartoons on the poem, the
first appearing in juxtaposition to it in the Forum issue of
November 4, 1945, the second on November 9. In the first,
entitled "Make Up Your Mind, Madam," a kindly middle-
aged lady named Civilization stood at a crossroads reading
a signpost. A finger was on her chin; her expression was one
of doubt. One sign pointed "To International Unity
Against War," the other "To the Atomic Incinerator for
All Mankind." Behind the lady was a procession of people,
including "the young and the old," "the rich and the poor,"
"the great and the small," and "the strong and the weak."
The second cartoon showed a blasted, pitted skeleton of
the globe, with enormous craters in the remains of the con-

tinents and the oceans entirely evaporated. On top of this globe stood a charred skeleton of a human being, talking into a telephone. "Hello! Hello!" he was saying. "If there's anyone left alive I'd like to unite with 'em in a world league to outlaw war."

Several scientists at the Oak Ridge project communicated with Corwin following the broadcast and publication of the poem, saying that "Set Your Clock" summed up their own views on the matter and offering collaboration in a task of informing the public, via radio, of the political ramifications of atomic energy.

Listener and reader response was fairly heavy, though not immediate, and never on the level of "Triumph," "Untitled," or "14 August."

Press criticism was favorable, the outstanding tributes coming from Walter Winchell and Magee Adams. Winchell wrote:

> Corwin's literary lace was admirably delivered by Paul Robeson's deep-throated eloquence . . . after listening to Corwin's word-weaving you gaze upon a dictionary with renewed reverence.

Miss Adams, in the Cincinnati *Enquirer,* wrote:

> Listeners had a tantalizing glimpse of what Paul Robeson might do as a radio actor . . . his rich, flexible voice brought the Corwin lines alive with an artistry that would have been hard to equal.

# GLOSSARY OF TERMS

# GLOSSARY OF TERMS USED IN THIS BOOK

**Ad lib:** To extemporize, improvise, invent, doodle—whether in speech, sound, or music. Actually, good ad libbing should be carefully written and rehearsed so as to *sound* impromptu, for in radio, as nowhere else, the literal meaning of the phrase (from the Latin *ad libitum*—"at one's pleasure," or "as one wishes") cannot be honored. In cases where it is important to create authentic atmosphere (as in the background of a street in Tel Aviv, a barroom in Perth Amboy, an operating room, ball game, street corner), ad libs should be appropriate to the language, jargon, inflection, situation, and time of day. The slightest background phrase, wriggling through the dialogue of principals on-mike, can do wonders in the way of heightening realism. For example, if the scene were a wartime civilian airport waiting-room and you overheard somebody saying "priority" or "damn delay," it would help you believe the situation.

**Back:** To support, as with music, sound or cast ad libs, any speech or effect which holds the center of the microphonic stage.

**Background:** Sound, speech or music, used either separately or in combination, to back other elements.

**Balance:** Relationship between two or more elements of a program. In music, the term usually refers to ratios between instruments and voices.

**Blend:** To mix the various components of an effect simultaneously. Thus, if the sound of a dive-bomber is coming from Microphone A, a movement of the Mahler 3rd from B, a stream of consciousness from C, and an echo effect of a beating heart from D, all at the same time, the engineer would obviously have to do some tall blending to form these into an intelligent combination. So would the author.

**Board:** The engineer's control panel, through which all elements of the show must pass. Each microphone on the studio floor is controlled by a volume-dial on the board and can be faded individually. On the average big network-studio board there are channels for eight microphones. Most boards have fewer.

**Build:** To increase the power of an effect.

**Cold:** Without support; solo; without preparation. If a program opens with a speech by the narrator unaccompanied by music or sound, the program "opens cold." Also, if an effect is produced without the anticipation of a fade-in, it is said to "come in cold."

**Contact mike:** A microphone about the size of a coat-button, which amplifies sound enormously by means of an intimate pick-up. It is the same type as those worn by bomber crews for intercommunication.

**Control room:** The chamber where the engineer, director and assistant director operate in isolation from the rest of the studio. It is usually a small room whose windows face on one or more studios. The engineer has a great deal of equipment at both elbows and in front of him, and the director's panel consists of a clock and a talk-back mechanism, through which he communicates to the company in the studio. A loudspeaker, usually overhead, "monitors" the program as it is blended and balanced on the board.

**Cross-fade:** To fade in one effect while another is faded out. It corresponds to the "dissolve" in motion pictures.

**Cue:** A sound or word or musical phrase used as a signal for the entrance of another sound or word or musical phrase. Director's cues are generally relayed by hand, although in complicated circumstances, light signals are used. The term "cue" is often used loosely to indicate a speech or a printed direction, and in mimeographed scripts where each speech and effect is separately numbered to facilitate reference in rehearsal, each number is called a cue. Thus, a director may refer to "cue 186 on page 23." That is the sense in which the word is most often used in this volume.

**Damping:** Quieting, or reducing the sound level of an effect, or the resonance characteristic of a studio, by physical rather than electrical means. The use of screens, curtains, and acoustical vanes is the most common method of damping. Piano tones may be muffled by interference with the vibration of strings. It is necessary to damp when a studio's "quality," or natural resonance, is so brilliant that it becomes harsh and uncontrollable. Such a studio is called "live," and the opposite kind "dead."

**Double:** To perform more than one role in the same play.

**Dress:** The final complete rehearsal, under actual broadcast conditions.

**Echo:** The effect produced either electrically or mechanically to give hollowness or the impression of space, as in a large auditorium.

**Engineer:** The technician who operates electrical equipment controlling the elements of a broadcast.

**Establish:** To register solidly an effect before reducing it in favor of another component of the program. Once a background has been convincingly established, it can be subordinated and yet maintain presence by a sort of carry-over suggestion. For instance, if the scene is a boiler factory, it is not necessary to make a loud din for more than a few seconds. After that, the listener will take your word for it, and there is no point in continuing to beat him over the head. You "bring down" the sound after having established it, so that when Burton the boilermaker speaks, he can be heard above the boilers.

**Fade:** To diminish or increase (fade in) volume, whether by changing positions relative to a microphone or by electrical means on the control board.

**Filter:** An electrical device used to alter tone characteristics by eliminating or augmenting various frequencies. Thus, low frequencies may be "filtered out" to leave only high frequencies. The "tone control" on the standard home receiver accomplishes filtering when you select a bass or treble register.

**Headphones:** Ordinary earphones used for cueing or for intrastudio communication during rehearsal or broadcast. In instances where an actor or conductor is isolated from a sound effect or other members of the company, he must wear earphones in order to hear what is going on.

**Highs:** (See **Filter**.)

**Isolate:** To separate one element (like an orchestra) from another (like the cast) in order to achieve absolute control in the blending of both on the control board. This separation can be accomplished either physically—by placing them far enough apart—or (in the case of a studio which is too small to keep elements from getting in each other's way) by constructing an isolation "booth" to serve as a studio-within-a-studio.

**Level:** The volume at which an effect takes its proper place in the balancing of a program. If an actor's voice is too low, the director may tell him to "give more level." Levels are "set," or fixed, on the control board early in rehearsal and, under optimum conditions, adhered to throughout subsequent readings.

**Live:** In the case of an effect, one which is produced physically as opposed to one produced electrically or by means of a recording. For the term as applied to a studio, see "Damping," above.

**Lows:** (See **Filter**.)

**Manual:** Hand-operated sound-effects as distinguished from electrically-operated. The term applies to effects such as hoof-beats, hammering, or stirring water in a splash-tank, as against "canned" or recorded effects. Very often manual and recorded effects are used together.

**Mix:** Same as blend.

**Montage:** A kaleidoscopic succession of brief scenes, speeches, sounds, music, or any of these in combination.

**Motif:** A thematic phrase or passage of music which is reproduced or varied through the course of a script; often, a short musical figure serving both as means of transition and as an aid to the identification of a character or setting. In a script these are sometimes specified by letter as, for example, Themes "X" and "Y," merely for the convenience of the composer or conductor, and the word "theme" in such an instance is practically synonymous with Motif.

**Nondirectional microphone:** A mike that can pick up sound from any direction. The most common type of mike for dramatic purposes is the "ribbon" or "velocity" microphone, which is sensitive on its front and back, but not on its sides. Limited sensitivity of a microphone permits a director to get better balance, clarity, and selectivity in sound pick-up than would be possible with an unlimited, or nondirectional, mike. But the latter has important uses, as with a spread-out effect like a chorus or the circular arrangement of people in a dinner scene.

**Overlap:** Two elements of speech or dialogue running at once. The technique is often used to approximate what occurs when an on-the-spot announcer describes an event.

**P.A.:** Public-Address system, used to amplify the voice of a speaker. It is the identical apparatus used in airports, bingo games, auditoriums, and baseball parks.

**Pacing:** The control of tempo, cadence, or the physical or intellectual rhythm of a performance.

**Peak:** As used in this volume, the height of an effect.

**Perspective:** The relation of an element to any other, or to the microphone. As with a movie camera visually, one must establish perspective aurally through the microphone. The listener must know where he is in relation to characters or scenes, and unless there are varying perspectives in a performance, the total impression will be one of flatness and unreality.

**Pipe:** To convey a program or effect by wire from a remote point. The term is never applied to wireless transmission.

**Print:** A standard published musical arrangement.

**Production:** A term whose definition varies according to company practice. Largely it means organizing, directing, and presenting programs, but when one speaks of "the production" on a program, it is meant to apply to the general artistic effect.

**Project:** To use more voice; to make one's self heard at a distance.

**Pyramid:** To build within an effect; musically, instrument by instrument.

**Reaction:** The response of an individual or of a group to a speech or happening.

**Reprise:** Musically, a return to an earlier theme.

**Resolve:** A term used somewhat loosely in radio to indicate completion of a musical statement started earlier. In its purest sense (musically), it means to progress from discord to concord.

**Ribbon mike:** (See Nondirectional microphone.)

**Schmaltz:** Excessive sentiment; bathos; corn.

**Segue** (pronounced "seg-way") : Musical transition, without a break, from one mood or number to another.

**Sneak:** To introduce music or sound softly behind dialogue or narration.

**Sock cue:** An immediate, sudden, and vigorous entrance. Musically, it is most often used to indicate a smash opening or climax.

**Straight:** As written; without changes, accent, or emotionalization. An actor cast as an Italian laborer or a German spy would have to be told whether to use an accent or play "straight." Another who was making too much of an emotion might be told the same thing.

**Transition:** The change, or passage, from one scene or time to another.

**Under:** Behind another effect.

**Up:** When applied to speech, a direction to distinguish between a personal, narrative, aside, inward, or contemplative quality, and direct address to another person.

**Up and Out:** A direction used to indicate that music which has for some time been supporting an effect should now flare up and come to a finish or fade quickly.

**Vignette:** A short scene; especially when it is a component of a montage (which see).

**Wipe out:** To obliterate, overwhelm, drown out, as when music takes a scene away from speech or sound.